EXPLAINABLE DEEP LEARNING AI

EXPLAINABLE DEEP LEARNING AI

Methods and Challenges

Edited by

JENNY BENOIS-PINEAU
Univ. Bordeaux, CNRS, Bordeaux INP, LaBRI, UMR 5800
Talence, France

ROMAIN BOURQUI
Univ. Bordeaux, CNRS, Bordeaux INP, LaBRI, UMR 5800
Talence, France

DRAGUTIN PETKOVIC
San Francisco State University, CS Department
San Francisco, CA, United States

GEORGES QUÉNOT
Univ. Grenoble Alpes, CNRS, Grenoble INP, LIG
Grenoble, France

ACADEMIC PRESS
An imprint of Elsevier

Academic Press is an imprint of Elsevier
125 London Wall, London EC2Y 5AS, United Kingdom
525 B Street, Suite 1650, San Diego, CA 92101, United States
50 Hampshire Street, 5th Floor, Cambridge, MA 02139, United States
The Boulevard, Langford Lane, Kidlington, Oxford OX5 1GB, United Kingdom

Notices

Knowledge and best practice in this field are constantly changing. As new research and experience broaden our understanding, changes in research methods, professional practices, or medical treatment may become necessary.

Practitioners and researchers must always rely on their own experience and knowledge in evaluating and using any information, methods, compounds, or experiments described herein. In using such information or methods they should be mindful of their own safety and the safety of others, including parties for whom they have a professional responsibility.

To the fullest extent of the law, neither the Publisher nor the authors, contributors, or editors, assume any liability for any injury and/or damage to persons or property as a matter of products liability, negligence or otherwise, or from any use or operation of any methods, products, instructions, or ideas contained in the material herein.

ISBN: 978-0-323-96098-4

For information on all Academic Press publications
visit our website at https://www.elsevier.com/books-and-journals

Publisher: Mara E. Conner
Acquisitions Editor: Tim Pitts
Editorial Project Manager: Isabella C. Silva
Production Project Manager: Selvaraj Raviraj
Cover Designer: Christian J. Bilbow

Typeset by VTeX

Working together
to grow libraries in
developing countries

www.elsevier.com • www.bookaid.org

Contents

List of contributors

Kamila Abdiyeva

Nanyang Technological University, School of Electrical and Electronic Engineering, Singapore, Singapore

Nazarbayev University, School of Engineering and Digital Sciences, Nur-Sultan, Kazakhstan

Narendra Ahuja

University of Illinois at Urbana-Champaign, Department of Electrical and Computer Engineering, Urbana, IL, United States

Mathias Anneken

Fraunhofer Institute of Optronics, System Technologies and Image Exploitation, Interactive Analysis and Diagnosis, Karlsruhe, Germany

David Auber

Univ. Bordeaux, CNRS, Bordeaux INP, LaBRI, UMR 5800, Talence, France

Meghna P. Ayyar

Univ. Bordeaux, CNRS, Bordeaux INP, LaBRI, UMR 5800, Talence, France

Romaissa Beddiar

University of Oulu, Faculty of ITEE, CMVS, Oulu, Finland

Jenny Benois-Pineau

Univ. Bordeaux, CNRS, Bordeaux INP, LaBRI, UMR 5800, Talence, France

Jesús Bescós

Universidad Autónoma de Madrid, Video Processing & Understanding Lab., Escuela Politécnica Superior, Madrid, Spain

Ilaria Boscolo Galazzo

University of Verona, Department of Computer Science, Verona, Italy

Romain Bourqui

Univ. Bordeaux, CNRS, Bordeaux INP, LaBRI, UMR 5800, Talence, France

Lorenza Brusini

University of Verona, Department of Computer Science, Verona, Italy

Nadia Burkart

Fraunhofer Institute of Optronics, System Technologies and Image Exploitation, Interactive Analysis and Diagnosis, Karlsruhe, Germany

Massimiliano Calabrese

University of Verona, Department of Neurosciences, Biomedicine and Movement, Verona, Italy

Federica Cruciani

University of Verona, Department of Computer Science, Verona, Italy

Eoin Delaney

School of Computer Science, University College Dublin, Dublin, Ireland

VistaMilk SFI Research Centre, Dublin, Dublin, Ireland

Rachid Deriche

Inria Sophia Antipolis-Méditerranée, Côte d'Azur University, Athena Project-Team, Sophia Antipolis, France

Marcos Escudero-Viñolo

Universidad Autónoma de Madrid, Video Processing & Understanding Lab., Escuela Politécnica Superior, Madrid, Spain

Andrija Gajić

Universidad Autónoma de Madrid, Video Processing & Understanding Lab., Escuela Politécnica Superior, Madrid, Spain

Damien Garreau

Université Côte d'Azur, Inria, CNRS, LJAD, UMR 7351, Nice CEDEX 2, France

Giorgio Giacinto

University of Cagliari, Department of Electrical and Electronic Engineering, Piazza d'Armi, Cagliari, Italy

Romain Giot

Univ. Bordeaux, CNRS, Bordeaux INP, LaBRI, UMR 5800, Talence, France

Oleksii Gorokhovatskyi

Simon Kuznets Kharkiv National University of Economics, Department of Informatics and Computer Engineering, Kharkiv, Ukraine

Volodymyr Gorokhovatskyi

Kharkiv National University of Radio Electronics, Department of Informatics, Kharkiv, Ukraine

Derek Greene

School of Computer Science, University College Dublin, Dublin, Ireland

VistaMilk SFI Research Centre, Dublin, Dublin, Ireland

Adrien Halnaut

Univ. Bordeaux, CNRS, Bordeaux INP, LaBRI, UMR 5800, Talence, France

Alexandre Hardouin

Pôle emploi, Information Technology Department, Nantes, France

Marco F. Huber

Institute of Industrial Manufacturing and Management IFF, University of Stuttgart, Stuttgart, Germany

Center for Cyber Cognitive Intelligence (CCI), Fraunhofer IPA, Stuttgart, Germany

Gaëlle Jouis

Nantes Université, École Centrale Nantes, CNRS, LS2N, UMR 6004, Nantes, France

Pôle emploi, Information Technology Department, Nantes, France

Mark T. Keane

School of Computer Science, University College Dublin, Dublin, Ireland

VistaMilk SFI Research Centre, Dublin, Dublin, Ireland

Eoin M. Kenny

School of Computer Science, University College Dublin, Dublin, Ireland

VistaMilk SFI Research Centre, Dublin, Dublin, Ireland

Alejandro López-Cifuentes

Universidad Autónoma de Madrid, Video Processing & Understanding Lab., Escuela Politécnica Superior, Madrid, Spain

Martin Lukac

Nazarbayev University, School of Engineering and Digital Sciences, Nur-Sultan, Kazakhstan

Gloria Menegaz

University of Verona, Department of Computer Science, Verona, Italy

Harold Mouchère

Nantes Université, École Centrale Nantes, CNRS, LS2N, UMR 6004, Nantes, France

Mourad Oussalah

University of Oulu, Faculty of ITEE, CMVS, Oulu, Finland

University of Oulu, Faculty of Medicine, MIPT Unit, Oulu, Finland

Olena Peredrii

Simon Kuznets Kharkiv National University of Economics, Department of Informatics and Computer Engineering, Kharkiv, Ukraine

Dragutin Petkovic

San Francisco State University, San Francisco, CA, United States

Fabien Picarougne

Nantes Université, École Centrale Nantes, CNRS, LS2N, UMR 6004, Nantes, France

Georges Quénot

Univ. Grenoble Alpes, CNRS, Grenoble INP, LIG, Grenoble, France

Gustavo Retuci Pinheiro

UNICAMP, MICLab, School of Electrical and Computer Engineering (FEEC), Campinas, Brazil

Konrad Rieck

Technische Universität Braunschweig, Institute of System Security, Braunschweig, Germany

Leticia Rittner

UNICAMP, MICLab, School of Electrical and Computer Engineering (FEEC), Campinas, Brazil

Wojciech Samek

Technical University of Berlin, Department of Electrical Engineering and Computer Science, Berlin, Germany

Fraunhofer Heinrich Hertz Institute, Department of Artificial Intelligence, Berlin, Germany

BIFOLD – Berlin Institute for the Foundations of Learning and Data, Berlin, Germany

Michele Scalas

University of Cagliari, Department of Electrical and Electronic Engineering, Piazza d'Armi, Cagliari, Italy

Francesco Setti

University of Verona, Department of Computer Science, Verona, Italy

Manjunatha Veerappa

Fraunhofer Institute of Optronics, System Technologies and Image Exploitation, Interactive Analysis and Diagnosis, Karlsruhe, Germany

Nataliia Vlasenko

Simon Kuznets Kharkiv National University of Economics, Department of Informatics and Computer Engineering, Kharkiv, Ukraine

Akka Zemmari

Univ. Bordeaux, CNRS, Bordeaux INP, LaBRI, UMR 5800, Talence, France

Mauro Zucchelli

Inria Sophia Antipolis-Méditerranée, Côte d'Azur University, Athena Project-Team, Sophia Antipolis, France

Preface

If you can't explain it simply, you don't understand it well enough.
Albert Einstein, Physicist

Artificial Intelligence (AI) techniques, especially those based on Deep Learning (DL), have become extremely effective on a very large variety of tasks, sometimes performing even better than human experts. However, they also have a number of problems: they generally operate in mostly opaque and/or intractable ways, their very good performance is only statistical and they can fail even on apparently obvious cases, they can make biased decisions, and they can be quite easily manipulated through adversarial attacks, to cite a few. These limitations prevent their adoption in applications of great economic or societal interest, especially for critical or sensible applications like autonomous driving, medical diagnosis, or loan approvals.

Considering this, a lot of research has been conducted in order to increase the trustworthiness of DL-based AI systems by providing explanations understandable by human users for the decisions made by these systems. The aim of this book is to present recent and original contributions covering the main approaches in the domain of explainable DL, either for expert or for layman users. Two main types of approaches are presented: the "post hoc" or "model agnostic" ones, in which the operation of an already available "black box" system is modeled and explained, and the intrinsic ones, in which systems are specifically designed as "white boxes" with an interpretable mode of operation.

This book is a follow-up of a very successful Workshop "Explainable Deep Learning-AI" which we have organized at ICPR'2020 IAPR and IEEE conference making a large tour of ongoing research in the field.

The question of the explainability is addressed in a variety of media domains, including images, text, temporal series, and tabular data. The difficult and important question of the evaluation of explanation methods is also specifically addressed in two chapters. Finally, still open challenges are mentioned in the concluding chapter.

Georges Quénot, Jenny Benois-Pineau, Dragutin Petkovic, and Romain Bourqui
LIG/CNRS, LABRI/University of Bordeaux (France), San Francisco State
University (USA), LABRI/University of Bordeaux (France)
April 5, 2022

CHAPTER 1

Introduction

Jenny Benois-Pineau[a] and Dragutin Petkovic[b]
[a]Univ. Bordeaux, CNRS, Bordeaux INP, LaBRI, UMR 5800, Talence, France
[b]San Francisco State University, San Francisco, CA, United States

Chapter points

- In this chapter we first give the rationale of the book.
- The content of each chapter will be shortly introduced.

We are witnessing the emergence of an "AI economy and society" where AI technologies are increasingly impacting many aspects of business as well as everyday life. We read with great interest about the recent advances in AI medical diagnostic systems, self-driving cars, the ability of AI technology to automate many aspects of business decisions like loan approvals, hiring, policing, etc. However, as evident by recent experiences, AI systems may produce errors, can exhibit overt or subtle bias, may be sensitive to noise in the data, and often lack technical and judicial transparency and explainability. These shortcomings have been documented in the scientific literature, but also, importantly, in the general press (accidents with self-driving cars, biases in AI-based policing, hiring, and loan systems, biases in face recognition systems for people of color, seemingly correct medical diagnoses later found to be made due to wrong reasons, etc.). These shortcomings are raising many ethical and policy concerns not only in technical and academic communities, but also among policymakers and general public, and will inevitably impede wider adoption of this potentially very beneficial technology. These broad concerns about AI are often grouped under an umbrella area of "AI Ethics and Values" or "Trustworthy AI." The technical community, potential adopters, popular media, as well as political and legal stakeholders, have recognized the problem and have begun to seek and ask for solutions. Many very high level political and technical bodies (e.g., G20, EU expert groups, Association of Computing Machinery in the USA), as well as major AI companies, have identified Trustworthy AI as a critical issue. The technical and academic community are also addressing these issues by dedicated conferences and workshops and academic centers. The governing bodies are issuing guidance and even laws like EU GDPR with "right to know" clauses for AI-driven decisions.

The problems related to Trustworthy AI are complex and broad, and encompass not only technical issues but also legal, political, and ethical ones. Trustworthy AI concerns seem to have some common components, such as bias/discrimination, need for human understanding and control, ethics, as well as judicial and human-centric transparency

Explainable Deep Learning AI
https://doi.org/10.1016/B978-0-32-396098-4.00007-7

1

and explainability. It is also a common belief that better methods for auditing and even certification of AI systems for Trustworthiness are going to be critical for its broader adoption in business and society.

One way to tackle broad problems like Trustworthy AI is to first work on its key components. We hence devote this book to AI explainability, which is what we believe of the critical issue in achieving Trustworthy AI – after all, how can one audit/certify, trust, and legally defend (that will come, too!) something one does not understand? More specifically, this book addresses explainability of Deep Learning (DL) AI technologies, which are very popular and powerful, but at the same time notoriously hard to explain. At a high level, explainability of AI systems should allow human users to gain insights into how they make their decisions. The human users of Explainable AI have to include not only AI experts but also domain experts (often the key adopters), as well as general public. AI explainability can be model based, where it offers insights on how the AI system works on a collection of data as a whole (e.g., the whole training database), and sample based, where it offers insights into how the trained Machine Learning system classifies a specific data sample ("why was I rejected for the loan?"). The latter has been shown to be critical in determining user trust in AI systems. AI explainers can be agnostic to AI methods they try to explain, or direct (tied to a specific AI algorithm). AI systems that are explainable achieve many benefits, e.g., they could increase user trust and adoption, improve AI quality control and maintenance, make them legally more transparent, and possibly even offer new insights into the analyzed domain. The need for explainability does not exclude the usefulness of black-box models since they are often tried first and may serve, among other things, to point to ultimate achievable accuracy. Explainable systems can also be used for development, verification, and testing of AI systems including otherwise hard to explain black box systems.

Challenges in achieving explainability of DL AI systems are very significant. Due to their structure (multiple layers of a very large number of interconnected weighted connections), they are extremely hard to explain compared to, for example, powerful ensemble tree based systems like Random Forests. The challenges for explainable DL include algorithms to extract explainable information from trained DL systems, ways to present and visualize explanation information such that it is understandable to target human users (experts or not) at the model as well as sample level, and methods for evaluation of such systems which have to involve target human users, thus making them time consuming and expensive.

This book covers the latest and novel contributions to all aspects of explainable DL, from area overview to specific approaches, including comprehensive evaluations of usefulness for human users. It comprises 13 contributing chapters which present methodological aspects, together with application examples.

Chapter 2 introduces the reader to the concepts, methods, and recent developments in the field of explainable AI. After discussing what it means to "explain" in the context of machine learning and presenting useful desiderata for explanations, a brief overview of established explanation techniques is provided, mainly focusing on the so-called attribution methods which explain the model's decisions by post hoc assigning importance scores to every input dimension (e.g., pixels in images). Furthermore, recent developments in XAI are discussed. In addition, the author presents ways to use explanations to effectively prune, debug, and improve a given model, as well as the concept of neuralization which easily allows one to transfer XAI methods specifically developed for neural network classifiers to other types of models and tasks. The chapter concludes with a discussion of the limits of current explanation methods and promising future research directions.

In *Chapter 3* the authors make use of information visualization approaches to present a method to help in the interpretability of trained deep neural networks. By depicting both their architecture and their way to process the different classes of a testing input dataset, the moment (i.e., the layer) where classes are being discriminated becomes visible. Similarly, they show how it is possible to detect degradation in the classification process, mainly because of the usage of an oversized network for a simpler classification task. The authors conduct their experiments on well-known Deep NN architectures, such as LeNet5 and VGG16 networks, when using popular MNIST and Fashion-MNIST data sets. Results show a progressive classification process which is extended to an improvement on an oversized network to solve a simpler task.

In *Chapter 4* the authors address the family of explanation methods by perturbation. These methods are based on evaluating the effect that perturbations applied to the input induce on the model's output. We note that the authors are in particular interested in image classification. In this chapter, they discuss the limitations of the existing perturbation-based approaches and contribute with a perturbation-based attribution method guided by semantic segmentation of images. This method inhibits specific image areas according to their semantic meaning, associated to an assigned semantic label. Hereby, perturbations are linked up with this semantic meaning and a complete attribution map is obtained for all image pixels. The potential capabilities of this attribution scheme are exemplified by automatically arranging image areas into semantic sets according to their relevance, irrelevance, and distracting potential for scene recognition of the semantic label assigned to them.

Chapter 5 presents a further development of recently introduced Feature Understanding Method (FEM) which explains DNN decisions also in the context of image classification tasks. The authors call the method "Modified FEM." It belongs to the family of the so-called "white-box" methods. It is based on the analysis of the features in the last convolution layer of the network with further backpropagation to identify the image pixels which contributed to the decision the most. The method explains the decision of a trained network for a specific sample image. The application example of the method is explanation of the network trained for the classification of chest

X-ray images for the recognition of COVID-19 disease. This chapter covers the intensive research in the XAI field despite its relatively rich set of methods which have been previously developed.

Chapter 6 is an example of the use of XAI methods in a clinical field. The authors do not propose new explainers. Instead, they use methods previously proposed in the literature, such as Backpropagation, Guided Backpropagation, and Layerwise Relevance Propagation. They hypothesize that the agreement across these methods is an indication of the robustness of the results in the problem of stratification of multiple sclerosis on brain images. The voxels of the input data mostly involved in the classification decision are identified and their association with clinical scores is assessed, potentially bringing to light brain regions which might reveal disease signatures. Indeed, presented results highlight regions such as the Parahippocampal Gyrus, among others, showing both high stability across the three visualization methods and a significant correlation with the Expanded Disability Status Scale (EDSS) score, witnessing in favor of the neurophysiological plausibility of these findings.

In *Chapter 7* as in *Chapter 4*, the authors focus on perturbation based methods which use some modifications of the initial signal (more often, in some neighborhood around it) and measure how the classification result changes. They propose a method recursively hides image parts to get an explanation for a particular decision of the black-box classifier. The core of this method is the division of the image being classified into separate rectangular parts, followed by the analysis of their influence on the classification result. Such divisions are repeated recursively until the explanation of the classification result is found, or the size of parts is too small. As a result, the pair of images with complementary hidden parts is discovered: the first image preserves both the most valuable parts and the classification result of the initial image. The second shows the result of hiding the most valuable parts of an initial image that leads to the different classification. Such a representation allows humans to see which parts of the image are significant for the particular decision and confirms that classification is not successful without these parts.

Chapter 8 focuses on the importance of trained convolutional filters in the convolutional neural networks. Removing some of them, the authors track classification results and thus also explain the network. Filter removal can lead to the increased accuracy, which explains the chapter title "Remove to improve."

Chapter 9 is interesting in the sense that it combines rule-based methods which are naturally explainable prediction models, with CNNs. The rule mining techniques such as SBRL, Rule Regularization, and Gini Regularization are adapted to produce an interpretable surrogate model, which imitates the behavior of the CNN classifier on time series data. This makes the decision process more comprehensible for humans. In the experiments the authors evaluate three methods on the classification task trained on AIS real-world dataset and compare the performance of each method in terms of metrics such as F1-score, fidelity, and the number of rules in the surrogate list. Besides, they illustrate the impact of support, and bins (number of discrete intervals), parameters on the model's performance along with the strengths and weaknesses of each method.

Chapter 10 addresses an extremely important and still open research question of the evaluation of explanation methods. It presents two protocols to compare different XAI methods. The first protocol is designed to be applied when no end users are available. An objective, quantitative metric is being compared to objective data expert's analysis. The second experiment is designed to take into account end-users feedback. It uses the quantitative metric applied in the first experiment, and compares it to users preferences. Then, the quantitative metric can be used to evaluate explanations, allowing multiple explanation methods to be tried and adjusted, without the cost of having systematic end-users' evaluation. The protocol can be applied on post hoc explaining approaches, as well as to self-explaining neural networks. The application example used is natural language processing tasks.

Chapter 11 is application oriented in the field of cybersecurity. As machine learning approaches are used for malware detection, XAI approaches allow for detecting the most characteristic features both in the static and dynamic analysis frameworks, which characterize malware. In this perspective, the authors focus on such challenges and the potential uses of explainability techniques in the context of Android ransomware, which represents a serious threat for mobile platforms. They present an approach that enables the identification of the most influential features and the analysis of ransomware. Their results suggest that the proposed methods can help cyber threat intelligence teams in the early detection of new ransomware families and could be extended to other types of malware.

The authors of *Chapter 12* are interested in explainability in medical image captioning tasks. Image captioning is the task of describing the content of the image using textual representation. It has been used in many applications such as semantic tagging, image retrieval, early childhood learning, human-like robot–robot interactions, visual question answering tasks, and medical diagnosis. In the medical field, automatic captioning assists medical professionals in diagnosis, disease treatment, and follow-up recommendations. As a general trend, deep learning techniques have been developed for image captioning task. They rely on encoder–decoder models which are black boxes of two components cooperating to generate new captions for images. Image captioning builds a bridge between natural language processing and image processing, making it difficult to understand the correspondence between visual and semantic features. The authors present an explainable approach that provides a sound interpretation of the attention-based encoder–decoder model for image captioning. It provides a visual link between the region of medical image and the corresponding wording in the generated sentence. The authors evaluate the performance of the model and provide samples from the ImageCLEF medical captioning dataset.

Chapter 13 is the second one which explicitly tackles the question of the evaluation of explainers. This chapter elaborates on some key ideas and studies designed to provide post hoc explanations-by-example to the problem of explaining the predictions of black-box deep learning systems. With a focus on image and time series data, the authors review several recent explanation strategies – using factual, counterfactual, and semifactual explanations – for Deep Learners. Several novel evaluations of these methods are reported, showing how well these methods work, along with representative outputs that are produced. The chapter also profiles the user studies being carried out on these methods, discussing the pitfalls that arise and results found.

Up to now a wide variety of XAI methods have been proposed. It is not always obvious for an AI practitioner which of them is the most applicable to the problem at hand, as the theoretical analysis of these methods and the conditions of their applicability remain rare. One of the popular methods in the family of black-box XAI approaches is Locally Interpretable Model-agnostic Explanation (LIME). It consists in masking pre-segmented regions in the data (images) and tracking the score changes, thus determining the regions important for classification. The exact operation of LIME, though, is often overlooked by practitioners, sometimes at a great expense. One example in particular is the nature of the sampling process, which can lead to misleading explanations if not adapted to the data at hand. Another point is the role of LIME's hyperparameters, of which the provided explanations depend in a complicated manner. In *Chapter 14*, the author summarizes some recent theoretical work focused on LIME with the goal to propose useful insights into the method.

Finally, *Chapter 15* concludes the book. We review the content of the book providing insights about the main concepts presented in the previous chapters. We also give two important directions for future work: the evaluation of XAI methods and the enrichment of the explanation methods with semantics in order to foster trust to nonexperts.

CHAPTER 2

Explainable deep learning: concepts, methods, and new developments

Wojciech Samek[a,b,c]

[a]Technical University of Berlin, Department of Electrical Engineering and Computer Science, Berlin, Germany
[b]Fraunhofer Heinrich Hertz Institute, Department of Artificial Intelligence, Berlin, Germany
[c]BIFOLD – Berlin Institute for the Foundations of Learning and Data, Berlin, Germany

ChapterPoints

- Why do we need explanations? From black-box models to explainable AI.

- What to explain? Definitions and desiderata of explanations.

- How to explain? Overview over post hoc explanation methods.

- Beyond explaining. From explanations to better models.

2.1. Introduction

In the last decade, deep learning has revolutionized the research in the field of artificial intelligence (AI) and is now slowly transforming the world we live in. Smart services, intelligent devices, and advanced analysis tools are becoming more and more available and are increasingly being used. Google Translate and Amazon's Alexa are popular services demonstrating the power of today's deep learning-centered AI. While the AI revolution has started in the field of computer vision and natural language processing, it is now also transforming many other application domains, including medicine, signal processing, and communications. This trend will intensify as more and more methods augmented with learning capabilities outperform traditional algorithms relying on hand-crafted features. Examples can be found in image compression (Toderici et al., 2017), physical layer communications (Qin et al., 2019) or ECG-based arrhythmia classification (Hannun et al., 2019).

Due to the complexity of commonly used deep neural networks, the question of interpretability is of central importance. The recent rise in the field of Explainable AI (XAI) (Samek et al., 2019) shows the growing need to understand the reasoning of these powerful learning machines. The reasons for making machine learning models explainable are diverse and range from more trust and verification capabilities (Holzinger et al., 2019), over the generation of deeper (scientific) insights (Roscher et al., 2020) and legal requirements (Hacker et al., 2020), to the ability to debug the model and identify

Explainable Deep Learning AI
https://doi.org/10.1016/B978-0-32-396098-4.00008-9

"Clever Hans" predictors[1] (Lapuschkin et al., 2019). One spectacular example of the last aspect is the unmasking of spurious correlations utilized by the AI model winning the PASCAL VOC competition (Everingham et al., 2010). The goal of this prestigious challenge was to train models, which reliably recognize objects such as boats, trains, or horses in real-word images crawled from Flickr. Since at the time of the challenge (2007–2012) explanation techniques were not available, the participating methods were solely evaluated on the basis of average classification precision. Several years after the challenge, however, it turned out that the seemingly well-performing competition winner was classifying many images correctly, but for the wrong reason (Lapuschkin et al., 2016). More precisely, it was recognizing boats in images solely by the presence of water, trains by the presence of rail tracks, and horses by the presence of a copyright watermark, which accidentally and unnoticedly was present in many horse images in the training and test dataset. This case demonstrates that models developed in lab settings not necessarily perform well when deployed in real applications (where horses do not carry a copyright watermark). Furthermore, it shows that a profound understanding of the model and its prediction strategies is a crucial step (though not sufficient) for the development of trustworthy AI models. Another popular application domain of explanation methods are the sciences, e.g., medicine (Lauritsen et al., 2020), pharmacology (Preuer et al., 2019), meteorology (Ebert-Uphoff and Hilburn, 2020), or astronomy (Zhu et al., 2019), where explanations are used to generate novel scientific hypotheses and help gaining deeper insights into the natural processes behind the observed data.

This chapter introduces the basic concepts and methods of explainable AI, and discusses new developments in this quickly evolving research field. It will mainly focus on XAI techniques designed (but not limited) to explain the predictions of deep neural networks, i.e., models which are commonly regarded black boxes due to their nonlinearity and enormous complexity. Despite the availability of these explanation methods, practitioners still often refrain from using black-box models and prefer machine learning algorithms such as (generalized) linear models, rule-based systems, decision trees, or Random Forests. These "simpler" models are commonly regarded more transparent and perform very well in many applications. However, while for a long time it has been common belief that there exists a fundamental trade-off between model complexity/performance and model explainability, recent work (Lipton, 2018; Lundberg et al., 2020) argues that this is not the case, i.e., that even the results of these simpler models can be hard to interpret for humans or the interpretations can be misleading.

The rest of this chapter is organized as follows. Section 2.2 starts with the question what it actually means to explain a prediction and what properties good and meaningful

---

[1] Clever Hans was a horse that was claimed to perform arithmetic tasks. However, a formal investigation in 1907 found that the horse was not really doing the calculations, but was solving the task by carefully watching the body language of its master. AI models basing their predictions on spurious correlations are therefore referred as to "Clever Hans" predictors (Lapuschkin et al., 2019).

explanations (and explanation methods) should fulfill. In particular, we focus on attribution methods assigning scores to every input dimension (e.g., pixel), reflecting the importance of this dimension with respect to the model's prediction. We formally introduce the concept of explanation for linear models and discuss possible extensions to nonlinear models such as deep neural networks. Throughout the chapter, we stress that the term explanation is very ambiguous and that we therefore should be always aware what we refer to when using it. We illustrate this often overlooked aspect by discussing the filter vs. pattern problem from the neuroimaging literature (Haufe et al., 2014).

Section 2.3 reviews explanation methods. In particular, we focus on XAI techniques proposed to compute explanations—in the form of attribution maps—for individual predictions of a deep classifier. These methods include perturbation-based approaches determining the relevant parts by relating the change in the output to changes in the input, surrogate-based techniques locally fitting a simple interpretable model (e.g., linear model) to the prediction, and propagation-based algorithms redistributing the model's decision in the form of relevance values from the output to the input. In addition, we briefly also discuss whole-dataset XAI analysis methods and approaches aiming to interpret the model itself rather than its predictions.

Section 2.4 discusses some of the recent developments in XAI. Since the field is very vibrant, we focus on only two directions. First, we present recent works aiming to integrate explanations into the model training in order to debug the model, improve its generalization ability, or make it more efficient by targeted pruning and quantization. Second, we present the concept of "neuralization," which allows one to transfer XAI techniques developed for explaining neural network classifiers to other model types or tasks such as clustering, regression, and outlier detection.

Section 2.5 concludes the chapter with a discussion on the limitations of current XAI methods and an outlook on interesting future directions.

2.2. Concepts

The term "explanation" is highly ambiguous and lacks a strict and uniformly accepted (mathematical) definition. Moreover, it can have different meanings in different contexts. For instance, if used in everyday life it usually refers to an interactive and iterative process, in which one person explains something (by using words, by referring to common concepts or by demonstration) to another person. In scientific context, an explanation, e.g., of a natural phenomenon, typically consists of deductive logic, a formal description or reference to the results of conducted experiments. When mentioning explanations in the context of machine learning, we usually refer to attribution maps computed for predictions of complex ML models (see Fig. 2.1). Misunderstandings can occur if we mix up these different types of explanations, e.g., if we expect the XAI method to generate human-like or formal descriptions of model behavior. Although

Image   Explanation

predicted as "pool table"   attribution map showing
                                         why this is a pool table

Figure 2.1 Explaining individual predictions by attribution maps. The attribution map highlights the pixels in the image, which are relevant for the model when classifying this particular image. The model seems (interpretation) to classify the image into the category "pool table" mainly by detecting a rectangular table (with feet), several pool balls, and two billiard cues in the image. The fact that the pool table is located in a bar seems to be not relevant for the model.

some progress has been recently made (e.g., Kim et al. (2018); Achtibat et al. (2022)), the computation of semantically richer (concept-based) explanations of model behavior is still an open research topic.

Another difficulty in defining the term explanation stems from its relative nature. More precisely, we usually explain a phenomenon with respect to a reference, e.g., "why classified as A and not as B", however, this reference is often not explicitly mentioned. In practice, it may make a big difference whether we explain the classification of an image as "dog" only relative to the class "cat" or relative to 1000 other classes. Furthermore, explanations can consist of different types of information, e.g., words, pixel values, or abstract concepts, and depend on the receiver (more fine-grained explanations for experts than for beginners) and the pursuit goal (i.e., what do we want the explanations for). Many XAI techniques allow one to adapt the explanation to these different purposes (e.g., by controlling the resolution and sparsity of the explanation), moreover, postprocessing techniques can be designed to highlight the information of interest (by pooling, thresholding, filtering, etc.) in the attribution map.

In summary, an explanation is an intrinsically ambiguous and relative concept, and one should therefore be fully aware of the specific setup (what do we exactly explain, relative to what, etc.) before applying the XAI algorithm.

2.2.1 Explaining, interpreting, and understanding

The terms *explaining*, *interpreting*, and *understanding* are often used interchangeably in the XAI literature. One possibility to distinguish these terms is to define them by the level of insight they provide into the functioning of the model.

In this case the term *explaining* refers to the process of computing an attribution map (or heatmap) quantifying the contribution of each input element (relevance value) to the prediction. This explanation neither tells us anything about the inner working of the model (i.e., which sequence of steps it takes to arrive at the prediction) nor is it necessarily comprehensible for a human, e.g., because the domain itself where the model operates (e.g., sensor readings) may not be comprehensible. Such explanations can be either computed post hoc using a dedicated XAI algorithm or provided by the model itself in form of an attention map.

The term *interpreting* refers to the process of assigning a meaning to the explanation. It naturally involves the human, who aims to comprehend (e.g., by mapping the attribution map to own mental concepts) and verify the model's decision making. Note that this term is sometimes also used when referring to the model's representation rather than the explanation of an individual prediction (Montavon et al., 2018).

Finally, the term *understanding* refers to a deeper functional insight which goes beyond the mere computation and interpretation of explanations. This understanding may comprise knowledge about the implemented mechanisms, learned rules, and prototypical behaviors of the model. Such knowledge can be very valuable for the development of more robust and trustworthy models,[2] as well as for gaining new scientific insights when applying deep learning to complex scientific datasets.

The definition of these three terms by the level of insight makes the "interpretation gap" in the field of XAI very explicit. In other words, although various techniques are available to explain our models and their predictions, e.g., in terms of attribution maps, we still often lack a profound understanding of their behaviors (Goebel et al., 2018).

2.2.2 Desiderata and explanation quality

In the following we will focus on the quality aspects of an explanation. Although the discussion about what exactly constitutes a good explanation and how to practically measure its quality is still ongoing, several useful desiderata for explanations have already crystallized out:

- Faithfulness. This property refers to the ability to accurately explain the function learned by the analyzed ML model. An explanation is faithful if it reflects the quantity being explained and not something else. In other words, it attributes the importance scores (relevance values) to each input element in a way so that they truly reflect the model's decision strategy. The "pixel-flipping" procedure (Samek et al., 2017) is a popular evaluation method for explanations, which indirectly tests

---

[2] Note that in many engineering domains, e.g., in the car or airplane industry, such a deep understanding of the system, its limitations, and the behavior of all its components is a prerequisite for passing the certification process. Similar auditing procedures are currently being investigated for AI-based systems (Berghoff et al., 2021). Since explanations foster a deeper understanding of the system's behavior, they play an important role in these testing procedures.

the faithfulness by disturbing the most relevant inputs and measuring the decay of the model's prediction ability. It assumes that a faithful explanation will lead to a much larger decay than, e.g., a random explanation.

- Conservation and Meaningful Sign. Relevance conservation ensures that the explanation remains connected to the model's output. It requires the summed up relevance values to match the evidence for the prediction (i.e., $f(\boldsymbol{x})$). This is a useful property, because it not only allows one to meaningfully compare explanations (if the model is more certain about the decision, then the corresponding explanation will have more relevance attributed), but also to aggregate them (e.g., compute clusters (Lapuschkin et al., 2019)). Explanations have a meaningful sign if positive relevance values indicate evidence supporting the prediction of the model and negative values refer to features speaking against it.

- Continuity. Explanation continuity requires explanations for two almost identical predictions (e.g., two images deviating in only a few pixels) to be very similar (Montavon et al., 2018). If fulfilled, this property ensures a certain level of robustness and smoothness of the explanation method.

- Understandability and Sufficiency. These properties require the explanation to be easy to understand by its receiver, typically a human, and provide sufficient information on how the model came up with its prediction. An insufficient explanation would provide incomplete (e.g., discard a part of the image) or uninformative information (e.g., Q: "Why has this image been classified as dog?", A: "Because there is a dog in the image."). An explanation of a sensor time series may be sufficient, but still hard to understand for the receiver. To make it more understandable, one could try to transform the explanation from the time domain to frequency–amplitude domain (which is often easier to interpret for time series data).

- Applicability and Runtime. Many other desirable properties can be defined for the explanation method. For instance, one such property is the specificity of the XAI method, e.g., is it only applicable for convolutional neural networks or widely applicable. Another property is its computational efficiency, e.g., whether the XAI method computes the explanation very efficiently or comes with a significant computational overhead.

This list of desiderata is not complete, e.g., additional properties such as implementation invariance (Sundararajan et al., 2017) or consistency (Lundberg et al., 2020) can be found in the literature. Also various desirable properties for explanations have been described for stakeholder groups, which are not ML experts. We refer the reader to the work of Miller (2019), who provides a social science perspective on XAI, and Bhatt et al. (2020), who explore how different stateholder groups in organizations view and use explanations. In addition to these desiderata, various approaches have been proposed to practically measure explanation quality, e.g., by pixel-flipping (Samek et al., 2017), by pointing games (Zhang et al., 2018) or by relying on a synthetic task with ground-truth information about the explanation (Arras et al., 2022). The latter work provides a freely available benchmark dataset,[3] which can be used to objectively evaluate and compare XAI methods. We also refer the reader to Quantus (Hedström et al., 2022), which is a recently proposed toolkit[4] for responsible evaluation of neural network explanations.

2.2.3 Explaining linear models

This section introduces the concept of an explanation as a prediction decomposition. Let us assume a trained ML model, e.g., a deep neural network, implementing an abstracted function

$$f : \mathbb{R}^d \to \mathbb{R}.$$

The input to the model can be, e.g., pixel intensities, and the output a binary classification decision. Thus, the function output $f(\boldsymbol{x})$ can be interpreted as the amount of evidence for $(f(\boldsymbol{x}) > 0)$ or against $(f(\boldsymbol{x}) < 0)$ the presence of a certain class (e.g., a dog) in the image.

An *explanation* (Samek et al., 2021) can be viewed as a "meaningful" decomposition of an individual prediction in terms of input-wise scores $\boldsymbol{R} = [R_1, R_2, \ldots, R_d] \in \mathbb{R}^d$, i.e.,

$$f(\boldsymbol{x}) \approx \sum_{i=1}^{d} R_i. \tag{2.1}$$

Since linear models are by definition decomposable into input-wise scores, they are immediately explainable

$$f(\boldsymbol{x}) = \sum_{i=1}^{d} w_i x_i + b \approx \sum_{i=1}^{d} R_i \quad \text{with} \quad R_i = w_i x_i. \tag{2.2}$$

Note that the bias b constitutes a fixed shift (not depending on the input) and is therefore not included into the explanation. In this decomposition the ith feature is regarded relevant if (1) it is present in the data (i.e., $x_i \neq 0$) and (2) it is actually used by the model (i.e., $w_i \neq 0$). The combination of these two factors determines the amount of relevance assigned to a feature. The more the feature is present and the more it is used by the model to arrive at its decision, the higher relevance it will have. Note that a feature can also have negative relevance. In this case it contradicts the model's decision $f(\boldsymbol{x}) > 0$, e.g., if it is present in the data in larger amounts than the zero reference value ($x_i > 0$), but it inhibits the model in arriving at large prediction values ($w_i < 0$). We would also like to stress that not all XAI methods reviewed in Section 2.3 fulfill the above definition

---

[3] The CLEVR-XAI dataset can be found at https://github.com/ahmedmagdiosman/clevr-xai.
[4] Quantus can be found at https://github.com/understandable-machine-intelligence-lab/Quantus.

of relevance. For instance, methods such as Sensitivity Analysis (Simonyan et al., 2014) do not explain the "model–data interaction" (i.e., the two factors: (i) is the model using the feature and (ii) is the feature present in the input), but just visualize the sensitivity of the model to the input dimensions. For linear models such methods would provide the same explanation (i.e., $R_i = w_i$) irrespectively of the input (for deep neural networks this is not necessarily the case due to pooling layers, etc.). Thus, it would certainly be technically more correct to refer to these attribution maps as sensitivity maps rather than explanations. However, in this chapter we will not follow this strict definition, but consider a wide range of approaches which have been proposed in the context of XAI and refer to them as explanation methods.

While an immediately meaningful decomposition of the prediction can be found for linear models, it becomes more challenging to find similarly adequate definitions for the nonlinear case. When viewing the nonlinear model as a function, one can naturally obtain a decomposition from its Taylor expansion

$$f(\boldsymbol{x}) \approx \sum_{i=1}^{d} R_i = \sum_{i=1}^{d} \underbrace{[\nabla f(\widetilde{\boldsymbol{x}})]_i \cdot (x_i - \widetilde{x}_i)}_{R_i}, \tag{2.3}$$

where $\widetilde{\boldsymbol{x}}$ is some nearby root point. Also this explanation considers an input dimension to be relevant if (1) the feature is present in the data, i.e., it differs from the reference value $\widetilde{x}_i$, and (2) the model output is sensitive to it, i.e., $[\nabla f(\widetilde{\boldsymbol{x}})]_i \neq 0$. Although this type of Taylor expansion offers a nice mathematical framework to decompose the model's prediction, it is not directly applicable to more complex models such as deep neural networks due to the gradient shattering problem and the difficulty of root point selection (Samek et al., 2021).

The approach of Deep Taylor Decomposition (Montavon et al., 2017) overcomes these challenges and provides a popular theoretical framework for deep neural network explanations.

2.2.4 Explaining signal vs. explaining noise

This section again focuses on the question of *what* to explain and demonstrates that in some settings naively computed explanations may not explain what we are interested in (i.e., the signal) but rather be affected by other factors (e.g., noise in the data). Most image datasets such as ImageNet, PASCAL VOC, or MS COCO are practically free of noise, i.e., the noise coming from the image sensor is negligible (except when the image is being taken in poor light conditions). This property makes the features extracted by the ML model (and identified by the XAI method) directly interpretable, e.g., pixels representing the wheels of the car or the nose of the dog. The same noise freeness property applies to natural language processing (i.e., words are not noisy), another domain where XAI has been successfully applied.

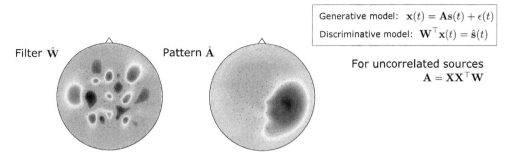

Filter $\hat{\mathbf{W}}$ Pattern $\hat{\mathbf{A}}$

Generative model: $\mathbf{x}(t) = \mathbf{A}\mathbf{s}(t) + \epsilon(t)$
Discriminative model: $\mathbf{W}^{\top}\mathbf{x}(t) = \hat{\mathbf{s}}(t)$

For uncorrelated sources
$$\mathbf{A} = \mathbf{X}\mathbf{X}^{\top}\mathbf{W}$$

Figure 2.2 Filter vs. pattern problem. Since the spatial filter is largely affected by the noise in the measured EEG signal, it is not directly interpretable. On the other hand, the spatial pattern is easily interpretable, here it visualizes the relevant source over the right sensorimotor cortex.

However, many domains in signal processing do not fulfill this property. For instance, EEG measurements are very noisy with the background noise often having a much larger power than the signal of interest. Here the measured signal $\boldsymbol{x}$ at time point t is usually represented as a linear combination of the sources $\boldsymbol{s}$ and some noise ϵ component, i.e.,

$$\boldsymbol{x}(t) = \boldsymbol{A}\boldsymbol{s}(t) + \epsilon(t).$$

Advanced signal processing methods have been proposed to extract and analyze the signal component and suppress the noise. For instance, in Brain–Computer Interfacing (BCI) (Wolpaw et al., 2000) one task is to decode the imagined motion of the person (e.g., left hand vs. right hand) solely from the EEG measurements. Since motion related information can be extracted from the power of the sources (the so-called ERD/ERS effect (Wolpaw et al., 2000)), various algorithms have been proposed to spatially filter the data and estimate sources $\hat{\boldsymbol{s}}$ containing this information (see Fig. 2.2). Technically, this is done by computing the so-called spatial filter $\boldsymbol{W}$, i.e.,

$$\boldsymbol{W}^{\top}\boldsymbol{x}(t) = \hat{\boldsymbol{s}}(t).$$

Since it is of neurophysiological interest to understand the location of the sources, explainability is a key requirement in this kind of analyses. However, visualizing the spatial filter weights on the scalp (i.e., $R_i = w_i$) does not give many insights (see Fig. 2.2). The reason for that is that the model (i.e., the learned $\boldsymbol{W}$) is largely affected by the noise component ϵ, which it tries to cancel out when extracting the sources. Thus, the explanation (in this case, the spatial filter) also largely shows the noise component.

There are techniques to suppress the noise in the explanation and just visualize the relevant signal locations. This so-called spatial pattern can be obtained from the spatial filter by multiplying it with the covariance matrix (Haufe et al., 2014). In this example it shows the right sensorimotor cortex as the source of one signal component responsible for distinguishing between imagined movements (see Fig. 2.2). This result is consistent with the knowledge in neurophysiology.

Although neither the spatial filter nor the spatial pattern constitute an explanation as defined in Section 2.2.3 (they can be rather regarded as sensitivity maps, one being and the other not being affected by the noise component), this example demonstrates that we should always be aware about what we are actually explaining. Not much work in the XAI literature explicitly targets this signal vs. noise problem, with (Kindermans et al., 2018; Pahde et al., 2022) being an exception.

2.3. Methods

The last decade has been a very active phase in the field of XAI. Various techniques have been developed to explain individual decisions of increasingly complex algorithms such as kernel-based Support Vector Machines (Baehrens et al., 2010; Lapuschkin et al., 2016), Decision Trees and Random Forests (Lundberg et al., 2020), Convolutional Neural Networks (Simonyan et al., 2014; Bach et al., 2015), LSTM networks (Arras et al., 2019), and other ML models (Kauffmann et al., 2020; Lundberg et al., 2020). This section gives an overview over the most popular explanation techniques, mainly focusing on deep neural networks. For a more complete overview, we refer the reader to other excellent review and survey papers (Samek et al., 2021; Gilpin et al., 2018; Linardatos et al., 2021), as well as to toolboxes implementing XAI methods and providing advanced analysis tools (e.g., Alber et al. (2019); Kokhlikyan et al. (2020); Anders et al. (2021)). For a systematic evaluation and comparison of XAI methods, we refer the reader to a recent study with ground-truth explanations (Arras et al., 2022).

2.3.1 Overview of attribution methods

Different approaches have been developed to explain single predictions of machine learning models (see Table 2.1 for an overview of four types of methods). These methods are based on different assumptions and come with specific limitations and benefits. Two theoretical XAI frameworks, one based on Deep Taylor Decomposition (Montavon et al., 2017) and the other based on Shapley values (Shapley, 1953), comprise some of the most popular methods as special cases (we refer the reader to Samek et al. (2021) for more information).

2.3.1.1 Perturbation-based methods

Perturbation-based explanation methods explain individual predictions by observing the changes in the model's output resulting from changes in the input. For instance, an occlusion of the object of interest (e.g., a ladybug in the image) will very likely drastically change the prediction of a ladybug classifier, whereas the occlusion of background pixels

Table 2.1 Overview of popular types of explanation methods. Four properties are compared, namely model agnosticism, computational efficiency, the ability to compute explanations in a deterministic manner, and potential artifacts affecting the explanation process. Perturbation-based methods produce samples which often lie out of the data manifold (OOD). Gradient-based methods are partly model agnostic (as they require access to the gradient) and are known to suffer from the gradient shattering problem (Balduzzi et al., 2017). Surrogate-based explanations may suffer from artifacts coming from a poor fit of the surrogate model. Propagation-based methods may require specific and layer-dependent redistribution rules.

Method	Examples	Agnostic	Efficient	Determ.	Challenges
Pert.–Based	Zeiler and Fergus (2014); Shapley (1953); Fong and Vedaldi (2017)	YES	NO	YES	OOD
Grad.–Based	Baehrens et al. (2010); Simonyan et al. (2014); Sundararajan et al. (2017)	PARTLY	YES	YES	Shattering
Sur.–Based	Ribeiro et al. (2016, 2018)	YES	NO	NO	Surrogate
Prop.–Based	Bach et al. (2015); Montavon et al. (2017); Zhang et al. (2018)	NO	YES	YES	Rules[a]

[a] Deep Taylor Decomposition (Montavon et al., 2017) offers a theoretical framework to design these rules.

will have no or only a minor effect. By systematically observing these changes, one can derive which parts of the input are truly relevant to the model (see Fig. 2.3).

Mathematically, the different perturbation–based XAI methods can be informally viewed as algorithms measuring the (expected) decrease or distortion D with respect to the prediction $f(x)$, resulting from the application of the perturbation function $\mathcal{P}$ to the input, e.g.,

$$D = \mathbb{E}\left[(f(x) - f(\mathcal{P}(x)))^2\right]. \tag{2.4}$$

The methods differ in the way they implement $\mathcal{P}$ and how they construct the relevance values R_i from this perturbation process.

In the simple occlusion analysis, an individual input dimension i (or a patch) is substituted by a fixed value (e.g., zero) or random noise sampled from an appropriate distribution. This procedure needs to be applied to each input dimension (or patch) and is therefore computationally demanding. The resulting decrease or distortion can be directly regarded as relevance value. This approach is applicable to a model without requiring to know its internal structure and parameters (model agnosticism). However, the perturbation process generates out of data manifold (OOD) inputs, which may make the evaluation unreliable in the case of complex models such as deep neural networks. Furthermore, occlusion analysis has a strong locality assumption as it only occludes one feature at a time, which makes the detection of relevant interactions of nonneighboring features very difficult. The use of a generative model can partially cope

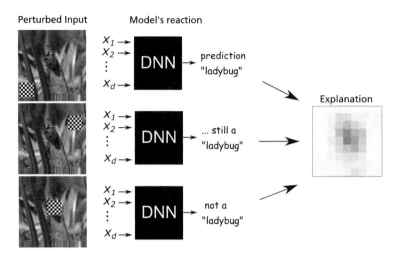

Figure 2.3 Example of a simple perturbation-based explanation method which constructs the explanation by tracking the model's reaction to local occlusions of the input image.

with the out of data manifold problem (Agarwal and Nguyen, 2020). Also Shapley values (Shapley, 1953) overcome many of the above mentioned problems and are regarded as solid mathematical framework for XAI. However, since the computation of Shapley values involves all combinations of possible occlusion patterns, it is intractable for most of the current ML models.[5] Approximation algorithms for computing Shapley values exist (Lundberg and Lee, 2017), but are nevertheless computationally demanding.

Other perturbation-based XAI methods do not rely on a fixed perturbation process $\mathcal{P}$, but try to optimize it under some sparsity constraints. For instance, the Meaningful Perturbation method (Fong and Vedaldi, 2017) aims to synthesize a sparse occlusion pattern, which maximizes the decrease, i.e., which leads to the maximum drop of the function value f. Since this occlusion pattern identifies the impactful input variables, it can be directly used as explanation. The work of MacDonald et al. (2019) follows a similar idea by splitting the variables into a relevant and irrelevant subset and casting the explanation problem into a rate-distortion framework. The method aims to find the smallest set of input variables (i.e., the relevant ones) that will make the model approximately arrive at the same predictions on average, when replacing the nonrelevant input variables by random noise. Unfortunately, finding such smallest set is computationally very demanding (MacDonald et al., 2019).

In summary, perturbation-based approaches represent the simplest and probably oldest category of XAI techniques. They have the advantage of being easy to implement and model agnostic, however, they are typically computationally very demanding and

[5] Tractable algorithms were recently proposed for tree-based models (Lundberg et al., 2020).

may suffer from out of manifold effects and restrictive locality assumptions. Shapley values and the rate-distortion approach are even intractable in practice, except for some very simple models, low-dimensional inputs, or when relying on approximations.

2.3.1.2 Gradient-based methods

This class of XAI approaches constructs explanations from gradient information. As gradients quantify the function's sensitivity to infinitesimally small changes, these methods can also be regarded as very local perturbation-based approaches. Sensitivity maps based on gradient magnitude have already been proposed over 25 years ago to visualize and explain neural network predictions (Morch et al., 1995). For RGB images, these methods compute sensitivity scores as

$$R_i = \left\| \left(\frac{\partial}{\partial x_{i,c}} f(\boldsymbol{x}) \right)_{c \in (r,g,b)} \right\|_{\ell_p}, \tag{2.5}$$

where ℓ_p indicates a p-norm. These methods have been also applied to explain more recent ML models (Baehrens et al., 2010; Simonyan et al., 2014). Although very efficient and simple to implement, major drawbacks have been reported for these explanation methods (Montavon et al., 2018), including their inability to capture global effects (e.g., they do not explain what features make this ladybug a ladybug, but rather what features–if infinitesimally changed—would make it more or less ladybugish), lack of sign information, and high levels of noise due to gradient shattering (Balduzzi et al., 2017). Thus, explaining neural networks predictions through sensitivity maps is of limited practical value as they do not decompose the predictions[6] and are often very hard to interpret due to a high level of noise (see Fig. 2.4).

Extensions such as Integrated Gradients (Sundararajan et al., 2017) overcome some of these major limitations and are therefore widely used today. This method constructs explanations by integrating the computed gradient $\nabla f(\boldsymbol{x})$ along a path connecting the point $\boldsymbol{x}$ with some reference point $\widetilde{\boldsymbol{x}}$, e.g., a point lying on the decision hyperplane. Mathematically, this can be expressed as

$$R_i(\boldsymbol{x}) = (x_i - \widetilde{x}_i) \cdot \int_0^1 [\nabla f(\widetilde{\boldsymbol{x}} + t \cdot (\boldsymbol{x} - \widetilde{\boldsymbol{x}}))]_i \, dt. \tag{2.6}$$

In contrast to sensitivity analysis, Integrated Gradients construct explanations which are consistent with the definition in Section 2.2.3.

Other popular extensions of sensitivity analysis exist. For instance, the SmoothGrad method (Smilkov et al., 2017) implements the seemingly paradoxical idea of removing

---

[6] Note that sensitivity maps do not decompose the prediction $f(\boldsymbol{x})$, but the change in prediction, i.e., $\sum_i R_i = \nabla f(\boldsymbol{x})$.

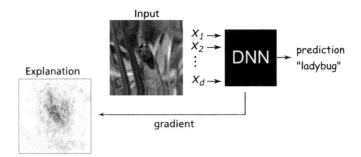

Figure 2.4 Example of a gradient-based explanation method which constructs a sensitivity map based on the model's gradient magnitude.

noise in the explanation by adding noise to the input sample. Technically, this method tackles the noise problem by sampling gradients in the neighborhood of the point of interest and averaging them. The result of the averaging process is a smoothed sensitivity map.

2.3.1.3 Surrogate-based methods

Surrogate-based XAI methods follow a different idea. Instead of directly explaining the prediction of the model of interest (e.g., a deep neural network classifier), they first approximate the prediction locally using a simple (and interpretable) surrogate model and explain the latter in a second step (see Fig. 2.5). LIME (Ribeiro et al., 2016) uses a linear surrogate model and is one of the most popular methods in this category. In the first step, LIME estimates the parameters w of a linear model by minimizing the error

$$err = \sum_i (f(x_i) - w^\top x_i)^2, \tag{2.7}$$

where x_i are sampled in the neighborhood of the point of interest x. Note that the quality of the fit depends on various factors, including the number of samples used. Thus, a good fit usually comes with a large computational overhead. In the second step, LIME uses the surrogate model to construct the explanation. As shown in Section 2.2.3 this is straightforward for linear models, resulting in $R_i = x_i w_i$. Other methods in this category, e.g., LORE (Guidotti et al., 2018) or Anchors (Ribeiro et al., 2018), aim to explain a local prediction by extracting a decision rule. Optimally, these decision rules are valid beyond the local prediction (i.e., have a larger coverage) and thus give more global insights into model behavior.

A benefit of surrogate-based methods is their model agnosticism, i.e., they explain predictions without requiring access to the model's internals such as topology structure, weights, activations, etc. This property makes these methods widely applicable. However, since they do not explain the ML model of interest but a surrogate of it, the

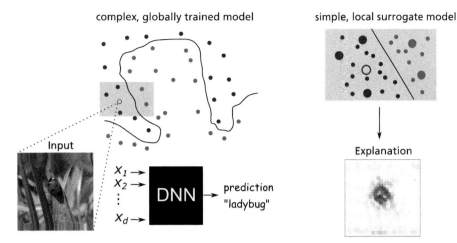

Figure 2.5 Surrogate-based explanation methods first locally approximate the prediction by fitting a simple (e.g., linear) model. Here, the empty blue (dark gray in print version) dot stands for the target prediction and the green (light gray in print version) rectangle represents its local neighborhood. A good fit of the surrogate model usually requires sampling in the local neighborhood (shown as small dots in the right panel). In a second step, an explanation is constructed from the surrogate model.

explanation quality largely depends on the quality of the surrogate fit. A good fit requires significant sampling, which makes these approaches computationally costly. The use of sampling also makes explanations nondeterministic, which can be disadvantageous in certain applications (e.g., when explanations are used for legal purposes).

2.3.1.4 Propagation-based methods

This class of methods simplify the explanation problem by utilizing the model's internal structure. For instance, in the case of deep neural networks these methods do not explain the complex model in one step (e.g., by approximating the model or fitting a surrogate model), but explain (i.e., decompose) the results layer by layer, starting from the model's output. Since the operations between layers (e.g., ReLU applied to a weighted sum of inputs) are much easier to explain than the highly nonlinear prediction function represented by the whole model, propagation-based methods provide high quality explanations at very low computational costs. Layer-wise Relevance Propagation (LRP) (Bach et al., 2015) is a popular approach in this category.

Fig. 2.6 shows the redistribution process implemented by LRP. Starting from the last layer, LRP iteratively redistributes the relevance values $R_j^{[i-1]}$ from the upper to the lower layer, i.e.,

$$R_j^{[i-1]} = \sum_{k=1}^{n_i} \frac{z_{jk}^{[i]}}{\sum_{l=1}^{n_{i-1}} z_{lk}^{[i]} + b_k^{[i]}} R_k^{[i]}, \tag{2.8}$$

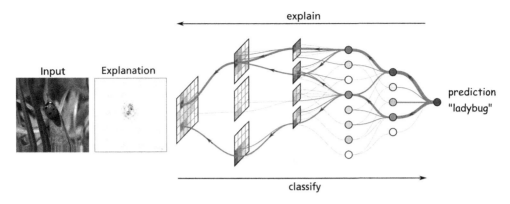

Figure 2.6 Propagation-based explanation methods rely on a meaningful layer-wise redistribution of relevance, starting from the output layer.

where the $R_k^{[i]}$ upper-layer relevance values are already known, and $z_{jk}^{[i]}$ denotes the (relevance) contribution of neuron j to neuron k.

The specific properties of the layers in a neural network (e.g., convolutional, fully-connected, input layer) should be taken into account in order to meaningfully measure the contribution of neuron j to neuron k, The simplest way to do so is to take two factors into account, namely the connection strength between these two neurons (i.e., the weight w_{jk}) and the activation of the lower-layer neuron j. Thus, more relevance is redistributed from neuron k to neuron j, if the latter is more activated (this is the case when the neuron detects structures which are present in the image, e.g., the ladybug's black dots or the green (light gray in print version) grass in the background) and if these two neurons strongly interact (i.e., the detected structure plays an important role in the upper layer processing). In this case we arrive at $z_{jk}^{[i]} = x_j^{[i-1]} w_{jk}^{[i]}$, resulting in the standard LRP rule. Since this rule may lead to numerical instabilities (due to vanishing denominator), extensions have been proposed which add a stabilizer term to the denominator (known as ϵ-LRP). Recent work showed that it is beneficial to use rules which take the specific properties of the different layers (e.g., positivity constraint after ReLU operation, convolution structure, box constraints such as [0 255] in the input layer) into account (Montavon et al., 2019). Luckily Deep Taylor Decomposition (Montavon et al., 2017) offers a theoretical framework to design such layer type-specific redistribution rules. Extensions of LRP have been also developed for models with recurrent structures (Arras et al., 2017).

Note that popular methods such as Excitation Backprop (Zhang et al., 2018) can be viewed as a specific realization of LRP, namely as the $\alpha\beta$-LRP method (Bach et al., 2015) with parameters $\alpha = 1$ and $\beta = 0$. Other approaches such as GradCAM (Selvaraju et al., 2016) and deconvolution (Zeiler and Fergus, 2014) also fall into the propagation-based category of XAI methods.

In summary, propagation-based methods offer an efficient[7] framework for computing explanations, which (at least in the case of LRP) are aligned with the definitions from Section 2.2. Since LRP does not use gradients, it does not suffer from gradient shattering, moreover, it fulfills the continuity property and allows one to compute signed explanations, where positive relevances indicate supporting evidence for a prediction and negative relevances represent information contradicting the prediction.

The price to pay for the great advantages of this class of XAI methods is the required knowledge about the model internals and the layer–type dependency of the redistribution rule, complicating the implementation and application of these approaches to nonneural network ML models. Luckily, highly efficient toolboxes have recently become available (Alber et al., 2019), as well as a generic "neuralization trick" (see Section 2.4) allowing one to transfer these methods beyond neural network classifiers.

2.3.2 Other types of XAI methods

To complement the above discussion, this section briefly summarizes a recently proposed metaanalysis techniques for explanations and presents some popular nonattribution XAI techniques.

The spectral relevance analysis (SpRAy) method (Lapuschkin et al., 2019) aims to find common patterns, i.e., prototypical decision strategies of the model, from a set of individual explanations by clustering. SpRAy applies spectral clustering to the preprocessed (e.g., blurred and standardized) heatmaps computed by a perturbation-, gradient-, surrogate- or perturbation-based XAI algorithm. The number of distinct clusters representing distinct prediction strategies can be identified from the gap in the eigenvalue spectrum. Furthermore, one can visualize the clustering by applying low-dimensional embedding methods such as tSNE. This type of dataset-wide analysis of explanation patterns can help to find flawed behaviors (Lapuschkin et al., 2019) and debug the model (Anders et al., 2022). Note that such clusterings not necessarily need to be performed on the input space explanations, but can be performed on the hidden representation (feature space) (Anders et al., 2022), which encodes more abstract concepts and is more invariant to translations, scaling, and other transformations of the input.

Other nonattribution-based methods aim to interpret the model, e.g., understand what concepts particular neurons encode, rather than explaining individual predictions. For instance, the network dissection approach (Zhou et al., 2018; Bau et al., 2019) identifies neurons encoding certain emergent concepts such as object parts, materials, or colors. Methods such as testing with concept activation vectors (TCAV) (Kim et al., 2018) allow one to identify and quantitatively test for hidden-layer patterns for every individual prediction. The recently proposed Concept Relevance Propagation (CRP)

---

[7] The computation of an explanation is of the order of a backward pass, thus can be very efficiently implemented with GPU support.

approach (Achtibat et al., 2022) combines the local and global XAI perspectives in order to explain individual predictions in terms of localized and human-understandable concepts. Other work focuses on concept whitening (Chen et al., 2020) and actively penalizes the concept activation vectors during training in order to force the model to learn decorrelated, and thus more interpretable, representations. Another approach (Chen et al., 2019) explains the model's decisions by comparing activations to prototypical patterns in the training data, e.g., it explains the prediction of a clay colored sparrow in terms of learned prototypical parts of clay colored sparrows from the training data. A similar concept of explaining by example is proposed in Koh and Liang (2017). This approach uses the influence function to identify the most relevant training samples, i.e., samples through which the model has learned to classify a particular test sample as it does. Another approach (Zhang et al., 2019) proposes to explain individual predictions at different levels of granularity by fitting a decision tree and mining all potential decision modes of the convolutional neural network. Finally, attention mechanisms (Larochelle and Hinton, 2010) are a common way to foster transparency, even in highly complex models such as Vision Transformers (Han et al., 2020).

2.4. New developments

This section discusses two interesting new developments in the field of XAI: first, the use of explanations for improving (different aspects of) the model, and second, the concept of neuralization, which allows transferring XAI methods developed for deep learning classifiers to other types of models and tasks.

2.4.1 XAI-based model improvement

As we discussed in previous sections, complex machine learning models potentially suffer from overfitting, can be biased and unreliable, moreover, in the worst case they become "Clever Hans" predictors. One source of the problem is that the information provided during training is usually very coarse. In particular, in classification tasks the error signal provided to the model is merely the correctness of the decision. Although more informed labeling procedures have been investigated in Binder et al. (2012), we still typically train our classifiers with integer labels denoting the correct category. Explanations offer a much more rich source of information, when included into the model training. Note that the integration of XAI can happen on different levels, e.g., it can be used to correct for the training data (e.g., identify and remove flawed samples) or as additional regularization target in the loss function.

Exemplar approaches using XAI to change the distribution of samples that are fed to the model or generate additional samples to prevent undesired behaviors (e.g., focusing on the copyright watermark) are Schramowski et al. (2020); Anders et al. (2022). Both approaches include the participation of a human user. In Schramowski et al. (2020) the user directly can correct the model prediction and the corresponding explanation provided by the XAI method. Thus, the human can actively include his/her rationale to improve the model, e.g., tell the model not to focus on the copyright watermark when classifying images of a horse. This user feedback can be either utilized by generating additional samples (e.g., without a copyright tag) helping the model learn the desired strategy, or by directly augmenting the loss function as proposed by Ross et al. (2017). Anders et al. (2022) use XAI to identify flawed prediction strategies. For that they compute explanations by using LRP, followed by a dataset-wide analysis and identification of artifactual strategies. An extension of SpRAy (Lapuschkin et al., 2019) is proposed to reliably identify common prediction patterns. Also here the human expert has to decide whether an observed decision strategy is desired or flawed. In the latter case, the artifact is added to other samples (either in the input space or in feature space as a concept activation vector) in order to encourage the model to ignore it. An alternative projection-based method is also proposed in Anders et al. (2022) to actively suppress artifacts during inference without the need for additional finetuning of the model.

A more direct way to guide the model training through XAI is to add an explanation-based term as regularizer to the loss function, i.e.,

$$\mathcal{L}(f_\theta(\boldsymbol{x}_i), y_i) = \mathcal{L}_{\text{pred}}(f_\theta(\boldsymbol{x}_i), y_i) + \lambda \mathcal{L}_{\text{xai}}(\boldsymbol{R}_i, \boldsymbol{M}_i), \tag{2.9}$$

where $\boldsymbol{R}_i = [R_1, R_2, \ldots, R_d]$ is the explanation computed for the prediction of sample $\boldsymbol{x}_i$, $\boldsymbol{M}_i$ is a ground-truth relevance mask of same dimensionality provided by the human, λ is a regularization parameter, $\mathcal{L}_{\text{pred}}$ denotes the standard prediction loss term between the true and predicted class probabilities including any non-XAI-based regularization terms. Ross et al. (2017), Liu and Avci (2019), Rieger et al. (2020), and Erion et al. (2020) propose an XAI-based loss term $\mathcal{L}_{\text{xai}}$ which compares the explanation to the human provided ground truth. The inclusion of such a term forces the model to learn prediction strategies, which are aligned with the human expert. In addition, one can also include XAI-based loss terms, which do not depend on human provided ground truth, but rather impose other properties (e.g., sparsity, locality) on the explanation (Ross and Doshi-Velez, 2018; Erion et al., 2020).

Yet another stream of work used explanations not to guarantee a human consistent prediction strategy, but to make the model computationally more efficient by pruning and quantization. Especially propagation-based XAI methods are well-suited for this task as they compute relevance scores not only for the input elements, but also for every component (neuron, weight) of a neural network. Thus, if we know which neurons or weights are not so relevant for a task, we can remove or strongly quantize them without much effect on the overall performance. Yeom et al. (2021) computed such average relevance values using LRP for a reference dataset and showed that such an XAI-based pruning criterion is more effective (e.g., one can prune much more weights and neurons) than when relying on the weight magnitude or gradient information (Sun et al., 2017; Molchanov et al., 2016; Li et al., 2017). Becking et al. (2022) generalized this approach by using these relevance values as guidance for a clustering-based quantization algorithm. With that the authors were able to increase model storage efficiency by generating low bit width and sparse networks, and simultaneously preserve or even improve (due to reduction in overfitting) performance.

2.4.2 The neuralization trick

Propagation-based XAI methods can be very efficiently implemented, have a profound mathematical foundation (Deep Taylor Decomposition) and fulfill various XAI desiderata, e.g., explanation continuity, signed relevances, conservation, etc. However, as discussed in Section 2.3 these methods have been originally developed for layered models such as convolutional neural networks. Many popular ML algorithms, e.g., k-means clustering (MacQueen, 1967), kernel density estimation (Parzen, 1962), and one–class Support Vector Machine (Li et al., 2003), do not have such a layered structure. Thus, propagation-based XAI methods are not directly applicable for explaining these algorithms.

The concept of *neuralization*, however, aims to make these methods applicable by constructing an equivalent neural network implementing the above-mentioned algorithms. In short, the idea of this approach is to map something which we do not know how to explain to a form (i.e., we "neuralize" it by constructing an equivalent neural network), which we can explain and for which we have established techniques and theory. One should stress here that we construct and do not train the surrogate neural network, i.e., this process is extremely fast and we do not need any training data for it. In the following, we will explain the neuralization of k-means as proposed by Kauffmann et al. (2019).

At first it may look counterintuitive to construct a neural network (which is commonly considered a black box) to explain an algorithm such as k-means (which is commonly considered a straightforward ML algorithm). However, our goal is to formulate the cluster assignment decision of k-means as a sequence of simple operations (layers of a neural network), which we know how to explain. Thus, we aim to simplify the explanation problem, without introducing any additional complexity or nonlinearity to the cluster assignment function. After neuralization we will be able to explain the assignment decision in terms of an attribution map, i.e., identify the input dimensions which have mostly contributed for a sample $\boldsymbol{x}$ to be assigned to cluster c.

Technically, we define the following function to represent the assignment to cluster c:

$$f_c(\boldsymbol{x}) = - \|\boldsymbol{x} - \boldsymbol{\mu}_c\|^2 + \min_{k \neq c} \left\{ \|\boldsymbol{x} - \boldsymbol{\mu}_k\|^2 \right\},$$

where $\boldsymbol{\mu}_c$ and $\boldsymbol{\mu}_k$ represent the cluster center of cluster c and k, respectively. If the output of this function is positive, then the sample $\boldsymbol{x}$ is assigned to cluster c. If it is zero, then the sample lies on the decision boundary, i.e., has the same distance to cluster c than to some other cluster k. This cluster assignment function represents the k-means clustering solution and can be rewritten as a two-layer network

$$h_k = \boldsymbol{w}_k^\top \boldsymbol{x} + b_k \qquad \text{(layer 1)},$$
$$f_c = \min_{k \neq c}\{h_k\} \qquad \text{(layer 2)},$$

where $\boldsymbol{w}_k = 2(\boldsymbol{\mu}_c - \boldsymbol{\mu}_k)$ and $b_k = \|\boldsymbol{\mu}_k\|^2 - \|\boldsymbol{\mu}_c\|^2$. Note that layer 1 is a standard linear layer and layer 2 a min-pooling layer. Predictions of this simple neural network (i.e., representing cluster assignments of the original k-means algorithm) can be easily explained by LRP.

Similar neuralization steps can be applied to many other algorithms, e.g., 1-class SVM (Li et al., 2003) or kernel density estimator (Montavon et al., 2022). Moreover, even within a neural network, multiple layers can be mapped to an equivalent form, which is more accessible to explanation. This "restructuring trick" has been proposed for the explanation of regression problems (Letzgus et al., 2022). The difficulty in neuralizing parts of a model or a nonneural algorithm is to find an equivalent (but easier explainable) form. This at the moment requires human involvement, but can potentially be automated in the future. Additionally, one should also be aware that different neuralizations of the same model may lead to different explanations as propagation-based XAI methods do not explain the function represented by the model irrespectively of its implementation, but the model's processing of the input sample (model–data interaction). More research is needed to better understand the impact of neuralization on the explanations and investigate respective desiderata (e.g., uniqueness, functional equivalence, minimalism principle).

Finally, the neuralization trick not only allows one to convert opaque algorithms into neural networks, which are explainable, but can also be used to apply all other things specifically developed for neural networks. For instance, by using the neuralized form, one could easily create adversarial examples for a nonneural network algorithm.

2.5. Limitations and future work

After reviewing the basic concepts and methods, as well as some of the new developments in the field of XAI, we would now like to focus on the limitations of current approach and highlight interesting future research directions. When applying XAI beyond images and text, the question quickly arises whether the explanations are at all interpretable to a human (understandability desideratum). For instance, explanations on time series data, e.g., indicating that certain points in the time series are relevant, can be very difficult to understand for the human. Thus in this case, one should consider transforming the data into a more interpretable domain (e.g., spectrogram) before training the model. In addition, a meaningful postprocessing of the explanation could help to enhance the interpretability. Future work needs to develop generic ways to interpret models trained on data from noninterpretable domains.

Of interest here are also more complex explanations going beyond individual attribution maps. In many applications, the most interesting aspects of a signal are not encoded in individual features, but in the interactions between features. For instance, in ECG signals the time interval between two peaks (RR interval) or the amplitude change between the reference value and the peak (T amplitude) convey relevant information, e.g., about a cardiac disorder. Clearly, the level on which we provide explanations can make a practical difference in many applications, as a high relevance value at a particular time point of the time series alone does not represent these interacting effects. Unfortunately, computing feature interactions is not easy and may be computationally very expensive (even for interactions between only two features). For specific models, low-dimensional input methods such as Shapley interaction index (Lundberg et al., 2020) are available. For state-of-the-art deep neural networks, relevant feature co-occurrences could potentially be captured post hoc by clustering or correlating relevances over a set of explanations. Promising steps towards tackling the feature interaction problem have also been taken with the BiLRP approach (Eberle et al., 2022), a method which efficiently allows decomposing similarity scores on pairs of input features.

A topic which goes beyond the scope of this chapter is the use of explanations for AI auditing and certification (Berghoff et al., 2021). XAI methods have successfully demonstrated their ability to identify flaws and biases in the model, in the extreme case Clever Hans behaviors can be detected from just seeing one explanation. Note that identifying such problems without explanations, i.e., solely based on prediction accuracy metrics, would require many well-curated samples (e.g., horses with and without copyright watermark). The trend to use XAI for detecting flaws and improving the model will continue and hopefully result in standardized benchmarking and auditing procedures, which can guarantee a certain level of trustworthiness of the AI model.

From an utilitarian perspective explanations are not computed for the sake of their own, but should provide a benefit. Future research will need to carefully investigate the possible benefits XAI can provide, especially in the context of human-AI interaction. A relevant question here is how explanations need to be constructed in order to become useful for the human operator and allow him or her to make better, faster, and more certain decisions. In this process, also the human will need to learn how to use explanations and understand their properties and limitations. The latter aspect is crucial as it is known that the wrong use of explanations by the human can even lead to worse decisions (Weller, 2019). An interesting concept potentially improving the human use of XAI are interactive explanations, i.e., explanations which allow the user to query the model in order to understand different aspects of its prediction strategy.

Acknowledgment

This work was supported by the German Federal Ministry of Education and Research (BMBF) under grants 01IS18025A, 01IS18037I, 031L0207C, and 01IS21069B. Furthermore, this work has received funding from the European Union's Horizon 2020 research and innovation program under grant agreement no. 965221.

References

Achtibat, Reduan, Dreyer, Maximilian, Eisenbraun, Ilona, Bosse, Sebastian, Wiegand, Thomas, Samek, Wojciech, Lapuschkin, Sebastian, 2022. From "Where" to "What": Towards Human-Understandable Explanations through Concept Relevance Propagation. arXiv preprint. arXiv:2206.03208.

Agarwal, Chirag, Nguyen, Anh, 2020. Explaining image classifiers by removing input features using generative models. In: Proceedings of the Asian Conference on Computer Vision.

Alber, Maximilian, Lapuschkin, Sebastian, Seegerer, Philipp, Hägele, Miriam, Schütt, Kristof T., Montavon, Grégoire, Samek, Wojciech, Müller, Klaus-Robert, Dähne, Sven, Kindermans, Pieter-Jan, 2019. iNNvestigate neural networks! Journal of Machine Learning Research 20 (93), 1–8.

Anders, Christopher J., Neumann, David, Samek, Wojciech, Müller, Klaus-Robert, Lapuschkin, Sebastian, 2021. Software for dataset-wide XAI: From local explanations to global insights with Zennit, CoRelAy, and ViRelAy. arXiv preprint. arXiv:2106.13200.

Anders, Christopher J., Weber, Leander, Neumann, David, Samek, Wojciech, Müller, Klaus-Robert, Lapuschkin, Sebastian, 2022. Finding and removing Clever Hans: Using explanation methods to debug and improve deep models. Information Fusion 77, 261–295.

Arras, Leila, Arjona-Medina, Jose A., Widrich, Michael, Montavon, Grégoire, Gillhofer, Michael, Müller, Klaus-Robert, Hochreiter, Sepp, Samek, Wojciech, 2019. Explaining and interpreting LSTMs. In: Explainable AI: Interpreting, Explaining and Visualizing Deep Learning. In: LNCS, vol. 11700. Springer, pp. 211–238.

Arras, Leila, Montavon, Grégoire, Müller, Klaus-Robert, Samek, Wojciech, 2017. Explaining recurrent neural network predictions in sentiment analysis. In: Proceedings of the EMNLP'17 Workshop on Computational Approaches to Subjectivity, Sentiment & Social Media Analysis (WASSA), pp. 159–168.

Arras, Leila, Osman, Ahmed, Samek, Wojciech, 2022. CLEVR-XAI: A benchmark dataset for the ground truth evaluation of neural network explanations. Information Fusion 81, 14–40.

Bach, Sebastian, Binder, Alexander, Montavon, Grégoire, Klauschen, Frederick, Müller, Klaus-Robert, Samek, Wojciech, 2015. On pixel-wise explanations for non-linear classifier decisions by layer-wise relevance propagation. PLoS ONE 10 (7), e0130140.

Baehrens, David, Schroeter, Timon, Harmeling, Stefan, Kawanabe, Motoaki, Hansen, Katja, Müller, Klaus-Robert, 2010. How to explain individual classification decisions. Journal of Machine Learning Research 11, 1803–1831.

Balduzzi, David, Frean, Marcus, Leary, Lennox, Lewis, J.P., Ma, Kurt Wan-Duo, McWilliams, Brian, 2017. The shattered gradients problem: If resnets are the answer, then what is the question? In: Proceedings of the 34th International Conference on Machine Learning, vol. 70. PMLR, pp. 342–350.

Bau, David, Zhu, Jun-Yan, Strobelt, Hendrik, Zhou, Bolei, Tenenbaum, Joshua B., Freeman, William T., Torralba, Antonio, 2019. GAN dissection: Visualizing and understanding generative adversarial networks. In: 7th International Conference on Learning Representations.

Becking, Daniel, Dreyer, Maximilian, Samek, Wojciech, Müller, Karsten, Lapuschkin, Sebastian, 2022. ECQ^x: Explainability-driven quantization for low-bit and sparse DNNs. In: xxAI - Beyond Explainable AI. In: LNAI, vol. 13200. Springer, pp. 271–296.

Berghoff, Christian, Biggio, Battista, Brummel, Elisa, Danos, Vasilios, Doms, Thomas, Ehrich, Heiko, Gantevoort, Thorsten, Hammer, Barbara, Iden, Joachim, Jacob, Sven, Khlaaf, Heidy, Komrowski, Lars, Kröwing, Robert, Metzen, Jan Hendrik, Neu, Matthias, Petsch, Fabian, Poretschkin, Maximilian, Samek, Wojciech, Schäbe, Hendrik, von Twickel, Arndt, Vechev, Martin, Wiegand, Thomas, 2021. Towards auditable AI systems: Current status and future directions. Whitepaper. BSI, VdTÜV and Fraunhofer HHI, pp. 1–32.

Bhatt, Umang, Xiang, Alice, Sharma, Shubham, Weller, Adrian, Taly, Ankur, Jia, Yunhan, Ghosh, Joydeep, Puri, Ruchir, Moura, José M.F., Eckersley, Peter, 2020. Explainable machine learning in deployment. In: Proceedings of the 2020 Conference on Fairness, Accountability, and Transparency, pp. 648–657.

Binder, Alexander, Müller, Klaus-Robert, Kawanabe, Motoaki, 2012. On taxonomies for multi-class image categorization. International Journal of Computer Vision 99 (3), 281–301.

Chen, Zhi, Bei, Yijie, Rudin, Cynthia, 2020. Concept whitening for interpretable image recognition. Nature Machine Intelligence 2 (12), 772–782.

Chen, Chaofan, Li, Oscar, Tao, Daniel, Barnett, Alina, Rudin, Cynthia, Su, Jonathan, 2019. This looks like that: Deep learning for interpretable image recognition. In: Advances in Neural Information Processing Systems 32, pp. 8928–8939.

Eberle, Oliver, Büttner, Jochen, Kräutli, Florian, Müller, Klaus-Robert, Valleriani, Matteo, Montavon, Grégoire, 2022. Building and interpreting deep similarity models. IEEE Transactions on Pattern Analysis and Machine Intelligence 44, 1149–1161.

Ebert-Uphoff, Imme, Hilburn, Kyle, 2020. Evaluation, tuning, and interpretation of neural networks for working with images in meteorological applications. Bulletin of the American Meteorological Society 101 (12), E2149–E2170.

Erion, Gabriel, Janizek, Joseph D., Sturmfels, Pascal, Lundberg, Scott, Lee, Su-In, 2020. Improving performance of deep learning models with axiomatic attribution priors and expected gradients. arXiv preprint. arXiv:1906.10670.

Everingham, Mark, Van Gool, Luc, Williams, Christopher K.I., Winn, John, Zisserman, Andrew, 2010. The Pascal visual object classes (VOC) challenge. International Journal of Computer Vision 88 (2), 303–338.

Fong, Ruth C., Vedaldi, Andrea, 2017. Interpretable explanations of black boxes by meaningful perturbation. In: IEEE International Conference on Computer Vision (ICCV), pp. 3449–3457.

Gilpin, Leilani H., Bau, David, Yuan, Ben Z., Bajwa, Ayesha, Specter, Michael, Kagal, Lalana, 2018. Explaining explanations: An overview of interpretability of machine learning. In: 2018 IEEE 5th International Conference on Data Science and Advanced Analytics (DSAA). IEEE, pp. 80–89.

Goebel, Randy, Chander, Ajay, Holzinger, Katharina, Lecue, Freddy, Akata, Zeynep, Stumpf, Simone, Kieseberg, Peter, Holzinger, Andreas, 2018. Explainable AI: The new 42? In: International Cross-Domain Conference for Machine Learning and Knowledge Extraction. Springer, pp. 295–303.

Guidotti, Riccardo, Monreale, Anna, Ruggieri, Salvatore, Pedreschi, Dino, Turini, Franco, Giannotti, Fosca, 2018. Local rule-based explanations of black box decision systems. arXiv preprint. arXiv: 1805.10820.

Hacker, Philipp, Krestel, Ralf, Grundmann, Stefan, Naumann, Felix, 2020. Explainable AI under contract and tort law: Legal incentives and technical challenges. Artificial Intelligence and Law 28, 415–439.

Han, Kai, Wang, Yunhe, Chen, Hanting, Chen, Xinghao, Guo, Jianyuan, Liu, Zhenhua, Tang, Yehui, Xiao, An, Xu, Chunjing, Xu, Yixing, et al., 2020. A survey on visual transformer. arXiv e-prints. arXiv:2012.12556.

Hannun, Awni Y., Rajpurkar, Pranav, Haghpanahi, Masoumeh, Tison, Geoffrey H., Bourn, Codie, Turakhia, Mintu P., Ng, Andrew Y., 2019. Cardiologist-level arrhythmia detection and classification in ambulatory electrocardiograms using a deep neural network. Nature Medicine 25 (1), 65–69.

Haufe, Stefan, Meinecke, Frank, Görgen, Kai, Dähne, Sven, Haynes, John-Dylan, Blankertz, Benjamin, Bießmann, Felix, 2014. On the interpretation of weight vectors of linear models in multivariate neuroimaging. NeuroImage 87, 96–110.

Hedström, Anna, Weber, Leander, Bareeva, Dilyara, Motzkus, Franz, Samek, Wojciech, Lapuschkin, Sebastian, Höhne, Marina M.-C., 2022. Quantus: An explainable AI toolkit for responsible evaluation of neural network explanations. arXiv preprint. arXiv:2202.06861.

Holzinger, Andreas, Langs, Georg, Denk, Helmut, Zatloukal, Kurt, Müller, Heimo, 2019. Causability and explainability of artificial intelligence in medicine. Wiley Interdisciplinary Reviews: Data Mining and Knowledge Discovery 9 (4), e1312.

Kauffmann, Jacob, Esders, Malte, Montavon, Grégoire, Samek, Wojciech, Müller, Klaus-Robert, 2019. From clustering to cluster explanations via neural networks. arXiv preprint. arXiv:1906.07633.

Kauffmann, Jacob, Müller, Klaus-Robert, Montavon, Grégoire, 2020. Towards explaining anomalies: A deep Taylor decomposition of one-class models. Pattern Recognition 101, 107198.

Kim, Been, Wattenberg, Martin, Gilmer, Justin, Cai, Carrie J., Wexler, James, Viégas, Fernanda B., Sayres, Rory, 2018. Interpretability beyond feature attribution: Quantitative testing with concept activation vectors (TCAV). In: Proceedings of the 35th International Conference on Machine Learning, vol. 80. PMLR, pp. 2673–2682.

Kindermans, Pieter-Jan, Schütt, Kristof T., Alber, Maximilian, Müller, Klaus-Robert, Erhan, Dumitru, Kim, Been, Dähne, Sven, 2018. Learning how to explain neural networks: PatternNet and PatternAttribution. In: International Conference on Learning Representations (ICLR).

Koh, Pang Wei, Liang, Percy, 2017. Understanding black-box predictions via influence functions. In: International Conference on Machine Learning. PMLR, pp. 1885–1894.

Kokhlikyan, Narine, Miglani, Vivek, Martin, Miguel, Wang, Edward, Alsallakh, Bilal, Reynolds, Jonathan, Melnikov, Alexander, Kliushkina, Natalia, Araya, Carlos, Yan, Siqi, et al., 2020. Captum: A unified and generic model interpretability library for PyTorch. arXiv preprint. arXiv:2009.07896.

Lapuschkin, Sebastian, Binder, Alexander, Montavon, Grégoire, Müller, Klaus-Robert, Samek, Wojciech, 2016. Analyzing classifiers: Fisher vectors and deep neural networks. In: Proceedings of the IEEE Conference on Computer Vision and Pattern Recognition (CVPR), pp. 2912–2920.

Lapuschkin, Sebastian, Wäldchen, Stephan, Binder, Alexander, Montavon, Grégoire, Samek, Wojciech, Müller, Klaus-Robert, 2019. Unmasking Clever Hans predictors and assessing what machines really learn. Nature Communications 10 (1), 1096.

Larochelle, Hugo, Hinton, Geoffrey E., 2010. Learning to combine foveal glimpses with a third-order Boltzmann machine. In: Advances in Neural Information Processing Systems 23, pp. 1243–1251.

Lauritsen, Simon Meyer, Kristensen, Mads, Olsen, Mathias Vassard, Larsen, Morten Skaarup, Lauritsen, Katrine Meyer, Jørgensen, Marianne Johansson, Lange, Jeppe, Thiesson, Bo, 2020. Explainable artificial intelligence model to predict acute critical illness from electronic health records. Nature Communications 11 (1), 1–11.

Letzgus, Simon, Wagner, Patrick, Lederer, Jonas, Samek, Wojciech, Müller, Klaus-Robert, Montavon, Grégoire, 2022. Toward explainable AI for regression models. Signal Processing Magazine.

Li, Kun-Lun, Huang, Hou-Kuan, Tian, Sheng-Feng, Xu, Wei, 2003. Improving one-class SVM for anomaly detection. In: Proceedings of the 2003 International Conference on Machine Learning and Cybernetics, vol. 5. IEEE, pp. 3077–3081.

Li, Hao, Kadav, Asim, Durdanovic, Igor, Samet, Hanan, Graf, Hans Peter, 2017. Pruning filters for efficient ConvNets. In: 5th International Conference on Learning Representations.

Linardatos, Pantelis, Papastefanopoulos, Vasilis, Kotsiantis, Sotiris, 2021. Explainable AI: A review of machine learning interpretability methods. Entropy 23 (1), 18.

Lipton, Zachary C., 2018. The mythos of model interpretability. ACM Queue 16 (3), 30.

Liu, Frederick, Avci, Besim, 2019. Incorporating priors with feature attribution on text classification. In: Proceedings of the 57th Conference of the Association for Computational Linguistics. ACL, pp. 6274–6283.

Lundberg, Scott M., Lee, Su-In, 2017. A unified approach to interpreting model predictions. In: Advances in Neural Information Processing Systems 30, pp. 4765–4774.

Lundberg, Scott M., Erion, Gabriel, Chen, Hugh, DeGrave, Alex, Prutkin, Jordan M., Nair, Bala, Katz, Ronit, Himmelfarb, Jonathan, Bansal, Nisha, Lee, Su-In, 2020. From local explanations to global understanding with explainable AI for trees. Nature Machine Intelligence 2 (1), 2522–5839.

MacDonald, Jan, Wäldchen, Stephan, Hauch, Sascha, Kutyniok, Gitta, 2019. A rate-distortion framework for explaining neural network decisions. arXiv preprint. arXiv:1905.11092.

MacQueen, J., 1967. Some methods for classification and analysis of multivariate observations. In: Proceedings of the Fifth Berkeley Symposium on Mathematical Statistics and Probability, Volume 1: Statistics. University of California Press, pp. 281–297.

Miller, Tim, 2019. Explanation in artificial intelligence: Insights from the social sciences. Artificial Intelligence 267, 1–38.

Molchanov, Pavlo, Tyree, Stephen, Karras, Tero, Aila, Timo, Kautz, Jan, 2016. Pruning convolutional neural networks for resource efficient transfer learning. arXiv preprint. arXiv:1611.06440.

Montavon, Grégoire, Binder, Alexander, Lapuschkin, Sebastian, Samek, Wojciech, Müller, Klaus-Robert, 2019. Layer-wise relevance propagation: An overview. In: Explainable AI: Interpreting, Explaining and Visualizing Deep Learning. In: LNCS, vol. 11700. Springer, pp. 193–209.

Montavon, Grégoire, Kauffmann, Jacob, Samek, Wojciech, Müller, Klaus-Robert, 2022. Explaining the predictions of unsupervised learning models. In: xxAI - Beyond Explainable AI. In: LNAI, vol. 13200. Springer, pp. 117–138.

Montavon, Grégoire, Lapuschkin, Sebastian, Binder, Alexander, Samek, Wojciech, Müller, Klaus-Robert, 2017. Explaining nonlinear classification decisions with deep Taylor decomposition. Pattern Recognition 65, 211–222.

Montavon, Grégoire, Samek, Wojciech, Müller, Klaus-Robert, 2018. Methods for interpreting and understanding deep neural networks. Digital Signal Processing 73, 1–15.

Morch, N.J.S., Kjems, Ulrik, Hansen, Lars Kai, Svarer, C., Law, I., Lautrup, B., Strother, S., Rehm, K., 1995. Visualization of neural networks using saliency maps. In: Proceedings of ICNN'95-International Conference on Neural Networks, vol. 4, pp. 2085–2090.

Pahde, Frederik, Weber, Leander, Anders, Christopher J., Samek, Wojciech, Lapuschkin, Sebastian, 2022. PatClArC: Using pattern concept activation vectors for noise-robust model debugging. arXiv preprint. arXiv:2202.03482.

Parzen, E., 1962. On estimation of a probability density function and mode. The Annals of Mathematical Statistics 33 (3), 1065–1076.

Preuer, Kristina, Klambauer, Günter, Rippmann, Friedrich, Hochreiter, Sepp, Unterthiner, Thomas, 2019. Interpretable deep learning in drug discovery. In: Explainable AI: Interpreting, Explaining and Visualizing Deep Learning. Springer, pp. 331–345.

Qin, Zhijin, Ye, Hao, Li, Geoffrey Ye, Juang, Biing-Hwang Fred, 2019. Deep learning in physical layer communications. IEEE Wireless Communications 26 (2), 93–99.

Ribeiro, Marco Túlio, Singh, Sameer, Guestrin, Carlos, 2016. "Why should I trust you?": Explaining the predictions of any classifier. In: Proceedings of the 22nd ACM SIGKDD International Conference on Knowledge Discovery and Data Mining, pp. 1135–1144.

Ribeiro, Marco Tulio, Singh, Sameer, Guestrin, Carlos, 2018. Anchors: High-precision model-agnostic explanations. In: Proceedings of the AAAI Conference on Artificial Intelligence, vol. 18, pp. 1527–1535.

Rieger, Laura, Singh, Chandan, Murdoch, W. James, Yu, Bin, 2020. Interpretations are useful: Penalizing explanations to align neural networks with prior knowledge. In: Proceedings of the 37th International Conference on Machine Learning, vol. 119. PMLR, pp. 8116–8126.

Roscher, Ribana, Bohn, Bastian, Duarte, Marco F., Garcke, Jochen, 2020. Explainable machine learning for scientific insights and discoveries. IEEE Access 8, 42200–42216.

Ross, Andrew Slavin, Doshi-Velez, Finale, 2018. Improving the adversarial robustness and interpretability of deep neural networks by regularizing their input gradients. In: Proceedings of the 32nd AAAI Conference on Artificial Intelligence, pp. 1660–1669.

Ross, Andrew Slavin, Hughes, Michael C., Doshi-Velez, Finale, 2017. Right for the right reasons: Training differentiable models by constraining their explanations. In: Proceedings of the 26th International Joint Conference on Artificial Intelligence, pp. 2662–2670.

Samek, Wojciech, Binder, Alexander, Montavon, Grégoire, Lapuschkin, Sebastian, Müller, Klaus-Robert, 2017. Evaluating the visualization of what a deep neural network has learned. IEEE Transactions on Neural Networks and Learning Systems 28 (11), 2660–2673.

Samek, Wojciech, Montavon, Grégoire, Vedaldi, Andrea, Hansen, Lars Kai, Müller, Klaus-Robert (Eds.), 2019. Explainable AI: Interpreting, Explaining and Visualizing Deep Learning. LNCS, vol. 11700. Springer.

Samek, Wojciech, Montavon, Grégoire, Lapuschkin, Sebastian, Anders, Christopher J., Müller, Klaus-Robert, 2021. Explaining deep neural networks and beyond: A review of methods and applications. Proceedings of the IEEE 109 (3), 247–278.

Schramowski, Patrick, Stammer, Wolfgang, Teso, Stefano, Brugger, Anna, Herbert, Franziska, Shao, Xiaoting, Luigs, Hans-Georg, Mahlein, Anne-Katrin, Kersting, Kristian, 2020. Making deep neural networks right for the right scientific reasons by interacting with their explanations. Nature Machine Intelligence 2 (8), 476–486.

Selvaraju, Ramprasaath R., Das, Abhishek, Vedantam, Ramakrishna, Cogswell, Michael, Parikh, Devi, Batra, Dhruv, 2016. Grad-CAM: Why did you say that? Visual explanations from deep networks via gradient-based localization. arXiv preprint. arXiv:1610.02391.

Shapley, L.S., 1953. 17. A value for *n*-person games. In: Contributions to the Theory of Games (AM-28), Volume II. Princeton University Press.

Simonyan, Karen, Vedaldi, Andrea, Zisserman, Andrew, 2014. Deep inside convolutional networks: Visualising image classification models and saliency maps. In: ICLR (Workshop Poster).

Smilkov, Daniel, Thorat, Nikhil, Kim, Been, Viégas, Fernanda B., Wattenberg, Martin, 2017. SmoothGrad: Removing noise by adding noise. arXiv preprint. arXiv:1706.03825.

Sun, Xu, Ren, Xuancheng, Ma, Shuming, Wang, Houfeng, 2017. meProp: Sparsified back propagation for accelerated deep learning with reduced overfitting. In: Precup, Doina, Teh, Yee Whye (Eds.), Proceedings of the 34th International Conference on Machine Learning, vol. 70. PMLR, pp. 3299–3308.

Sundararajan, Mukund, Taly, Ankur, Yan, Qiqi, 2017. Axiomatic attribution for deep networks. In: International Conference on Machine Learning. PMLR, pp. 3319–3328.

Toderici, George, Vincent, Damien, Johnston, Nick, Hwang, Sung Jin, Minnen, David, Shor, Joel, Covell, Michele, 2017. Full resolution image compression with recurrent neural networks. In: IEEE Conference on Computer Vision and Pattern Recognition (CVPR), pp. 5306–5314.

Weller, Adrian, 2019. Transparency: Motivations and challenges. In: Explainable AI: Interpreting, Explaining and Visualizing Deep Learning. In: LNCS, vol. 11700. Springer, pp. 23–40.

Wolpaw, Jonathan R., McFarland, Dennis J., Vaughan, Theresa M., 2000. Brain–computer interface research at the Wadsworth center. IEEE Transactions on Rehabilitation Engineering 8 (2), 222–226.

Yeom, Seul-Ki, Seegerer, Philipp, Lapuschkin, Sebastian, Binder, Alexander, Wiedemann, Simon, Müller, Klaus-Robert, Samek, Wojciech, 2021. Pruning by explaining: A novel criterion for deep neural network pruning. Pattern Recognition 115, 107899.

Zeiler, Matthew D., Fergus, Rob, 2014. Visualizing and understanding convolutional networks. In: European Conference Computer Vision – ECCV 2014, pp. 818–833.

Zhang, Jianming, Bargal, Sarah Adel, Lin, Zhe, Brandt, Jonathan, Shen, Xiaohui, Sclaroff, Stan, 2018. Top-down neural attention by excitation backprop. International Journal of Computer Vision 126 (10), 1084–1102.

Zhang, Quanshi, Yang, Yu, Ma, Haotian, Wu, Ying Nian, 2019. Interpreting CNNs via decision trees. In: Proceedings of the IEEE/CVF Conference on Computer Vision and Pattern Recognition, pp. 6261–6270.

Zhou, Bolei, Bau, David, Oliva, Aude, Torralba, Antonio, 2018. Interpreting deep visual representations via network dissection. IEEE Transactions on Pattern Analysis and Machine Intelligence 41 (9), 2131–2145.

Zhu, Xiao-Pan, Dai, Jia-Ming, Bian, Chun-Jiang, Chen, Yu, Chen, Shi, Hu, Chen, 2019. Galaxy morphology classification with deep convolutional neural networks. Astrophysics and Space Science 364 (4), 55.

CHAPTER 3

Compact visualization of DNN classification performances for interpretation and improvement

Adrien Halnaut, Romain Giot, Romain Bourqui, and David Auber
Univ. Bordeaux, CNRS, Bordeaux INP, LaBRI, UMR 5800, Talence, France

3.1. Introduction

Deep learning (LeCun et al., 2015) based approaches are used in many contexts and usually surpass historical methods, especially for classification problems. Even when training datasets are not large enough to train Deep Neural Networks (DNNs), it is possible to use transfer learning with a pretrained DNN by fine-tuning it (Ghazi et al., 2017), or by extracting features and feeding them to a conventional classifier (Tang, 2013). A DNN can be represented by a graph with nodes representing the model computational blocks (i.e., layers). Each node connection represents how the output of each block is processed by the rest of the network. These blocks are applying a simple function defined during the model construction whose parameters (name weights) are defined during the training phase of the model.

The black-box nature is one of the largest issues (Benítez et al., 1997). Indeed, even if each block is individually well understood mathematically, its behavior depends mainly on the training data (i.e., their impact on the learned weights). As a consequence, one can hardly know what processing these blocks are doing and why. However, it is well accepted that the model's first layers extract low-level features, while the latest ones extract high-level features specific to the application problem (Erhan et al., 2009). Two nonexclusive strategies can help to open this black box: (i) *Explainable deep learning* where the architecture of the DNN emphasizes its explainability (Zhang et al., 2018), even if it could negatively impact its performance, and (ii) *Interpretable deep learning* where additional processes extract information from the tested model by computing a more explainable one (Zhang et al., 2019), computing some saliency information (Binder et al., 2016; Fuad et al., 2020), or using information visualization techniques (Hohman et al., 2018). Understanding, even partially, the classification process of a trained network helps in both understanding which data classes are easier to classify than others and where the network can be further improved for its task, in a different way than what layer pruning techniques do (He et al., 2017).

Explainable Deep Learning AI
https://doi.org/10.1016/B978-0-32-396098-4.00009-0

This chapter extends the work of Halnaut et al. (2021), presenting a new method for interpretable deep learning based on information visualization techniques. The task to solve corresponds to visualization of the progressive classification aspect of DNNs, regardless of the nature of the studied DNN and dataset. It aims at analyzing how all input samples of a dataset are globally treated by any part of the network. In contrast to most papers of the literature on attribution-based methods, the focus is not on a specific sample but on a full testing dataset. The method *allows focusing on* successive layers that better (or worse) discriminate the samples. It also displays the complete network and the data behavior for each of its computational blocks.

The method's originality relies on the fact it focuses on both all samples and full architecture and has the advantages of (i) using less screen space than existing methods despite the amount of information to display without overlapping elements, or *overplot*; (ii) fitting to any network that can be represented as a directed acyclic graph; (iii) using the same encoding for input data, inner blocks, and final result.

The rest of the chapter is organized as follows. Section 3.2 presents previous works in visualization for DNNs and usages of space filling curves. Section 3.3 describes the proposed method. Section 3.4 provides the details of the experimental protocol. Section 3.5 discusses the results and provide directions for future work. We finally draw conclusions in Section 3.6.

3.2. Previous works

Our proposed method aims at visually interpreting how DNNs behave using a space-efficient method. This section first presents previous works on deep neural networks visualization, then focuses on dense, pixel-oriented visualization methods.

3.2.1 Visualization for the interpretation of deep neural networks

Some works focus on *single views* that can be reused in other works or embedded in more complex applications. GradCam (Selvaraju et al., 2017) aims at generating a heatmap for a single input to highlight the spatial location that greatly supports the final decision. It is computed using gradients from the model's output of a target class up to the latest convolutional layer. When the input feature is an image, the heatmap can be straightforwardly visualized and interpreted as what features the model used to classify the data. Other methods rely on different concepts to achieve the same objective such as Layer-wise Relevance Propagation (LRP) (Binder et al., 2016) on the concept of relevance propagation, or other work (Fuad et al., 2020) that only uses information collected during the forward pass. Instead of focusing on a single input sample, it is also possible to focus on the complete dataset. Some methods use Sankey-diagram analogy (Halnaut et al., 2020) to highlight the processing flows. Others project activations obtained at a specific layer in a 2D space to verify how the network sees the data at this specific point (Rauber et al., 2016). Such an approach is also common in the literature using T-SNE projection (van der Maaten and Hinton, 2008); however, an important draw-back remains: the representation is not space efficient and there is no guarantee that no overlap occurs. Our proposed method solves these two issues. Other works create *applications for educational purpose* to visually explain how some specific deep systems perform. For example, TensorFlow playground (Smilkov et al., 2017) focuses on a simple DNN, CNN-101 (Wang et al., 2020) focuses on a CNN, Ganlab (Kahng et al., 2018b) focuses on a GAN system, and Adversarial Playground (Norton and Qi, 2017) illustrates the concept of adversarial examples. Even if they are visually appealing, these systems can hardly be used for industrial scenarios.

In contrast, several complete tools treat *industrial problems*. Some of them are general enough to be used in almost any scenario, such as Activis (Kahng et al., 2018a) (it focuses on the visualization and comparison of activation of a single selected layer), while some others are restricted to some specific networks or evaluation scenarios. CNNVIS (Liu et al., 2017) is tailored for CNNs and uses a visualization that relies on aggregation of layers (not all layers are depicted), filters (filters that behave similarly are grouped), and data (a subset of the samples are depicted). DQNVIZ (Wang et al., 2019) has been designed for Deep Q-Network explanation in the specific context of Atari play.

3.2.2 Hilbert curve in information visualization

Dense pixel-oriented methods aim at improving both the data–ink ratio (Tufte, 2001) and the visualization size by displaying a unit of information on a single pixel while avoiding unused pixels. Keim reviewed various pixel-oriented visualizations (Keim, 2000) and asserts that space-filling curves, such as that of Hilbert (1935), are among the bests to project ordered elements in a screen space while preserving the distance of the one-dimensional ordering in the two-dimensional arrangement. Blanchard et al. (2005) have shown that to display images, reduced to a one pixel representation, on a Hilbert curve produces coherent and identifiable clusters. Auber et al. (2007) have also shown the interest of such visualization, when complemented by tailored interaction techniques, to explore datacubes of several dozen million elements. Based on previous successes, we have selected the Hilbert curve to project our data in a square; a curve of order n contains 4^n elements (Auber et al., 2007).

3.3. Proposed method for compact visualization of DNN classification performances

Fig. 3.1 describes our proposed method with the "Nested blocks and guidelines model" (Meyer et al., 2015) among various description levels: *domain* (which is concerned by which problem), *abstraction* (which data is used or generated to solve which task),

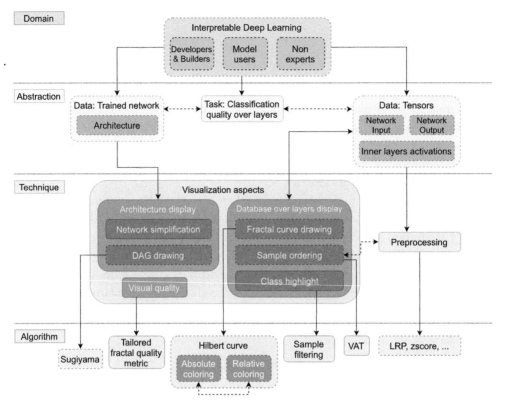

Figure 3.1 Nested blocks and guidelines (Meyer et al., 2015) representation of the proposed method. Dashed blocks correspond to existing ones; straight blocks are defined in the work.

technique (which methods are used), and *algorithm* (how these methods are implemented).

Additionally, Fig. 3.2 lists the successive steps involved in our method. The requirement of the proposed method is to be *space efficient* (R1) while displaying information from *all samples* (R2) in *all layers* (R3) of the network to solve the *task "classification quality analysis over layers"* (R4).

3.3.1 Domain level

The proposed method fits the needs of *networks designers* and *trainers* that want to verify *how* the samples are *grouped* by the various *layers* of their *classification network*. From the *analysis* of these groupings, they could infer *hypotheses* that aim at being verified with other techniques. Such hypotheses are related to input sample properties and network errors. *Nonexperts* would better understand how DNNs work by looking at the representation of simple networks and datasets.

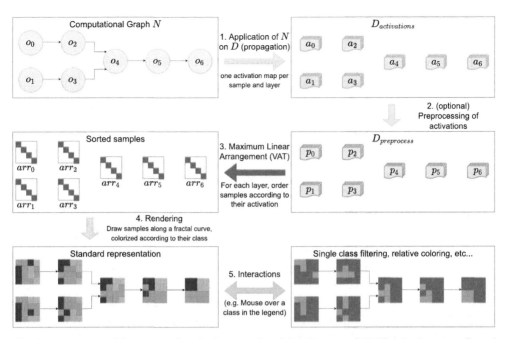

Figure 3.2 Summary of the proposed method. Dataset *D* is fed to the network *N*. All activations are collected, eventually preprocessed, and finally ordered at each layer. The ordered samples are drawn along a fractal curve at each operation of the network that is placed on the screen using a graph drawing method.

3.3.2 Abstraction level

The proposed method considers N, an already trained DNN, with a compatible test dataset D_{test}. This N is a network (i.e., graph) of operations (i.e., nodes) $N = (O, E)$. Its sources $s_{\bullet} \in O$ are the identity function on data input (i.e., samples), and its sinks $t_{\bullet} \in O$ are its outputs (i.e., output classes probability). Also N has multiple sources for a multimodal system, but always a single sink as we are restricted to the use case of standard classification. The other nodes $o_{\bullet} \in O \setminus \{s_{\bullet} \cup t_{\bullet}\}$ correspond to any operations (e.g., convolution, pooling, etc.) that compose N; operations related to optimization (e.g., dropout) are not included. The edges $E = O \times O$ model the flow of data over the operations of the network (i.e., they link successive layers).

Each sample $d_i \in D_{test}$ is fed into the network and the output (i.e., activations) of each operation o^j is stored in d_i^j; we assume operations are ordered depending on the execution flow. These activations consist of tensors whose order depends on the underlying operation and whose dimensions depend on the input data of the network. Each operation o^j consumes at least one result $d_i^k | k < j$ computed by a previous operation except for the sources where $a_i^{\bullet}$ corresponds to the raw data (of the targeted modality in a multimodal scenario). Thus, a sample d_i is represented by a set of activations $A_i = \bigcup_j \{d_i^j\}$ and the complete dataset D_{test} is represented by an ensemble of sets of activations $D_{activations} = \bigcup_i \{A_i\}$.

The activations can be optionally preprocessed to fall within compatible domains as their initial domain is not controlled, $D_{preprocess} = \bigcup_i \bigcup_j \left\{ Preprocessed\left(d_i^j\right) \right\}$. This preprocessing method is a parameter of the proposed framework.

3.3.3 Technique level

As our method aims to display (a) the dataset and its *ground truth* (R2), (b) the *architecture of the network* (R3) and (c) its impact on the *complete dataset* (R4), we propose an encoding relying on both $D_{preprocess}$ and N.

Ground–truth encoding. The ground truth of the dataset is depicted with a legend where each class is represented by a colored rectangle (similar to the one of the sample encoding) followed by a black text (class name).

Network Encoding. It is straightforward to layout N operations with a graph-drawing algorithm tailored for Directed Acyclic Graphs (networks are always DAGs). Such a technique is common in the literature (Kahng et al., 2018a; Wongsuphasawat et al., 2017) and aims at computing the coordinates of each node (operation) in a plane, while emphasizing the order of operations in the computing flow. Each node is depicted by a glyph that represents the whole dataset as viewed by the network after this layer operation. Thus, a specific encoding is used to map the activations $\bigcup_i \{Preprocessed(d_i^j)\}$ of each node o^j in the screen space.

Similarly to Ganlab (Kahng et al., 2018b), a dotted line is drawn between nodes that represents consecutive operations; the flow of data is revealed by the dots moving in the flow direction. Some networks can be very deep with successive layers that do not bring additional information because they only consist of data reordering. We allow the user to request the visualization of a simplified network where the corresponding nodes are removed (thus, their successors are linked to their predecessors), as such information brings noise to the representation. No special encoding is used to represent this information shrinking.

Sample encoding. As previously mentioned, we have chosen a pixel-oriented technique that relies on fractal curves (R1). For a given node o^j, a maximal linear arrangement method is used to order the representation d_i^j of each sample d_i in such a way that samples are positioned closely in the ordering according to a *distance* function. We assume that close samples in the output space of o^j correspond to samples treated similarly by the network (i.e., considered to be similar). Once the samples are ordered, they are projected into a discrete pixel grid using a fractal curve that respects proximity relations. This way, screen space usage can be maximized (e.g., 1 pixel per sample) and we are assured that close samples are drawn closely on the screen (however close pixels on the screen are not necessarily close in data space). We provide two visual encodings to represent this curve. The first, *absolute coloring*, explicitly draws samples of each class with the same color (and thus is limited to scenarios with a limited number of classes). The second, *relative coloring*, uses a gray scale to emphasize label difference between adjacent nodes and identify zones where different labels are present. It can be used *de facto* when the number of classes is too high to be efficiently discernable by a human using regular class colorization. When using the *absolute coloring* scheme, the user can choose to only visualize a specific class to observe the spread of its samples over the layer. The name of the layer is written above its fractal representation, and a quality metric (presented later in this chapter) is written below it.

3.3.4 Algorithm level

The model topology is drawn using the Sugiyama algorithm (Sugiyama et al., 1981) and each node (i.e., operation) is depicted with a specific fractal-based glyph that represents the ordered samples. The Euclidean distance is used to compare the activations generated for all the samples on the same operation. It reflects the dissimilarity between samples; we consider that each neuron activation has the same impact as others in the full network processing. These distances are then compiled into an $n \times n$ distance matrix, n being the number of compared samples. During the full processing of a sample by a DNN, it is frequently the case that several neurons in each layer have minor contributions in the decision layer. Euclidean distance does not differentiate between neurons with minor contributions and those with major contributions. Some pre- or postprocessing methods, such as the LRP (Binder et al., 2016) method as done in Halnaut et al. (2020), can be applied to the activation maps to reflect that behavior and prioritize more important neurons than less important ones in the dissimilarity computation. However, we decided not to apply those methods because of the unsure interpretation on model topologies using branches, such as our chimeric *DoubleLeNet5* (Section 3.4) or the widely used ResNet (He et al., 2016) which uses residual connections. Using ordering methods (Behrisch et al., 2016), data can be ordered in a queue with similar elements placed next to each other using their dissimilarity matrix. The VAT algorithm (da Silva and Wunsch, 2018) computes such order on dissimilarity matrices. Indeed, the order of the row and column of the dissimilarity matrix computed by VAT results in similar values being next to each other. The order computed by this algorithm can then be applied on a 1D-space to display similar data indexes next to each other. Using a fractal curve, we project this 1D-space into a 2D-space which is more suitable for data visualization. The fractal curve chosen to map each sample into a pixel grid is the Hilbert curve (Hilbert, 1935) because of its ability to place points in a discrete space (which is not the case of Gosper curve (Gardner, 1976)) and the absence of "jumps" in the curve (which is not the case of the Z-order curve (Morton, 1966)) which ensures that two consecutive samples are adjacent. The order in which each sample is positioned is following the same order computed by VAT on the previous step. When the number of test samples is less than the number of pixels available in the curve, we skip half of the missing positions in the beginning of the curve (and thus half of the missing positions at the end of the curve); making a "hole" in the curve but keeping the sample centered in the glyph.

In the absolute coloring, each pixel sample is being colored according to its ground-truth class color. In the relative coloring, the colors depend on the number of similar labels for the pixel of interest in its sample ordering. That gives three possible values (0 for an outlier with no neighbors of the same class, 1 for a previous or next label different, and 2 when the three successive samples are of the same class). The absolute colors come from a palette of diverging colors, while the relative colors or black (0), gray (1), and white (2). Computing in the ordering space instead of the picture allows not highlighting the visual border inherent to the fractal curve. Placing the cursor on a class in the legend selects this specific class and draws only its samples with the appropriate absolute color.

The machine learning community provides various evaluation metrics (e.g., cross-entropy) to evaluate the accuracy of the network by comparing its output to a ground truth. By definition, they cannot be applied at each layer, but we still need to provide hints to the user of their individual contribution to the final classification. We have defined a quality metric, based on the local homogeneity of the layer's visual representations, which counts the number of neighbors of a given pixel that are of the same color (i.e., the number of samples that belong to the same class). We normalized it between 0 and 1 to ease its comparison (however, as the normalization does not consider the mandatory borders, 1 is an unreachable value). We assume that to quantify the quality of the visualization is strongly related to the ability of the layer to separate data.

3.3.5 Output interpretation

The high-dimensional output of each layer is encoded into a compact glyph which describes how data is scattered into that high-dimensional space. Because of the DAG representation of the model, experts and nonexperts know which glyph corresponds to which layer output, and where the data is being transformed in the classification process. Glyph composition gives a quick and understandable overview of the classification progress; a group of pixels of same color indicates a group of input data of the same class are being processed in a similar way, which means that the model managed to extract features that is common to this class. However, a group of pixels of mixed colors indicates a group of input data that are not close to other groups in the high-dimensional space, and thus do not possess features that enable to recognize them with others from their class. With those visual clues, experts and nonexperts can recognize layers (i.e., glyphs) that are helpful to the classification process (i.e., grouped pixels of same color) or hindering it (i.e., degradation of previously grouped pixels of same color). The contribution of a layer to the classification on all classes is also noticeable by looking at how less noisy the glyphs are from a layer to the next one.

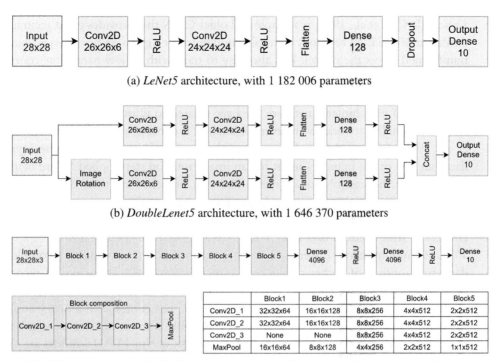

(a) *LeNet5* architecture, with 1 182 006 parameters

(b) *DoubleLenet5* architecture, with 1 646 370 parameters

	Block1	Block2	Block3	Block4	Block5
Conv2D_1	32x32x64	16x16x128	8x8x256	4x4x512	2x2x512
Conv2D_2	32x32x64	16x16x128	8x8x256	4x4x512	2x2x512
Conv2D_3	None	None	8x8x256	4x4x512	2x2x512
MaxPool	16x16x64	8x8x128	4x4x256	2x2x512	1x1x512

(c) *VGG16* architecture, with 33 638 218 parameters. Convolution blocks are resized to handle MNIST dataset

Figure 3.3 Models used in our evaluation with their total number of parameters. In the case of *VGG16*, convolutional blocks are pretrained with the ImageNet dataset.

3.4. Experimental protocol

Several scenarios that rely on a *test dataset* and a *trained network* illustrate the efficiency of the proposed method. In this section, we present these datasets and networks.

Datasets. *MNIST* (LeCun, 1998) is a standard dataset used in handwritten digit recognition with 28×28 grayscale images. Even simple networks are able to perform almost perfectly on this 10-class dataset. We use it to illustrate classification on easy data. *Fashion-MNIST* (Xiao et al., 2017) shares a similar distribution as *MNIST* but is composed of images of clothes instead of digits. Classification performance is usually lower than with *MNIST*. We use it to illustrate classification on averagely difficulty dataset, closer to real-world classification problems.

Both datasets are composed of 60 000 samples to train the model and 10 000 samples to evaluate it.

Networks. In our evaluation, we make use of three networks summarized in Fig. 3.3:

- *LeNet5* (LeCun et al., 1998) is a simple and older CNN that provides good accuracy results on *MNIST*. Its topology is simple enough to get a grasp on how data is being transformed across the model. It is also easy to train with its low parameter count, but that simplicity comes at the cost of lower accuracy results in more complex recognition tasks.
- *DoubleLeNet5* is a chimeric network we have created to illustrate the ability of the system to handle networks with several branches. It consists of two *LeNet5* (LeCun et al., 1998) without the prediction layer that process in parallel the same input data, but one of the branches input has an image rotation step applied before being processed by the convolutional layers. The two branches are then concatenated before being fed to the prediction layer. The image rotation step is not depicted on the diagrams as it has no weights in the network. Performance-wise this model targets the same kinds of data as *LeNet5*, with a minor performance gain.
- *VGG16* (Simonyan and Zisserman, 2014) is a deep CNN usually used on complex datasets composed of higher resolution, colored images, with thousands of recognizable classes, such as ImageNet (Russakovsky et al., 2015). Its robustness allows it to reach fairly good accuracy results on target tasks, but comes with a heavy computation cost and it cannot be trained in a reasonable amount of time on standard computers. In this chapter, the convolutional blocks of the *VGG16* model are already pretrained with the ImageNet dataset, and are not retrained when training the prediction layers.

3.4.1 Scenarios

We have selected meaningful combinations of network and dataset for each scenario.
- *Easy scenario.* *LeNet5* uses *MNIST* which illustrates a well performing system.
- *Generalization scenario.* *LeNet5* uses *Fashion-MNIST* which illustrates a system with more classification errors.
- *Branch scenario.* *DoubleLeNet5* predicts *Fashion-MNIST* which illustrates a usage case with nonlinear network architecture.
- *Simplification scenario.* *VGG16* is processing *MNIST*. It illustrates the use of a complex network to solve a simple task. By applying the visualization pipeline and observing resulting glyphs, we propose an improvement for the model's architecture resulting in better accuracy performances and simpler complexity for the model.

3.4.2 Implementation and execution infrastructure

The TensorFlow framework (Abadi et al., 2015) is used along with Keras (Chollet et al., 2015) to train the studied models for each scenario. Each layer output, processed as potentially very large high-dimensional data (e.g., output of *VGG16* convolutional layers), is saved into distributed computation infrastructure as $n \times s$ matrices, with n being the size of the tested dataset and s the number of dimensions of the layer output.

This distributed computation infrastructure is handling the dissimilarity matrix computation, which makes use of a large pool of memory (around 2 terabytes). The resulting matrices are small enough (for our experiments) to fit and be processed on a recent laptop. The matrix manipulations of the original VAT algorithm (da Silva and Wunsch, 2018) are implemented using the ArrayFire library (Yalamanchili et al., 2015) for their efficient matrix computation abilities. This part of the process only produces the data for the visualization tool and thus can be seen as a backend infrastructure. Fractal images (i.e., glyphs) are then generated by relying on the Rust *hilbert* library, based on Skilling (2004). The visual and interactive part corresponds to an HTML application relying on D3.js (Bostock et al., 2011) for the visualization and D3-dag (Brinkman, 2018) for the Sugiyama implementation. For each scenario, an additional glyph is displayed under the labels prediction to graphically present the accuracy of the model only based on its output.

3.5. Results and discussion

The complete results are accessible at the following address: https://pivert.labri.fr/frac/index.html. We strongly recommend viewing the results online as the images here are severely undersized on the paper where 1 pixel represents several samples because of the image compression. Figs. 3.5 to 3.8 depicts still resized representations of the proposed method for several scenarios, while their confusion matrices are presented in Fig. 3.4.

3.5.1 Visual analysis of method results

The accuracy for the system of the *easy scenario* in Fig. 3.5 is 98.96%. This is clearly reflected by the heterogeneous organization of the 09-prediction glyph in the visualization.

When looking at the successive operations that correspond to activation functions (01-relu0, 03-relu1, 06-relu2, 09-prediction), we observe that uniformly colored parts of the glyphs are growing as the classification goes. This improvement in glyph composition indicates a better discriminability over layers. Light and dark blue pixels, corresponding to 1 and 0 classes, are grouped in the first glyphs of the DAG, which indicates that these classes are discriminated early in the network and can be considered as "easy" classes for the model. Several elements of the 6, 7, and 8 classes are mixed together in the upper parts of the first glyphs. This indicates that these classes are also recognized early, but not yet completely distinctive between each other. The first dense layer 05-dense0 brings a dramatic improvement of the discriminability in the classification as many pixels of the same color are grouped together compared to the previous glyph.

The accuracy in the *Generalization scenario* in Fig. 3.6 is 73.44%. Compared to the prediction layer's glyph from the *Easy scenario*, this one is a bit noisier and reflects the

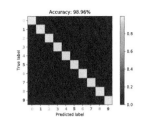

Easy scenario (*LeNet5 + MNIST*)

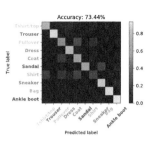

Generalization scenario (*LeNet5 + Fashion-MNIST*)

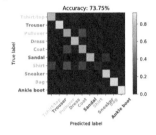

Branch scenario (*DoubleLeNet5 + MNIST*)

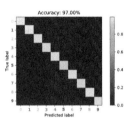

Simplification scenario (*VGG16 + MNIST*)

Figure 3.4 Confusion matrices of the models evaluated in each scenario. Easy and Simplification scenarios present models that are well performing on their datasets with clear distinction between each class. Those results are reflected on the well-organized last glyphs in our results. Generalization and Branch scenarios present much more confused networks, which is also reflected on the less-organized last glyphs in our results.

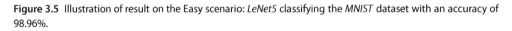
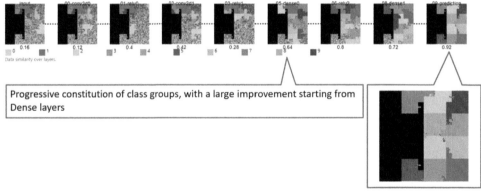

Figure 3.5 Illustration of result on the Easy scenario: *LeNet5* classifying the *MNIST* dataset with an accuracy of 98.96%.

difference in classification accuracy. The previous layers overall are also less organized, which reflects the overall lower performances of the model on this dataset. The T-shirt and Trouser classes are differentiated early in the classification process (i.e., their corre-

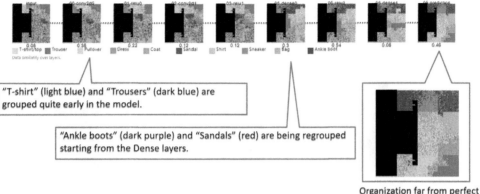

Figure 3.6 Illustration of result on the Generalization scenario: *LeNet5* classifying the *Fashion-MNIST* dataset with an accuracy of 73.45%.

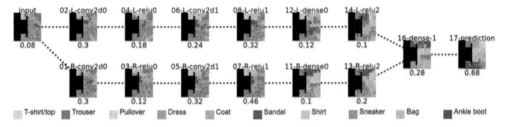

Figure 3.7 Illustration of result on the Branch-model scenario: *DoubleLeNet5* classifying the *Fashion-MNIST* dataset with an accuracy of 73.75%.

sponding pixels are grouped together in the first glyphs of the DAG) while `Ankle boots` or `Sandal` are discriminated only at the end of the network (i.e. their corresponding pixels are grouped only toward the last glyphs).

The *Realistic scenario* in Fig. 3.7 illustrates the ability to draw networks with branches. The 73.75% accuracy of the model is very close to its linear counterpart in the *Generalization scenario*. We observe the same tendencies in both branches, as well as a similar sample organization than in the *Generalization scenario*. They are also confident on the same classes.

The *Simplification scenario* in Fig. 3.8 has the accuracy of 97% (lower than *LeNet5* despite the more complex architecture). During the progressive classification, we can notice a succession of improvements and decreases in sample organization in the glyph (i.e. pixels of same color are getting grouped but are separated on the next glyph). We assume that this less efficient classification comes from several reasons: networks are pretrained and not specialized for the task, and/or the model is too deep and layers

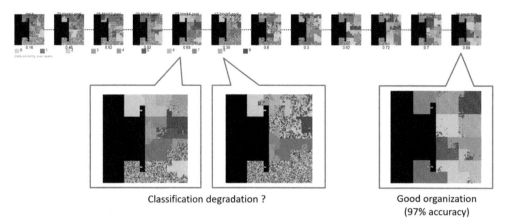

Classification degradation ?   Good organization
                                                 (97% accuracy)

Figure 3.8 Illustration of result on the Simplification scenario: *VGG16* classifying the *MNIST* dataset with an accuracy of 97.00%.

are redundant. In the next subsection, we propose an improvement of the network architecture based on this observation.

3.5.2 Improvement to simplification scenario

The glyph representing the fifth convolutional block of $VGG16$, 17-block5-pool, shows a large degradation of the classification process, with fewer subsets of data being similarly processed than at the end of the fourth convolutional block, namely 13-block4-pool: red (class 5), yellow (class 6), and light green (class 2) pixels are dispersed, and other groups are slightly shrunk compared to previous glyph. We assume that data is being overprocessed by convolution operations, which degrades the model performance. Thanks to the perlayer glyph construction, we focus our improvement effort to the concerned glyph, which is the fifth convolutional block. We propose two ways to improve the model architecture based on this assumption:

- **VGG16-B4**. Remove the fifth convolutional block and directly connect the fourth block (13-block4-pool) to the next dense layer of the model (19-dense0).
- **VGG16-B4+**. Remove the fifth convolutional block but keep the pooling layer before connecting the next dense layer of the model (i.e., only remove layers 14-block5_conv1, 15-block5-conv2, and 16-block5-conv3). This ensures that the number of weight parameters for each neuron of the next layer is not increased after the modification.

In both cases, the dense layers of the model are being retrained from scratch (convolution blocks keep their pretrained ImageNet parameters) to ensure that any noticeable improvement is due to the architecture modification instead of possible transfer learning from a previous iteration.

Table 3.1 Performances of different *VGG16* architectures following modification based on observations of progressive classification. *VGG16-B4* architecture has 1.67% more accuracy than the original model while having 2.34% less parameters and having 27.1% smaller footprint in RAM. *VGG16-B4+* has 1.37% more accuracy than the original but with 21% less parameters. However, its RAM footprint is only 22.2% smaller than that of the original model.

Architecture	Accuracy	Parameters
VGG16	97.00%	33 638 218
VGG16–B4	98.65%	32 850 250
VGG16–B4+	98.35%	26 558 794

Table 3.1 shows the results of *VGG16*'s simplification. Removing the fifth convolutional block of VGG16 improved the classification performance of the model while reducing its complexity. Which improvement is better for the use case is up to the user's decision. However, even without knowing the parameters of each VGG16's layer, or the nature of the processed data, the user can notice the classification degradation behavior of the network, and engage in network simplification manually.

3.5.3 Discussion

Compared to widely used t–SNE projection (e.g., visualizing layer outputs using t–SNE (Rauber et al., 2016)), the method presented in this chapter has a fairly more efficient use of the screen space. Furthermore, all of the layer activations can be displayed on the same screen space without overplotting data. The focus on pixel-scale usage is emphasized, but not all points of the curves are used; black pixels correspond to unused pixels because test datasets are smaller than what is technically possible with such display size. Indeed, in the case of Hilbert's curve, only datasets of size 4^n can entirely fit into the curve. In our experiment, $4^7 - 10\,000$ pixels are lost, which is roughly 39% of the picture for each layer. It is thus possible to evaluate larger datasets without using more space on the screen, resulting in better data–ink usage. Another observation is the effectiveness of samples projection over the fractal curve to depict the classification performance over layers. Usually, representation of sample ordering is getting better over layers which means the network is progressively better at separating classes of samples. Dataset and subsets of dataset classification difficulty are also represented: *Fashion-MNIST*, which is a problem more difficult than *MNIST*, is thus less well organized.

By construction, the very first node corresponds to the projection of the raw dataset; the noisier it is, the more complex it is to distinguish its samples without extracting additional features. The representation clearly depicts this point and its quality metric is worse for *Fashion-MNIST* than *MNIST*. The very last node corresponds to the projection of the softmax values; the noisier it is, the worse the network's accuracy. This final

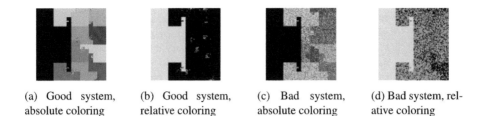

| (a) Good system, absolute coloring | (b) Good system, relative coloring | (c) Bad system, absolute coloring | (d) Bad system, relative coloring |

Figure 3.9 Comparison of the absolute and relative color schemes. No data is depicted in black for absolute and light blue for relative color schemes.

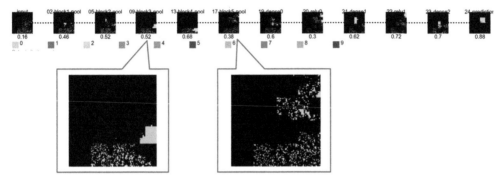

Figure 3.10 Analysis of the spread of samples of class 2 over layers. Such a representation could indicate an oversizing of the network by looking at the separation effect around layer 17-block5-pool.

representation is complementary to a confusion matrix (see Fig. 3.4) as it provides more information about classification efficiency of the models.

A labeled dataset is currently needed to color the pixels. This limits the use of the method to a test dataset and not a real world unlabeled dataset. However, it is still possible to use the predicted labels instead of the ground-truth ones to obtain a view of how the network interprets the data. Fig. 3.9 compares the absolute and relative color schemes for one operation able to differentiate the samples and another which is not able to differentiate them yet. Thanks to the color, absolute colorization allows us to clearly see which classes are subject to more noise than the others, while the relative colorization rule allows better seeing the relative quantity of errors, and by construction it is also able to handle many classes.

Focusing on a specific class helps track the evolution of the sample processing for that chosen class over layers. Fig. 3.10 illustrates the oversizing of the *VGG16* network on *MNIST* by observing that samples of selected class tend to be processed similarly at the 09-block3-pool layer, whereas it is not the case anymore around layer 17-block5-pool.

3.5.4 Future work

Our method presented in this chapter is resource consuming, mainly due to the need for storing dissimilarity matrices in memory, which are of size N^2, with N being the size of the tested dataset. Future works should compute the order of the elements without relying on a full dissimilarity matrix, as it becomes expensive for the method to be applied on larger datasets. Additionally, the ordering of the samples highly depends on the Euclidean distance that is known to not be efficient in high-dimensional spaces; other metrics need to be compared. The approach is satisfactory using interaction, but is not yet self-sufficient. Indeed, it provides a good overview of how the classification is handled but lacks interactions to track the progression of a single sample or group of samples (in contrast to our previous work that specifically focuses on this point (Halnaut et al., 2020)) in the network. Such investigations have to be performed; for example, some sort of consistency in the sample position between two successive glyphs would help in tracking elements. Furthermore, being able to focus on a single sample instead of the whole class would help in determining the cause of misclassification by the network (e.g., the model was confused between a 6 and an 8 at the first convolutional layer, which led to misclassification for the rest of the processing).

The Hilbert curve is very efficient in placing the samples in its reserved space. However, there is a high probability that the number of elements in the dataset to visualize is lower than what is possible with the curve. It would be interesting to implement additional interactions that use this additional space; or use grid-based projection methods (e.g., IsoMatch (Fried et al., 2015) or Self-Sorting Maps (Strong and Gong, 2014)) instead of fractal ones. Subsampling or sampling with replacement the dataset with a number of samples equals to the curve length, and that follows data distribution, which could also be interesting. The standard Sugiyama algorithm does not consider the screen space size; a modified method should be used in order to project the graph on the screen in a way that does not necessitate horizontally scrolling the screen to see it (Liu et al., 2018).

Finally, as this work is an attempt to visually explain CNN innerworking and decisions to both experts and nonexperts, it is essential to conduct user studies on this method for both populations. The ease of comprehension, result interpretation, and efficiency in detecting classification-related issues are evaluation topics that would give good insight on how to improve the mentioned point and the method in general.

3.6. Conclusion

Deep learning classifiers are progressively replacing handcrafted and understood standard feature detection methods for various fields. This significant gain in performance and accuracy is counterbalanced by a significant difficulty in understanding how and why they perform so well. Information visualization is one solution to fill this lack of interpretability. We have presented a pipeline containing a trained network and a dataset which produces an interactive representation depicting both the network's architecture and the behaviors of each layer when they process the test samples. Such a system allows visually analyzing the classification quality over layers of a dataset and could be used to visually detect patterns in the data. This analysis would lead to a hypothesis about the performance of the network. However, such hypothesis would need then to be verified by other means.

This approach has been validated on various scenarios and shows its potential and limits that could be overcome in the future. Extensions with various specific interaction methods should also focus on individual data, efficient data subsampling, and dense pixel-based glyph construction with better screen-space usage and/or less restrictions which would improve the method for more complex and precise network analysis.

Acknowledgments

This work has been carried out with financial support from the French State. Experiments presented in this chapter were carried out using the Labo's in the Sky with Data (LSD), the LaBRI data platform partially funded by Region Nouvelle Aquitaine.

References

Abadi, Martín, Agarwal, Ashish, Barham, Paul, Brevdo, Eugene, Chen, Zhifeng, Citro, Craig, Corrado, Greg S., Davis, Andy, et al., 2015. TensorFlow: Large-scale machine learning on heterogeneous systems. Software available from tensorflow.org.

Auber, David, Novelli, Noël, Melançon, Guy, 2007. Visually mining the datacube using a pixel-oriented technique. In: 2007 11th International Conference Information Visualization (IV'07). IEEE, pp. 3–10.

Behrisch, Michael, Bach, Benjamin, Henry Riche, Nathalie, Schreck, Tobias, Fekete, Jean-Daniel, 2016. Matrix reordering methods for table and network visualization. Computer Graphics Forum 35 (3), 693–716.

Benítez, José Manuel, Castro, Juan Luis, Requena, Ignacio, 1997. Are artificial neural networks black boxes? IEEE Transactions on Neural Networks 8 (5), 1156–1164.

Binder, Alexander, Montavon, Grégoire, Lapuschkin, Sebastian, Müller, Klaus-Robert, Samek, Wojciech, 2016. Layer-wise relevance propagation for neural networks with local renormalization layers. In: Lecture Notes in Computer Science, vol. 9887. Springer, Berlin / Heidelberg, pp. 63–71.

Blanchard, Frédéric, Herbin, Michel, Lucas, Laurent, 2005. A new pixel-oriented visualization technique through color image. Information Visualization 4 (4), 257–265.

Bostock, Michael, Ogievetsky, Vadim, Heer, Jeffrey, 2011. D^3 data-driven documents. IEEE Transactions on Visualization and Computer Graphics 17 (12), 2301–2309.

Brinkman, Erik, 2018. D3-DAG. https://github.com/erikbrinkman/d3-dag.

Chollet, François, et al., 2015. Keras. https://keras.io.

da Silva, L.E.B., Wunsch, D.C., 2018. A study on exploiting VAT to mitigate ordering effects in fuzzy art. In: 2018 International Joint Conference on Neural Networks (IJCNN), pp. 1–8.

Erhan, Dumitru, Bengio, Yoshua, Courville, Aaron, Vincent, Pascal, 2009. Visualizing higher-layer features of a deep network. Technical report. University of Montreal.

Fried, Ohad, DiVerdi, Stephen, Halber, Maciej, Sizikova, Elena, Finkelstein, Adam, 2015. IsoMatch: Creating informative grid layouts. Computer Graphics Forum 34, 155–166. Wiley Online Library.

Fuad, Kazi Ahmed Asif, Martin, Pierre-Etienne, Giot, Romain, Bourqui, Romain, Benois-Pineau, Jenny, Zemmari, Akka, 2020. Features understanding in 3D CNNs for actions recognition in video. In: The Tenth International Conference on Image Processing Theory, Tools and Applications (IPTA 2020), p. 6.

Gardner, Martin, 1976. Mathematical games—in which "monster" curves force redefinition of the word "curve". Scientific American 235 (6), 124–133.

Ghazi, Mostafa Mehdipour, Yanikoglu, Berrin, Aptoula, Erchan, 2017. Plant identification using deep neural networks via optimization of transfer learning parameters. Neurocomputing 235, 228–235.

Halnaut, Adrien, Giot, Romain, Bourqui, Romain, Auber, David, 2020. Deep dive into deep neural networks with flows. In: 15th International Joint Conference on Computer Vision, Imaging and Computer Graphics Theory and Applications, pp. 231–239.

Halnaut, Adrien, Giot, Romain, Bourqui, Romain, Auber, David, 2021. Samples classification analysis across DNN layers with fractal curves. In: ICPR 2020's Workshop Explainable Deep Learning for AI.

He, Kaiming, Zhang, Xiangyu, Ren, Shaoqing, Sun, Jian, 2016. Deep residual learning for image recognition. In: Proceedings of the IEEE Conference on Computer Vision and Pattern Recognition, pp. 770–778.

He, Yihui, Zhang, Xiangyu, Sun, Jian, 2017. Channel pruning for accelerating very deep neural networks. In: Proceedings of the IEEE International Conference on Computer Vision, pp. 1389–1397.

Hilbert, David, 1935. Über die stetige Abbildung einer Linie auf ein Flächenstück. In: Dritter Band: Analysis· Grundlagen der Mathematik· Physik Verschiedenes. Springer, pp. 1–2.

Hohman, Fred, Kahng, Minsuk, Pienta, Robert, Chau, Duen Horng, 2018. Visual analytics in deep learning: An interrogative survey for the next frontiers. IEEE Transactions on Visualization and Computer Graphics 25 (8), 2674–2693.

Kahng, M., Andrews, P.Y., Kalro, A., Chau, D.H., 2018a. Activis: Visual exploration of industry-scale deep neural network models. IEEE Transactions on Visualization and Computer Graphics 24 (1), 88–97.

Kahng, Minsuk, Thorat, Nikhil, Chau, Duen Horng Polo, Viégas, Fernanda B., Wattenberg, Martin, 2018b. GAN Lab: Understanding complex deep generative models using interactive visual experimentation. IEEE Transactions on Visualization and Computer Graphics 25 (1), 1–11.

Keim, Daniel A., 2000. Designing pixel-oriented visualization techniques: Theory and applications. IEEE Transactions on Visualization and Computer Graphics 6 (1), 59–78.

LeCun, Yann, 1998. The MNIST database of handwritten digits. http://yann.lecun.com/exdb/mnist/.

LeCun, Yann, Bottou, Léon, Bengio, Yoshua, Haffner, Patrick, 1998. Gradient-based learning applied to document recognition. Proceedings of the IEEE 86 (11), 2278–2324.

LeCun, Yann, Bengio, Yoshua, Hinton, Geoffrey, 2015. Deep learning. Nature 521 (7553), 436–444.

Liu, Mengchen, Liu, Shixia, Su, Hang, Cao, Kelei, Zhu, Jun, 2018. Analyzing the noise robustness of deep neural networks. In: 2018 IEEE Conference on Visual Analytics Science and Technology (VAST). IEEE, pp. 60–71.

Liu, Mengchen, Shi, Jiaxin, Li, Zhen, Li, Chongxuan, Zhu, Jun, Liu, Shixia, 2017. Towards better analysis of deep convolutional neural networks. IEEE Transactions on Visualization and Computer Graphics 23 (1), 91–100.

van der Maaten, Laurens, Hinton, Geoffrey, 2008. Visualizing data using t-SNE. Journal of Machine Learning Research 9, 2579–2605.

Meyer, Miriah, Sedlmair, Michael, Quinan, P. Samuel, Munzner, Tamara, 2015. The nested blocks and guidelines model. Information Visualization 14 (3), 234–249.

Morton, Guy M., 1966. A computer oriented geodetic data base and a new technique in file sequencing. Technical report. International Business Machines Company, New York.

Norton, Andrew P., Qi, Yanjun, 2017. Adversarial-playground: A visualization suite showing how adversarial examples fool deep learning. In: Visualization for Cyber Security (VizSec), 2017 IEEE Symposium on. IEEE, pp. 1–4.

Rauber, Paulo E., Fadel, Samuel G., Falcao, Alexandre X., Telea, Alexandru C., 2016. Visualizing the hidden activity of artificial neural networks. IEEE Transactions on Visualization and Computer Graphics 23 (1), 101–110.

Russakovsky, Olga, Deng, Jia, Su, Hao, Krause, Jonathan, Satheesh, Sanjeev, Ma, Sean, Huang, Zhiheng, Karpathy, Andrej, Khosla, Aditya, Bernstein, Michael, et al., 2015. ImageNet large scale visual recognition challenge. International Journal of Computer Vision 115 (3), 211–252.

Selvaraju, R.R., Cogswell, M., Das, A., Vedantam, R., Parikh, D., Batra, D., 2017. Grad-CAM: Visual explanations from deep networks via gradient-based localization. In: 2017 IEEE International Conference on Computer Vision (ICCV), pp. 618–626.

Simonyan, Karen, Zisserman, Andrew, 2014. Very deep convolutional networks for large-scale image recognition. preprint. arXiv:1409.1556.

Skilling, John, 2004. Programming the Hilbert curve. AIP Conference Proceedings 707, 381–387. American Institute of Physics.

Smilkov, Daniel, Carter, Shan, Sculley, D., Viégas, Fernanda B., Wattenberg, Martin, 2017. Direct-manipulation visualization of deep networks. arXiv preprint. arXiv:1708.03788.

Strong, Grant, Gong, Minglun, 2014. Self-sorting map: An efficient algorithm for presenting multimedia data in structured layouts. IEEE Transactions on Multimedia 16 (4), 1045–1058.

Sugiyama, Kozo, Tagawa, Shojiro, Toda, Mitsuhiko, 1981. Methods for visual understanding of hierarchical system structures. IEEE Transactions on Systems, Man and Cybernetics 11, 109–125.

Tang, Yichuan, 2013. Deep learning using linear support vector machines. In: ICML.

Tufte, Edward Rofl, 2001. The Visual Display of Quantitative Information. Graphic Press, Cheshire, Connecticut.

Wang, Junpeng, Gou, Liang, Shen, Han-Wei, Yang, Hao, 2019. DQNViz: A visual analytics approach to understand deep q-networks. IEEE Transactions on Visualization and Computer Graphics 25 (1), 288–298.

Wang, Zijie J., Turko, Robert, Shaikh, Omar, Park, Haekyu, Das, Nilaksh, Hohman, Fred, Kahng, Minsuk, Chau, Duen Horng, 2020. CNN 101: Interactive visual learning for convolutional neural networks. In: Extended Abstracts of the 2020 CHI Conference on Human Factors in Computing Systems, pp. 1–7.

Wongsuphasawat, Kanit, Smilkov, Daniel, Wexler, James, Wilson, Jimbo, Mane, Dandelion, Fritz, Doug, Krishnan, Dilip, Viégas, Fernanda B., Wattenberg, Martin, 2017. Visualizing dataflow graphs of deep learning models in TensorFlow. IEEE Transactions on Visualization and Computer Graphics 24 (1), 1–12.

Xiao, Han, Rasul, Kashif, Vollgraf, Roland, 2017. Fashion-MNIST: A novel image dataset for benchmarking machine learning algorithms. arXiv preprint. arXiv:1708.07747.

Yalamanchili, Pavan, Arshad, Umar, Mohammed, Zakiuddin, Garigipati, Pradeep, Entschev, Peter, Kloppenborg, Brian, Malcolm, James, Melonakos, John, 2015. ArrayFire – A high performance software library for parallel computing with an easy-to-use API. https://github.com/arrayfire/arrayfire.

Zhang, Quanshi, Wu, Ying Nian, Zhu, Song-Chun, 2018. Interpretable convolutional neural networks. In: Proceedings of the IEEE Conference on Computer Vision and Pattern Recognition, pp. 8827–8836.

Zhang, Quanshi, Yang, Yu, Ma, Haotian, Wu, Ying Nian, 2019. Interpreting CNNs via decision trees. In: Proceedings of the IEEE Conference on Computer Vision and Pattern Recognition, pp. 6261–6270.

CHAPTER 4

Characterizing a scene recognition model by identifying the effect of input features via semantic-wise attribution

Marcos Escudero-Viñolo, Jesús Bescós, Alejandro López-Cifuentes, and Andrija Gajić

Universidad Autónoma de Madrid, Video Processing & Understanding Lab., Escuela Politécnica Superior, Madrid, Spain

Chapter points

- A novel perturbation-based method that generates complete attribution maps aligned with the objects' boundaries and also enables the study of interclass relationships.
- A study of the scene interdependencies of a scene-recognition model trained on the Places-365 dataset.
- The proposed method is of potential interest for profiling failure cases, identifying dataset biases and comparing knowledge encoding capabilities of several models.

4.1. Introduction

The use of Convolutional Neural Networks (CNNs) has spread rapidly during the last years. In addition to their discriminative and generative power, strategies such as transfer learning allow one to start from heavily and richly trained CNNs (models) and adapt them for specific tasks, partially inheriting the potential of the source model but also inheriting its biases. In order to detect these biases, help the foretelling of the models' behavior in real-world applications and design adequate training approaches in accordance with their learning processes, the success of CNNs comes together with the need to explain their decisions. To this aim, model interpretability is a matter of great concern and interest, a research area that encompasses different methodologies for generating visual representations of trained models focused on aiding human interpretation of their operation.

4.1.1 Model interpretability

In model interpretability, the performance of the model is not measured solely by accounting for its global accuracy or learning evolution, but is also analyzed qualitatively by representing and studying the learned concepts. One of the most simple methodologies to achieve this is the use of two- or three-dimensional *cluster-like representations*

Explainable Deep Learning AI
https://doi.org/10.1016/B978-0-32-396098-4.00010-7

obtained by grouping features extracted from the last layers of the model as a response to sets of (generally annotated) validation images, as in t-SNE (Van der Maaten and Hinton, 2008). A finer grained description of the model can be extracted using *feature visualization*. This includes a set of methods that aim to generate a visual representation of the learned/encoded knowledge. These representations can be computed via optimization for an individual neuron, complete layers, specific channels, or arbitrary groups of neurons (Olah et al., 2017). The idea is to generate an artificial input image that maximizes a specific response of the selected parts of the model. Differently, *attribution methods* are focused on analyzing the input data. Specifically, the collection of attribution methods can be understood as the set of strategies and techniques that characterize the response of CNNs by identifying the input image features responsible for a model decision (Simonyan et al., 2014). In other words, their aim is to identify *what the CNN is looking at*.

The majority of attribution methods can be broadly organized into four categories: methods based on backpropagation (Selvaraju et al., 2019; Simonyan et al., 2014), perturbation-based methods (Petsiuk et al., 2018; Zeiler and Fergus, 2014), approximation-based methods (Ribeiro et al., 2016), and methods for the visualization of intermediate neurons' activations (Ulyanov et al., 2018; Olah et al., 2017).

4.1.2 Perturbation methods

In this chapter we focus on perturbation-based attribution methods to aid the human interpretation of image-fed CNNs. In this context, perturbation methods propose to measure attribution by modifying the input image and then collecting and observing the effect of that perturbation in the model's output. Seminal works in this topic include the study of Zeiler and Fergus (2014) where the effect of systematically covering up different portions of an image with a gray square is analyzed, yielding coarse square-shaped, yet revealing, attribution maps at the image level. Following the same idea, Fong and Vedaldi (2017) proposed to replace these fixed-size perturbations with meaningful ones obtained by blurring specific areas of an image. The spatial extension of these blurred areas was defined by spatial masks resulting from the optimization of changes in the model outputs. The same authors extended their idea by regularizing a set, not just a single region, of representative perturbations (Fong et al., 2019). The arrangement of the regions in this set, together with their association to the model output, led to the concept of *extremal perturbations*. An extremal perturbation is the inhibition of a certain key neuron in a model for classification caused by the perturbation of the corresponding relevant area in the input image. In all these methods, the masks are obtained through an optimization process that originates at the last layer of the CNN and goes back by unpooling processes to the original image resolution according to the neurons' receptive fields. Therefore, despite being extremely informative, these relevant areas are usually blurry-defined, comprehending regions which extensions are misaligned with the image objects' boundaries, hence hindering the interpretative power of these methods. Kapishnikov et al. (2019) proposed XRAI, an attribution method based on superpixels that also builds upon integrated gradients to obtain perturbed versions of images. In this case, by constraining to areas defined by superpixels, the resulting attribution maps comprising the most important regions for the classification of an image are not blurred but aligned with the image edges. However, while this method solves the proper identification of image regions, a semantic interpretation of these regions is still missing and hence left to the observer.

4.1.3 Scope of perturbation methods

Although some of the indicated perturbation methods permit the definition of multiple (but few) relevant regions, their use has been primarily assessed on image classification tasks like those defined by the ImageNet Challenge (Deng et al., 2009). In these tasks there are mainly one or two objects that define or impact on the image class. Differently, for tasks such as scene recognition, the scene class is determined by several objects and by their spatial arrangement. Therefore, a more object-systematic interpretation covering all the image is required for better assessing these models. Without detracting from this issue, and as the estimated relevant areas are not assigned a semantic meaning, a critical limitation of the existing methods is the lack of references that allow to associate results throughout sets of images without human intervention. This limitation impedes the use of attribution on a per-class basis, a procedure that enables interesting studies, as we explore along this chapter for scene-recognition. For the practicability of these studies it is also paramount to generate automatic relationships between the semantic meaning of the attribution regions and the model outputs. These relationships are not provided by any of the aforementioned methods.

This chapter describes a novel perturbation-based attribution method guided by cues or labels obtained via a semantic segmentation of the input images. The method is based on perturbing color images by inhibiting or adapting specific areas according to their assigned semantic labels. Through this process, the perturbation areas are no longer of a fixed shape (Zeiler and Fergus, 2014), nor is their extension optimized according to the output (Fong et al., 2019) or constrained by superpixel shapes according to low-level image features (Kapishnikov et al., 2019); instead, perturbation areas have a semantic labeling that empowers the attribution study on a per-class basis by enabling the automatic association of different images of the same scene class. Furthermore, the use of this method yields complete attribution maps, i.e., maps composed of attribution scores for **all** pixels, not just for the *relevant* ones. Moreover, the particularization of the method for the scene recognition task enables delving deeper into the interpretability of the scene recognition task, allowing to identify relevant, irrelevant, and distracting semantic labels for each scene class.

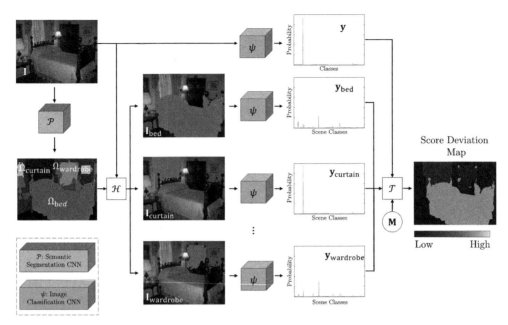

Figure 4.1 Diagram of the proposed method: A given image **I** is forwarded to a trained scene classification CNN Ψ obtaining prediction **y**. In parallel, **I** is segmented into regions using a semantic segmentation network $\mathcal{P}$ obtaining a segmented image **M**. This is used to remove or inhibit objects of **I** creating a set of perturbed images. Each perturbed image $\mathbf{I}_l$ derived from color image **I**, with l being the semantic class of the inhibited object, is forwarded to Ψ to obtain the corresponding probability distribution $\mathbf{y}_l$. Using the semantic segmentation **M**, the original prediction **y** and the set of predictions for the perturbed images $\mathbf{y}_l$, the proposed Score Deviation Map is obtained. Better viewed in color.

4.1.4 Overview of the proposed interpretation method

Fig. 4.1 graphically depicts the per-image operation of the proposed method. Given an input image, a trained semantic segmentation model and a scene recognition model—albeit any other image-wise model can be also used—the method measures the impact in the scene prediction of the image areas assigned to each semantic region. Toward this goal, the process entails the perturbation of the image areas associated to each one of the semantic classes (e.g., to the bed class in Fig. 4.1). Then, the perturbed image is fed to the scene recognition model resulting in a score vector containing the likelihoods of the image being an instance of each trained scene class. This score vector is compared to that obtained for the unperturbed image. The impact of the semantic class in the prediction is obtained by measuring the deviation or change between the two score vectors. Repeating this process for all the semantic classes and creating an image by associating the resulting deviation to the semantic segmentation area, a Score Deviation

Map is assembled. This map graphically provides attribution evidence of each image region in the scene prediction.

Differently from other attribution methods, the proposed one leverages the spatial information and distinctness of semantic segmentation to provide complete score maps aligned with the objects' boundaries, rather than isolated salient blurry areas. However, the main advantage of the proposed interpretation method is that semantic labels enable the automatic association of evidences from all the images of the same scene class by grouping the deviation scores according to the semantic class. In other words, instead of providing evidences to assess questions such as: *How important is this image area for predicting this image as a bedroom?* It provides semantically meaningful evidence for appraising more general questions as: *How important are beds for predicting images as bedroom ones?*

These aggregated attribution evidences lead to the creation of two sets of semantic classes for each scene class: those that are relevant for the prediction and those that are irrelevant, according to their average deviation score. This classification can be very useful for analyzing performance and flaws, as it eases the interpretation of the model's encoded knowledge by providing information in a semantic abstraction level closer to an object-wise human interpretation of the image. To provide additional semantic cues that may be specially useful for explaining model's mispredictions, the proposed interpretation method also defines sets of distracting semantic classes. These Distracting semantic classes are image areas (usually associated to Relevant semantic classes) that may be *confusing* the model leading to incorrect scene predictions: images perturbed by inhibiting these areas lead to a correct prediction of the scene class.

The rest of the chapter formalizes this attribution processes and exemplifies them with several illustrative examples.

4.2. Semantic-wise attribution

This section first describes the process for measuring attribution of each semantic class in the scene prediction of a given image by perturbing the image region associated to each semantic class (Sections 4.2.1 and 4.2.2). Then, it follows by introducing alternatives for the perturbation process (Section 4.2.3). The section is closed by outlining the protocols used for aggregating attribution results on a per image basis—creating what we called a Score Deviation Map (Section 4.2.4), and on per-scene class basis (Section 4.2.5), i.e., accounting for the attribution results of all the images labeled as instances of a given scene class. Toward the latter goal, the proposed methodology allows identifying the sets of Relevant, Irrelevant, and Distracting semantic classes for the prediction of each scene class.

4.2.1 Preliminaries

Scene recognition model

Let $\mathbf{I}$ be a color image, and let $\Psi : \mathbb{R}^{W \times H \times 3} \to \mathbb{R}^K$ be a classification model that maps $\mathbf{I}$ to a vector of nonnormalized predictions $\mathbf{f} = \Psi(\mathbf{I})$, one for each of the K learned scene classes.

The inference of class posterior probabilities $\mathbf{y} = [\gamma_1, \ldots, \gamma_k, \ldots, \gamma_K] \in \mathbb{R}^K$ is obtained from $\mathbf{f}$ by using a logarithmic normalized exponential function $\gamma(\mathbf{f}) : \mathbb{R}^K \to \mathbb{R}^K$,

$$\gamma_k = \gamma(\mathbf{f}) = \log\left(\frac{\exp(f_k)}{\sum_i^K \exp(f_i)} \right), \qquad (4.1)$$

for the posterior probability of class k. Generally, $\mathbf{I}$ is classified as an instance of class k^* if $k^* = \mathrm{argmax}_k(\mathbf{y})$.

Semantic segmentation model

Let Ω be the spatial support of $\mathbf{I}$, and let $\mathcal{P} : \mathbb{R}^{W \times H \times 3} \to \mathbb{N}^{W \times H}$ be a semantic segmentation model that maps $\mathbf{I}$ to $\mathbf{M}$, which consists of a partition of $\mathbf{I}$ into regions with a semantic coherence,

$$\mathbf{M} = \mathcal{P}(\mathbf{I}) = \left\{ \Omega_1, \ldots, \Omega_n : \Omega = \bigcup_{j=1}^{n} \Omega_j \quad \text{such that } \left(\Omega_{j_1} \cap \Omega_{j_2} = \emptyset, \forall j_1 \neq j_2 \right) \right\}, \qquad (4.2)$$

where each region is assigned a semantic label $\ell(\Omega_j) = l$, $\{l \in \mathbb{N} : 1 \leq l \leq L\}$, with L being the number of semantic classes learned by the model $\mathcal{P}$.

4.2.2 Score deviation

Some studies have confirmed that there is a significant texture-bias in the prediction of classification models (Geirhos et al., 2019). According to these studies, we propose to remove or inhibit the texture of each region or regions associated to each semantic class in $\mathbf{I}$ in order to evaluate the impact or influence of those regions in the prediction of the scene class $\Psi(\mathbf{I})$.

Toward this goal, we rely on an operator $\mathcal{H}$ that, given an image, its semantic segmentation, and a categorical semantic label, returns a perturbed image $\mathbf{I}_l$ which is $\mathbf{I}$ changed by modifying the set of pixels $\mathbf{p}$ belonging to regions tagged in $\mathbf{M}$ as instances of the semantic class l.

For the sake of simplicity, we here assume a simple perturbation strategy, namely texture inhibition, which simply consists in assigning all the pixels in this region a reference color value $\boldsymbol{\mu}$, hence removing the region texture:

$$\mathcal{H}(\mathbf{I}, \mathbf{M}, l) = \mathbf{I}_l, \quad \mathbf{I}_l(\mathbf{p}) = \begin{cases} \boldsymbol{\mu}, & \forall \mathbf{p} \in \{\Omega_j \quad \text{such that } \ell(\Omega_j) = l\}, \\ \mathbf{I}(\mathbf{p}), & \text{elsewhere.} \end{cases} \quad (4.3)$$

Alternative perturbation strategies are briefly presented in Section 4.2.3.

Once the image has been modified, the effect in the prediction of the area(s) associated to the semantic class l that defines the modified part can be evaluated by measuring what we called the score deviation $s(\mathbf{I}, l)$. The score deviation is simply the difference in the predictions obtained by the original and modified image. Therefore, for the originally predicted class k^*, it can be obtained by subtracting the inferred probability obtained for the modified image from that obtained for the original image:

$$s(\mathbf{I}, l) = y_{k^*} - y_{k^*}(l), \quad \text{where} \quad \mathbf{y}_l = \{y_1(l), \dots, y_k(l), \dots, y_K(l)\} = \gamma(\Psi(\mathbf{I}_l)). \quad (4.4)$$

Interpretation of score deviation

As far as y_{k^*} and $y_{k^*}(l)$ are probabilities, $s(\mathbf{I}, l)$ is theoretically bounded in the interval $[-1, 1] \subset \mathbb{R}$. Given that $\mathbf{y}$ and $\mathbf{y}_l$ are just evaluated for the class of maximum probability, obtaining large negative values is rare, as the class probability for the original image is usually large. Notwithstanding, negative values of $s(\mathbf{I}, l)$ are interesting, as they indicate prediction gains, i.e., an increase in the score of the predicted class after the perturbation of the areas tagged as l; hence, negative values are not indicative of the impact of these areas, but may suggest areas potentially hindering a correct prediction. Nevertheless, identifying larger values of $s(\mathbf{I}, l)$ is of a higher relevance for the method: the larger the value, the higher the impact of the inhibited semantic region in the prediction, as this inhibition decreases the score. Finally, values close to zero indicate low impact, as the prediction score remains nearly unchanged.

By repeating this process for all the L semantic classes, one can obtain a vector of score deviations $\mathbf{s(I)} = \{s(\mathbf{I}, l), l \in \mathbb{N} : 1 \leq l \leq L\}$.

4.2.3 Perturbation strategies

The aim of the perturbation strategy is to avoid the influence of an area, delimited by the extension of a class region in the semantic segmentation, in the prediction of the analyzed image.

In Eq. (4.3) we proposed a simple perturbation method consisting in inhibiting the texture of the region of interest by replacing the color of all the pixels in the region by a reference color value $\boldsymbol{\mu}$. The effectiveness of this method is validated in Section 4.3, suggesting that even a simple inhibition strategy enables the study of relevant explainable characteristics of the model. However, there are alternative perturbation mechanisms that may provide additional insight into the influence of a region.

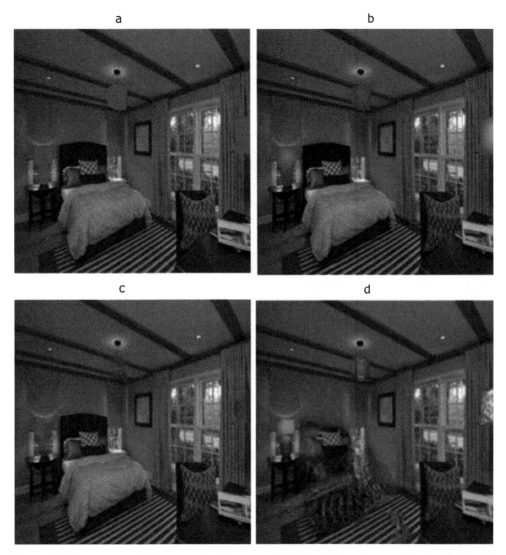

Figure 4.2 Alternative perturbation strategies. The texture inhibition of the region associated to the *lamp* (a) can be replaced by its Gaussian blurring (b) or its inpainting (c). The inpainting strategy (Yu et al., 2018), effective for small regions such as the lamp, may produce undesirable artifacts for larger objects like the *bed* (d). Better viewed in color.

For instance, texture inhibition does not eliminate the information of the inhibited region boundaries; hence, information on the inhibited region is still present in the image. An alternative would be to smooth the region, e.g., by Gaussian filtering the inner values and boundaries (see Fig. 4.2(b)) or to use some sort of inpainting strategy such as in Yu et al. (2018) (see Figs. 4.2(c)–(d)) which can be very effective for small objects (see Fig. 4.2(c)) but usually lacks enough information to correctly identify coherent regions when inpainting large regions (see Fig. 4.2(d)). In this chapter we do not delve deeper into these perturbation methods, but rather suggest that the study of alternative perturbation strategies is an interesting research path to be explored in the future.

4.2.4 Score deviation map

To visualize the attribution of each region in the input image, one can create a Score Deviation Map $\mathbf{SDM}$ by relying on an operator $\mathcal{T}$ that assigns to the spatial support of each region Ω_j of the semantic segmentation $\mathbf{M}$ the score deviation obtained after modifying the input image by inhibiting the regions tagged as $\ell(\Omega_j)$,

$$\mathcal{T}(\mathbf{M}, \mathbf{s}, l) = \mathbf{SDM}, \quad \mathbf{SDM}(\mathbf{p}) = s(\mathbf{I}, l), \forall \mathbf{p} \in \left\{ \Omega_j \quad \text{such that } \ell(\Omega_j) = l \right\}. \qquad (4.5)$$

4.2.5 Class-wise statistics

Differently than previous methods for measuring image attribution, the set of scores for each image obtained using the semantic-wise perturbation is parametrized by the semantic classes. This parametrization eases the creation of a complete nonbinary attribution measure, the Score Deviation Map, where every pixel, not just the relevant ones, has an attribution score. Furthermore, it also enables the automatic extraction of class-wise relationships between scene and semantic classes.

To exemplify the potential of this strategy, three types of class-wise statistics are studied in this chapter: relevant semantic classes for the prediction, irrelevant semantic classes for the prediction, and distracting semantic classes.

Relevant semantic classes

Let $\mathbf{I}_k$ be the set of images predicted as instances of the scene class k, and let $\mathbf{S}_l = \left\{ s(\mathbf{I}, l) \ \forall \mathbf{I} \in \mathbf{I}_k \right\}$ be the score-set obtained by following the scoring procedure defined in equations (4.3) and (4.4) for images in $\mathbf{I}_k$ and semantic class l.

If the process is repeated in the set $\mathbf{I}_k$ for every semantic class, a set of score-sets $\mathbf{S} = \left\{ \mathbf{S}_l, l \in \mathbb{N} : 1 \leq l \leq L \right\}$ is yielded.

The expectation $\mathbb{E}(\mathbf{S}_l)$, median, and standard deviation of each score-set $\mathbf{S}_l$ can be used as class-wise statistics of the impact of the semantic class l in the prediction of class k for a classification model and a dataset. Arranging one of these statistics, different relevance sets $\mathbf{S}^R$ can be obtained; $\mathbf{S}^R$ is here defined as the ranked set of semantic classes obtained by arranging the score-sets according to their average score:

$$\mathbf{S}^R = \left\{ \mathbf{S}_{(1)}, \dots, \mathbf{S}_{(l)}, \dots, \mathbf{S}_{(L)} \right\} \to \mathbb{E}(\mathbf{S}_{(1)}) \geq \cdots \geq \mathbb{E}(\mathbf{S}_{(l)}) \geq \cdots \geq \mathbb{E}(\mathbf{S}_{(L)}). \qquad (4.6)$$

To remove noisy segmentation cues, this relevance set can be shortened by using a significance score value α. Thereby, removing all the score-sets which average is smaller than α. We refer to this relevant truncated set as $\mathbf{S}^R(\alpha)$ through the rest of the chapter.

Irrelevant semantic classes

Similarly, for a given significance level α, the set of irrelevant semantic classes, $\mathbf{S}^I(\alpha)$, can be simply defined as the relative complement of $\mathbf{S}^R(\alpha)$ with respect to $\mathbf{S}^R$, namely $\mathbf{S}^I(\alpha) = \mathbf{S}^R \setminus \mathbf{S}^R(\alpha)$.

This set can be again shortened to reduce the impact of a noisy segmentation by removing all the score-sets associated to semantic classes that are lowly represented in the set of images $\mathbf{I}_k$. To this aim, the density of each semantic class l in $\mathbf{I}_k$ can be estimated by dividing the number of pixels tagged as l in the partitions of the whole set $\{\mathcal{P}(\mathbf{I}), \forall \mathbf{I} \in \mathbf{I}_k\}$ by the total number of pixels in $\mathbf{I}_k$. Then, using a significance density value β, all the score-sets in the irrelevant set which density is smaller than or equal to β can be removed. Hereinafter, we refer to this irrelevant truncated set as $\mathbf{S}^I(\alpha, \beta)$.

Distracting semantic classes

The previous sets measure the impact of semantic classes in the prediction of a scene class. A careful reader may have noticed that this does not require knowledge of the scene ground truth, as only the predictions are used. In a different manner, in order to extract the set of distracting semantic classes, one requires the ground-truth class, k_{GT}, for each image $\mathbf{I}$.

Using this information, the set of distracting semantic classes $\mathbf{D}(\mathbf{I}_k)$ for the set of images $\mathbf{I}_k$ can be defined as the set of semantic classes which inhibition changes the prediction from a wrong class (i.e., a false positive) to the ground-truth one. That is, a distracting semantic class is one that has the ability to *confuse* the model:

$$\mathbf{D}(\mathbf{I}_k) = \left\{ l \quad \text{such that } \operatorname{argmax}_k(\mathbf{y}) \neq k_{GT} \wedge \operatorname{argmax}_k(\mathbf{y}_l) = k_{GT} \right\}. \tag{4.7}$$

4.3. Experimental results

Although the semantic-wise attribution method described in this chapter can be applied on the output activation, class prediction scores, or intermediate layers of any image-wise classification model, we believe that scene recognition is a representative task to illustrate its potential benefits. This touchstone condition mainly comes from the need of effective scene recognition models to rely on multifocus learning; as the scene is detected by aggregating cues from several objects and their context.

Along this section, we illustrate the potential of the method by a series of results. For the sake of reproducibility, it starts by compiling the implementation details and describing the adopted dataset in Section 4.3.1. Then, attribution results using the simplest perturbation method (texture inhibition) are presented, covering qualitative examples at the image (Section 4.3.2) and scene class (Section 4.3.3) levels.

4.3.1 Overview of the experiments

Our aim is to aid interpretability and understanding of any classification model and, specifically in this chapter, of any scene recognition model. Therefore, the qualitative analysis that follows is suitable to be applied on any state-of-the-art scene recognition method disregarding its architecture.

The semantic segmentation used for defining the regions is also replaceable by any other approach in the literature, and the complete method may benefit from better semantic segmentation models. The better the semantic segmentation model in terms of mean class accuracy, number of semantic classes L, and diversity of these trained classes, the more reliable the analysis will be.

Implementation details

The results reported in this chapter have been obtained using as the probe model a scene recognition model trained with data from the training set of the Places365 dataset (Zhou et al., 2017a) on a ResNet-18 architecture (He et al., 2016). For the semantic segmentation counterpart used to define the attribution regions, we opted for the stable UPerNet-50 architecture (Xiao et al., 2018) trained using the ADE20K dataset (Zhou et al., 2017b), which encompasses samples from $L = 150$ semantic objects classes and stuff classes.

For the texture inhibition perturbation method (see Section 4.2.2), we have set $\mu = [0.485, 0.456, 0.406]$, the mean color value of the ImageNet dataset which is also used to mean-normalize the input images in the trained scene recognition model.

Scope of the experiments

Results are extracted on the 36000 validation images from $K = 365$ scene classes that constitute the Places365 validation set (Zhou et al., 2017a), i.e., for an unbiased estimation of the performance, we extract results on images unused for training. For each of these images, we extract the associated Score Deviation Map. Aggregating results for all the images of each of the $K = 365$ scene classes and using a fixed α value, we extract 365 sets of relevant, irrelevant and distracting semantic classes. All these sets are available at Semantic-Wise Attribution Results. We include here a subset of illustrative examples of the three sets to stress on the semantic similarities, connections, and dissimilarities among scene classes.

4.3.2 Score deviation maps

Fig. 4.3 represents several examples of the obtained **SDM** for a given image. Yellowish colors in the **SDM** represent objects/areas whose inhibition decreases the probability—more relevant for scene prediction. On the other hand, blueish colors represent areas that do not modify the probability; hence, are irrelevant for scene prediction. In the

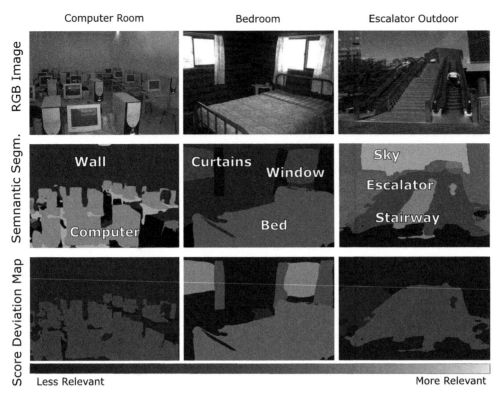

Figure 4.3 Several examples of the proposed method for a given image. Top row includes the analyzed RGB images. Middle row depicts the corresponding semantic segmentation. Bottom row represents the corresponding Score Deviation Map. Yellowish colors in the map, i.e., $s(\mathbf{I}, l) \rightarrow 1$, represent objects/areas with higher relevance in the prediction. On the other hand, blueish colors, i.e., $s(\mathbf{I}, l) \rightarrow -1$, represent areas with lower relevance in the prediction. Better viewed in color.

examples included in Fig. 4.3, the impact of specific sets of pixels in the prediction of the scene class is clear: when the computers, bed, and windows or the stairs and escalators are inhibited, the score for the originally predicted class strongly descends. This indicates that the pixels identified as samples of these semantic classes are relevant for the prediction. Differently, the inhibition of the pixels assigned to the wall or the sky classes does not really produce a decrease in the originally predicted score, suggesting that their role in the prediction is minimal.

4.3.3 Relevant, irrelevant, and distracting semantic classes

SDM can be used to visually interpret how different areas of an image directly affect a scene prediction (see Section 4.3.2). Specifically, attribution-scored regions in the **SDM** define an image generalization of the maximal activation regions used by other attribution methods. Along with this per image study on the attribution, the semantic labels associated to these regions enable the study on a per scene class basis, i.e., aggregating results for all the images of the same scene class. In particular, we here include examples of qualitative studies designating the set of semantic classes that are relevant, irrelevant, or distracting, for predicting a specific scene class.

4.3.3.1 Relevant semantic classes for scene prediction

Fig. 4.4 depicts an example of the relevant semantic classes for *lagoon* and *lake natural* scene classes. The ranked set of relevant semantics (Eq. (4.6)) for each scene is presented using two representations: first, a word count represents the full set of relevant semantic labels $\mathbf{S}^R(\alpha = 0.00)$ using a font size relative to each $\mathbf{S}_l$ value. Second, a box–plot represents a qualitative analysis of the set; but, to ease visualization, just the most relevant semantic classes are presented, i.e., a larger α is used, namely $\mathbf{S}^R(\alpha = 0.01)$; see the project website for nontruncated representations.

Results from Fig. 4.4 lead to a two-fold analysis. First, solely studying the attribution evidences, one can obtain reliable information, albeit constrained by the L learned semantic classes, of how semantic classes affect the prediction of a given scene. In this line, results for *lagoon* suggest that the set of relevant stuff learned by the CNNs as representative of *lagoon(s)* is primarily composed by sea, sky, and water semantic classes (sorted from a higher to a lower score), with small contributions from other semantic classes such as palm tree. Otherwise, for the *lake natural* class, results suggest that tree, water, sky, river, and mountain pixels are the most relevant. In our opinion, for both scene classes, the relevant semantic classes are somehow connected with potential human decomposition of the scenes' gist, yet a deeper and rigorous study is required for further assessment.

Secondly, we can use the attribution results to partially understand the knowledge encoded in the scene recognition model. Interestingly, pixels assigned to the tree class are slightly more relevant for the prediction than those assigned to the aquatic semantic classes (water, sea, river). As stated before, one of the main challenges in Scene Recognition is the high overlap between similar scenes. In these examples, images from *lagoon* and *lake natural* have a low interclass variability, i.e., are expressed by somehow close semantic manifolds in the domain of natural images (Bengio et al., 2013). In fact, these manifolds can be abstracted by using the semantic classes as explanatory factors. According to this premise, we can hypothesize that the prevalence of the tree semantic class over the aquatic ones may be derived from the training process focusing the model to encode differentiating representations that (may) help discriminating between similar scene classes. The rest of the set of most populated semantic classes for these two scene classes supports this: tree is irrelevant for the prediction of *lagoon* and the relevance of river for this scene class is smaller than for *lake natural*, with sea being its counterpart: it has a significant smaller impact for *lake natural* than for *lagoon*.

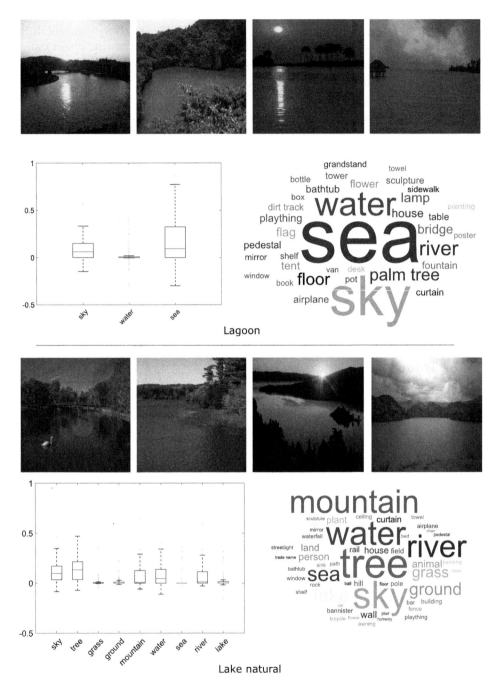

Figure 4.4 Relevant Semantic Classes for *lagoon* (top) and *lake natural* (bottom) scene classes. In each subfigure, the top row represents different samples from the Places365 validation set, whereas the bottom row depicts a box-plot (obtained using $\alpha = 0.01$ for the sake of visualization) and a word count representation (obtained using $\alpha = 0$) showing which objects and stuff are relevant for each scene class. Better viewed in color.

The attribution statistics can be also used to speculate on the learning pathways. Note that, among the aquatic semantic classes, the scene recognition model does not have at prediction time the key semantic distinction provided by the semantic segmentation differentiating between sea (common in *lagoon*) and water or river (more representative of *lake natural*). Yet, the implicit encoding of different intermediate representations for these two kinds of aquatic concepts during the training process of the scene recognition model is also a plausible possibility.

In this vein, attribution statistics can provide specifics on the implicit difference between two scene classes. Fig. 4.5 is a clear example to illustrate this potential and includes the relevant semantic concepts for the prediction of the *patio* and *restaurant patio* scene classes. First, one may notice that the amount of relevant semantic classes is larger in this example than in the one included in Fig. 4.4. This is a combination of a larger scene clutter in both categories (as contain human-made objects not present in the previous natural images) and the human-bias of the semantic segmentation dataset used to train the semantic segmentation model (that considerably contains more human-made semantic categories than natural stuff).

These two scene classes are one a version of the other. This agrees with the similarity between the sets of relevant semantic categories: 9 out of the 10 most relevant semantic classes for *patio* are also relevant for *restaurant patio*. Furthermore, classes as building, chair, and table are of a high relevance for both scene classes. From the word clouds, it is evident that the differentiating class is here person, suggesting that in the annotation process their presence was used for the disambiguation of these two classes. The relevance of additional human-related semantic classes such as awning (to protect from the sun while eating outside) support this hypothesis. The only semantic class that is exclusively relevant for the *patio* class is the ground one, probably because *restaurant patio* samples are crowded, with persons occluding the ground.

Another interesting example is that included in Fig. 4.6 to compare relevant semantic classes for three scenes classes strongly entangled: *field cultivated, vegetable garden,* and *farm.* In Fig. 4.6 instead of the box-plots of the relevant categories, we include the prior distributions of the semantic classes in each scene class (fourth row). If we account for semantic classes that are assigned to at least 1% of the scene class pixel instances, we discover that five of the most common semantic classes are shared among the three scene types, namely field, grass, ground, sky, and tree. Furthermore, two other semantic categories are common in two scene classes (plant, building, and person), whereas the rest are class specific: mountain for *field cultivated*, wall, floor, fence, rock, flower, and water for usually urban-sited *vegetable garden,* and animal for *farms.* In spite of starting from similar prior distributions, the model is trained to focus on different objects and stuff to differentiate each scene class, according to the relevance word clouds in the fifth row of Fig. 4.6. Intriguingly, the scene-specific objects are not the main focus (yet are relevant), probably due to the effect of other scene classes sharing these specifics in

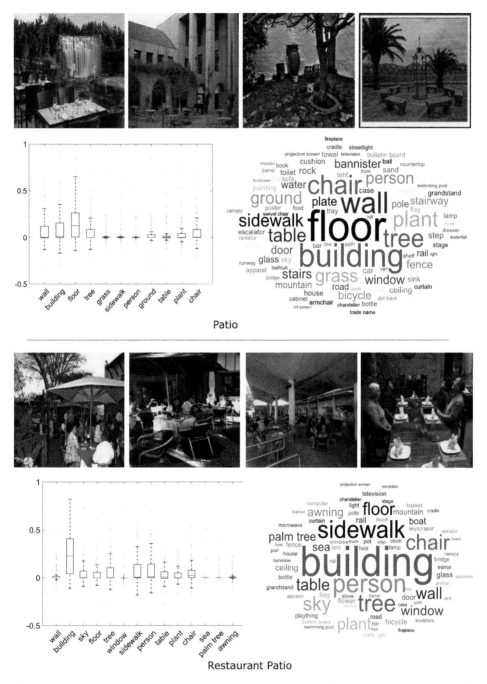

Figure 4.5 Relevant Semantic Classes for *patio* (top) and *restaurant patio* (bottom) scene classes. In each subfigure, the top row represents different samples from the Places365 validation set, whereas the bottom row depicts a box-plot (obtained using $\alpha = 0.01$ for the sake of visualization) and a word count representation (obtained using $\alpha = 0$) showing which objects and stuff are relevant for each scene class. Better viewed in color.

Figure 4.6 Relevant Semantic Classes for *field cultivated* (left column), *vegetable garden* (middle column) and *farm* (right column) scene classes. In each column, the top three rows represent different samples from the Places365 validation set, whereas the fourth row depicts the distribution of the main semantic classes for the semantic segmentation of scene class images in the training set (only semantic classes with more than 1% of total pixel samples have been included). The fifth row includes word count representations (obtained using $\alpha = 0$) of the relevant objects and stuff for each scene class. Better viewed in color.

the dataset. In any case, the distinguishing encoding of each scene is evidenced by the presence of a different top-relevant semantic for each scene class: field for *field cultivated*, plant for *vegetable garden*, and grass for *farm*.

It is important to highlight that these relevance analyses are constrained by the quality of the semantic segmentation model, but also by the diversity of the examples in the scene recognition training dataset: real-world representations of the scene classes may differ. Accordingly, the study of the attribution statistics can be also useful for uncovering dataset biases. These biases may have been inadvertently included during the harvest and annotation processes, hindering the proper training and evaluation of scene recognition methods, as identifying them usually requires exhaustive human inspection.

4.3.3.2 Irrelevant semantic classes for scene prediction

Fig. 4.7 results complement those presented in Figs. 4.4, 4.5, and 4.6. Specifically, Fig. 4.7 depicts *lagoon, lake natural, patio, restaurant patio, field cultivated, vegetable garden,* and *farm*, irrelevant semantic classes using word counts representing the irrelevant truncated sets $\mathbf{S}^{I}(\alpha = 0.01, \beta = 0.00)$.

Observing the word clouds of irrelevant objects and stuff, some evidences are aligned with the relevant analysis. Specifically, in these examples, it can be observed how relevant semantic classes for some classes are, in turn, irrelevant for potentially confusing scene classes. For instance, tree is part of the set of irrelevant semantic classes for *lagoon*, whereas it was the most relevant one for *lake natural*. Similarly, the irrelevance of plant for the prediction of the *farm* class may be producing a better discrimination between this class and *vegetable garden* to which it represents top relevance.

For understanding the irrelevant nature of other semantic classes, we need to analyze the scene recognition problem holistically, i.e., accounting for all the scene classes. Thereby, we may hypothesize that the sand pixels in *lagoon* images or the bridge pixels in *lake natural* images may be irrelevant for the prediction as they are relevant for the prediction of other scene classes such as *beach* and *bridge* that also share similarities with *lagoon* and *lake natural* respectively (see the website of the project).

Another remarkable factor is how these irrelevant semantic classes are also aligned with the nature of the scene class. For instance, the sky is the most irrelevant for the *patio* class, whereas its equivalent for the *restaurant patio* class is ceiling. This is indicative of a difference in the top part of the images of these two classes: a semantic stuff or object cannot be irrelevant for a given scene class if it is not sufficiently-sampled in the semantic distribution of the class.

The analysis brought forth by this irrelevance representations could additionally be helpful to outline, with human inspection, if irrelevant objects might be useful even if they are currently not part of the encoded knowledge of the model.

Figure 4.7 Irrelevant semantic classes for *lagoon, lake natural, patio, restaurant patio, field cultivated, vegetable garden,* and *farm* scene classes. Better viewed in color.

4.3.3.3 Distracting semantic classes for scene prediction

Fig. 4.8 depicts examples of the set **D** (Eq. (4.7)) of distracting semantic classes for missclassified samples from the *lagoon, lake natural, patio, restaurant patio, field cultivated, vegetable garden,* and *farm* scene classes. Scene classes are represented as graph nodes while semantic classes are represented as graph edges. The center node of the graph

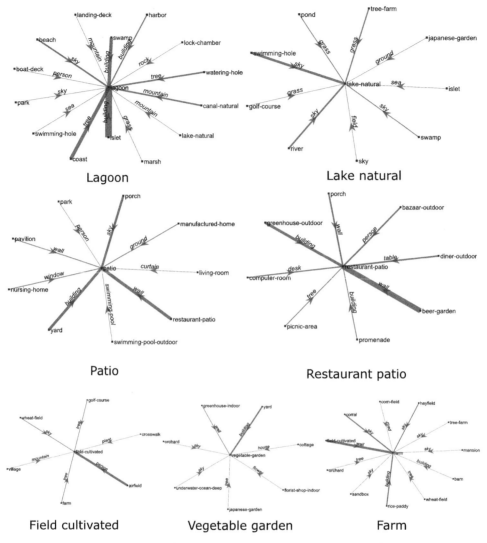

Figure 4.8 Distractor semantic classes for *lagoon, lake natural, patio, restaurant patio, field cultivated, vegetable garden,* and *farm*. Scene classes are represented as graph nodes whereas semantic classes are represented as graph edges. The center node of the graph (bold node) is the ground-truth scene class. The exterior nodes represent predictions for missclassified samples of the ground-truth class. The edge joining an exterior node with the center node represents the semantic class whose inhibition shifts the prediction to the ground-truth one. The width of the edge is proportional to the number of samples in which this change occurs. Better viewed in color.

(bold font) represents the ground-truth scene class. The exterior nodes represent the model wrong scene predictions for the considered ground-truth class. The edge joining an exterior node with the center node represents the semantic class whose inhibition shifts the prediction to the ground truth. The size of the edge is proportional to the times the shift occurs.

Usually, profiling of missclassified samples for a scene class is carried out by analyzing which is the scene that agglutinates most of the wrong predictions (analysis of nodes from Fig. 4.8). This information is useful to detect problematic sets of similar scene classes, e.g., *lagoon–islet* or *restaurant patio–beer–garden*. However, such analysis does not provide evidences on the reasons behind the confusion. The proposed visualization strategy of distracting semantic classes might aid for the identification of problematic semantic classes, which then may lead to the definition of new tailored training schemes.

Results from Fig. 4.8 suggest that, for some of the presented scene classes, building and wall are usually potentially distracting semantic classes. Building and walls may be distracting semantic classes due to their discriminative appearance. Their solely presence may move the prediction from a natural to a urban scene class, e.g., a *yard* can contain a small *vegetable garden* at the back of a building.

Note that, the presence of building pixels in *lagoon* images does not necessarily entail that *lagoon* examples contain buildings, but rather that there are image areas that resemble building structures. These areas are confusing the semantic segmentation that missclassifies them, and seem to be confusing also the scene recognition model as their inhibition corrects the prediction.

4.4. Conclusions

This chapter describes a simple, yet effective, approach for the problem of attribution in image classification tasks, i.e., the characterization of the response of the deep learned models by identifying the input features responsible for the model predictions. The proposed method perturbs color images leveraging specific areas according to semantic segmentation labels obtained using a complementary state-of-the-art semantic segmentation model. Complete attribution maps are obtained for images. The main novelty of the proposed method is that the class-semantic relation allows performing a per-scene (rather than per-image) analysis. This analysis encompasses the definition of sets of semantic classes, providing a deep interpretability of relevant, irrelevant, and distracting semantic labels for each scene category. This analysis enables researchers and developers to deeply profile the trained models and training datasets.

The presented analyses can boost research on the Scene Recognition task, and comparable recognition processes, by increasing the understanding of how the trained models are encoding the information that is driving scene recognition predictions. This may be of great interest for profiling failure cases, identifying dataset biases, and comparing the current and potential knowledge encoding capabilities of several models.

The presented results and analyses are only the tip of the iceberg of what the proposed attribution strategy might offer, and we invite other researchers to explore the website of the project that contains all the examples that did not fit into this chapter. In addition, future work will continue exploring this line of research extending the number of analyzed models, evaluating alternative perturbation strategies, and expanding the results to other computer vision tasks.

Acknowledgments

This study has been partially supported by the Spanish Government through its TEC2017-88169-R MobiNetVideo project.

References

Bengio, Yoshua, Courville, Aaron, Vincent, Pascal, 2013. Representation learning: A review and new perspectives. IEEE Transactions on Pattern Analysis and Machine Intelligence 35 (8), 1798–1828.

Deng, Jia, Dong, Wei, Socher, Richard, Li, Li-Jia, Li, Kai, Fei-Fei, Li, 2009. ImageNet: A large-scale hierarchical image database. In: Proceedings of the IEEE Conference on Computer Vision and Pattern Recognition (CVPR). IEEE, pp. 248–255.

Fong, Ruth, Patrick, Mandela, Vedaldi, Andrea, 2019. Understanding deep networks via extremal perturbations and smooth masks. In: Proceedings of the IEEE International Conference on Computer Vision (ICCV), pp. 2950–2958.

Fong, Ruth C., Vedaldi, Andrea, 2017. Interpretable explanations of black boxes by meaningful perturbation. In: Proceedings of the IEEE International Conference on Computer Vision (ICCV), pp. 3429–3437.

Geirhos, Robert, Rubisch, Patricia, Michaelis, Claudio, Bethge, Matthias, Wichmann, Felix A., Brendel, Wieland, 2019. ImageNet-trained CNNs are biased towards texture; increasing shape bias improves accuracy and robustness. In: Proceedings of the International Conference on Learning Representations (ICLR).

He, Kaiming, Zhang, Xiangyu, Ren, Shaoqing, Sun, Jian, 2016. Deep residual learning for image recognition. In: Proceedings of the IEEE Conference on Computer Vision and Pattern Recognition (CVPR), pp. 770–778.

Kapishnikov, Andrei, Bolukbasi, Tolga, Viégas, Fernanda, Terry, Michael, 2019. XRAI: Better attributions through regions. In: Proceedings of the IEEE International Conference on Computer Vision (ICCV), pp. 4948–4957.

Olah, Chris, Mordvintsev, Alexander, Schubert, Ludwig, 2017. Feature visualization. Distill 2 (11), e7.

Petsiuk, Vitali, Das, Abir, Saenko, Kate, 2018. RISE: Randomized input sampling for explanation of black-box models. In: Proceedings of the British Machine Vision Conference (BMVC).

Ribeiro, Marco Tulio, Singh, Sameer, Guestrin, Carlos, 2016. "Why should I trust you?" Explaining the predictions of any classifier. In: Proceedings of the International Conference on Knowledge Discovery and Data Mining (SIGKDD), pp. 1135–1144.

Selvaraju, R.R., Cogswell, M., Das, A., Vedantam, R., Parikh, D., Batra, D., et al., 2019. Visual explanations from deep networks via gradient-based localization. In: Proceedings of the IEEE Conference on Computer Vision and Pattern Recognition (CVPR), pp. 618–626.

Simonyan, Karen, Vedaldi, Andrea, Zisserman, Andrew, 2014. Deep inside convolutional networks: Visualising image classification models and saliency maps. In: Proceedings of the Workshop at International Conference on Learning Representations (ICLR).

Ulyanov, Dmitry, Vedaldi, Andrea, Lempitsky, Victor, 2018. Deep image prior. In: Proceedings of the IEEE Conference on Computer Vision and Pattern Recognition (CVPR), pp. 9446–9454.

Van der Maaten, Laurens, Hinton, Geoffrey, 2008. Visualizing data using t-SNE. Journal of Machine Learning Research 9 (11).

Xiao, Tete, Liu, Yingcheng, Zhou, Bolei, Jiang, Yuning, Sun, Jian, 2018. Unified perceptual parsing for scene understanding. In: Proceedings of the European Conference on Computer Vision (ECCV), pp. 418–434.

Yu, Jiahui, Lin, Zhe, Yang, Jimei, Shen, Xiaohui, Lu, Xin, Huang, Thomas S., 2018. Generative image inpainting with contextual attention. In: Proceedings of the IEEE Conference on Computer Vision and Pattern Recognition (CVPR).

Zeiler, Matthew D., Fergus, Rob, 2014. Visualizing and understanding convolutional networks. In: Proceedings of the European Conference on Computer Vision (ECCV). Springer, pp. 818–833.

Zhou, Bolei, Lapedriza, Agata, Khosla, Aditya, Oliva, Aude, Torralba, Antonio, 2017a. Places: A 10 million image database for scene recognition. IEEE Transactions on Pattern Analysis and Machine Intelligence 40 (6), 1452–1464.

Zhou, Bolei, Zhao, Hang, Puig, Xavier, Fidler, Sanja, Barriuso, Adela, Torralba, Antonio, 2017b. Scene parsing through ADE20K dataset. In: Proceedings of the IEEE Conference on Computer Vision and Pattern Recognition (CVPR), pp. 633–641.

CHAPTER 5

A feature understanding method for explanation of image classification by convolutional neural networks

Meghna P. Ayyar, Jenny Benois-Pineau, and Akka Zemmari
Univ. Bordeaux, CNRS, Bordeaux INP, LaBRI, UMR 5800, Talence, France

5.1. Introduction

The objective of eXplainable AI (XAI)/Deep learning is to design and develop methods that can be used to understand how these systems produce their decisions. Explanation methods aid in the unmasking of such spurious correlations and biases in the model or data and also help in explaining the failures of the system. Inspecting the recent trends, the major methods that exist for the explanation of a CNN can be classified into two major categories of (i) black-box methods and (ii) white-box methods. Black-box methods are typically those that inspect the output of the network by changing the input to draw conclusions and insights. They do not require any knowledge about the model like the different layers, parameters or different connections amongst the layers. In contrast, the methods of XAI which access internal model parameters and structure are called **white–box** approaches. These methods have been designed to study the network architecture and the parameters that have been learnt during training to perform attribution of the results of the network. Such methods have been intensively developed during recent years, but universal solutions have not been found, yet.

5.2. Principles of white-box explanation methods

An explanation method can be categorized as a white-box method based on the following salient features:

- **Accessing the parameters of the network.** Unlike black-box methods, white-box methods utilize the parameters of the networks, e.g., weights and activations of the intermediate layers of a CNN.
- **Being Model Specific.** Based on the type of the network and its architecture, the calculations of the explanation methods would vary. In addition, as it accesses the parameters of the network, the architecture of the network affects the type of explanations that are produced by the method. The explanations given by a method for a network are directly influenced by how well the network has been trained.

Explainable Deep Learning AI
https://doi.org/10.1016/B978-0-32-396098-4.00011-9

79

- **Post-hoc explanations.** Generally, these methods provide explanations for a pre-built model, i.e., the models for which the training has been completed. As the methods use the internal parameters of the model like the weights and activations of the layers, they typically are employed when these parameters have already been learnt after training has been completed.

Furthermore, white-box methods can be differentiated based on the type of explanations they produce. Based on recent trends, the methods make two major types of explanations:

- **Local Explanations** that explain an individual prediction. These methods explain the output of the network given a particular input. This provides insights about the reasons for the decision of the network, i.e., if the decision has been made in accordance to the right features (similar to human perception).
- **Global Explanations** that attempt to explain the behavior of the complete model. It is a high-level analysis to understand if the model has learnt relevant features for a class, e.g., gradient backpropagation (Simonyan et al., 2014) – class saliency maps.

Our focus for this chapter will be on the methods designed to explain Convolutional Neural Networks (CNNs) that have been trained on the classification task. We term the output of these methods as an Explanation map, that is, a map to be superimposed on the original image to highlight pixels in it which have contributed the most to the decision of the classifier. Further we also use the term *importance map* – a binary map containing 1 if the feature in this spatial position (x, y) is selected as a **strong** feature, i.e., it is important for decision making. These maps are useful visualizations that aid the users in gleaning insights from the results of the explanation methods.

5.3. Explanation methods

Ayyar et al. (2021) proposed a detailed review of some of the existing white-box methods and presented a taxonomy for the methods to be able to understand them better. The following section contains a short overview of some of the most interesting explanation methods for CNNs.

5.3.1 Gradient backpropagation

One of the first methods proposed to explain the decision of a CNN is gradient back-propagation (Simonyan et al., 2014). It is a local explanation based method that explains the prediction of a network on the basis of the *locally evaluated gradient*. The *gradient* is calculated similar to the backpropagation of the loss gradient during the training of the network. The term *local* signifies that the gradient is calculated for the particular image whose prediction by the network is to be explained.

To elaborate, consider an image x_0 whose output classification score S_c for the class c is to be explained for the trained CNN. Any CNN can be described by a nonlinear classifier function $f(x)$ that maps the images from the data set in the space X to the output score space S_x. Here S is the prediction given by the CNN. Then, this nonlinear $f(x)$ can be approximated by a linear mapping as

$$S_c(x) \approx w^T \cdot x + b, \tag{5.1}$$

where S_c denotes the score for a particular class c, x the input image, w are the weights, and b the bias in the network. Gradient Backpropagation proposes that the *weights* that are assigned to the input pixels of x are representative of their contribution to the final score S_c. Thus the weights are approximated as shown in Eq. (5.2). The magnitude of the derivatives that have been calculated could be interpreted to indicate the input pixels to which the output classification is the most sensitive. The gradient value would correspond to the pixels that need to be changed the least to affect the final class score the most:

$$w = \left. \frac{\partial S_c}{\partial x} \right|_{x_0}. \tag{5.2}$$

The partial derivative of the output classification score with respect to the input corresponds to the gradient calculation for a single backpropagation pass for a particular input image x. The final heat map relevance scores R_{ij}^c for a particular pixel i, j and class c, in the input 2D image are calculated as

$$R_{ij}^c = \left\| \frac{\partial}{\partial x_{ij}} S_c \right\|. \tag{5.3}$$

5.3.2 SmoothGrad

The gradient backpropagation method suffers from an instability for the explanations as slight changes in the input can cause large changes in the gradient that is calculated. This changes the explanation maps drastically. For example, a small perturbation to the input pixel values does not change it visually for humans. However, the gradients of this image would be different and lead to a different saliency map.

SmoothGrad method (Smilkov et al., 2017) is based on the idea of reducing the issue of noisy maps by averaging multiple maps to get sharper visualizations. This is done by adding small noise vectors sampled from a Gaussian distribution $\mathcal{N}(0, \sigma^2)$ to each pixel of the image x_0; n such samples of the image x_0 are created and an explanation method like the gradient backpropagation is applied to each of these samples. The average of the maps of all these n samples forms the final explanation map for the image x_0 as shown in Eq. (5.4) where R_x^c is the relevance score for the image x for the prediction of class c

by the network:

$$x_i = x + \mathcal{N}(0, \sigma^2),$$

$$\hat{R}^c(x) = \frac{1}{n} \sum_{i=1}^{n} R^c(x_i). \tag{5.4}$$

5.3.3 Grad-CAM

Gradient Class Activation Mapping (Grad-CAM) (Selvaraju et al., 2017) is a class-discriminative visualization method for a network, i.e., the explanations map highlights the pixels of the images that contributed to the prediction of a particular class. It has been designed on the observation that the deeper layers of a CNN act as a high-level feature extractors (Bengio et al., 2013). This means that the feature maps of the last convolutional layer of the network contain structural information of the objects in the image. Unlike gradient backpropagation, Grad-CAM propagates the gradient only till the last convolution (conv) layer of the network.

The feature maps of the last conv layer contain information regarding all the classes present in the data set. Hence, the method calculates the importance of each feature map with respect to the prediction. Assuming that $A^1, A^2, \ldots, A^k$ are the k activation maps of the last conv layer for an image x_0, the importance of each map is calculated as the global average pooling of the gradient of the classification score $S_c(x)$ with respect to the activation values A^k. This assigns a single weight value α_k^c with respect to the class c to each of k maps, namely

$$\alpha_k^c = \frac{1}{Z} \sum_i \sum_j \frac{\partial S_c(x)}{\partial A_{ij}^k}. \tag{5.5}$$

Here $Z = h \times w$, where h and w are the height and width of each feature map, respectively.

Every feature in the k feature maps is weighted with the corresponding α_k^c and averaged to get the relevance score map R^c. To retain only the positive features (≥ 0), an ReLU (rectification) function is applied over this map, see Eq. (5.6). The map R_c has the same spatial dimension as the last conv layer feature maps and is upsampled by an interpolation method to have a correspondence with the input image x,

$$R^c = ReLU\left(\sum_k \alpha_k^c A^k\right). \tag{5.6}$$

5.3.4 Layer-wise Relevance Propagation (LRP)

The authors introduce the method of Layer-wise Relevance Propagation (LRP) (Bach et al., 2015) for the purpose of assigning an importance score to each pixel in the image x_0. They formulate LRP as a method defined by a set of constraints. LRP in general assumes that the network can be decomposed as a composition of several layers. The first constraint, namely Relevance (R) conservation law between each layer in the network, is given by

$$f(x) = \cdots = \sum_{d \in l+1} R_d^{(l+1)} = \sum_{d \in l} R_d^{(l)} = \cdots = \sum_d R_d^{(1)}. \tag{5.7}$$

The relevance is the local contribution of the neuron to the prediction function $f(x)$ and the relevance of the output layer is the prediction itself.

Let two consecutive layers in the network be l and $l+1$ and let i, j neurons belong to these layers, respectively. The relevance of neuron j based on $S_c(x)$ can be written as R_j^c. If neurons i and j are connected then neuron i receives a relevance value of R_j^c, weighted by the activation a_i and the weight of the connection between the two neurons w_{ij}. Similarly, i is assigned relevance from all the neurons it is connected to in layer $l+1$. The relevance of neuron i, R_i^c, is calculated as the sum of all the relevance it receives from the neurons it is connected to as shown in Eq. (5.8). The denominator term in Eq. (5.8) is the normalization that is used to ensure the relevance conservation rule in Eq. (5.7). This rule is termed as the LRP-0 rule (Montavon et al., 2019):

$$R_i^c = \sum_j \frac{a_i w_{ij}}{\sum_{0,q} a_q w_{qj}} R_j^c. \tag{5.8}$$

These rules and the method have been proposed only for rectifier networks, i.e., networks that use only ReLU nonlinearity.

5.3.5 Feature-based Explanation Method (FEM)

Feature-based Explanation Method (FEM), first proposed by Fuad et al. (2020), employs the observation that deeper convolutional layers of the network act as high-level feature extractors. The learned filters of a deeper convolution layers of a CNN behave similarly to a high-pass filter on the top of the Gaussian pyramid (some examples are given in Zemmari and Benois-Pineau (2020)). The implication is that the information in the feature maps of the last convolution layer corresponds to the main object that has been detected by the network for the image x.

Therefore, the proposal by FEM is that the contribution of the input pixels for the network decision can be inferred from the *strong* features of x detected by the last convolution layer. FEM supposes that the k feature maps of the last convolutional layer have a Gaussian distribution. Hence, the *strong* features of the maps correspond to the *rare* features. A K-sigma filtering rule is used to identify these *rare* and *strong* features. The kth feature map in the layer is thresholded based on this rule to get binary maps $B_k(a_{i,j,k})$, where i, j denote the spatial dimension of the kth feature maps as shown in

Eq. (5.9). The mean μ_k and standard deviation σ_k are calculated for each feature map and thresholded to get binary maps (B_k); K is the parameter that controls the threshold value and is set to 1 by the authors in their work:

$$B_k(a_{i,j,k}) = \begin{cases} 1 & \text{if } a_{i,j,k} \geq \mu_k + K * \sigma_k, \\ 0 & \text{otherwise.} \end{cases} \qquad (5.9)$$

In addition, the authors propose to weigh each feature map based on contribution of the positive features in the channels. The weight term is calculated as the mean of the initial feature maps $w_k = \mu_k$ for each binary map B_k. The final importance map R is computed as the linear combination of all the weighted binary maps B_k and normalized to [0, 1]. The importance map R is then upsampled by interpolation to have the same spatial resolution as the input image x.

FEM eliminates the calculation of gradients and is faster and simpler method to get importance scores for input pixels only from the features extracted by the network.

5.4. The proposed improvement – modified FEM

In the original implementation of FEM, the mean of the activations of each of the feature maps from the last convolution layer is considered as its weighting term. This makes the assumption that the importance is related to the sample image feature itself and its contribution is indicated by its value. Our proposal is to improve this method by using a Multi-Layer Perceptron (MLP) based approach to learn the weights of the features of the last convolution layer of network rather than using a mean weighting approach.

The following section presents a well-known method called the Squeeze–Excitation Block (Hu et al., 2018), which has been used in the design for Modified FEM.

5.4.1 Squeeze-Excitation (SE) block

The Squeeze-Excitation block is a method to apply "global attention," by learning the importance to be assigned to the filters learnt by each convolutional layer. The number of filters in a convolution layer is a hyperparameter often decided by performing multiple experiments but by using a weighting mechanism to select the optimal filters helps with network optimization.

In a CNN, the tensor that is computed at a 2D-convolutional layer has dimension of ($B \times H \times W \times C$) where B denotes the batch size, $H \times W$ is the product of spatial dimension of the feature map at the layer, and C is the channels that are derived from the convolutional filters of the layer. Hu et al. (2018) propose that not every channel C has the same importance in terms of the features that it learns. They propose a form of attention module, called the *Squeeze-Excitation (SE) Block,* that can be used in tandem

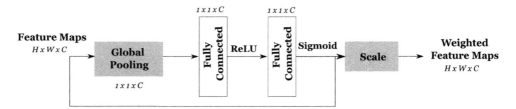

Figure 5.1 Squeeze-Excitation (SE) Block, $H \times W$ – the height times width of the feature map; C – channels at the layer.

with any convolutional layer to apply weights to the channels based on their importance before propagation to the next layer. This form of weighting provides extra information of higher importance to those maps that have more relevant features when compared to the other maps. The overall framework for the SE block is summarized by Fig. 5.1.

The squeeze module is used to decompose the information of each feature map from the previous convolution layer to a singular value per channel using Global Average Pooling (GAP). Thus, the dimensions of the input feature maps ($H \times W \times C$) after the GAP operation reduce to a tensor of ($1 \times 1 \times C$).

The next part of the block is the excitation module that learns the adaptive scaling weights for each of these channels during the training of the network. It is a fully connected (FC) Multi–Layer Perceptron (MLP) that could map the channel information from the Squeeze module to the scaling weights. The MLP has an input layer, a single hidden layer, and an output layer. The hidden layer has a reduction block where the input is reduced by a factor r, empirically chosen as 16, to get better results. The output layer has a sigmoid (Eq. (5.10)) activation in order to scale the weights between 0 to 1 to get a tensor of size ($1 \times 1 \times C$):

$$sig(x) = \frac{1}{1 + e^{-x}}. \qquad (5.10)$$

These scaling weights are then applied to the feature maps obtained from the convolutional layer by an element-wise multiplication such that it scales each ($H \times W$) feature map in the input with the corresponding weight that has been learned by the MLP. This forms the Scale module of the SE block shown in Fig. 5.1.

5.4.2 Modified FEM

A single SE-Block from Section 5.4.1 is attached to the last convolution layer of a CNN. Once the training is completed, the network has learnt the attention weights for each channel of the last conv layer with the use of the SE block. In CNNs it is supposed that the training data set has a distribution similar to the images that are to be tested on. This forms the basis for the training of any network. Subsequently, the

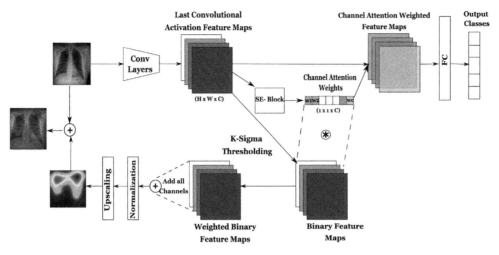

Figure 5.2 Framework of the modified FEM method with the addition of the Squeeze-Excitation (SE) Block. The binary feature maps are multiplied with the channel attention weights. FC – Fully Connected Layers. ($H \times W \times C$) – product of Height, Width, number of Channels of the last convolutional layer.

importance of the features from each image should be based on the feature attention learnt from the whole data set, i.e., the channel attention weights from the SE Block. Hence, modified FEM has been designed for the networks with SE–Blocks to use the channel weights learnt during training to weight each binary feature map calculated by the K-sigma thresholding. Fig. 5.2 shows an overview of the modified FEM using the channel weights learnt from the SE-Block.

The major change is that, by using a low computation, simple global attention weight would help the method weigh the important features in a better way. This is essential to ensure that the explanation maps that are produced by the methods have better resolution and highlight the exact image features that contributed to a decision of the network.

5.4.3 Application of FEM and modified FEM for COVID-19 classification

The novel coronavirus disease (COVID-19) causes severe respiratory infections and has been declared as a pandemic by the World Health Organization (WHO). It has had devastating effects on the human life, economy, and functioning of many countries in the world. Chest X-Ray (CXR) images have been shown to be effective to be used alongside the RT-PCR test to triage patients with suspected cases of COVID-19 (Schiaffino et al., 2020).

Fig. 5.3 shows a sample CXR image that has been annotated by an expert radiologist to show the primary areas that are observed by the medical doctors to make a diagnosis.

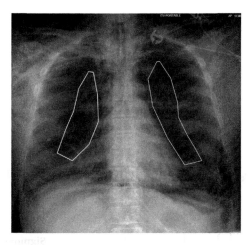

Figure 5.3 Sample annotation of Chest X-Ray (CXR) image that has been affected with the regions showing the presence of pneumonia that could be COVID-19 as annotated by a radiologist.

In this chapter we present an application of the FEM and Modified FEM for the explanation of well-known networks, like ResNet and Inception, that have been trained for the classification of COVID-19 images from Chest X-Ray (CXR) images.

5.4.4 Evaluation metrics for the evaluation of explanation maps

The two common benchmarking metrics for the prediction and comparison of different visual attention maps are (1) similarity, (2) Pearson correlation coefficient (PCC) metrics (Bylinskii et al., 2018). These metrics can be used to directly compare the importance maps P_1 and P_2 given by two explanation methods.

The *similarity (SIM)* is given by Eq. (5.11), where iteration is over the discrete pixel i, and $\sum_i P_{1i} = \sum_i P_{2i} = 1$. A maximum similarity of 1 is achieved when the two maps completely overlap and 0 when they do not overlap:

$$\mathbf{SIM}(P_1, P_2) = \sum_i \min(P_{1i}, P_{2i}). \tag{5.11}$$

The *Pearson correlation coefficient (PCC)* is a measure of the correlation or dependence between the two maps. It is 1 for perfectly correlated and 0 when they are not correlated at all. It is given by Eq. (5.12), where $\sigma(P_1, P_2)$ is the covariance between the maps:

$$\mathbf{PCC}(P_1, P_2) = \frac{\sigma(P_1, P_2)}{\sigma(P_1) \times \sigma(P_2)}. \tag{5.12}$$

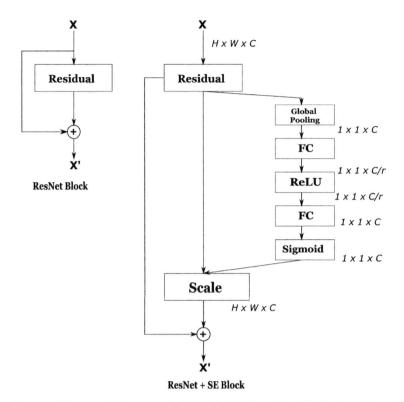

Figure 5.4 Schema of the original ResNet residual block (right), the residual block after adding the SE Block (left).

5.5. Experimental results

A transfer learning approach has been adopted to train two popular pretrained models ResNet50 (He et al., 2016) and InceptionV3 (Szegedy et al., 2014). The networks have been retrained to perform the classification of COVID-19 vs. Normal images. No changes to the basic architecture were made, except for changing the last layer of the network to match the classes in the data set. The pretrained ImageNet (Deng et al., 2009) weights were used for initialization of both networks and all the layers were retrained for the classification.

To test the modified FEM method both these networks have been updated by adding the SE-Block to the last convolution layer as shown in Figs. 5.4 and 5.5. The SE-Block is added only with the last residual block and the last convolution layer, respectively.

In addition, the performance of these retrained networks is compared to the COVID-Net, a network that has been proposed to work on the COVIDx dataset. It has been tailor-made for the dataset. The goal is to compare the performance of a rel-

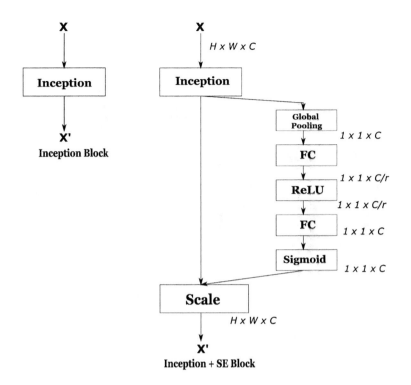

Figure 5.5 Schema of the original Inception block (right), the inception block after adding the SE Block (left).

atively new network created specially to work on a dataset and that of the well-known and well-tested network architectures to see how comparable they are.

The following section presents in detail the dataset used for the training of the networks (CNNs) for COVID-19 classification from CXR images. It also discusses the explanation maps that are obtained by applying different explanation methods to these trained networks. Two types of comparisons of the maps are done:

- FEM vs. Grad-CAM to check the performance of the trained network as these two methods have similar explanation results (Fuad et al., 2020).
- FEM vs. Modified FEM to compare how the modification helps in improving the resolution of the final explanation map.

5.5.1 Dataset details

The open-access COVIDx dataset (Wang et al., 2020a) has been used for the study. It consists of 13,975 images across 13,870 patient cases and has been created by combining five other publicly available data repositories, namely (a) COVID-19 Image Data

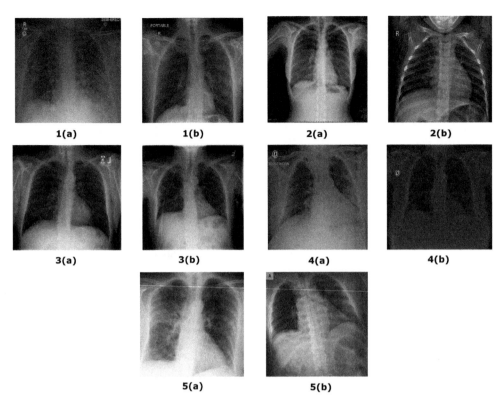

Figure 5.6 Sample images from COVIDx dataset comprising of images from multiple repositories: (1) COVID-19 Image Data Collection (Cohen et al., 2020), (2) COVID-19 Chest X-Ray Dataset Initiative [1], (3) RSNA Pneumonia Detection challenge dataset [3], (4) ActualMed COVID-19 Chest X-Ray Dataset Initiative [2], and (5) COVID-19 radiography database [4].

Collection (Cohen et al., 2020), (b) COVID-19 Chest X-ray Dataset Initiative,[1] (c) ActualMed COVID-19 Chest X-ray Data set Initiative,[2] established in collaboration with ActualMed (Wang et al., 2020b), (d) RSNA Pneumonia Detection Challenge data set,[3] which used publicly available CXR data, and (e) COVID-19 radiography database.[4] Fig. 5.6 shows the different images taken from each of these datasets to create the final COVIDx dataset.

The COVIDx dataset contains three classes: Normal (X-Rays that do not contain Pneumonia or COVID-19), Pneumonia (X-Rays that have some form of bacterial or viral

---

[1] https://github.com/agchung/Figure1-COVID-chestxray-dataset.
[2] https://github.com/agchung/Actualmed-COVID-chestxray-dataset.
[3] https://www.kaggle.com/c/rsna-pneumonia-detection-challenge/data.
[4] https://www.kaggle.com/tawsifurrahman/covid19-radiography-database.

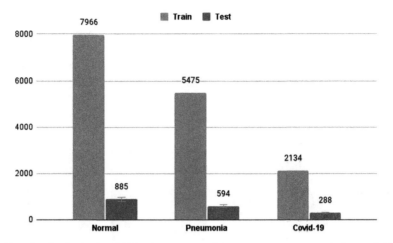

Figure 5.7 Class distribution in the COVIDx dataset created. Due to some images not being available, the class counts for COVID-19 vary from the official data set.

pneumonia, but no COVID-19), and COVID-19 (X-Rays that are COVID-19 positive). Fig. 5.7 shows the distribution of the images.

5.5.2 Binary classifier explanation maps

FEM and Grad-CAM methods have been chosen to visualize the relevance maps for the binary classifier networks. It has been observed by the authors of FEM that the heat maps visualized by FEM are the most similar to Grad-CAM (Fuad et al., 2020). The heat maps for the FEM and Grad-CAM methods for the three networks (trained on normal vs. COVID-19) – ResNet50, InceptionV3, and COVID-Net – are shown in Fig. 5.8. In the case of ResNet50, the FEM map essentially highlights the regions belonging to the lungs but has a low resolution on the exact features. Grad-CAM for ResNet50 has a slightly better visualization as the important regions are better localized and not spread out, though it still highlights some regions outside the lungs. This kind of inspection is useful to understand that the network somehow still focuses on these features which indicates to it having a low performance.

For InceptionV3, both methods highlight similar regions on the image. Grad-CAM has better importance assigned to regions within the lungs when compared to FEM. The heat maps for COVID-Net with FEM and Grad-CAM look visually the most similar. In both these images, similar areas of the lungs have been highlighted, though with FEM the important areas have higher relevance scores and are highlighted better. Table 5.1 gives the similarity and PCC metrics for the heat maps of FEM vs. Grad-CAM on the complete test set. Similar to Fig. 5.8, it can be seen that COVID-Net has the highest similarity and correlation between FEM and Grad-CAM.

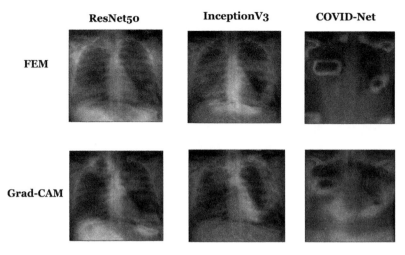

Figure 5.8 Visualization of heat maps for the FEM and Grad-CAM methods for the trained networks – ResNet50, InceptionV3, and COVID-Net – for the binary classification of COVID-19 vs. Normal classes.

Table 5.1 Metric analysis for the FEM vs. Grad-CAM explanation maps on the test set for the networks for COVID-19 vs. Normal classification.

	SIM	PCC
ResNet50	$0.5599 \pm 0.0.86$	0.3791 ± 0.230
InceptionV3	0.5158 ± 0.137	-0.1050 ± 0.415
COVID-Net	**0.7525 ±0.139**	**0.6520 ±0.286**

Thus it can be seen that explanation methods and their results are dependent on how well the network performs and the kind of features it has learnt from the dataset. Hence, a network that has better performance metric scores would have explanation maps where the important regions that have been highlighted correspond to the features that are relevant for the identification of the disease. It can be concluded that amongst the three networks COVID-Net indeed is better trained to focus on relevant features and shows better performance.

5.5.3 FEM vs. modified FEM

The networks ResNet50 and InceptionV3 that have been trained using the addition of the SE-Block are used to compare the maps produced by FEM and Modified FEM for the same networks.

Visualizations of explanation maps from FEM and modified FEM for two images from the data set for the ResNet50 + SE and InceptionV3 + SE networks are shown in Figs. 5.9 and 5.10, respectively. From the comparison of the maps of FEM denoted by (1) and the maps of modified FEM denoted by (2), it can be seen that using channel

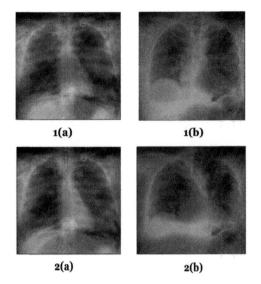

Figure 5.9 Visualization of heat maps for two corresponding images for the ResNet50 + SE network where 1(a) and 1(b) are original FEM, while 2(a) and 2(b) are modified FEM.

attention based weighting improves the visualizations significantly. In the case of the ResNet50 + SE explanation maps, using the modified FEM reduces the importance that is assigned to the regions that do not belong to the lung areas. They are visually similar to the results of FEM in terms of the regions of the image that is highlighted but with modified FEM the non-lung areas are assigned much lower importance.

For the heat maps of InceptionV3 + SE, it is evident that the modified FEM is visually more holistic. For the first image labeled 2(a), the modified FEM has high relevance scores only over the lung areas where the lung tissue is present. This is unlike the case of 1(a) where with FEM some portion of the region right below the rib cage gets assigned a high relevance value. With the image in Fig. 5.10 labeled 2(b), the region that is highlighted is over both lungs and it can be seen that the middle portion between the two lungs gets assigned a lower score. The heat maps of modified FEM have a better overlap between the relevant lung areas in the image and the regions assigned higher relevance scores.

The results for the similarity and PCC scores between the FEM and modified FEM for the two networks are given in Table 5.2. For both networks the heat maps of FEM and modified FEM have high similarity and correlation with a small error margin. Observing the metrics and the visual results, it can be said that modified FEM indeed produces better results while not drastically changing the explanations produced with FEM.

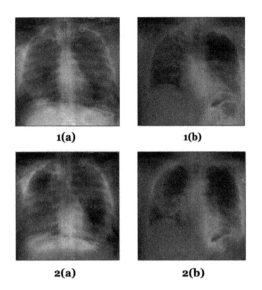

Figure 5.10 Visualization of heat maps for two corresponding images for the InceptionV3 + SE network where 1(a) and 1(b) are original FEM, while 2(a) and 2(b) are modified FEM.

Table 5.2 Metrics for the comparison of the explanation maps for the FEM and Modified FEM for the ResNet50 + SE and InceptionV3 + SE networks.

	ResNet50 + SE		InceptionV3 + SE	
	SIM	PCC	SIM	PCC
FEM vs Modified FEM	0.7072 ± 0.058	0.7374 ± 0.099	0.7917 ± 0.044	0.8370 ± 0.071

It can be concluded that FEM uses channel weighting with the mean of the features themselves, i.e., it assigns importance to the channels based on the properties of the sample image. Channel attention weights from the SE-Block have learnt the importance of features based on the whole data set. Hence, when using a sample-based explanation method like FEM for an image belonging to the same distribution as the data set, using the trained attention weights along with FEM (Modified FEM) describes the results better.

5.6. Conclusion

This chapter presents an explanation method based on the understanding the features that have been learnt by a CNN for the purpose of image classification. The explanation is performed by identifying the pixels in the input images that contributed to the model prediction. The FEM method that has been described in this chapter does this by using the idea that the last convolution layer of the network contains the high level information about the objects in the image.

FEM is then applied to the problem of the classification and explanation of the results on Chest X-Ray images, for a problem with high societal impact – detection of COVID-19 disease. Medical image explanations require explanation maps with finer resolution for the pixels of high importance. Our contribution is the proposal of the modified FEM method wherein we use a weighting learnt from a Multi-Layer Perceptron (MLP) instead of mean weighting for the features from the last convolutional layer. The further weighting of the feature maps with these learnt weights is shown to yield better explanations that are more focused on the regions of relevance in the X-ray images.

The presented results show promise in being useful for medical experts to gain more trust in the results of CNN-based solutions. It would also be useful in determining the reliability of such networks and help in making these solutions robust for the use in the real world applications. Further work in improving the method could propel the adoption of deep learning and CNN-based solutions in a highly sensitive domain of medical image analysis. Future work will focus on creating ground-truth explanation maps with the help of experts and fine tuning the method to obtain results with better resolution.

Acknowledgments

We would like to thank Dr. I. Saurin from Institute Bergonié, Bordeaux for her kind advice on the visual analysis of SARS-CoV2 and pneumonia affected Chest X-ray images.

References

Ayyar, Meghna P., Benois-Pineau, Jenny, Zemmari, Akka, 2021. Review of white box methods for explanations of convolutional neural networks in image classification tasks. Journal of Electronic Imaging 30 (5), 050901.

Bach, Sebastian, Binder, Alexander, Montavon, Grégoire, Klauschen, Frederick, Müller, Klaus-Robert, Samek, Wojciech, 2015. On pixel-wise explanations for non-linear classifier decisions by layer-wise relevance propagation. PLoS ONE 10 (7), 1–46.

Bengio, Yoshua, Courville, Aaron, Vincent, Pascal, 2013. Representation learning: A review and new perspectives. IEEE Transactions on Pattern Analysis and Machine Intelligence 35 (8), 1798–1828.

Bylinskii, Zoya, Judd, Tilke, Oliva, Aude, Torralba, Antonio, Durand, Frédo, 2018. What do different evaluation metrics tell us about saliency models? In: Proceedings of the IEEE Trans on Pattern Analysis and Machine Intelligence, pp. 740–757.

Cohen, Joseph Paul, Morrison, Paul, Dao, Lan, Roth, Karsten, Duong, Tim Q., Ghassemi, Marzyeh, 2020. COVID-19 image data collection: Prospective predictions are the future. arXiv preprint. arXiv: 2006.11988.

Deng, Jia, Dong, Wei, Socher, Richard, Li, Li-Jia, Li, Kai, Fei-Fei, Li, 2009. ImageNet: A large-scale hierarchical image database. In: Proceedings of IEEE Conference on Computer Vision and Pattern Recognition. IEEE, pp. 248–255.

Fuad, Kazi Ahmed Asif, Martin, Pierre-Etienne, Giot, Romain, Bourqui, Romain, Benois-Pineau, Jenny, Zemmari, Akka, 2020. Features understanding in 3D CNNs for actions recognition in video. In: Proceedings of the Tenth International Conference on Image Processing Theory, Tools and Applications (IPTA). IEEE, pp. 1–6.

He, Kaiming, Zhang, Xiangyu, Ren, Shaoqing, Sun, Jian, 2016. Deep residual learning for image recognition. In: Proceedings of the IEEE Conference on Computer Vision and Pattern Recognition, pp. 770–778.

Hu, Jie, Shen, Li, Sun, Gang, 2018. Squeeze-and-excitation networks. In: Proceedings of the IEEE Conference on Computer Vision and Pattern Recognition, pp. 7132–7141.

Montavon, Grégoire, Binder, Alexander, Lapuschkin, Sebastian, Samek, Wojciech, Müller, Klaus-Robert, 2019. Layer-wise relevance propagation: An overview. In: Samek, Wojciech, Montavon, Grégoire, Vedaldi, Andrea, Hansen, Lars Kai, Müller, Klaus-Robert (Eds.), Explainable AI: Interpreting, Explaining and Visualizing Deep Learning. In: Lecture Notes in Computer Science, vol. 11700. Springer, pp. 193–209.

Schiaffino, Simone, Tritella, Stefania, Cozzi, Andrea, Carriero, Serena, Blandi, Lorenzo, Ferraris, Laurenzia, Sardanelli, Francesco, 2020. Diagnostic performance of Chest X-ray for COVID-19 pneumonia during the SARS-CoV-2 pandemic in Lombardy, Italy. Journal of Thoracic Imaging 35 (4), W105–W106.

Selvaraju, Ramprasaath R., Cogswell, Michael, Das, Abhishek, Vedantam, Ramakrishna, Parikh, Devi, Batra, Dhruv, 2017. Grad-CAM: Visual explanations from deep networks via gradient-based localization. In: Proceedings of the IEEE International Conference on Computer Vision, pp. 618–626.

Simonyan, Karen, Vedaldi, Andrea, Zisserman, Andrew, 2014. Deep inside convolutional networks: Visualising image classification models and saliency maps. In: Proceedings of 2nd International Conference on Learning Representations, ICLR 2014, Workshop Track Proceedings.

Smilkov, Daniel, Thorat, Nikhil, Kim, Been, Viégas, Fernanda B., Wattenberg , Martin, 2017. SmoothGrad: Removing noise by adding noise. CoRR. arXiv:1706.03825 [abs], pp. 1–10.

Szegedy, Christian, Wojciech, Zaremba, Ilya, Sutskever, Joan, Bruna, Dumitru, Erhan, Goodfellow, Ian J., Fergus, Rob, 2014. Intriguing properties of neural networks. In: ICLR (Poster), pp. 1–10.

Wang, Linda, Lin, Zhong Qiu, Wong, Alexander, 2020a. COVID-Net: A tailored deep convolutional neural network design for detection of COVID-19 cases from chest X-ray images. Scientific Reports 10 (1), 19549.

Wang, Linda, Wong, Alexander, Qiu, Z.L., McInnis, Paul, Chung, Audrey, Gunraj, Hayden, 2020b. Actualmed COVID-19 Chest X-ray Dataset Initiative. https://github.com/agchung/Actualmed-COVID-chestxray-dataset.

Zemmari, Akka, Benois-Pineau, Jenny, 2020. Deep Learning in Mining of Visual Content. Springer. ISBN 9783030343750.

CHAPTER 6

Explainable deep learning for decrypting disease signatures in multiple sclerosis

Federica Cruciani[a]**, Lorenza Brusini**[a]**, Mauro Zucchelli**[b]**,
Gustavo Retuci Pinheiro**[c]**, Francesco Setti**[a]**, Rachid Deriche**[b]**, Leticia Rittner**[c]**,
Massimiliano Calabrese**[d]**, Ilaria Boscolo Galazzo**[a]**, and Gloria Menegaz**[a]

[a]University of Verona, Department of Computer Science, Verona, Italy
[b]Inria Sophia Antipolis-Méditerranée, Côte d'Azur University, Athena Project-Team, Sophia Antipolis, France
[c]UNICAMP, MICLab, School of Electrical and Computer Engineering (FEEC), Campinas, Brazil
[d]University of Verona, Department of Neurosciences, Biomedicine and Movement, Verona, Italy

6.1. Introduction

Convolutional Neural Networks (CNNs) recently gained popularity thanks to their ability in solving complex classification tasks. Especially in the last few years, CNNs are starting to be employed to address clinical questions such as patient stratification, that is, classifying patients based on the disease stage, or disease detection. Besides the lack of big data for training, one of the main bottlenecks for the use of these techniques for medical purposes is that they are notoriously hard to interpret in retrospect. This is a bottleneck that cannot be overlooked in diagnostics and treatment monitoring. In this respect, Deep Learning (DL) methods, including CNNs, are often criticized for being nontransparent and are still considered as black boxes. Therefore, the availability of a means for interpreting the network decisions becomes the key element for their exploitability in the clinical context.

EXplainable Artificial Intelligence (XAI) recently emerged as one of the hottest topics aimed at overcoming this limitation by proposing strategies for understanding the *why* and the *how* of the outcomes of Machine (ML) and Deep Learning (DL), allowing to disentangle the contributions of the different features of the input shaping the CNN final output.

In this context, the stratification of patients with Multiple Sclerosis (MS) would highly benefit from the use of such techniques since the mechanisms driving this pathology are still mostly unknown. MS affects the brain and the spinal cord, potentially leading to physical and cognitive disability (Compston and Coles, 2008; Popescu et al., 2013). Among the identified MS phenotypes, Relapsing–Remitting and Primary Progressive MS (RRMS and PPMS, respectively) are the most known forms (Hurwitz,

Explainable Deep Learning AI
https://doi.org/10.1016/B978-0-32-396098-4.00012-0

2009; Lublin et al., 2014). The sooner the clinician can distinguish between them, the sooner personalized treatments can be devised for each patient (Lublin et al., 2014; Manca et al., 2018). Though demyelination and atrophy could be found in both PPMS and RRMS, the relative structure and patterns vary quantitatively and qualitatively (Huang et al., 2017) across the two forms of disease. This suggests that the differentiation could be driven by different mechanisms in the two phenotypes (Lucchinetti et al., 2000; Popescu et al., 2013). Different studies aimed at MS stage stratification, grounding on classical statistics and white matter derived features (Miller et al., 2003; De Santis et al., 2019), but more recently it has been hypothesized that the distinction might be related to the appearance of lesions in the Grey Matter (GM) whose impairment has been found to be associated with the early onset of the pathology (Calabrese et al., 2010; Calabrese and Castellaro, 2017).

Several Magnetic Resonance Imaging (MRI) studies confirmed the GM involvement, detecting both demyelination and atrophy in cortical and deep GM structures (Calabrese et al., 2015; Calabrese and Castellaro, 2017; Lassmann, 2018; Nourbakhsh and Mowry, 2019). Such findings were confirmed by recent studies relying on advanced MRI techniques such as diffusion MRI (dMRI) relying on ML and DL methods (Boscolo Galazzo et al., 2021; Marzullo et al., 2019; Cruciani et al., 2021) such as support vector machines, graph-, 2D-, and 3D-CNNs. Moreover, Zhang et al. (2021) and Cruciani et al. (2021) applied interpretability methods for feature visualization.

In this work, we built on top of our previous results (Cruciani et al., 2021), proposing a 3D-CNN architecture trained on T1-weighted (T1-w) MRI data. We aim at providing hints for the interpretation of the mechanisms at the basis of the MS disease course, besides the primary classification task, opening new perspectives for diagnosis, prognosis, and treatment. To this end, the CNN outcomes were analyzed relying on three feature visualization methods, namely Backpropagation (BP) (Simonyan et al., 2014), Guided Backpropagation (GBP) (Springenberg et al., 2014), and Layerwise Relevance Propagation (LRP) (Bach et al., 2015). A consensus analysis across the feature visualization methods was also carried out based on Normalized Mutual Information (NMI) (Studholme et al., 1999), under the assumption that stability across methods would be an indication of the neuroanatomical plausibility of the outcomes.

This chapter is organized as follows. Section 6.2 provides an overview of the state-of-the-art (SOA) with a focus on XAI methods and applications to MS disease, including a short overview on the feature visualization methods considered in this work. Section 6.3 illustrates the proposed approach describing the study cohort, the T1-w MRI preprocessing, and the CNN architecture. In particular, Section 6.3.3 regards the implementation of the feature visualization methods, their analysis and the discussion of the consensus analysis across the different methods, as well as their neuroanatomical plausibility. In Section 6.4 the main results are provided, which are then discussed in Section 6.5. In Section 6.5.1 the main limitations of the proposed work are highlighted, and the conclusions are drawn in Section 6.6.

6.2. State-of-the-art

This chapter provides an overview on XAI, briefly introducing the relevant taxonomy (Section 6.2.1). The three XAI methods employed in this work, namely BP, GBP, and LRP, are then detailed. Finally, the state-of-the-art of XAI methods applied to MS pathology is presented in Section 6.2.2.

6.2.1 EXplainable Artificial Intelligence (XAI)

Multiple categorizations of interpretability methods can be found in the literature. Referring to Holzinger et al. (2019), such methods can be divided into *post-hoc* methods, which explain what the model predicts after its application, and *ante-hoc*, which instead are methods that incorporate explainability directly into their structure. This categorization maps straightforwardly to the most commonly known methods presented in Linardatos et al. (2021) which separates the interpretability models based on their purpose, namely *explain black-box models* and *create white-box models*. Following Boscolo Galazzo et al. (2022), the post-hoc models would sit in the first category and ante-hoc models in the second. This chapter focuses on post-hoc models, particularly tailored for the clinical field. Following Kohoutová et al. (2020), on a feature-probing level, each interpretability method targets three feature properties: (i) Stability that measures how stable each feature contribution is over multiple models trained on held-out datasets using resampling methods or cross-validation; (ii) Importance which assesses the impact of a feature on the prediction output; and (iii) Visualization, in the form of saliency maps, or heatmaps, which provide ways to make a model human understandable.

Interpretability methods aiming at feature visualization will be the core of our discussion since, for volumetric inputs and DL models like CNNs, they allow highlighting the voxels having the strongest impact on the model output. As described in Samek et al. (2021), the basic approaches are: (i) methods relying on gradients, where each gradient quantifies to which extent a change in each input would change the predictions in a small neighborhood around the voxel (Simonyan et al., 2013; Bach et al., 2015; Montavon et al., 2018; Shrikumar et al., 2017); (ii) LRP, which makes explicit use of the layered structure of the neural network and operates iteratively to produce the explanation, mapping the model output score back to the input space (Bach et al., 2015); (iii) occlusion analysis, in which the feature relevance is measured by comparing the model outputs with respect to an input and a modified copy of the input (Zeiler and Fergus, 2014; Zintgraf et al., 2017); (iv) methods generating interpretable local surrogates aiming at replacing the decision function with a local surrogate model structured in a self-explanatory way (Ribeiro et al., 2016). An extensive review of the SOA of visualization methods is out of the scope of this chapter and can be found in Xie et al. (2020); Linardatos et al. (2021); Kohoutová et al. (2020).

Gradient-based methods are the most used in the biomedical field since they allow examining the fine-grained pixel/voxel importance, relying on saliency maps at the network input. Moreover, they are easily applicable to different models.

The simple BP and the GBP were initially presented in Simonyan et al. (2014); Springenberg et al. (2014) and applied, for example, to MRI-based classification problems and contrasted to perturbation methods for Alzheimer's disease (AD) diagnosis in Rieke et al. (2018) and Hu et al. (2021). However, methods relying on gradients only measure the susceptibility of the output to changes in the input that might not necessarily coincide with those areas on which the network based its decision (Böhle et al., 2019). To overcome these limitations, LRP aims at decomposing directly the network output score into individual contributions of the input neurons, keeping the total amount of relevance constant across layers. This method, originally presented in Bach et al. (2015), was applied to visualize the most relevant features influencing CNNs decisions in Böhle et al. (2019) and Eitel et al. (2019) for MRI-based classification tasks, involving the differentiation of patients from controls in diseases such as AD or MS.

A detailed overview of the BP, GBP, and LRP interpretability methods is given in what follows.

6.2.1.1 Backpropagation

BP (Simonyan et al., 2014) relies on the visualization of the gradient of the network output probability with respect to the input image. For a given voxel, this gradient describes how much the output probability changes when the voxel value changes. In CNNs, the gradient is straightforwardly available since it can be easily computed via the backpropagation algorithm used for training, and it is equivalent to the visualization of the partial derivatives of the network output with respect to each input feature scaled by its value. Given an input x and a function S_c that describes the model output for the class c, the BP can be expressed as

$$BP(x) = \frac{\partial S_c}{\partial x}.$$

(6.1)

Differently from the backpropagation algorithm used for training, to obtain the saliency map, what is backpropagated is not the classification error, or loss, but directly the classification probability for a given class. The absolute value of the resulting coefficients is taken as the relevance score representing the feature importance.

For an intuition of this method, following the example in Springenberg et al. (2014) and Fig. 6.1, we can exemplify what happens in the backward pass to obtain the saliency maps for the convolutional and, in particular, for the Rectified Linear Unit (ReLU) layer which holds the difference between GB and GBP. The ReLU layer is responsible for adding the nonlinearity to the neural network. For short, it is a piecewise linear

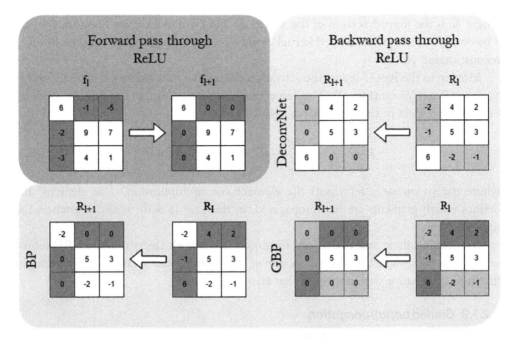

Figure 6.1 Differences between Backpropagation (BP), Guided Backpropagation (GBP), and DeconvNet in the backpropagation through the Rectified Linear Unit (ReLU) layers, following the example proposed in Springenberg et al. (2014).

function that is defined to be zero for all negative values of the node input and one otherwise, thus keeping unchanged the positive input values while annihilating the negative ones.

Given the input image or volume **x**, during the forward pass, each CNN layer l returns a feature activation map f^l till the last layer L. Then, starting from f^L, it is possible to generate the backpropagation map R^L by zeroing all the neuron activations except that to be backpropagated, that is, the one related to the target class, and starting the backward pass to reconstruct the input image **x** showing the part of the input image that is most strongly activating this neuron. Each R^l represents an intermediate step in the calculation of the BP, for the intermediate layer l. When reaching the CNN input layer, the reconstruction R^1 will have the same size of the input **x**.

Starting from the convolutional layers, the respective activation in the forward pass can be expressed as $f_{l+1} = f_l \circledast K_l$, where K_l is a convolutional kernel. The gradient with respect to the output feature map R^L, for layer l is then

$$R^l = \frac{\partial R^L}{\partial f_l} = \frac{\partial R^L}{\partial f_{l+1}} \circledast \hat{K}_l, \qquad (6.2)$$

where $\hat{K}_l$ is the flipped version of the kernel K_l and f is the visualized neuron activity. The convolution with the flipped kernel exactly corresponds to computing the lth layer reconstruction R_l.

Moving to the ReLU layers, the activation during the forward pass can be defined as $f_{l+1}(x) = ReLU(f_l) = \max(f_l, 0)$. The respective backpropagation computes the gradient of R^L with respect to the ReLU layer l as

$$R^l = \frac{\partial R^L}{\partial f_l} = \frac{\partial R^L}{\partial f_{l+1}} \cdot (f_l > 0) = R^{l+1} \cdot (f_l > 0) \tag{6.3}$$

where the $(\cdot)$ operator represents the elementwise multiplication. The element that defines which gradients are backpropagated, in this case $(f_l > 0)$, is also known as the sign operator.

By iterating these steps backward through the network layers results in R^1, representing the image-specific class saliency map, highlighting the areas of the given input that is discriminative with respect to that class.

6.2.1.2 Guided backpropagation

This method was presented by Springenberg et al. (2014) and is a modified version of BP with respect to the backward pass through the ReLU layer. More in detail, GBP combines the approach used for the Deconvolution Network (DeconvNet) (Zeiler and Fergus, 2014) with the one described for the BP, leading to more focused heatmaps.

Here, we briefly present the DeconvNet in order to introduce the GBP. The focus will be on the backpropagation through the ReLU layer which holds the main difference between BP and DeconvNet. Following the same mathematical framework as for the BP, the DeconvNet backward pass through the ReLU layer l can be described as

$$R^l = \frac{\partial R^L}{\partial f_l} = \frac{\partial R^L}{\partial f_{l+1}} \cdot (R^{l+1} > 0) = R^{l+1} \cdot (R^{l+1} > 0). \tag{6.4}$$

This differs from the BP since the sign indicator is based on the output reconstruction R^{l+1} of the precedent layer and not on the input activation f_{l+1} to the precedent layer as for BP. This allows only positive error signals to be backpropagated through the net to obtain the final saliency map.

Moving to the GBP, this method defines the backpropagation through the ReLU layer l as

$$R^l = \frac{\partial R^L}{\partial f_l} = \frac{\partial R^L}{\partial f_{l+1}} \cdot (R^{l+1} > 0) \cdot (f_l > 0) = R^{l+1} \cdot (R^{l+1} > 0) \cdot (f_l > 0). \tag{6.5}$$

Like DeconvNets, in GBP only positive error signals are backpropagated, setting the negative gradients to zero, which amounts to the application of the ReLU to the error signal itself during the backward pass. Moreover, like in BP, only positive inputs are considered. The advantage of retaining only positive gradients is to prevent a backward flow of negative contributions corresponding to neurons which inhibit the activation of the higher level neuron. As opposed to BP, this can act as an additional guidance signal when traversing the network. As above, the absolute value of the gradient is taken as the relevance score.

6.2.1.3 Layerwise relevance propagation

LRP (Bach et al., 2015) is slightly different from both BP and GBP since it does not rely on the gradient computation. This technique is based on a backward procedure which is a conservative relevance redistribution of the output prediction probability through the CNN layers till the input volume.

The core rule of the LRP procedure is the relevance conservation per layer. Let s and $s+1$ be two successive layers of the network and j and k two neurons of those layers, respectively. The relevance of the neuron k for the prediction $f(x)$, where x is the input, can be written as R_k^{s+1}. This relevance is redistributed to the connected neurons in layer s through the following equation:

$$\sum_j R_{j \leftarrow k}^s = R_k^{s+1}. \tag{6.6}$$

Iterating Eq. (6.6) through all the CNN layers allows decomposing the relevance of the prediction function $f(x)$, R_f, in terms of the input to the first layer.

Multiple rules can be applied for the distribution of the relevance (Montavon et al., 2018). In this work we used the β-rule as in Bach et al. (2015); Binder et al. (2016):

$$R_{i \leftarrow j}^{r,r+1} = \left((1+\beta) \frac{w_{ij}^+}{w_j^+} - \beta \frac{w_{ij}^-}{w_j^-} \right) R_j^{r+1}. \tag{6.7}$$

In this equation, $w_{i,j}^{+/-}$ is the amount of positive/negative contribution that node j transfers to node i, divided by the sum over all positive/negative contributions of the nodes in layer r. In fact, $w_j^{+/-} = \sum_i w_{i,j}^{+/-}$ so that the relevance is conserved from layer $r+1$ to layer r.

We set $\beta = 0$, hence allowing only positive contribution to the relevance score, following Böhle et al. (2019) where they demonstrated the LRP robustness relative to the β-value. Higher β-values would decompose the relevance in positive and negative contributions, the latter usually considered when dealing with patients/controls classification task.

6.2.2 EXplainable AI: application to multiple sclerosis

The classification between MS patients and healthy controls has been largely investigated in the literature. As an example, Zhang et al. (2018) and Wang et al. (2018) used a 2D-CNN model on T1-w MRI data, with 676 axial slices for MS patients and 681 axial slices for healthy controls. However, their main focus was on the optimization of the CNN architecture for this specific classification task. Zhang et al. (2018) indeed proposed a 10-layer deep CNN with seven convolutional layers and three fully connected layers, reaching an accuracy of 98.23%. Conversely, Wang et al. (2018) exploited a 14-layer CNN combined with batch normalization, dropout, and stochastic pooling, achieving higher accuracy of 98.77%.

Focusing on XAI applications, this precise task was previously approached by Eitel et al. (2019), which employed 3D-CNNs for the classification between MS subjects and healthy controls based on structural MRI data. They initially pretrained a 3D-CNN consisting of four convolutional layers followed by exponential linear units and four max-pooling layers on a large data sample (921 subjects) from the Alzheimer's Disease Neuroimaging Initiative. Afterwards they specialized the CNN to discriminate between MS patients and controls on a smaller dataset of 147 subjects, reaching a classification accuracy of 87.04%. As final analysis, they used the LRP heatmaps to assess the most relevant regions for the classification, analyzing both positive and negative relevance given their patients *versus* controls classification task. Feature visualization was also employed in Lopatina et al. (2020) to distinguish 66 control subjects from 66 MS patients. They relied on susceptibility-weighted imaging (SWI) and a 2D-CNN, since for each SWI volume they considered only one single 2D projection in transverse orientation. The CNN was composed of five convolutional layers with ReLU activation functions followed by max-pooling layers and two final fully-connected layers. To interpret the classification decisions, they investigated three different feature visualization methods, namely LRP, DeepLIFT (Shrikumar et al., 2017), and BP as reference. The resulting maps were analyzed with perturbation analysis. In perturbation analysis, information from the image is perturbed regionwise from most to least relevant according to the attribution map. The target output score of the classifier is affected by this perturbation and quickly drops if highly relevant information is removed. The faster the classification score drops, the better an interpretability method is capable to identify the input features responsible for correct classification. Their results highlighted the outstanding performance of LRP maps and DeepLIFT over simpler methods, strengthening the suitability of such methods to address clinically relevant questions.

However, the specific problem of stratifying MS patients according to their phenotype is still unexplored in literature. Only few works were found addressing this task. Marzullo et al. (2019) combined graph-based CNN with structural connectivity information from dMRI, relying in particular on a network-based representation of the structural connectome. They aimed at distinguishing between 90 MS patients divided in four clinical profiles, namely clinically isolated syndrome, RRMS, Secondary-Progressive MS (SPMS), and PPMS, and 24 healthy controls. The combination of different local graph features, such as node degree, clustering coefficient, local efficiency, and betweenness centrality allowed achieving accuracy scores higher than 80%. Zhang et al. (2021) moved a step further by introducing feature-visualization methods to investigate the MS patients stratification. They relied on structural MRI and compared six different 2D-CNN architectures for classification into three classes, namely RRMS, SPMS, and controls. Furthermore, they applied three different feature visualization techniques (Class Activation Mapping (CAM), Gradient (Grad)-CAM, and Grad-CAM++ (Selvaraju et al., 2017; Chattopadhay et al., 2018)) to achieve increased generalizability for CNN interpretation. Their results showed that Grad-CAM had the best localization ability in finding differences between RRMS and SPMS for discriminating brain regions.

To the best of our knowledge, only our preliminary work (Cruciani et al., 2021) attempted the exploitation of 3D-CNNs to differentiate the PPMS and the RRMS, applying only the LRP method to detect the most impacting regions to the CNN outcome. In that study we exploited only GM features derived from both T1-w and dMRI brain acquisitions for a total of 91 subjects equally split in PPMS and RRMS categories. Our results demonstrated that LRP heatmaps highlighted areas of high relevance which relate well with what is known from literature for the MS disease.

6.3. Materials and methods

This chapter illustrates the experimental pipeline. An overview of the whole process is provided in Fig. 6.2. The description of the population is given in Section 6.3.1, reporting demographical information, MRI acquisition parameters, and image processing and processing details. Section 6.3.2 presents the 3D-CNN architecture for the classification between PPMS and RRMS patients including the training and validation parameters. Section 6.3.2.1 describes the procedure for the assessment of the impact of the confounds in the classification outcomes. Finally Sections 6.3.4 and 6.3.3 detail the applied XAI methods, as well as the resulting relevance heatmaps and their post-hoc comparative analysis. The latter aims at the assessment of the stability of relevant regions across XAI methods, under the assumption that the extent of the heatmaps overlap provides evidence in favor of the robustness of the outcomes, as well as of their potential neuroanatomical plausibility.

6.3.1 Population, data acquisition, and image processing

The population consisted of 91 subjects, including 46 RRMS (35 females, 52.5 ± 10.4 years old) and 45 PPMS (25 females, 47.2 ± 9.5 years old) patients. Expanded Disability Status Scale (EDSS) score was 2.8 ± 1.4 and 4.8 ± 1.3 for the two groups, respectively.

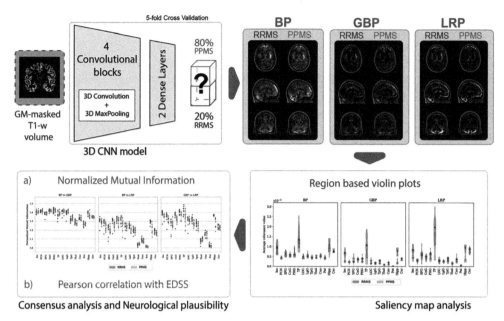

Figure 6.2 Overview of the interpretability and validation pipeline adopted for Multiple Sclerosis (MS) patients stratification. The Grey Matter (GM) masked T1-weighted volumes were given as input to a 3D convolutional Neural Network (CNN) architecture trained and validated through a 5-fold Cross Validation (CV) procedure. The Backpropagation (BP), Guided BP (GBP), and the Layerwise Relevance Propagation (LRP) maps were derived for 20 subjects, 10 for each class, namely Primary Progressive MS (PPMS) and Relapsing Remitting MS (RRMS). For each visualization technique, a quantitative analysis was carried out by computing region based violin plots across 14 regions of interest (ROIs). In order to assess the robustness of the results, the ROI based Normalized Mutual Information between all the possible combinations of BP, GBP, and LRP was computed. Finally, the neuroanatomical plausibility was investigated through the assessment of the Spearman correlation between the relevance value in each ROI and the Expanded Disability Status Scale (EDSS), separately for BP, GBP, and LRP heatmaps.

MRI acquisitions were performed on a 3T Philips Achieva scanner (Philips Medical Systems, the Netherlands) equipped with an 8-channel head coil. The following sequences were acquired for all patients: (1) 3D T1-w Fast Field Echo (repetition time [TR]/echo time [TE] $= 8.1/3$ ms, flip angle [FA] $= 8°$, field of view [FOV] $= 240 \times 240$ mm^2, 1-mm isotropic resolution, 180 slices); (2) 3D Fluid-Attenuated Inversion Recovery (FLAIR) image (TR/TE $= 8000/290$ ms, inversion time [TI] $= 2356$ ms, FA $= 90°$, FOV $= 256 \times 256$ mm^2, $0.9 \times 0.9 \times 0.5$ mm^3 resolution, 180 slices). All patients were recruited in our center according to their diagnosis based on the McDonald 2010 diagnostic criteria. The study was approved by the local ethics committee, and informed consent was obtained from all patients. All procedures were performed in accordance with the Declaration of Helsinki (2008).

For each subject, the FLAIR image was linearly registered to the T1-w one (FSL flirt tool, (Jenkinson and Smith, 2001)) and the Lesion Prediction Algorithm (Schmidt et al., 2012) of the SPM software (Penny et al., 2011) was used to automatically segment and fill the white matter lesions in the native T1-w image. Each filled T1-w image was then imported in the FreeSurfer software (Fischl, 2012) to perform a complete brain parcellation with 112 anatomical Regions-of-Interest (ROIs). The binary mask representing the GM tissue probability with threshold at 95% was derived for each subject (FSL `fast` tool, Zhang et al. (2000)) and multiplied to all the filled T1-w.

6.3.2 3D-CNN network architecture

A Visual Geometry Group (VGG) like 3D-CNN (Simonyan and Zisserman, 2014) was employed. This model has been used in combination with MRI data in few recent studies (Korolev et al., 2017; Böhle et al., 2019; Rieke et al., 2018), and it has been demonstrated to achieve similar accuracy as a Residual Neural Network (ResNet) model (He et al., 2016) in distinguishing Alzheimer's disease patients from healthy controls (Korolev et al., 2017). The advantage of the VGG model in this context is its suitability to the application of visualization methods such as LRP.

The architecture implemented in this work consists of four volumetric convolutional blocks for feature extraction, two deconvolutional layers with batch normalization, and one output layer with `softmax` nonlinearity. More in detail, each convolutional block consists of a convolutional layer followed by ReLU, batch normalization and 3D pooling. A graphical representation of the 3D-CNN structure highlighting the main parameters for each layer is provided in Fig. 6.3.

Data augmentation was performed during the training/validation phase in order to improve the generalization capabilities of our model due to the scarcity of the data. In detail, data augmentation consisted in: (i) addition of random Gaussian noise ($\mu = 0$, $\sigma = 0.1$); (ii) random affine transformation from -5 to $+5$ degrees in the Z axis, and from -3 to $+3$ degrees in the X axis; (iii) random volume translation from -3 to $+3$ voxels along each of the three axis; and (iv) flipping across the X axis. In addition, clipping of the values to the 99th percentile was performed.

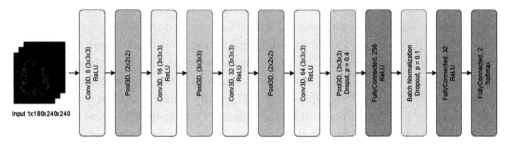

Figure 6.3 3D Convolutional Neural Network architecture with 3D T1-weighted input (masked to retain Grey Matter voxels only).

The CNN was trained using a 5-fold Cross-Validation (5-fold CV) strategy over a training/validation set of 91 subjects. On each fold, the 91 subjects were randomly split in five groups of 18 subjects each (except one of 19 subjects). The experiment was repeated five times and, for each repetition, four groups were considered as training and the remaining one for validation. The cross-entropy loss was optimized by means of the Adam optimizer (Kingma and Ba, 2014) during the training phase.

The CNN performance was reported as the average over the validation set of the five models, in terms of accuracy, sensitivity and specificity, while precision for each class was defined as detailed in what follows. True Positives (TrueP) and True Negatives (TrueN) represent the number of correctly classified PPMS and RRMS subjects, respectively, while False Positives (FalseP) and False Negatives (FalseN) count the wrongly classified RRMS and PPMS, respectively. The class-specific precision was defined as $precision_{PPMS} = TrueP/(TrueP + FalseP)$ and $precision_{RRMS} = TrueN/(TrueN + FalseN)$. The whole DL analysis was carried out using the software toolkit PyTorch (Paszke et al., 2017). The computation was performed on a laptop (Ubuntu 18.6, Nvidia GeForce GTX 1050, Intel Core i7, 16 GB RAM). Torchsample wrapper was used as high-level interface.

6.3.2.1 Confounding variables influence assessment

Confounding variables or confounders are often defined as the variables correlated (positively or negatively) with both the dependent and independent variables. In consequence, their presence affects the results of the study that do not reflect the actual relationship between them. To assess the influence of confounding variables on the classification outcome we adopted a *post-hoc* analysis following the method proposed by Dinga et al. (2020). Indeed, there exist two main approaches to deal with confounds in ML and DL methods. First, a direct deconfounding of the input that amounts to removing the contribution of the confounds from the input voxel values, most often using linear regression. This is a widely used approach, in particular when applying linear methods for the subsequent analyses. The main drawback is the possible failure of such methods to completely eliminate the confound influence on the input data, especially when there exists a nonlinear relationship between them. To solve this issue, an alternative solution based on *post-hoc* analyses can be performed. In particular, Dinga et al. (2020) proposed to control for confounds at the level of ML predictions relying on logistic classification models. This allows understanding what information about the outcome can be explained using model predictions that is not already explained by confounding variables. Following Dinga et al. (2020), this information can be obtained by calculating the Likelihood Ratio (LR), or difference in log-likelihood, of two models, namely (i) the model predicting the outcome using only confounding variables and (ii) the model predicting the outcome using both confounding variables and the CNN predictions as calculated during the training phase, under the assumption that the statistical significance of the LR, assessed through a χ^2 test, would reveal that the role of the confounds in shaping the classification outcomes is not prevalent.

In our study this method was used to assess the role of age, sex, and EDSS in the differentiation between PPMS and RRMS phenotypes.

6.3.3 Convolutional neural networks visualization methods

To identify the regions on which the CNN model based the classification decision, we employed three interpretability methods, namely BP, GBP, and LRP (Section 6.2). As the classification aims at differentiating two groups of patients, relevance maps were derived for both TrueP (PPMS) and TNs (RRMS) samples and were referred to as *winning class* heatmaps. More in detail, in a multiclass classification task, the CNN prediction function $f(x)$ consists of multiple values indicating the probability for the input x to belong to each of the classes c_i, e.g., $f(x) = \{f_{C_1(x)}, f_{C_2(x)}, \ldots, f_{C_N(x)}\}$, where N represents the total number of classes. Indeed, to obtain relevance maps, a target class has to be defined and the resulting maps are strongly dependent on the class. Let n be the class index and the BP the algorithm used to compute the saliency map. Then, $C_n - BP(x)$ is obtained by backpropagating $R_L = f_{C_n(x)}$ through the network. Following this notation, in this work the prediction $f(x)$ is defined as $f(x) = \{f_{C_{PPMS}(x)}, f_{C_{RRMS}(x)}\}$. In particular, since the two classes share the same importance, there is not a fixed target class. For the correctly classified PPMS subjects, the relative PPMS-BP, PPMS-GBP, and PPMS-LRP were calculated starting from the respective $f_{C_{PPMS}(x)}$. On the contrary, for the correctly classified RRMS subjects the RRMS-BP, RRMS-GBP, and RRMS-LRP were calculated starting from the relative $f_{C_{RRMS}(x)}$.

In this way, the resulting winning class relevance maps will answer to two questions: (i) "What speaks for PPMS in this subject?", for the subjects correctly classified as PPMS, and (ii) "What speaks for RRMS in this subject?" for those correctly predicted as RRMS. To cope with the low dataset size, the heatmaps were derived for 20 randomly sampled subjects, 10 per class, using the best model out of the 5-fold CV model set, resulting in three maps per subject that were subsequently analyzed as detailed hereafter.

6.3.4 Relevance heatmap analysis

The Captum library (Kokhlikyan et al., 2020) was used to compute BP and GBP maps, while the iNNvestigate library (Alber et al., 2019) was employed for LRP. The relevance maps were registered to the standard MNI space (voxel size = 1 mm isotropic) and averaged over the two groups of patients separately, for visualization purposes.

Fourteen brain ROIs were selected based on MS literature (Hulst and Geurts, 2011; Geurts et al., 2012; Calabrese et al., 2015; Eshaghi et al., 2018; Boscolo Galazzo et al., 2022): thalamus (Thal), caudate (Cau), putamen (Put), hippocampus (Hipp), insular cortex (Ins), temporal gyrus (TpG), superior frontal gyrus (SFG), cingulate gyrus (CnG), lateral occipital cortex (LOC), pericalcarine (PCN), lingual gyrus (LgG), cerebellum

(Cer), temporal pole (TP), and parahippocampal gyrus (PHG). The reference atlas was the Desikan–Killiany available in FreeSurfer.

The mean relevance values for each of the 14 ROIs was computed, for each of the three heatmaps in the subjects' space per condition. Each heatmap was previously normalized by the respective L^2-norm for direct comparison, following Zhang et al. (2019).

In order to assess the robustness of the heatmaps as descriptors of the relevance of the different ROIs for the considered task, a consensus analysis was performed across the outcomes of the visualization methods. The underlying assumption is that the agreement across methods witnesses in favor of the robustness, or stability, of the outcome. However, this does not guarantee the neuroanatomical plausibility of the so detected regions, which needs to be probed relying on additional criteria as will be discussed hereafter. Jointly, such two steps can be regarded as a cross-method validation of the relevance maps.

Assessing the stability of the heatmaps

To this end, the NMI was used as metric, calculated as presented in Studholme et al. (1999). More in detail, given two images I and K, the NMI is calculated as

$$NMI(I; K) = \frac{H(I) + H(K)}{H(I, K)},$$ (6.8)

where $H(I)$ and $H(K)$ represent the marginal entropy for the images I and K, respectively, while $H(I, K)$ is the joint entropy of I and K. In this study the entropy was estimated on the probability density function relying on the joint histogram of I and K. Following this definition, the NMI ranges from 1 to 2, where $NMI = 1$ means independent variables while $NMI = 2$ corresponds to $I = K$. The NMI was calculated at the region level between all the possible combinations of the normalized BP, GBP, and LRP.

Assessing the neuroanatomical plausibility of the heatmaps

As explorative analysis, we investigated the plausibility of the outcomes of the three considered feature visualization methods. Inspired by Eitel et al. (2019) and Böhle et al. (2019), the Spearman correlation between the average BP, GBP, and LRP relevance values for each ROI and the EDSS score were calculated, together with the corresponding p-value, both uncorrected and adjusted with Bonferroni correction for multiple comparisons. A total of 42 comparisons were performed (equal to the number of the considered regions multiplied by the number of feature visualization methods).

6.4. Results

A preliminary analysis revealed that the EDSS score and the age were significantly different between RRMS and PPMS subjects ($p < 0.05$), and thus constituted confounding variables. The same held with gender numerosity ($p < 0.05$), the latter observation reflecting the epidemiology of the disease.

The proposed CNN achieved an average accuracy on the validation sets equal to 0.81 ± 0.08 over the five models derived from the 5-fold CV, one for each fold. The sensitivity and specificity were 0.74 ± 0.22 and 0.80 ± 0.11, respectively, showing that the CNN minimized the FalsePs, that is, the wrongly classified RRMS subjects. This trend was confirmed by the $precision_{RRMS}$ which was 0.80 ± 0.15 while the $precision_{PPMS}$ was 0.76 ± 0.15.

Concerning the influence of the three confounds on the CNNs classification outcomes, the LR test revealed that the logistic classification model to which the CNN outcomes were added as predictor was significantly different (χ^2 test, $p < 0.05$) from the logistic classification model employing only the confounds as predictors, confirming that the classification was not driven by the confounding variables.

6.4.1 Qualitative assessment of the relevance heatmaps

Fig. 6.4 shows the BP, GBP, and LRP heatmaps averaged over the correctly classified subjects for each class, respectively. For ease of visualization, the maps were clipped between the 50th and 99.5th percentile, calculated over the respective target group heatmap. As expected, considering that winning class heatmaps were calculated for each method, high relevance was found in both PPMS and RRMS classes.

In general, a shared relevance pattern could be detected across ROIs, with the TrueP in the RRMS maps showing the highest similarity. Considering that the colormap is based on the percentile calculated for each class separately for each method, it is evident that BP shows widespread high voxel sensitivity values that do not correspond to regions of major interest, with the exception of the TrueP for the RRMS. The BP heatmap was more spread and noisier compared to those resulting from the other feature visualization techniques. A similar pattern was found between GBP and LRP maps for both PPMS and RRMS maps, with the GBP showing overall a more widespread and scattered relevance compared to the LRP.

More in detail of the different techniques, starting from the BP maps, the noisy pattern was particularly evident for the PPMS-BP. Both RRMS-BP and PPMS-BP highlighted higher relevance in the temporal lobe, particularly evident in the coronal and temporal views. Moving to the GBP maps, even if widespread relevance values were present in both classes, the pattern was slightly different. In fact, the RRMS-GBP map showed high activation in the temporal lobe and Cer, as highlighted in both the coronal and sagittal views. On the contrary, the PPMS-GBP maps showed low relevance

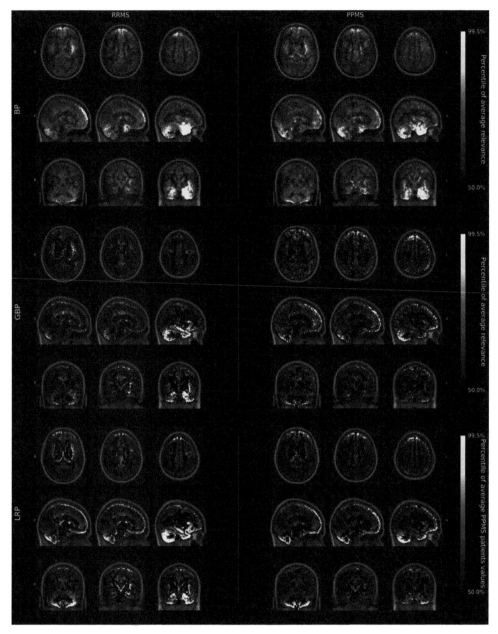

Figure 6.4 Backpropagation (BP), Guided Backpropagation (GBP), and Layerwise Relevance Propagation (LRP) heatmaps obtained from the T1-weighted based Convolutional Neural Network model. The heatmaps are shown for both Relapsing Remitting Multiple Sclerosis (RRMS) and Primary Progressive Multiple Sclerosis (PPMS) patients, and are overlaid to the MNI152 template in coronal, sagittal, and axial views (columns). Each interpretability map is averaged across the correctly classified RRMS and correctly classified PPMS subjects, respectively. The reported values are clipped to the range from the 60th to 99.5th percentile, calculated over the RRMS and the PPMS class group mean heatmaps.

in the temporal lobe, while high relevance was assigned to the frontal lobe as can be observed in the sagittal view. The LRP maps replicated the same trend described for GBP. However, a sharper and less scattered pattern was found for LRP maps, better highlighting only the most relevant regions.

6.4.2 Quantitative assessment of the heatmaps

ROI-based analysis was performed to quantitatively assess the relevant areas for the classification task, as a first step towards the clinical validation of the outcomes. Fig. 6.5 illustrates the average L^2-norm normalized relevance per ROI for the correctly classified patients, separately for the two classes and for the three visualization methods adopted in this study.

Starting from a general overview, a similar trend can be detected between the BP, GBP, and LRP, all showing high relevance for both subject classes in regions such as TP, Ins, Cer, and Hipp, with the LRP maps showing a generally higher relevance score. The RRMS mean relevance values were consistently higher compared to those of the PPMS for all the feature visualization methods, with the exception of the SFG, LOC, and LgG where the PPMS relevance mean values were higher than that of RRMS. The BP maps median relevance values for the two classes were highly overlapped in almost all the considered regions. On the contrary, the GBP and LRP maps showed a distinct

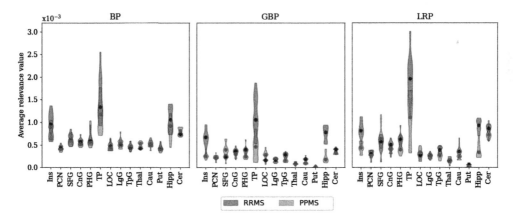

Figure 6.5 Size-normalized importance metric extracted from the Backpropagation (BP), Guided Backpropagation (GBP), and Layerwise Relevance Propagation (LRP) maps (columns). The mean relevance value for each region is reported for all the correctly classified Primary Progressive Multiple Sclerosis (PPMS) and Relapsing Remitting Multiple Sclerosis (RRMS) subjects. The median relevance for PPMS (orange circle, mid gray in print version) and RRMS (blue circle, dark gray in print version) groups are also shown. The relevance values are also normalized by the L^2-norm for direct comparison. *Abbreviations: thalamus (Thal), caudate (Cau), putamen (Put), hippocampus (Hipp), insular cortex (Ins), temporal gyrus (TpG), superior frontal gyrus (SFG), cingulate gyrus (CnG), lateral occipital cortex (LOC), pericalcarine (PCN), lingual gyrus (LgG), cerebellum (Cer), temporal pole (TP), and parahippocampal gyrus (PHG).*

relevance distribution for the two classes, as it is particularly evident in the Hipp where the two distributions resulted completely disjoint, with higher difference for GBP maps.

Stability analysis

The consensus analysis was performed to assess differences and similarities across the three feature visualization methods. Fig. 6.6 shows the NMI obtained for 14 brain regions. The NMI was calculated on the L^2-norm normalized relevance heatmaps, for the three combinations, namely BP versus GBP, BP versus LRP, and GBP versus LRP. In general, a similar NMI trend can be observed across the methods, with the cortical regions showing a higher NMI compared to the subcortical ones. The highest NMI was found, as expected, between BP and GBP maps, which showed an NMI value greater than 1.2 for all the ROIs. More in detail, the PHG resulted as the region featuring the highest similarity between the heatmaps derived from the two methods, followed by PCN, Ins, CnG, and TpG. Of note, the Cer showed the lowest variability in the NMI across subjects. Moving to the similarity between LRP and the two gradient-based methods, the NMI resulted generally lower for the comparison between BP and LRP compared to the GBP vs LRP, though sharing the same trend. Noteworthy, the RRMS showed higher similarity across methods compared to the PPMS class. The TrueP appeared as the most similar for both the comparisons, followed by the PHG and the Ins. The subcortical regions showed the lowest NMI, with the exception of the

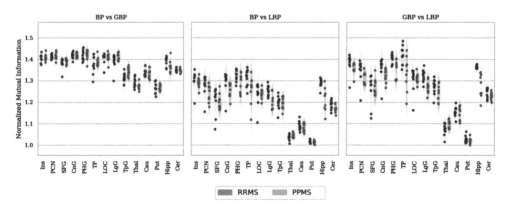

Figure 6.6 Region based Normalized Mutual Information (NMI) metric extracted from the comparison between Backpropagation (BP) and Guided Backpropagation (GBP), BP and Layerwise Relevance Propagation (LRP), GBP and LRP (columns). The NMI value for each region of interest is reported for all the correctly classified Primary Progressive Multiple Sclerosis (PPMS) (orange dots, mid gray in print version) and Relapsing Remitting Multiple Sclerosis (RRMS) subjects (blue dots, dark gray in print version). *Abbreviations: thalamus (Thal), caudate (Cau), putamen (Put), hippocampus (Hipp), insular cortex (Ins), temporal gyrus (TpG), superior frontal gyrus (SFG), cingulate gyrus (CnG), lateral occipital cortex (LOC), pericalcarine (PCN), lingual gyrus (LgG), cerebellum (Cer), temporal pole (TP), and parahippocampal gyrus (PHG).*

Hipp which instead showed high NMI values when comparing BP and LRP, and GBP and LRP, respectively.

Neuroanatomical plausibility

The Spearman correlation analysis between the ROI-wise mean relevance values for BP, GBP, and LRP and the EDSS scores are reported in Table 6.1. Significant positive correlations (p-value < 0.05, uncorrected) were detected for the SFG, for the three interpretability methods. Among the other regions, PHG, TP, Ins, TpG, and Hipp showed a significant negative correlation with EDSS for both GBP and LRP heatmaps. In particular, the largest negative correlation with the EDSS was found for LRP and GBP mean relevance in the PHG ($\rho = -0.81$ and -0.74, respectively), followed by the TpG which showed a negative ρ value of -0.65 and -0.64 for GBP and LRP, respectively. Finally, when applying Bonferroni correction for multiple comparisons, the PHG still showed a significant correlation with EDSS for both GBP and LRP (adjusted p-value of 0.011 and 0.001, respectively).

Table 6.1 Spearman correlation results between the mean Backpropagation (BP), Guided Backpropagation (GBP), and Layerwise Relevance Propagation (LRP) heatmap values for each ROI and the Expanded Disability Status Scale (EDSS) score (uncorrected p-values). *Abbreviations: thalamus (Thal), caudate (Cau), putamen (Put), hippocampus (Hipp), insular cortex (Ins), temporal gyrus (TpG), superior frontal gyrus (SFG), cingulate gyrus (CnG), lateral occipital cortex (LOC), pericalcarine (PCN), lingual gyrus (LgG), cerebellum (Cer), temporal pole (TP), and parahippocampal gyrus (PHG).*

	BP		GBP		LRP	
	ρ	*p*-value	ρ	*p*-value	ρ	*p*-value
Ins	−0.06	0.782	**−0.56**	**0.015**	**−0.56**	**0.012**
PCN	**−0.61**	**0.005**	−0.19	0.43	0.13	0.596
SFG	**0.52**	**0.022**	**0.58**	**0.008**	**0.52**	**0.021**
CnG	0.11	0.664	−0.34	0.148	−0.26	0.285
PHG	−0.29	0.221	<u>**−0.74**</u>	**0.001**	<u>**−0.81**</u>	**3e−05**
TP	−0.32	0.185	**−0.57**	**0.011**	**−0.56**	**0.013**
LOC	0.12	0.630	0.40	0.088	0.30	0.214
LgC	−0.16	0.505	−0.08	0.726	**−0.54**	**0.016**
TpG	−0.18	0.459	**−0.65**	**0.003**	**−0.64**	**0.003**
Thal	0.35	0.133	−0.08	0.746	0.13	0.599
Cau	0.09	0.686	−0.31	0.196	−0.36	0.132
Put	−0.08	0.729	**−0.55**	**0.016**	**−0.54**	**0.017**
Hipp	−0.31	0.188	**−0.59**	**0.008**	**−0.59**	**0.007**
Cer	0.04	0.890	**−0.52**	**0.022**	−0.43	0.068

The ρ score and relative p-values (rows) are reported for each region of interest (columns). The significant correlations (p-value < 0.05) are highlighted in bold. The correlations surviving after the Bonferroni correction are shown underlined.

6.5. Discussion

In this work we addressed the stratification problem between RRMS and PPMS patients based on T1-w data. A 3D-CNN was used to this aim, and three different interpretability methods for feature visualization were applied, namely BP, GBP, and LRP, in order to highlight the key brain regions involved in the classification of the two patients populations. A comparison between the different visualization techniques was also carried out to assess the stability of the outcomes across methods. Then, Spearman correlation was used to assess the concordance between the ROI-wise mean relevance and the individual EDSS scores for each of the 14 considered ROIs.

Distinguishing PPMS from RRMS based on GM features is one of the current challenges in MS research (Magliozzi et al., 2018), and the identification of a biomarker allowing one to capture the differences between these two disease phenotypes holds great importance in the field of personalized medicine (Inojosa et al., 2021).

The accuracy of 0.81 ± 0.08 suggests that the combination of T1-w and CNNs can help in the classification task between MS subtypes. The performance is comparable with that presented in Marzullo et al. (2019) (average precision of 0.84 and average recall of 0.8 on a dataset of 604 acquisitions) although achieved with different methods and protocols. The other classification metrics, as formalized in this work, express the ease of classification of each class of patients. In our results, the $precision_{RRMS}$ was close to the specificity, both being higher compared to the $precision_{PPMS}$ and the sensitivity, indicating that the CNN better characterized the RRMS subjects with respect to PPMS. Finally, the LR test between the two models for the *post-hoc* assessment of the prevalence of the confounding variables revealed that the classification results were not dominated by the confounds.

The differentiation between healthy and pathological subjects is much more common in the literature than patient stratification across disease phenotypes. In Wang et al. (2018) and Zhang et al. (2018), two different 2D-CNN architectures were combined with conventional structural MRI data to this end reaching high accuracy scores (98.77% and 98.23%, respectively). Using the different 2D images of each subject as a separate input led to a much larger sample size (e.g., amounting to 1357 images in total for the 64 subjects (Wang et al., 2018)) which brings a clear advantage for training. A 3D-CNN based approach was proposed in Eitel et al. (2019), showing an accuracy of 87.04% on a set of 147 fully volumetric structural MRI acquisitions. Despite the lower accuracy compared to the 2D-CNN based approaches, the use of a 3D-CNN architecture facilitated the interpretation of the CNN performance through the use of feature visualization techniques. However, the essential difference in the research question makes these works not directly comparable to ours. Concerning the feature visualization, Lopatina et al. (2020) compared different techniques applied to a 2D-CNN trained on 66 healthy controls and 66 MS patients SWI data. Their results highlighted the superiority of LRP and Deep Learning Important FeaTures (DeepLIFT) (Shriku-mar et al., 2017) over simpler methods, relying on the perturbation based analysis on the derived heatmaps, strengthening the exploitability of such methods to address clinically relevant questions.

The application of the BP, GBP, and LRP provides a means for CNNs interpretabil-ity and, when used in combination with other clinical and imaging data, could support diagnosis and treatment decisions. By relying on these techniques, it was possible to identify the regions playing a prominent role in the classification between the two MS phenotypes as the regions of highest difference in relevance across groups. In our results, the relevance maps of both RRMS and PPMS showed that BP was highly sensitive for both classes, highlighting a scarce class related relevance which was instead found for the other methods. Moreover, high relevance was found also in brain regions that were masked in the input, revealing the noisy pattern of BP maps and rising a warning on the interpretation of such results. We recall that only the GM-masked T1-w values were given as input to the CNN model. A more focused pattern was instead found for GBP and LRP which consistently showed relevance values only in the GM regions of the in-put volume. More in depth of the ROI-based analysis of the three feature visualization methods, the ROIs leading the CNN classification were coherent across methods and were in agreement with the clinical literature findings. Indeed, TP, which showed the highest relevance for BP, GBP, and LRP, as well as the highest NMI for all the compar-isons, has been reported to be present in MS cortical atrophy patterns (Steenwijk et al., 2016). The Ins, which was the second region for mean relevance value for all methods and NMI for all the comparisons, has been shown to reveal high probability of focal GM demyelination in MS pathology (Geurts et al., 2012). The Cer has been demon-strated to be a major site for demyelination, especially in PPMS patients (Kutzelnigg et al., 2007). Finally, an important feature for MS is a lower diffusion restriction and mas-sive neuronal loss and demyelination in Hipp (Geurts et al., 2007; Boscolo Galazzo et al., 2021), which was a region holding high relevance for all three feature visualization methods, as well as high NMI for all the considered comparisons.

It is important to note that the focus in interpreting feature visualization maps was not on the absolute values of the relevance, but on the differences and overlaps between the violin plots of the considered ROIs in the two classes of patients. This means that the relevance values allowed understanding how the voxels of certain ROIs contributed to the classification, but still did not allow identifying the subserving mechanism (lesion load, atrophy, etc.) (Böhle et al., 2019).

In general, the NMI between all the possible couplings of the three methods was, as expected, the highest between BP and GBP, the two methods both being based on gradients and having a similar computation with the exception for the ReLU layers. This was confirmed by the larger difference found instead between both BP and GBP, with respect to LRP. In fact, the LRP, as detailed in Section 6.2, is not directly based on gradients but on the backpropagation of the prediction values constrained by the relevance conservation rule. Of interest, higher NMI was found for the RRMS, particularly in the comparison between the gradient based methods and LRP, reflecting the clinically assessed higher variability in PPMS subjects compared to RRMS. However, the ROIs showing the highest NMI were the same for all the combinations, confirming their importance for the CNN outcome and providing evidence of the plausibility of the results.

In order to investigate whether high importance scores could correspond to clinically assessed difference across classes, the association between the mean relevance value in each ROI and the EDSS was also computed. All the regions featuring high relevance and NMI across methods showed also a significant Spearman correlation with EDSS. Of note, the PHG was the only region surviving the Bonferroni correction showing a significant and negative correlation with the EDSS, although it was not among the ROIs showing the highest relevance. For clinical assessment, this region has been associated with fatigue, particularly in RRMS (Calabrese et al., 2010).

Although deeper investigation would be needed to drive strong conclusions, these results, together with Böhle et al. (2019) and Eitel et al. (2019), provide evidence of the potential of the joint exploitation of CNNs and visualization methods for identifying relevant disease biomarkers for the considered disease phenotypes, as well as of the core role of visualization methods in pursuing the objective assessment of the plausibility and clinical relevance of the results.

6.5.1 Limitations and future works

One of the obvious possible improvements to our work would be the increase of the number of subjects, even though the classification performance and the consensus across the heatmaps obtained by different visualization methods witness in favor of the robustness and reliability of the results. Moreover, for the stability analysis, different metrics are being proposed in the literature focusing not only on assessing the similarity between heatmaps, but also on their stability and bias, such as the mutual verification proposed in Zhang et al. (2019). In a clinical context it is mandatory to obtain highly reliable and still understandable explanations in order to spread the use of ML and DL methods.

Another possible improvement would be single-subject analysis. Since the interpretability methods adopted provide a heatmap for each subject, indicating the contribution of each voxel to the final classification decision, a subject-specific analysis could be carried out, moving step forward the personalized precision medicine.

Then, additional feature visualization methods could be exploited, such as DeepLIFT analyzed also in Lopatina et al. (2020), in order to further investigate the consensus across more advanced interpretability methods.

Overall, we consider these outcomes as a valuable evidence of the potential of the proposed method in splitting apart the two MS phenotypes and providing hints on the signatures of possible subserving mechanisms of disease progression. We leave the open issues mentioned above for future investigation.

6.6. Conclusions

This work corroborated the capability of T1–w combined with a 3D–CNN classifier in distinguishing the different typologies of MS disease. In addition, we could highlight, through the application and the stability analysis across the three considered feature visualization techniques, that the CNN classification was based on ROIs holding clinical relevance whose heatmap NMI was high and which mean values significantly correlated with EDSS score. From a clinical perspective, our results strengthen the hypothesis of the suitability of GM features as biomarkers for MS pathological brain tissues. Moreover, this work has the potential to address clinically important problems in MS, like the early identification of the clinical course for diagnosis, personalized treatment, and treatment decision.

Acknowledgments

This work has received funding from the European Research Council (ERC) under the European Union's Horizon 2020 research and innovation program (ERC Advanced Grant agreement no. 694665: CoBCoM – Computational Brain Connectivity Mapping) and from the French government, through the 3IA Côte d'Azur Investments in the Future project managed by the National Research Agency (ANR) with the reference number ANR-10-P3IA-0002. This work was also partly supported by fondazione CariVerona (Bando Ricerca Scientifica di Eccellenza 2018, EDIPO project – reference number 2018.0855.2019)

References

Alber, Maximilian, Lapuschkin, Sebastian, Seegerer, Philipp, Hägele, Miriam, Schütt, Kristof T., Montavon, Grégoire, Samek, Wojciech, Müller, Klaus-Robert, Dähne, Sven, Kindermans, Pieter-Jan, 2019. Investigate neural networks! Journal of Machine Learning Research 20 (93), 1–8.

Bach, Sebastian, Binder, Alexander, Montavon, Grégoire, Klauschen, Frederick, Müller, Klaus-Robert, Samek, Wojciech, 2015. On pixel-wise explanations for non-linear classifier decisions by layer-wise relevance propagation. PLoS ONE 10 (7), e0130140.

Binder, Alexander, Montavon, Grégoire, Lapuschkin, Sebastian, Müller, Klaus-Robert, Samek, Wojciech, 2016. Layer-wise relevance propagation for neural networks with local renormalization layers. In: Villa, Alessandro E.P., Masulli, Paolo, Pons Rivero, Antonio Javier (Eds.), Artificial Neural Networks and Machine Learning – ICANN 2016. Springer International Publishing, Cham, pp. 63–71.

Böhle, Moritz, Eitel, Fabian, Weygandt, Martin, Ritter, Kerstin, 2019. Layer-wise relevance propagation for explaining deep neural network decisions in MRI-based Alzheimer's disease classification. Frontiers in Aging Neuroscience 11, 194.

Boscolo Galazzo, Ilaria, Brusini, Lorenza, Akinci, Muge, Cruciani, Federica, Pitteri, Marco, Ziccardi, Stefano, Bajrami, Albulena, Castellaro, Marco, Salih, Ahmed M.A., Pizzini, Francesca B., et al., 2021. Unraveling the MRI-based microstructural signatures behind primary progressive and relapsing-remitting multiple sclerosis phenotypes. Journal of Magnetic Resonance Imaging 55, 154–163.

Boscolo Galazzo, Ilaria, Cruciani, Federica, Brusini, Lorenza, Salih, Ahmed M.A., Radeva, Petia, Storti, Silvia Francesca, Menegaz, Gloria, 2022. Explainable artificial intelligence for MRI aging brainprints: Grounds and challenges. IEEE Signal Processing Magazine 39 (2), 99–116.

Calabrese, Massimiliano, Castellaro, Marco, 2017. Cortical gray matter MR imaging in multiple sclerosis. Neuroimaging Clinics 27 (2), 301–312.

Calabrese, Massimiliano, Rinaldi, Francesca, Grossi, Paola, Mattisi, Irene, Bernardi, Valentina, Favaretto, Alice, Perini, Paola, Gallo, Paolo, 2010. Basal ganglia and frontal/parietal cortical atrophy is associated with fatigue in relapsing–remitting multiple sclerosis. Multiple Sclerosis Journal 16 (10), 1220–1228. PMID: 20670981.

Calabrese, Massimiliano, Reynolds, Richard, Magliozzi, Roberta, Castellaro, Marco, Morra, Aldo, Scalfari, Antonio, Farina, Gabriele, Romualdi, Chiara, Gajofatto, Alberto, Pitteri, Marco, et al., 2015. Regional distribution and evolution of gray matter damage in different populations of multiple sclerosis patients. PLoS ONE 10 (8), e0135428.

Chattopadhay, Aditya, Sarkar, Anirban, Howlader, Prantik, Balasubramanian, Vineeth N., 2018. Grad-CAM++: Generalized gradient-based visual explanations for deep convolutional networks. In: 2018 IEEE Winter Conference on Applications of Computer Vision (WACV). IEEE, pp. 839–847.

Compston, Alastair, Coles, Alasdair, 2008. Multiple sclerosis. The Lancet 372 (9648), 1502–1517.

Cruciani, Federica, Brusini, Lorenza, Zucchelli, Mauro, Retuci Pinheiro, G., Setti, Francesco, Boscolo Galazzo, I., Deriche, Rachid, Rittner, Leticia, Calabrese, Massimiliano, Menegaz, Gloria, 2021. Interpretable deep learning as a means for decrypting disease signature in multiple sclerosis. Journal of Neural Engineering 18 (4), 0460a6.

De Santis, Silvia, Bastiani, Matteo, Droby, Amgad, Kolber, Pierre, Zipp, Frauke, Pracht, Eberhard, Stoecker, Tony, Groppa, Sergiu, Roebroeck, Alard, 2019. Characterizing microstructural tissue properties in multiple sclerosis with diffusion MRI at 7 T and 3 T: the impact of the experimental design. Neuroscience 403, 17–26.

Dinga, Richard, Schmaal, Lianne, Penninx, Brenda W.J.H., Veltman, Dick J., Marquand, Andre F., 2020. Controlling for effects of confounding variables on machine learning predictions. BioRxiv. https://doi.org/10.1101/2020.08.17.255034.

Eitel, Fabian, Soehler, Emily, Bellmann-Strobl, Judith, Brandt, Alexander U., Ruprecht, Klemens, Giess, René M., Kuchling, Joseph, Asseyer, Susanna, Weygandt, Martin, Haynes, John-Dylan, et al., 2019. Uncovering convolutional neural network decisions for diagnosing multiple sclerosis on conventional MRI using layer-wise relevance propagation. arXiv preprint. arXiv:1904.08771.

Eshaghi, Arman, Marinescu, Razvan V., Young, Alexandra L., Firth, Nicholas C., Prados, Ferran, Jorge Cardoso, M., Tur, Carmen, De Angelis, Floriana, Cawley, Niamh, Brownlee, Wallace J., et al., 2018. Progression of regional grey matter atrophy in multiple sclerosis. Brain 141 (6), 1665–1677.

Fischl, Bruce, 2012. FreeSurfer. NeuroImage 62 (2), 774–781.

Geurts, Jeroen J.G., Bö, Lars, Roosendaal, Stefan D., Hazes, Thierry, Daniëls, Richard, Barkhof, Frederik, Witter, Menno P., Huitinga, Inge, van der Valk, Paul, 2007. Extensive hippocampal demyelination in multiple sclerosis. Journal of Neuropathology and Experimental Neurology 66 (9), 819–827.

Geurts, Jeroen J.G., Calabrese, Massimiliano, Fisher, Elizabeth, Rudick, Richard A., 2012. Measurement and clinical effect of grey matter pathology in multiple sclerosis. The Lancet Neurology 11 (12), 1082–1092.

He, Kaiming, Zhang, Xiangyu, Ren, Shaoqing, Sun, Jian, 2016. Deep residual learning for image recognition. In: The IEEE Conference on Computer Vision and Pattern Recognition (CVPR), pp. 770–778.

Holzinger, Andreas, Langs, Georg, Denk, Helmut, Zatloukal, Kurt, Müller, Heimo, 2019. Causability and explainability of artificial intelligence in medicine. Wiley Interdisciplinary Reviews: Data Mining and Knowledge Discovery 9 (4), e1312.

Hu, Jingjing, Qing, Zhao, Liu, Renyuan, Zhang, Xin, Lv, Pin, Wang, Maoxue, Wang, Yang, He, Kelei, Gao, Yang, Zhang, Bing, 2021. Deep learning-based classification and voxel-based visualization of frontotemporal dementia and Alzheimer's disease. Frontiers in Neuroscience 14, 1468.

Huang, Wen-Juan, Chen, Wei-Wei, Zhang, Xia, 2017. Multiple sclerosis: pathology, diagnosis and treatments. Experimental and Therapeutic Medicine 13 (6), 3163–3166.

Hulst, Hanneke E., Geurts, Jeroen J.G., 2011. Gray matter imaging in multiple sclerosis: What have we learned? BMC Neurology 11 (1), 153.

Hurwitz, Barrie J., 2009. The diagnosis of multiple sclerosis and the clinical subtypes. Annals of Indian Academy of Neurology 12 (4), 226.

Inojosa, Hernan, Proschmann, Undine, Akgün, Katja, Ziemssen, Tjalf, 2021. A focus on secondary progressive multiple sclerosis (SPMS): Challenges in diagnosis and definition. Journal of Neurology 268 (4), 1210–1221.

Jenkinson, Mark, Smith, Stephen, 2001. A global optimisation method for robust affine registration of brain images. Medical Image Analysis 5 (2), 143–156.

Kingma, Diederik P., Ba, Jimmy, 2014. Adam: A method for stochastic optimization. arXiv preprint. arXiv:1412.6980.

Kohoutová, Lada, Heo, Juyeon, Cha, Sungmin, Lee, Sungwoo, Moon, Taesup, Wager, Tor D., Woo, Choong-Wan, 2020. Toward a unified framework for interpreting machine-learning models in neuroimaging. Nature Protocols 15 (4), 1399–1435.

Kokhlikyan, Narine, Miglani, Vivek, Martin, Miguel, Wang, Edward, Alsallakh, Bilal, Reynolds, Jonathan, Melnikov, Alexander, Kliushkina, Natalia, Araya, Carlos, Yan, Siqi, Reblitz-Richardson, Orion, 2020. Captum: A unified and generic model interpretability library for PyTorch. arXiv preprint. arXiv:2009.07896.

Korolev, Sergey, Safiullin, Amir, Belyaev, Mikhail, Dodonova, Yulia, 2017. Residual and plain convolutional neural networks for 3D brain MRI classification. In: 2017 IEEE 14th International Symposium on Biomedical Imaging (ISBI 2017). IEEE, pp. 835–838.

Kutzelnigg, Alexandra, Faber-Rod, Jens C., Bauer, Jan, Lucchinetti, Claudia F., Sorensen, Per S., Laursen, Henning, Stadelmann, Christine, Brück, Wolfgang, Rauschka, Helmut, Schmidbauer, Manfred, et al., 2007. Widespread demyelination in the cerebellar cortex in multiple sclerosis. Brain Pathology 17 (1), 38–44.

Lassmann, Hans, 2018. Multiple sclerosis pathology. Cold Spring Harbor Perspectives in Medicine 8 (3), a028936.

Linardatos, Pantelis, Papastefanopoulos, Vasilis, Kotsiantis, Sotiris, 2021. Explainable AI: A review of machine learning interpretability methods. Entropy 23 (1), 18.

Lopatina, Alina, Ropele, Stefan, Sibgatulin, Renat, Reichenbach, Jürgen R., Güllmar, Daniel, 2020. Investigation of deep-learning-driven identification of multiple sclerosis patients based on susceptibility-weighted images using relevance analysis. Frontiers in Neuroscience 14, 609468.

Lublin, Fred D., Reingold, Stephen C., Cohen, Jeffrey A., Cutter, Gary R., Sørensen, Per Soelberg, Thompson, Alan J., Wolinsky, Jerry S., Balcer, Laura J., Banwell, Brenda, Barkhof, Frederik, et al., 2014. Defining the clinical course of multiple sclerosis: The 2013 revisions. Neurology 83 (3), 278–286.

Lucchinetti, Claudia, Brück, Wolfgang, Parisi, Joseph, Scheithauer, Bernd, Rodriguez, Moses, Lassmann, Hans, 2000. Heterogeneity of multiple sclerosis lesions: implications for the pathogenesis of demyelination. Annals of Neurology: Official Journal of the American Neurological Association and the Child Neurology Society 47 (6), 707–717.

Magliozzi, Roberta, Howell, Owain W., Nicholas, Richard, Cruciani, Carolina, Castellaro, Marco, Romualdi, Chiara, Rossi, Stefania, Pitteri, Marco, Benedetti, Maria Donata, Gajofatto, Alberto, Pizzini, Francesca B., Montemezzi, Stefania, Rasia, Sarah, Capra, Ruggero, Bertoldo, Alessandra, Facchiano, Francesco, Monaco, Salvatore, Reynolds, Richard, Calabrese, Massimiliano, 2018. Inflammatory intrathecal profiles and cortical damage in multiple sclerosis. Annals of Neurology 83 (4), 739–755.

Manca, Riccardo, Sharrack, Basil, Paling, David, Wilkinson, Iain D., Venneri, Annalena, 2018. Brain connectivity and cognitive processing speed in multiple sclerosis: A systematic review. Journal of the Neurological Sciences 388, 115–127.

Marzullo, Aldo, Kocevar, Gabriel, Stamile, Claudio, Durand-Dubief, Françoise, Terracina, Giorgio, Calimeri, Francesco, Sappey-Marinier, Dominique, 2019. Classification of multiple sclerosis clinical profiles via graph convolutional neural networks. Frontiers in Neuroscience 13, 594.

Miller, D.H., Thompson, A.J., Filippi, M., 2003. Magnetic resonance studies of abnormalities in the normal appearing white matter and grey matter in multiple sclerosis. Journal of Neurology 250 (12), 1407–1419.

Montavon, Grégoire, Samek, Wojciech, Müller, Klaus-Robert, 2018. Methods for interpreting and understanding deep neural networks. Digital Signal Processing 73, 1–15.

Nourbakhsh, Bardia, Mowry, Ellen M., 2019. Multiple sclerosis risk factors and pathogenesis. Continuum: Lifelong Learning in Neurology 25 (3), 596–610.

Paszke, Adam, Gross, Sam, Chintala, Soumith, Chanan, Gregory, Yang, Edward, DeVito, Zachary, Lin, Zeming, Desmaison, Alban, Antiga, Luca, Lerer, Adam, 2017. Automatic differentiation in PyTorch. In: Conference on Neural Information Processing Systems (NIPS).

Penny, William D., Friston, Karl J., Ashburner, John T., Kiebel, Stefan J., Nichols, Thomas E., 2011. Statistical Parametric Mapping: The Analysis of Functional Brain Images. Elsevier.

Popescu, Veronica, Agosta, Federica, Hulst, Hanneke E., Sluimer, Ingrid C., Knol, Dirk L., Sormani, Maria Pia, Enzinger, Christian, Ropele, Stefan, Alonso, Julio, Sastre-Garriga, Jaume, Rovira, Alex, Montalban, Xavier, Bodini, Benedetta, Ciccarelli, Olga, Khaleeli, Zhaleh, Chard, Declan T., Matthews, Lucy, Palace, Jaqueline, Giorgio, Antonio, De Stefano, Nicola, Eisele, Philipp, Gass, Achim, Polman, Chris H., Uitdehaag, Bernard M.J., Messina, Maria Jose, Comi, Giancarlo, Filippi, Massimo, Barkhof, Frederik, Vrenken, Hugo, 2013. Brain atrophy and lesion load predict long term disability in multiple sclerosis. Journal of Neurology, Neurosurgery and Psychiatry 84 (10), 1082–1091.

Ribeiro, Marco Tulio, Singh, Sameer, Guestrin, Carlos, 2016. "Why should I trust you?" Explaining the predictions of any classifier. In: Proceedings of the 22nd ACM SIGKDD International Conference on Knowledge Discovery and Data Mining, pp. 1135–1144.

Rieke, Johannes, Eitel, Fabian, Weygandt, Martin, Haynes, John-Dylan, Ritter, Kerstin, 2018. Visualizing convolutional networks for MRI-based diagnosis of Alzheimer's disease. In: Understanding and Interpreting Machine Learning in Medical Image Computing Applications. Springer, pp. 24–31.

Samek, Wojciech, Montavon, Grégoire, Lapuschkin, Sebastian, Anders, Christopher J., Müller, Klaus-Robert, 2021. Explaining deep neural networks and beyond: A review of methods and applications. Proceedings of the IEEE 109 (3), 247–278.

Schmidt, Paul, Gaser, Christian, Arsic, Milan, Buck, Dorothea, Förschler, Annette, Berthele, Achim, Hoshi, Muna, Ilg, Rüdiger, Schmid, Volker J., Zimmer, Claus, et al., 2012. An automated tool for detection of flair-hyperintense white-matter lesions in multiple sclerosis. NeuroImage 59 (4), 3774–3783.

Selvaraju, Ramprasaath R., Cogswell, Michael, Das, Abhishek, Vedantam, Ramakrishna, Parikh, Devi, Batra, Dhruv, 2017. Grad-CAM: Visual explanations from deep networks via gradient-based localization. In: Proceedings of the IEEE International Conference on Computer Vision, pp. 618–626.

Shrikumar, Avanti, Greenside, Peyton, Kundaje, Anshul, 2017. Learning important features through propagating activation differences. arXiv preprint. arXiv:1704.02685.

Simonyan, Karen, Vedaldi, Andrea, Zisserman, Andrew, 2013. Deep inside convolutional networks: Visualising image classification models and saliency maps. arXiv preprint. arXiv:1312.6034.

Simonyan, Karen, Vedaldi, Andrea, Zisserman, Andrew, 2014. Deep inside convolutional networks: Visualising image classification models and saliency maps. In: Workshop at International Conference on Learning Representations. Citeseer.

Simonyan, Karen, Zisserman, Andrew, 2014. Very deep convolutional networks for large-scale image recognition. arXiv preprint. arXiv:1409.1556.

Springenberg, Jost Tobias, Dosovitskiy, Alexey, Brox, Thomas, Riedmiller, Martin, 2014. Striving for simplicity: The all convolutional net. arXiv preprint. arXiv:1412.6806.

Steenwijk, Martijn D., Geurts, Jeroen J.G., Daams, Marita, Tijms, Betty M., Wink, Alle Meije, Balk, Lisanne J., Tewarie, Prejaas K., Uitdehaag, Bernard M.J., Barkhof, Frederik, Vrenken, Hugo, et al., 2016. Cortical atrophy patterns in multiple sclerosis are non-random and clinically relevant. Brain 139 (1), 115–126.

Studholme, Colin, Hill, Derek L.G., Hawkes, David J., 1999. An overlap invariant entropy measure of 3D medical image alignment. Pattern Recognition 32 (1), 71–86.

Wang, Shui-Hua, Tang, Chaosheng, Sun, Junding, Yang, Jingyuan, Huang, Chenxi, Phillips, Preetha, Zhang, Yu-Dong, 2018. Multiple sclerosis identification by 14-layer convolutional neural network with batch normalization, dropout, and stochastic pooling. Frontiers in Neuroscience 12.

Xie, Ning, Ras, Gabrielle, van Gerven, Marcel, Doran, Derek, 2020. Explainable deep learning: A field guide for the uninitiated. arXiv preprint. arXiv:2004.14545.

Zeiler, Matthew D., Fergus, Rob, 2014. Visualizing and understanding convolutional networks. In: European Conference on Computer Vision. Springer, pp. 818–833.

Zhang, Yongyue, Brady, J. Michael, Smith, Stephen, 2000. Hidden Markov random field model for segmentation of brain MR image. In: Medical Imaging 2000: Image Processing, vol. 3979. International Society for Optics and Photonics, pp. 1126–1137.

Zhang, Hao, Chen, Jiayi, Xue, Haotian, Zhang, Quanshi, 2019. Towards a unified evaluation of explanation methods without ground truth. arXiv preprint. arXiv:1911.09017.

Zhang, Yunyan, Hong, Daphne, McClement, Daniel, Oladosu, Olayinka, Pridham, Glen, Slaney, Garth, 2021. Grad-CAM helps interpret the deep learning models trained to classify multiple sclerosis types using clinical brain magnetic resonance imaging. Journal of Neuroscience Methods 353, 109098.

Zhang, Yu-Dong, Pan, Chichun, Sun, Junding, Tang, Chaosheng, 2018. Multiple sclerosis identification by convolutional neural network with dropout and parametric ReLU. Journal of Computational Science 28, 1–10.

Zintgraf, Luisa M., Cohen, Taco S., Adel, Tameem, Welling, Max, 2017. Visualizing deep neural network decisions: Prediction difference analysis. arXiv preprint. arXiv:1702.04595.

CHAPTER 7

Explanation of CNN image classifiers with hiding parts

Oleksii Gorokhovatskyi[a]**, Olena Peredrii**[a]**, Volodymyr Gorokhovatskyi**[b]**, and Nataliia Vlasenko**[a]

[a]Simon Kuznets Kharkiv National University of Economics, Department of Informatics and Computer Engineering, Kharkiv, Ukraine
[b]Kharkiv National University of Radio Electronics, Department of Informatics, Kharkiv, Ukraine

Chapter points

- The goal of the research is to create a method to search for explanations of the black-box model with perturbation of images using hidden parts.
- The idea of complementary images as an explanation pair is described.
- The idea to evaluate the quality of black-box models in terms of explainability is proposed.

7.1. Introduction

Artificial neural networks (ANNs) and, especially, convolutional neural networks (CNNs) are used to solve a lot of artificial intelligence (AI) problems in computer vision, pattern recognition, and image processing domains. The application of deep neural networks often allows achieving the state-of-the-art or at least very good results.

The black-box nature of the neural network (NN) concept is one of the most severe drawbacks. ANNs can help to deal with a great variety of different problems effectively, but they are almost nonexplainable in terms of human language (Gunning and Aha, 2019).

The lack of interpretability of AI methods generates a trust problem, which is about whether a responsible person could trust automatic processing results. This problem becomes more acute in case we are talking about sensitive environments, like the identification of a person, medical diagnostic and health care, safety, and security, etc.

Interpretability of the model may help control the fairness of its usage, e.g., whether this model takes into account only those features it should, but not some accidental ones.

There are various opinions (sometimes philosophic) related to understanding and usage of the "explainability" and "interpretability" terms in the scope of our topic (Gunning and Aha, 2019; Gilpin et al., 2018; Johnson, 2020; Rudin, 2019), and in a lot of cases they are used interchangeably. From our point of view, "interpretability" makes more common sense (e.g., when the causality and data flow for the work of the entire

Explainable Deep Learning AI
https://doi.org/10.1016/B978-0-32-396098-4.00013-2
125

model is clear) compared to "explainability" (which allows us to understand only the probable cause for the decision being made). In this chapter, we talk about the search for the local explanation of the particular black-box decision in a human-friendly form.

Explainability is often classified also as model-specific or model-agnostic. The first type depends on the model (or the set of similar models) and uses specific features of the model to find explanations. Model-agnostic approaches do not depend on the model type, e.g., perturbation-based methods which change the input of the model and verify its output may be applied to the model of any type (Molnar, 2019).

Recently the usage of AI systems became the subject of regulations, e.g., General Data Protection Regulation (GDPR) (The European Union, 2016; Gorokhovatskyi et al., 2020; Wachter et al., 2017), introduced in the European Union in 2016 and implemented in 2018, guarantees the right to have a local explanation about the logic involved in automatic decision-making systems. The authors of the Montreal Declaration of responsible AI development proposed such interpretability statement (Université de Montréal, 2018): "The decisions made by AIS affecting a person's life, quality of life, or reputation should always be justifiable in a language that is understood by the people who use them or who are subjected to the consequences of their use. Justification consists in making transparent the most important factors and parameters shaping the decision, and should take the same form as the justification we would demand of a human making the same kind of decision". Finally, policy guidelines on Artificial Intelligence, which contain the "Transparency and Explainability" chapter, were adopted by OECD and partner countries in May 2019 (OECD, 2019).

There is also an interesting research (Rudin, 2019) that raises the questions about the accuracy of explanations and trust to them, the absence of correspondence between explanation and model it is trying to explain, and proposes the idea of using interpretable models instead of search for the explanations for the black-box ones.

In this chapter, we are searching for a simple and effective way to explain the CNN classification result in a form of a pair of images that confidently shows the importance of particular parts of the initial image for decision making.

The chapter is organized as follows. Section 7.2 includes the review of existing explanation approaches and methods. Section 7.3 describes the recursive division method, complementary images definition, and implementation details. The value to estimate the quality of CNN in terms of explainability is then proposed in Section 7.4. Section 7.5 contains the description of the main experimental modeling results, such as neural network architectures used for different classification problems, the results of estimation of the explanation quality values for them, also some examples of the application of the proposed method are included. Finally, the chapter ends with the conclusion in Section 7.6.

7.2. Explanation methods

There are different approaches to build explanations for black-box CNN models (Du et al., 2019; Petsiuk et al., 2018; Wagner et al., 2019; Zhang and Zhu, 2018).

The first class of methods involves backpropagation. They are used to measure the importance or influence of each pixel on the common classification result using the investigation of how a signal propagates back (Springenberg et al., 2015; Simonyan et al., 2014; Zeiler and Fergus, 2014). Backpropagation of the gradient is usually performed, followed by visualization of its magnitudes, the larger values of which show the more important features/pixels in the initial image (Simonyan et al., 2014). Famous methods in this field are SmoothGrad (Smilkov et al., 2017), DeepLift (Shrikumar et al., 2017), Integrated Gradients (Sundararajan et al., 2017), etc.

The second family of methods used is activation-based. They use linear combinations of convolutional layers' activations (Wagner et al., 2019). Class Activation Mapping (CAM) that allows visualizing the part of an image which is important for the particular classification is proposed in Zhou et al. (2016), the generalized versions of CAM were produced in Du et al. (2018); Selvaraju et al. (2017).

Both sets of methods described above are model-specific or require the building of additional supporting models.

In this chapter, we focus on the perturbation-based method. It allows finding model-agnostic local explanations without the utilizing of signal backpropagation or involving/analysis of the model's architecture. The idea of perturbation-based methods is the modification of input signal/image (often with hiding of some of its parts) followed by the investigation of how these changes influence classification result.

LIME (Local Interpretable Model-Agnostic Explanations) (Gorokhovatskyi et al., 2020; Ribeiro, 2016; Ribeiro et al., 2016) and SHAP (SHapley Additive exPlanations) (Lundberg and Lee, 2017; Molnar, 2019; Lundberg and Lee, 2022) are amongst the most famous perturbation methods used to search for interpretations. LIME uses the construction of a separate explainable model that uses points in a local neighborhood of the input features vector as a training set. The issues of this approach relate to the need to select some limited quantity of initial features and the overall instability (Molnar, 2019).

Superpixel analysis was applied in LIME (Ribeiro, 2016; Ribeiro et al., 2016) to search for explanations about the influence of separate parts of an image on the classification result. However, the effective selection of separate superpixels and combinations of them are unclear, except for the brute force method.

Dabkowski and Gal (2017), Seo et al. (2020), and Zhou et al. (2015) refer to iterative replacing of some image fragments preserving their mean color, but this method is computationally expensive.

"What-If" tool (Wexler, 2018), presented by Google, demonstrates the search for the counterfactuals approach. One of its functions is the search of the closest vector from the existing dataset that requires minimal changes and represents another class.

The occlusion of input image parts with a gray square is used for the researching and visualizing of the activity in the intermediate layers of the deep neural network (Zeiler and Fergus, 2014).

The generation of random occlusion masks (RISE – Randomized Input Sampling for Explanation of Black-Box Models) to measure the importance of each pixel in the overall decision is proposed in Petsiuk et al. (2018). The creation of perturbations with replacing with constant color, blurring, and noising is proposed in Fong and Vedaldi (2017). A comparison of hiding the image parts with superpixels versus grid masks, as well as the benefit of superpixels in terms of intersection over union, is shown in Seo et al. (2020). The generation of a superpixel score map visualization along with the interactive building of explanations when the user selects the superpixel is proposed in Wei et al. (2018).

Research of occlusion strategies is limited by hiding superpixels or rectangular parts of images with black/gray colors or blurring them. The performance of these approaches is not very high or is unclear. Additionally, it is also unknown whether the process of searching the explanations via brute force hiding of parts may fail, hence the probability of success is uncertain.

So, the most significant disadvantage of perturbation methods is the computational complexity. Another one is the chance that the perturbation changes in the initial image may involve new features significant for the model but not related to absence of these features (Dabkowski and Gal, 2017). For instance, we may perturb the initial image cautiously by hiding its parts with black color when black is the main feature color of some of the classes being classified by a model (Gorokhovatskyi and Peredrii, 2020, 2021).

Some of our previously presented results include:
-   measuring of the stability of the decision as well as searching for the explanations in the form of counterfactual cases in the neighborhood of the initial signal, which are proposed in Gorokhovatskyi et al. (2019);
-   research of different known image segmentation methods to form clusters in the image to create perturbation samples with hiding as well as research of different perturbation distortions and complementary images; this idea is shown in Gorokhovatskyi and Peredrii (2020);
-   research of the success explanation rate in the part analysis of the image, where it is shown that rate depends on the accuracy of the model and may be low even for models with good accuracy (Gorokhovatskyi et al., 2020);
-   image recursive division (RD) method and its application for the search of explanations of shallow CNN classification, shown in Gorokhovatskyi and Peredrii (2021).

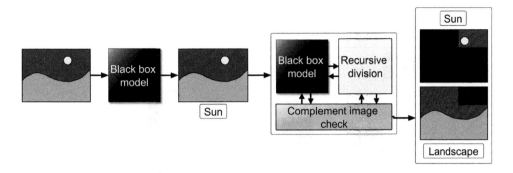

Figure 7.1 Searching for the explanations with recursive division.

7.3. Recursive division approach

The key idea of the chapter relates to the search for the explanation of the particular black-box classification result in the form of the pair of perturbation images (we call them complementary), generated from the initial one. The method includes the classification of the perturbed images built recursively from the image being classified by replacing some parts of it with black/white colors or blurring.

As a result of recursive division, we get a pair of complementary images with hidden parts, the first of which preserves both the most valuable parts and the classification result of the initial image. The second image represents the result of hiding the most valuable parts that leads to a different classification outcome. The entire idea is shown in Fig. 7.1.

7.3.1 Division

Let us investigate the way to find the most important parts of images that affect a certain classification decision without analyzing the image context (Gorokhovatskyi and Peredrii, 2021; Gorokhovatskyi et al., 2020). An example of such division process is shown in Fig. 7.2.

We denote by $O = B(I)$ the output vector that includes K elements (number of classes). This vector is the result of the classification of input image I by black-box model B. We refer to C as the decision class for image I.

We split the initial image I into $w \times h$ nonintersecting parts, where w is the number of horizontal parts, h is the number of vertical ones. Replacing each part with black color in turn, we obtain a set of images $\{I^{i,j}\}$, $i = \overline{1, w}$, $j = \overline{1, h}$. It is worth noting that the selection of color to hide a part should not affect classification results itself.

After that, we classify each perturbed image and retrieve output vector $\{o^{i,j}\}$ and classification results $\{c^{i,j}\}$. We compare each result $c^{i,j}$ with the initial one C, looking for

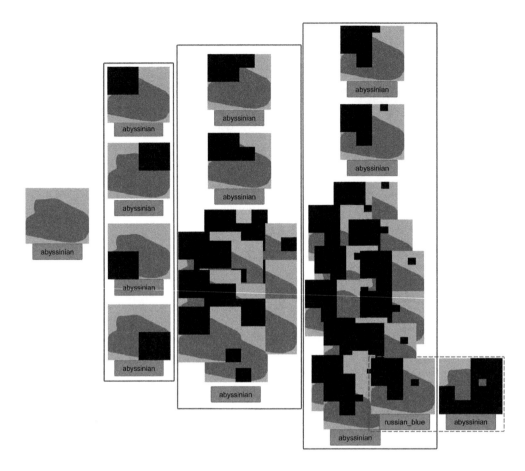

Figure 7.2 Recursive division process.

mismatches. If mismatches are found, the corresponding complementary $I - I^{i,j}$ images are formed and verified.

All four perturbation images created at the first division stage (Fig. 7.2, first column) were classified as "abyssinian." If all classification results $c^{i,j}$ are the same as the initial C, we reassign the initial image as

$$I^* = I^{i^* j^*}, \quad (i^*, j^*) = \underset{i,j}{\operatorname{argmax}}\, d(o^{i,j}, O), \tag{7.1}$$

where d is the distance between vectors (e.g., Euclidean), and divide image again into w^* horizontal parts and h^* vertical ones. For this particular abstract example, the first image out of four perturbed after the first stage has been chosen as a base for the next stage. Perturbed images for it are shown in the second column of Fig. 7.2.

At the next division stage, we see that one image exists, that is classified differently as a "russian_blue" representative. In this case, we immediately build and classify its complementary image. If the classification result corresponds to the initial one ("abyssinian"), we are done and an explanation in the form of the complementary image pair (CIP) is found. If there are several such pairs we may leave only the most reliable one or return all of them. For this particular example (Fig. 7.2), only the first CIP was found (early stop).

During this processing, we may face the case when a successful combination of an image with hidden parts and the complementary one is absent (both classification results are of the same classes, not opposite ones). In this situation, we give one more chance with the division of the most suitable (the farthest from the initial classification result) part of the image again to find more explanations. This allowed increasing the number of successful explanations up to 20% (Gorokhovatskyi and Peredrii, 2021).

There is no sense to process very small parts of images, so searching for explanations is stopped if either width or height of a part is less than 32 pixels. The visual quality of explanations found may vary depending on initial w and h, as well as on w^* and h^* used on deeper division levels.

Comparing to our previous works (Gorokhovatskyi and Peredrii, 2020, 2021; Gorokhovatskyi et al., 2020), the current modification of the RD approach includes early stopping implementation.

7.3.2 Complementary images

Our idea in showing the explanation for the particular image classification by the particular CNN model is the forming of two complementary images (CIP – complementary images pair). From our point of view, having a single image with the parts which are important for its classification is not enough. The motivation for this is that if the part of an image is important for the classification, this does not guarantee that the other parts are not important enough to ensure a successful classification result.

Let us assume that we have some black-box classifier and we used it to predict the class for some initial image; the classification result has the label of class L. Our goal is to find such complementary images (created with perturbations from the initial one), the first of which is still classified as L, but the second is classified as not L. Both these images should have different parts hidden in the same way, and each part of the initial image may be hidden only in one of the complementary parts. The common algorithm with early stopping (searching for only the first pair of complementary images) may be presented in such a form (Gorokhovatskyi and Peredrii, 2020, 2021; Gorokhovatskyi et al., 2020):

1. Classify the initial image to search explanation for and get its class label L.
2. Generate perturbation image using some method (hiding with black, white, etc.).
3. Classify this perturbation image getting its class label L_c.

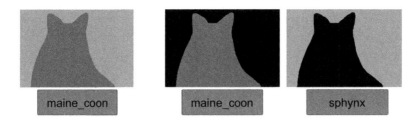

Figure 7.3 Complementary images' pair idea.

3.1. If $L_c = L$, return to step 2 (the perturbation may be changed, appended to the previous one, etc.).

3.2. If $L_c \neq L$, generate a complementary image to the initial perturbed and verify whether it is classified as class with the initial label L. If it is true, a complementary pair is found. If it is not, return back to step 2 (the perturbation may be changed, appended to the previous one, etc.).

4. If there is no such CIP found the algorithm fails. It means that all parts of the image are important for the classification or perturbation of image is not effective enough.

The example of CIP and classification labels are shown in Fig. 7.3. The initial abstract image has been classified as "maine_coon", two complementary images have been found. The first preserves the foreground and initial classification result, the second preserves background and has been classified differently ("sphynx" class label).

7.3.3 RD algorithm

So, the final steps to implement the recursive division parts' hiding may be described as follows.

Step 1. Prepare the black–box model and the test image to search for an explanation. We consider only the cases when this image is classified correctly with the current black–box model.

Step 2. Choose the way for the generation of perturbed images: hide parts with black or white color, or blurring. The additional blur strength parameter should be selected for the last approach. We used a value to make a significant blur in such a way so that part preserves only main colors and it is not easy to recognize its content by a human.

Step 3. Select hiding level parameters w and h for the first division level and w^* and h^* for next ones. We used mostly $w = h = w^* = h^* = 2$ and formed 4 parts (2×2) in the first level, 16 in the second, and so forth. If the width or the height of the part of an image is less than 32 pixels, we stop the processing.

Step 4. Divide the image for the first time, generate $w \times h$ perturbed images hiding a part in the initial one, and classify all of them with the initial black–box model.

Step 5. Search for such a perturbed image which has incorrect (assuming the test image was classified correctly in step 1) classification label compared to the initial one.

For each such image, build the complementary image and classify it. If the complementary image has the correct class label (the same as the initial test image), the explanation in the form of CIP is found. At this point, we stop the algorithm, but it is possible to continue in order to find more explanation CIPs.

Step 6. If there are no incorrect classification cases for the perturbed images after the first division or there is no CIP found, we move to the next step. Select one of the perturbed images with the correct class label (e.g., having the maximum absolute difference between current vector predictions and the correct class vector values) as the basic image for the next division stage with updated w and h values. In our experiments, we again divided each part into four fragments. Go to step 4 and generate perturbed images again.

Step 7. If the algorithm fails to find a CIP with the steps above, choose again the most suitable perturbed image with a correct class label from the last division stage and use it to generate a new perturbed image with $w = h = 2$. Go to step 4 again.

Step 8. At this step, the algorithm fails. This means that all parts of the test image may be important in the scope of the current classification result. We took this situation as it is in our experiments, but there are ways to continue searching for the CIP in this case, too.

7.4. Quality of the model

There are some typical ways to estimate the quality of the created neural network model. The easiest one includes the calculation of the classification accuracy for the test dataset that is usually supplemented by the confusion matrix. But this will not work well for imbalanced datasets when the quantity of train/test items differs significantly for different classes. Additionally, the analysis of the confusion matrix, which is done mostly manually, may not be convenient for the case when the quantity of classes is more than 20. There are also F-scores and ROC (receiver operating characteristic) curves to estimate the quality of the model numerically or visually.

All the above-mentioned approaches estimate the quality of the model using only the final classification results which do not allow us to understand whether the classification has been performed based on the correct reasoning. That is why it is possible to have such models that have good quality in terms of accuracy but bad explainability due to unknown internal biases.

One of the possible ways to estimate the quality of the black-box classifier in terms of explainability is the hiding parts' strategy. It allows us to understand whether really important parts of the image matter for the classification result. It is possible to implement this verification automatically if the data with ground-truth labeling (e.g., in the form of bounding boxes or binary masks) for the dataset exist.

In the estimation of the quality in terms of the explainability, we will use the explanation success rate (ESR) that is calculated according to

$$ESR = \frac{N_s}{N},\qquad(7.2)$$

where N is the total number of correctly classified images in the train/test dataset parts, N_s is the number of correctly classified test images we successfully found a pair of CIPs for.

So, in the scope of a particular CNN and the dataset, ESR value shows how many correctly classified test images have a correct explanation in the form of the CIP. We think this value may be useful in the entire process of the CNN quality estimation along with the total accuracy value.

7.5. Experimental modeling

This section includes the information about the experiments we performed in order to explore the usage of the proposed RD approach.

Sections 7.5.1–7.5.3 include the information about datasets and CNN models which were used. There are also details about the training process and quality for each CNN.

The analysis about using ESR as a CNN quality value is shown in Section 7.5.4. Section 7.5.5 includes a comparison of ESR values for different ways to split an image into parts to hide them including RD and image clustering methods. Section 7.5.6 contains a comparison of explanation quality for two RD and LIME methods in terms of intersection over union. Finally, Section 7.5.7 contains a short comparison of timings for previously presented in Gorokhovatskyi and Peredrii (2021) and current RD versions, and Section 7.5.8 shows the use cases of RD.

7.5.1 CNN for The Oxford-IIIT Pet Dataset

We used The Oxford-IIIT Pet Dataset (Parkhi et al., 2012a,b), which contains 37 classes of cats' (12) and dogs' (25) breeds with nearly 200 images per class (7393 images in total) to estimate the quality of the black-box model. Each image has an associated ground-truth annotation of breed, region of interest containing the head, and background/foreground/undefined pixel masks. All images are of different sizes, positioning, and scene conditions.

We have changed the initial training/validation split from 1846/1834 images to 3310/370, leaving only 10 first validation images for each class from the initial validation set. The test set contained 3669 images.

Our convolutional model has been built from two parts. The first included feature extraction for each image, and we used DenseNet201 (Huang et al., 2017) CNN with weights that were trained on ImageNet but without output layers. At the top of this, we added one flatten layer and batch normalization layer. After that, a dense layer containing 512 neurons, with ReLU activation function followed by a dropout (with 0.5 probability) layer, was added. A final batchnorm layer, followed by output 37 neurons with softmax activation function, was applied. All images at the preprocessing stage were scaled to 300×300 pixels.

The training of the model has been performed using Adam optimizer with 500 iterations with an early stop procedure that stopped after 50 iterations without validation dataset accuracy improving and saving only the best model weights.

The accuracy we achieved on the test set was 0.8817. Compared to the state-of-the-art results, this is not so high, but sufficient for such a straightforward model we have used.

Looking at the confusion matrix, we may notice that the accuracy for "american_pit_bull_terrier" class is only 0.45, this is the lowest value amongst all classes. Seven classes have accuracy in the range 0.68–0.8, 8 classes in the range 0.81–0.9; and 21 classes have accuracy of more than 0.9. The Gini index of this distribution is 0.07, with an average accuracy of 0.88 per class.

7.5.2 CNN for food and crack datasets

We built and tested another CNN that contained 8 layers only (Gorokhovatskyi and Peredrii, 2021). There were two convolutional layers ($32 \times 3 \times 3$) with ReLU activation function, two maxpooling (2×2) layers after each of these. This feature–detection part of the CNN followed by a dropout (0.25) layer, dense ReLU layer that contained 512 neurons, dropout (0.25) again, and the last output layer containing only 2 sigmoid neurons (as we talk about binary classification datasets in this section).

The initial images for this CNN have been rescaled down to 64×64 pixels, Adam optimizer was used, and batch size during training was set to 128 images.

Keras (Chollet, 2015) software with different backends (Theano, Tensorflow) was used for the experimental modeling.

7.5.2.1 Food-5K dataset

Food-5K dataset (Singla et al., 2016) that contains 2500 food and 2500 nonfood images was used for training of the shallow 8-layer model described above. In total, 3000 images were used for training, while testing and validation sets contained 1000 images each. Learning of the network has been stopped after 30 epochs, achieving an accuracy of 99.6% on the test set (according to Singla et al. (2016), fine-tuned GoogLeNet (22 layered CNN) reaches 99.2% accuracy).

7.5.2.2 UEC FOOD 100/256 dataset

UEC FOOD 100 dataset (Matsuda et al., 2012a,b) contains 14361 images and bounding-box ground-truth information about food location. Some images contain multiple food items or repeat in different folders, so we removed them from analysis to preserve correct comparison. In total, 10067 images from this dataset were used. Classification accuracy for UEC FOOD 100 dataset was 81.6% (11720 images were classified as food).

UEC FOOD 256 dataset (Kawano and Yanai, 2015, 2014) contains 31395 food images (27043 unique ones). The classification accuracy of the model was 87.57% (27495 "food" results).

7.5.2.3 Crack dataset

This dataset (Özgenel and Sorguç, 2018; Zhang et al., 2016) contains 20000 images without cracks and 20000 images with cracks. We split initial images into three parts: 14000 were used for training, and 3000 for validation and testing, respectively. The same shallow net described above has been trained, achieving an accuracy of 98.1% on the test set.

The Crack images dataset does not contain ground-truth labels, so we generated them for the "positive" part of the dataset (we used Otsu thresholding followed by inverting Gorokhovatskyi and Peredrii (2021)).

7.5.3 CNN for image scene classification problem dataset

We trained one more convolutional neural network to solve the Image Scene Classification problem (Intel image classification, 2019). There are six classes in this dataset: building, forest, glacier, mountain, sea, and street. The training part of the dataset contains 14034 images (approximately from 2100 to 3500 images per class), the testing part contains 3000 images with approximately the same quantity, representing different classes. All images are 150 by 150 pixels.

We applied the transfer learning model here (as well as for The Oxford-IIIT Pet Dataset), our model included the VGG16 network (Simonyan and Zisserman, 2015) pretrained on the ImageNet dataset as the feature extraction part. Additionally, we added two fully connected layers: the first contained 50 ReLU neurons and the last output layer had 6 neurons with a sigmoid activation function. The additional dropout layer that ignores 50% of random neurons was added in-between these two dense layers.

The training of this model has been performed with Adam optimizer according to the following partial procedure. We reduced the size of the images to 128×128 pixels, split the initial training set into parts with 2000 images in each. After that, we trained the model over 15 epochs with 32 images in a batch for each this part in turn. The training time was about 50 minutes, the accuracy of this network was 0.9230 for the training set and 0.8697 for the testing one. The confusion matrix showed (Gorokhovatskyi and Peredrii, 2020) that the best accuracy per class is 0.968 for the "forest" class. The worst case (accuracy of 0.8) was for the "glacier" class which was classified as "mountain" in 16% of cases.

Table 7.1 The ESR for the background/foreground and head bounding boxes hiding.

	Black hiding	White hiding	Blur
Train part (3310 images)			
Background	0.7568	0.7556	0.3414
Head	0.2204	0.2361	0.0836
Test part (3669 images)			
Background	0.8451	0.8646	0.5829

7.5.4 The quality of black-box model

Let us look at the implementation of the model quality evaluation approach, described in Section 7.4 above. The Oxford-IIIT Pet Dataset (Parkhi et al., 2012b,a) contains background/foreground/undefined ground-truth pixel masks for all images in it, but regions with animal heads are present only for train and validation images, but not for the test part of the dataset. So, we performed the head region importance analysis for only the train part. The "undefined" pixel mask was included in the "foreground" mask in our experiments.

We tested three different hiding approaches using black and white color, as well as Gaussian blur with the kernel size of 45, to distort the region significantly (Gorokhovatskyi and Peredrii, 2020). We skipped images that were not classified by model correctly (434 for test set).

The testing of each image was performed in two steps. We applied the distortion (with black, white, or blur) to the background part of the image according to its ground-truth mask. In this case, we expected that the initial classification would remain the same because background should not be important. Then we checked the opposite case: we hid only the foreground mask of the image with the same distortion and verified whether the classification result changed (that meant the foreground part was really important). The experiment with this particular image was successful only in case both these conditions were met. The same approach for measuring the importance of the head bounding box was applied.

Common results are shown in Table 7.1. As one can see, at least 75% of the experiments were successful when covered with black and white. At most 23% were successful with the hiding of regions with animal heads, but this can be explained easily just because the head area is much smaller than the background/foreground of the entire image. The blurring of parts of an image is not so helpful in searching for explanations.

The distribution of all images for train/test parts of the dataset for different hiding methods is shown in Fig. 7.4. The yellow circle shows the size of all train images we have tried to process. The red circle shows the images which were explained with hiding of background/foreground with black color, green shows the same for white color, and blue shows the cases with blurring. In total, 490 of train samples (14.8%) were not

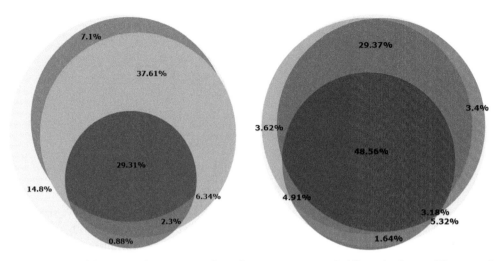

Figure 7.4 Split of the cases with explanations found for train/test parts with different background/foreground hiding methods: yellow shows all images, red presents images explained with black hiding, green gives those with white hiding, while blue shows those obtained with blurring. Diagrams were created based on Hulsen et al. (2008).

possible to explain with any of the hiding approaches (black, white, and blur); 2215 images (66.91%) were successfully explained with both black and white hiding at the same time, 29 images (0.88%) were explained by blurring only.

The analysis of the ESR for each separate class shows that both for train and test set, as well as for black, white hiding and blurring of background/foreground, "Sphynx" class is not possible to explain with perturbation images (ESR < 0.1). At the same time, classification accuracy for this class is 95%.

It is interesting to note that hiding with white color is much more effective than hiding with black for the "Bombay" class, and the reason is that all cats of this bread are black in all test/train images. The situation is the opposite for the "great_pyrenees" when hiding with black color is more successful and all species of this dog breed are white in the dataset.

Gini indices for the train set vary from 0.133 to 0.253 for different black/white/blur distortions with average $ESR = 0.75$ per class for black/white and $ESR = 0.34$ for blur. Corresponding indices for the test set are in the range 0.076–0.148 having an average $ESR = 0.85$ per class for black/white and $ESR = 0.59$ for blur.

We compared ESR values from Table 7.1 with those calculated for two other neural networks we have trained in a similar way. Test accuracies for these nets were 0.8860 and 0.8814 (compared to the 0.8817 value for the first net discussed above). ESR results for all three nets are similar and differ only by 2–3%. Using several such nets may help in finding more explanations because results of some nets' classification may be successfully explained for some images but failed for others. For example, for the case with hiding background of an image with black color 84.51% of images were explained with the first net (Table 7.1), but 90% were explained with at least one of the three nets we used for the comparison.

7.5.5 Explanation success rate for different clustering methods

We compared (Gorokhovatskyi and Peredrii, 2020) the *ESR* level for the Image Scene Classification problem for different image partition methods: K-means, mean shift, SLIC, DBSCAN, and the proposed recursive hiding parts. We calculated the *ESR* value for all the above-mentioned methods, trying to find explanations in a form of complementary images. We considered only hiding or changing just one part of the image, not a combination of both. For example, if there were 5 clusters in an image, we took into account 5 perturbation images with some cluster hidden or replaced in it, but not all combinations of tuples, triples, etc., of hidden parts.

While comparing ESR values, we controlled the real quantity of clusters for all methods because, e.g., the searching for explanation makes no sense when cluster count is equal to 1 (this means hiding the entire image but not its part). So we put such parameters in all methods, that allowed us to create at least 3 clusters.

The results of such a comparison showed that SLIC seems to be the most successful, but it is difficult to control it with the number of superpixels. The best $ESR = 0.5$ has been achieved for 4 superpixels, but only 327 images had exactly 4 superpixels, 750 contained 3 superpixels, and more than 1500 contained 1 or 2 superpixels.

It is worth noting that the recursive hiding approach shows a very different *ESR* value when the image is split vertically ($ESR = 0.36$) and horizontally ($ESR = 0.82$) at the first stage, but this may refer to this particular dataset though.

The results of hiding with white color instead of black are a bit worse (*ESR* values were smaller) but all trends for all methods are stable (Gorokhovatskyi and Peredrii, 2020).

The experiments for the last type of hiding parts – blurring – showed the effectiveness of the recursive approach. We compared (Gorokhovatskyi and Peredrii, 2020) *ESR* results for different methods using Gaussian blurring with square kernels, from 3×3 to 61×61. The results with the big kernel are the most interesting because such cases distort the parts of an image in such a way that makes it complex for a human to classify.

Again, the SLIC method with 4 clusters allowed achieving the maximum value of $ESR = 0.36$. But the average quantity of superpixels was only 2.28, so we analyzed the SLIC method that forms 6 clusters (in reality, only 3.07 on average). In this case $ESR = 0.31$, which is less than for the recursive hiding approach that brings $ESR = 0.34$ ($w = h = 2$, $w^* = h^* = 2$).

So, for the significant level of blur, recursive hiding of parts outperforms all methods except for SLIC for 4 superpixels.

7.5.6 Quality of explanation: LIME vs RD

To understand the dependency of explanation quality on different input variables, we performed LIME (Ribeiro, 2021) explanation with 3, 5, and 10 features (with 1000 building samples in LIME default model) and varied w, h, w^*, h^* values for RD.

We took into account only explanation attempts that successfully generate complementary images as an explanation output (as described above) and considered only images that were explained successfully with both methods being compared.

The summarized results for different input parameters, methods, and options are shown in Table 7.2. The quality of explanation is used in terms of pixelwise intersection over union (IOU) between ground-truth valuable bounding boxes and our explanations by complementary images.

The first four rows (experiments #1–4) contain a comparison of average IOU values for the explanations obtained with the LIME 3-features model and RD models with different parts quantity. For example, line #1 shows the average IOU value for LIME and RD when at each processing stage we split the previous image into four parts ($w = h = w^* = h^* = 2$), two vertical and two horizontal ones. As one can see, LIME has a bigger IOU value, which means it showed better results. In total, 6774 images were explained successfully by both methods for this case. In 53% of cases, the explanation provided by LIME was better.

Varying the number of LIME features (5 features were used for experiments #5–8, 10 features for #9–12) made almost no difference. It looks like the increase of the number of features for LIME decreases its average IOU values.

We used LIME configuration with 5 features to explore UEC FOOD 256 Dataset. RD parameters were set up to $w = h = w^* = h^* = 2$. In total, 21159 images were successfully explained by LIME, 21973 by RD, 15299 images were explained by both methods at the same time. LIME had an IOU value of 0.17 compared to ground-truth images, while RD had 0.1686. When we set RD options to $w = h = 3$, $w^* = h^* = 2$, we received average $AIOU_{LIME} = 0.1688$ and $AIOU_{RD} = 0.1863$ (12829 images were compared).

Experiments #13–15 contain the results for the Crack dataset. Superpixel-based explanation approaches are not applicable when parts of an image are hidden with black color. Hiding superpixels with black immediately leads to the classification of such image as "crack." So, in this case, we hid parts of images in RD with white color. As one can see, RD outperformed LIME in all cases.

7.5.7 Time performance

We measured the time required to perform RD analysis for our previous RD approach (Gorokhovatskyi and Peredrii, 2021) and for the updated one that used the early stop procedure. The previous implementation used to generate perturbation images and analyze them by division levels, so all perturbation images in each level were processed

Table 7.2 Quality Comparison of Explanations for LIME vs RD on different datasets with different options.

#	$AIOU_{LIME}$ (features)	$AIOU_{RD}$ (options)	Images compared
		UEC Food 100 dataset	
1	0.2129 (3)	0.1867 ($w = h = 2$, $w^* = h^* = 2$)	6774
2	0.2118 (3)	0.2161 ($w = h = 3$, $w^* = h^* = 2$)	4687
3	0.2156 (3)	0.1963 ($w = h = 2$, $w^* = h^* = 3$)	6302
4	0.2196 (3)	0.2237 ($w = h = 3$, $w^* = h^* = 3$)	3973
5	0.1935 (5)	0.1882 ($w = h = 2$, $w^* = h^* = 2$)	6480
6	0.1950 (5)	0.2174 ($w = h = 3$, $w^* = h^* = 2$)	4539
7	0.1970 (5)	0.1976 ($w = h = 2$, $w^* = h^* = 3$)	5537
8	0.2035 (5)	0.2244 ($w = h = 3$, $w^* = h^* = 3$)	3836
9	0.1923 (10)	0.1878 ($w = h = 2$, $w^* = h^* = 2$)	6439
10	0.1938 (10)	0.2167 ($w = h = 3$, $w^* = h^* = 2$)	4516
11	0.1959 (10)	0.1971 ($w = h = 2$, $w^* = h^* = 3$)	6302
12	0.2027 (10)	0.2238 ($w = h = 3$, $w^* = h^* = 3$)	3825
		Crack dataset	
13	0.3022 (3)	0.6534 ($w = h = 2$, $w^* = h^* = 2$)	806
14	0.3058 (5)	0.6559 ($w = h = 2$, $w^* = h^* = 2$)	755
15	0.2998 (10)	0.6544 ($w = h = 2$, $w^* = h^* = 2$)	777

even if the explanation was already found. The updated version stops generating perturbation images and processing immediately after the explanation result at some division level is found. According to time measurement for train and tests parts of the Oxford-IIIT Pet Dataset, the current implementation requires 30–40% less time compared to the previous one proposed in Gorokhovatskyi and Peredrii (2021).

7.5.8 Examples

Some interesting explanation examples are presented in Fig. 7.5. Initial images with a class label, as well as complementary image pairs with corresponding class labels, are shown, too.

The first row shows the result of the British shorthair image explanation with hiding using black color. It is interesting to note that the eye of the cat is an extremely important part. Almost the same parts of the image are important if we hide parts with white color, too.

Both explanations with hiding in black and white are shown for the next beagle image. As one can see, CIP in explanations shows the importance of the region with the head of a dog which is expected.

Figure 7.5 Complementary image pairs' examples.

The next image contains a miniature pinscher and both CIPs (for black and white hiding modes) confirmed that the region with the small dog matters.

The example with pomeranian shows the importance of the region with the head of a dog according to the complementary image pairs found both with black and white color hiding. Explanations obtained with both colors are very close for the next samoyed example too.

The last example shows the explanation results for the image with the Scottish terrier.

7.6. Conclusion

The building of interpretable models is a promising approach, which might make the embedding of artificial intelligence tools into sensitive data processing fields much easier.

We proposed the RD method to search for the explanation of the CNN image classifier. It is based on the building of the perturbation images (with hiding of parts) recursively. As a result, we have a pair of complementary images with hidden parts, the first of which preserves both the most valuable parts and the classification result of the initial image. The second image represents the result of hiding the most valuable parts that leads to a different classification result.

The RD method may be used to estimate the quality of the black-box NN classifier in terms of explainability in addition to the traditional model quality metrics like accuracy. This may help understand whether the model is probably stealthy biased, preserving high accuracy at the same time.

We performed a comparison of RD approach and the most popular LIME method based on superpixels. One of the benefits of recursive division is its performance while preserving the explanation quality at a level close to attainable by LIME. The improved RD version that includes an early stop procedure without the generation of perturbed images if the explanation is already found requires 30–40% less time. Additionally, RD is stable and reproducible.

The bottlenecks of the RD approach relate to the necessity of w, h, w^*, h^* parameters' selection, as well as the selection of the proper hide color and not very aesthetic view of visual explanations.

Acknowledgments

We would like to thank Nataly Krashchenko for the help with making test pictures and all other happy owners of wonderful pets which were patient enough to make great pictures.

We dedicate this chapter and thank the Army of Ukraine, all related Forces, and divisions, doctors, volunteers, everyone who stands for Ukraine. You had an enormous impact on the completion of this work. Proud to be Ukrainians.

References

Chollet, Francois, et al., 2015. Keras. GitHub, https://github.com/keras-team/keras. (Accessed 8 June 2021).

Dabkowski, Piotr, Gal, Yarin, 2017. Real time image saliency for black box classifiers. In: Proceedings of the 31st International Conference on Neural Information Processing Systems, NIPS'17. Curran Associates Inc., Red Hook, NY, USA, pp. 6970–6979.

Du, Mengnan, Liu, Ninghao, Hu, Xia, 2019. Techniques for interpretable machine learning. Communications of the ACM 63 (1), 68–77.

Du, Mengnan, Liu, Ninghao, Song, Qingquan, Hu, Xia, 2018. Towards explanation of DNN-based prediction with guided feature inversion. In: Guo, Yike, Farooq, Faisal (Eds.), Proceedings of the 24th ACM SIGKDD International Conference on Knowledge Discovery & Data Mining, KDD 2018. London, UK, 19–23 August, 2018. ACM, pp. 1358–1367.

The European Union, 2016. Regulation (EU) 2016/679 of the European Parliament and of the Council of 27 April 2016 on the Protection of Natural Persons with Regard to the Processing of Personal Data and on the Free Movement of Such Data, and Repealing Directive 95/46/EC (General Data Protection Regulation). Official Journal of the European Union (OJ L 119 4.5.2016, 1-88).

Fong, Ruth C., Vedaldi, A., 2017. Interpretable explanations of black boxes by meaningful perturbation. In: 2017 IEEE International Conference on Computer Vision (ICCV), pp. 3449–3457.

Gilpin, Leilani H., Bau, David, Yuan, Ben Z., Bajwa, Ayesha, Specter, Michael A., Kagal, Lalana, 2018. Explaining explanations: An overview of interpretability of machine learning. In: 2018 IEEE 5th International Conference on Data Science and Advanced Analytics (DSAA), pp. 80–89.

Gorokhovatskyi, Oleksii, Peredrii, Olena, 2020. Multiclass image classification explanation with the complement perturbation images. In: DSMP, pp. 275–287.

Gorokhovatskyi, Oleksii, Peredrii, Olena, 2021. Recursive division of image for explanation of shallow CNN models. In: Escalante, Hugo Jair, Vezzani, Roberto (Eds.), Alberto Del Bimbo, Rita Cucchiara, Stan Sclaroff, Giovanni Maria Farinella, Tao Mei, Marco Bertini. In: Pattern Recognition. ICPR International Workshops and Challenges. Springer International Publishing, Cham, pp. 274–286.

Gorokhovatskyi, Oleksii, Peredrii, Olena, Gorokhovatskyi, Volodymyr, 2020. Interpretability of neural network binary classification with part analysis. In: 2020 IEEE Third International Conference on Data Stream Mining Processing (DSMP), pp. 136–141.

Gorokhovatskyi, O., Peredrii, O., Zatkhei, V., Teslenko, O., 2019. Investigation of random neighborhood features for interpretation of MLP classification results. In: ISDMCI, pp. 581–596.

Gunning, David, Aha, David, 2019. DARPA's explainable artificial intelligence (XAI) program. AI Magazine 40 (2), 44–58.

Huang, Gao, Liu, Zhuang, Weinberger, Kilian Q., 2017. Densely connected convolutional networks. In: 2017 IEEE Conference on Computer Vision and Pattern Recognition (CVPR), pp. 2261–2269.

Hulsen, T., de Vlieg, J., Alkema, W., 2008. BioVenn – a web application for the comparison and visualization of biological lists using area-proportional Venn diagrams. BMC Genomics 9, 488. https://doi.org/10.1186/1471-2164-9-488.

Intel image classification. https://www.kaggle.com/puneet6060/intel-image-classification. (Accessed 13 February 2022).

Johnson, Jonathan, 2020. Interpretability vs explainability: The black box of machine learning. https://www.bmc.com/blogs/machine-learning-interpretability-vs-explainability/. (Accessed 8 June 2021).

Kawano, Y., Yanai, K., 2014. UECFOOD-256 dataset ver. 1.0. http://foodcam.mobi/dataset256.html. (Accessed 8 June 2021).

Kawano, Yoshiyuki, Yanai, Keiji, 2015. Automatic expansion of a food image dataset leveraging existing categories with domain adaptation. In: Agapito, L., Bronstein, M.M., Rother, C. (Eds.), Computer Vision – ECCV 2014 Workshops. Springer International Publishing, Cham, pp. 3–17.

Lundberg, Scott M., Lee, Su-In, 2017. A unified approach to interpreting model predictions. In: Guyon, I., Luxburg, U.V., Bengio, S., Wallach, H., Fergus, R., Vishwanathan, S., Garnett, R. (Eds.), Advances in Neural Information Processing Systems 30. Curran Associates, Inc., pp. 4765–4774.

Lundberg, Scott M., Lee, Su-In, 2022. SHAP (SHapley Additive exPlanations). https://github.com/slundberg/shap. (Accessed 26 July 2022).

Matsuda, Y., Hoashi, H., Yanai, K., 2012a. Recognition of multiple-food images by detecting candidate regions. In: Proc. of IEEE International Conference on Multimedia and Expo (ICME).

Matsuda, Y., Hoashi, H., Yanai, K., 2012b. UECFOOD-100 dataset ver. 1.0 (945 MB). http://foodcam.mobi/dataset100.html. (Accessed 8 June 2021).

Molnar, Christoph, 2019. Interpretable Machine Learning. https://christophm.github.io/interpretable-ml-book/.

OECD, Recommendation of the Council on Artificial Intelligence, OECD/LEGAL/0449, Forty-two countries adopt new OECD principles on artificial intelligence. https://www.oecd.org/science/forty-two-countries-adopt-new-oecd-principles-on-artificial-intelligence.htm. (Accessed 8 June 2021).

Özgenel, Ç.F., Sorguç, Arzu Gönenç, 2018. Performance comparison of pretrained convolutional neural networks on crack detection in buildings. In: Teizer, J. (Ed.), Proceedings of the 35th International Symposium on Automation and Robotics in Construction (ISARC). Taipei, Taiwan. International Association for Automation and Robotics in Construction (IAARC), pp. 693–700.

Parkhi, O.M., Vedaldi, A., Zisserman, A., Jawahar, C.V., 2012a. The Oxford-IIIT pet dataset. https://www.robots.ox.ac.uk/~vgg/data/pets/. (Accessed 8 June 2021).

Parkhi, Omkar M., Vedaldi, Andrea, Zisserman, Andrew, Jawahar, C.V., 2012b. Cats and dogs. In: IEEE Conference on Computer Vision and Pattern Recognition, pp. 3498–3505.

Petsiuk, Vitali, Das, Abir, Saenko, Kate, 2018. RISE: Randomized input sampling for explanation of black-box models. In: BMVC.

Ribeiro, Marco Tulio, 2016. LIME – local interpretable model-agnostic explanations. https://homes.cs.washington.edu/~marcotcr/blog/lime/. (Accessed 8 June 2021).

Ribeiro, M.T., 2021. LIME. https://github.com/marcotcr/lime. (Accessed 8 June 2021).

Ribeiro, Marco Tulio, Singh, Sameer, Guestrin, Carlos, 2016. "Why should I trust you?": Explaining the predictions of any classifier. In: Proceedings of the 22nd ACM SIGKDD International Conference on Knowledge Discovery and Data Mining, KDD '16. Association for Computing Machinery, New York, NY, USA, pp. 1135–1144.

Rudin, Cynthia, 2019. Stop explaining black box machine learning models for high stakes decisions and use interpretable models instead. Nature Machine Intelligence 1 (5), 206–215.

Selvaraju, Ramprasaath R., Cogswell, Michael, Das, Abhishek, Vedantam, Ramakrishna, Parikh, Devi, Batra, Dhruv, 2017. Grad-CAM: Visual explanations from deep networks via gradient-based localization. In: 2017 IEEE International Conference on Computer Vision (ICCV), pp. 618–626.

Seo, Dasom, Oh, Kanghan, Oh, Il-Seok, 2020. Regional multi-scale approach for visually pleasing explanations of deep neural networks. IEEE Access 8, 8572–8582.

Shrikumar, Avanti, Greenside, Peyton, Kundaje, Anshul, 2017. Learning important features through propagating activation differences. In: Precup, Doina, Teh, Yee Whye (Eds.), Proceedings of the 34th International Conference on Machine Learning. In: Proceedings of Machine Learning Research, vol. 70. PMLR, pp. 3145–3153.

Simonyan, K., Vedaldi, A., Zisserman, Andrew, 2014. Deep inside convolutional networks: Visualising image classification models and saliency maps. CoRR. arXiv:1312.6034 [abs].

Simonyan, K., Zisserman, A., 2015. Very deep convolutional networks for large-scale image recognition. In: International Conference on Learning Representations (ICLR).

Singla, Ashutosh, Yuan, Lin, Ebrahimi, Touradj, 2016. Food/non-food image classification and food categorization using pre-trained GoogLeNet model. In: Proceedings of the 2nd International Workshop on Multimedia Assisted Dietary Management, MADiMa '16. Association for Computing Machinery, New York, NY, USA. ISBN 9781450345200, pp. 3–11. https://doi.org/10.1145/2986035.2986039.

Smilkov, D., Thorat, Nikhil, Kim, Been, Viégas, F., Wattenberg, M., 2017. SmoothGrad: removing noise by adding noise. arXiv:1706.03825 [abs].

Springenberg, J.T., Dosovitskiy, A., Brox, T., Riedmiller, M., 2015. Striving for simplicity: The all convolutional net. In: ICLR (Workshop Track).

Sundararajan, Mukund, Taly, Ankur, Yan, Qiqi, 2017. Axiomatic attribution for deep networks. In: Proceedings of the 34th International Conference on Machine Learning – Volume 70, ICML'17. JMLR.org, pp. 3319–3328.

Université de Montréal, 2018. The Montreal Declaration for a responsible development of artificial intelligence. https://www.montrealdeclaration-responsibleai.com/context. (Accessed 8 June 2021).

Wachter, Sandra, Mittelstadt, B., Russell, Chris, 2017. Counterfactual explanations without opening the black box: Automated decisions and the GDPR. Cybersecurity 31, 841–887.

Wagner, Jorg, Kohler, Jan Mathias, Gindele, Tobias, Hetzel, Leon, Wiedemer, Jakob Thaddaus, Behnke, Sven, 2019. Interpretable and fine-grained visual explanations for convolutional neural networks. In: 2019 IEEE/CVF Conference on Computer Vision and Pattern Recognition (CVPR), pp. 9097–9107.

Wei, Yi, Chang, Ming-Ching, Ying, Yiming, Lim, Ser Nam, Lyu, Siwei, 2018. Explain black-box image classifications using superpixel-based interpretation. In: 24th International Conference on Pattern Recognition (ICPR), pp. 1640–1645.

Wexler, James, 2018. The what-if tool: Code-free probing of machine learning models. https://ai.googleblog.com/2018/09/the-what-if-tool-code-free-probing-of.html. (Accessed 8 June 2021).

Zeiler, Matthew D., Fergus, Rob, 2014. Visualizing and understanding convolutional networks. In: Fleet, David, Pajdla, Tomas, Schiele, Bernt, Tuytelaars, Tinne (Eds.), Computer Vision – ECCV 2014. Springer International Publishing, Cham, pp. 818–833.

Zhang, Lei, Yang, Fan, Zhang, Yimin Daniel, Zhu, Ying Julie, 2016. Road crack detection using deep convolutional neural network. In: 2016 IEEE International Conference on Image Processing (ICIP), pp. 3708–3712.

Zhang, Quan-shi, Zhu, Song-chun, 2018. Visual interpretability for deep learning: A survey. Frontiers of Information Technology & Electronic Engineering 19 (1), 27–39.

Zhou, Bolei, Khosla, A., Lapedriza, À., Oliva, A., Torralba, A., 2015. Object detectors emerge in deep scene CNNs. CoRR. arXiv:1412.6856 [abs].

Zhou, Bolei, Khosla, Aditya, Lapedriza, Agata, Oliva, Aude, Torralba, Antonio, 2016. Learning deep features for discriminative localization. In: 2016 IEEE Conference on Computer Vision and Pattern Recognition (CVPR), pp. 2921–2929.

CHAPTER 8

Remove to improve?
Understanding CNN by pruning

Kamila Abdiyeva[a,b], Martin Lukac[b], and Narendra Ahuja[c]

[a]Nanyang Technological University, School of Electrical and Electronic Engineering, Singapore, Singapore
[b]Nazarbayev University, School of Engineering and Digital Sciences, Nur-Sultan, Kazakhstan
[c]University of Illinois at Urbana-Champaign, Department of Electrical and Computer Engineering, Urbana, IL, United States

Chapter points

- the study on how different class-specific filter groups affect each other;
- an experimental demonstration that class-wise based pruning can lead to classification accuracy improvement for selected set of classes.

8.1. Introduction

Convolutional Neural Networks (CNNs) provide solutions to a range of problems, from computer vision (Ouyang et al., 2015; Wang et al., 2016; Lin et al., 2017; Hu et al., 2019; Zhou et al., 2014; Ren and Li, 2015; Girshick et al., 2014; Husain et al., 2017), raw audio generation (van den Oord et al., 2016), to general data analytics (Najafabadi et al., 2015). Each network consists of a set of layers, where each layer transforms its input using a set of filters and produces a multichannel output. The outputs of the filters are combined to obtain a likelihood that an input image belongs to a given set of classes. The network's core is the set of filters located in different layers and tuned to different features. Each filter offers a different contribution for each class recognition indicated by filter weights. The weights are obtained by the network training process in order to balance the needs of different classes and provide the best average results over the entire training data, e.g., the highest average accuracy of classification of given samples from all classes. This chapter extends the current understanding of the roles played by the filters in Convolutional Neural Network (CNN) and their interactions.

8.2. Previous work

8.2.1 Neural network visualization and understanding

A number of attempts have been made to interpret the operation of CNNs (Kindermans et al., 2017; Morcos et al., 2018; Olah et al., 2018; Yosinski et al., 2015; Zhou et al., 2019). Many of these (Olah et al., 2018; Yosinski et al., 2015; Zhou et al., 2019)

Explainable Deep Learning AI
https://doi.org/10.1016/B978-0-32-396098-4.00014-4
147

focused on explaining the functions of individual neurons. They search for the inputs and/or objects that maximize the response of a specific neuron, which is then seen as a "single-cell object identifier." Since neurons work as a network, single-neuron feature visualization provides limited insight into the understanding of neural network decision making. However, it is also challenging to analyze decisions made by groups of neurons, due to the combinatorial complexity created by the large number of network parameters. Visualization of groups of neurons was studied through visualization of activations in 2D space using PCA or t-SNE (van der Maaten and Hinton, 2008) dimensionality reduction methods. Lastly, in Carter et al. (2019), in addition to single neuron visualization, the authors approximate how variation in neuron value changes the logits of each class.

8.2.2 Pruning

Currently, available pruning methods (Anwar et al., 2015; Li et al., 2016; Zhu and Gupta, 2017; Raghu et al., 2017; Morcos et al., 2018; Ma et al., 2019) can be split mainly into three groups, based on weights, activations, and accuracy/loss based optimizations. The simplest line of work is based on removing filters with the smallest values (Iandola et al., 2016). Pruning based on activations is the closest to our approach, as it focuses on removing the least active neurons. One of such works is Luo et al. (2017). However, this method is not applicable in our case as the authors remove those filters that do not change the activation map, thus not providing sufficient information about the filters' contributions to a specific class. Accuracy/loss based optimization (Molchanov et al., 2017; Suzuki et al., 2020) methods try to estimate the contribution of a filter to the overall loss function or model accuracy, and usually involve a training component. Comparatively, for instance, Taylor pruning of Molchanov et al. (2017) is much more efficient, but it is optimized towards the final loss function with additional retraining. Both of these criteria are not suitable for our work, as we want to investigate the original filter contribution to classification of individual classes. Besides, we do not want to affect the model accuracy by applying retraining. Hence, we use the simplest pruning method, namely, prune neurons directly related to a particular object class, as opposed to pruning based on overall data statistics.

8.3. Definitions

In order to study the roles and relationships among filters in a convolutional network, we propose to use an activation-based pruning method, referred to as *Response Based Pruning (RBP)*. Below we first briefly present the main aspects and definitions related to RBP.

Let $\mathbb{F} = \{\mathbf{F}_1, \ldots, \mathbf{F}_t\}$ be the set of all filters in a convolutional neural network (CNN) and $\mathbf{F}_i \in \mathbb{R}^{M \times M \times d}$ be a filter, where M is the filter's spatial dimension and d is the depth.

Also, let a subset of filters for a given CNN layer l be denoted as $\mathbb{L}$ with $\mathbb{L} \subseteq \mathbb{F}$. Let $\mathbf{B} \in \mathbb{R}^{X \times Y \times d}$ be an input tensor to l (X and Y are spatial dimensions). To calculate the output tensor $\mathbf{B}'$ of the layer l, the input tensor $\mathbf{B}$ is convolved with the set of filters $\mathbb{L} = \{\mathbf{F}_1, \ldots, \mathbf{F}_{d'}\}$ (as illustrated in Fig. 8.1a). The output of the convolution between the input tensor $\mathbf{B}$ and a single filter $\mathbf{F}_i$ is $\mathbf{R}_i \in \mathbb{R}^{X' \times Y'}$ (later referred to as a **feature map**) given as

$$\mathbf{R}_i = \mathbf{F}_i \odot \mathbf{B} \quad \text{and} \quad \mathbf{B}'_{(:,:,i)} = \mathbf{R}_i. \tag{8.1}$$

Let $\mathbb{D}$ be a dataset containing the N data samples, $\mathbb{C} = \{c_1, \ldots, c_m\}$ be the set of all object classes in the dataset. Let $\mathbb{D}_c = \{\mathbf{I}_1^c \ldots \mathbf{I}_{N'}^c\}$ be a subset of $\mathbb{D}$ ($\mathbb{D}_c \subset \mathbb{D}$) containing all data samples ($\mathbf{I}_j^c$) with the class label $c \in \mathbb{C}$. The number of samples in $\mathbb{D}_c$ is denoted as N' such that $N' \leq N$.

Finally, we denote by $\mathbf{R}_i(\mathbf{I}_j^c)$ the feature map for the filter $\mathbf{F}_i$ and the input data sample $\mathbf{I}_j^c \in \mathbb{D}_c$.

Definition 8.1 (**Pruning,** $\wp(\cdot)$). Specifically, pruning a layer l is a process of removing one or more $\mathbf{F}_i$ from $\mathbb{L}$ using some predefined criteria, resulting in a new set of filters $\wp(\mathbb{L}) = \hat{\mathbb{L}} = \{\mathbf{F}_1, \ldots, \mathbf{F}_{\hat{d}}\}$. Hence, a new output is $\hat{\mathbf{B}}' = \hat{\mathbb{L}} \odot \mathbf{B}$ with $\hat{\mathbf{B}}' \in \mathbb{R}^{X' \times Y' \times \hat{d}}$ and $\hat{d} \leq d$.

As pruning criteria – conditions to determine which filters to remove from the network – we propose to threshold filters' **accumulated response** values.

Definition 8.2 (**Accumulated response** (r_i^c)). An accumulated response (r_i^c) for a class c and a filter $\mathbf{F}_i$ is defined as an average sum of all elements in a feature map $\mathbf{R}_i$ for all samples in $\mathbb{D}_c$. It is computed by

$$r_i^c = \frac{1}{X'Y'N'} \sum_{j=1}^{N'} \sum_{x=1}^{X'} \sum_{y=1}^{Y'} \mathbf{R}_{x,y,i}(\mathbf{I}_j^c), \tag{8.2}$$

where $\mathbf{R}_{x,y,i}$ is a single element at a position (x, y) ($x \in X'$, $y \in Y'$) in a feature map $\mathbf{R}_i$.

A schematic representation for calculating r_i^c for an input $\mathbf{B}$ is shown in Fig. 8.1b: the response of a filter is calculated as an average over each resulting channel of the convolution.

Definition 8.3 (**Response–Based Pruning (RBP)**). Let $\mathbf{r}^c = \{r_1^c, r_2^c, \ldots, r_t^c\}$ be a vector of accumulated responses of all filters in the network for a class c. For a given pruning ratio $\theta \in [0, 1]$, Response-Based Pruning (RBP) refers to a process of removing $|\mathbf{r}^c|\theta$ filters $\mathbf{F}_i$ with the smallest r_i^c values in $\mathbf{r}^c$, where $|\mathbf{r}^c|$ is a cardinality of $\mathbf{r}^c$.

For instance, for $\theta = 0.1$, 10% of filters with the lowest accumulated responses will be removed.

The experiments will throughout involve several measures, which we list below.

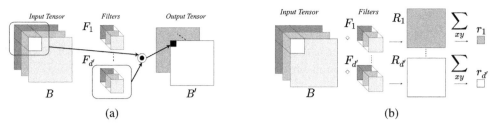

Figure 8.1 (a) Convolutional layer operation and (b) computation of the accumulated response r_i^c (for simplicity of visualization, superscript c was omitted in the figure).

Definition 8.4 (Accuracy ($\mathcal{A}_c^\theta$)). Accuracy is the performance of a model on a class c (viewed as a binary classification problem) for a given pruning ratio θ and computed using

$$\mathcal{A}_c^\theta = \frac{tp + tn}{tp + fp + fn + tn}, \tag{8.3}$$

where tp (true positive) stands for correctly classified samples (belonging to a class c), tn (true negative) stands for correctly classified samples (not belonging to a class c), fn (false negative) stands for misclassified samples (not belonging to a class c), and fp (false positive) stands for misclassified samples (belonging to a class c).

Definition 8.5 (Pruned Filter Similarity ($\mathcal{P}$)). Let $\bar{\mathbb{F}}_c = \{\mathbf{F}_1, \ldots, \mathbf{F}_z\}$ be a set of filters pruned at some θ for a class c. Then the similarity between two sets of filters $\bar{\mathbb{F}}_{c_1}$ and $\bar{\mathbb{F}}_{c_2}$ pruned separately for two classes (c_1, c_2) is computed by

$$\mathcal{P}(c_1, c_2) = \frac{|\bar{\mathbb{F}}_{c_1} \cap \bar{\mathbb{F}}_{c_2}|}{|\bar{\mathbb{F}}_{c_1} \cup \bar{\mathbb{F}}_{c_2}|}, \tag{8.4}$$

where $|\cdot|$ is the cardinality of a set.

Definition 8.6 (Highly Overlapping Classes (HOC)). If two classes have pruned filter similarity higher than a specified similarity threshold σ, $\mathcal{P}(c_1, c_2) \geq \sigma$, then classes c_1 and c_2 are referred to as Highly Overlapping Classes (HOC).

Definition 8.7 (Group of Classes ($\mathbb{G}$)). A group of classes $\mathbb{G}$ is a set consisting of multiple highly overlapping classes, $\mathbb{G} = \{c_i, c_j \in \mathbb{C} \mid \mathcal{P}(c_i, c_j) \geq \sigma \text{ and } 1 \leq i, j \leq m \text{ and } i \neq j\}$, where m is the number of classes in the dataset.

Definition 8.8 (k-Closest Neighbors ($\mathbb{K}$)). A family of k classes with the highest pruned filter similarity $\mathcal{P}$ to a class $c \in \mathbb{C}$ are referred to as k-Closest Neighbors $\mathbb{K}$ for a class c.

Definition 8.9 (Semantic Similarity ($\mathcal{S}$)). Semantic similarity between two classes $c_1, c_2 \in \mathbb{C}$ is measured using Wu–Palmer similarity (Wu and Palmer, 1994) between nodes in the WordNet graph structure corresponding to the ImageNet class names,

$$Wu - Palmer = 2\frac{depth(LCS(c_1, c_2))}{depth(c_1) + depth(c_2)}, \tag{8.5}$$

where LCS is a common ancestor of two concepts c_1, c_2 found in WordNet graph.

We use Wu–Palmer similarity (Wu and Palmer, 1994) as it provides a normalized, bounded value for the similarity, $\mathcal{S} \in (0, 1]$.

Definition 8.10 (Semantically Related Neighbors (SRN)). If the semantic similarity between two classes satisfies $\mathcal{S}(c_1, c_2) \geq \sigma$, where σ is a similarity threshold, then classes c_1 and c_2 are semantically related, and are referred to as Semantically Related Neighbors (SRN).

Definition 8.11 (Semantically Unrelated Neighbors (SUN)). If the semantic similarity between two classes satisfies $\mathcal{S}(c_1, c_2) < \sigma$, then classes c_1 and c_2 are referred to as Semantically Unrelated Neighbors (SUN), where σ is a similarity threshold.

8.4. Experiments

The first set of experiments was conducted in order to observe the changes in classification accuracy at different pruning ratios θ (Section 8.4.2). As expected, similar to the previous works, an average classification accuracy over all classes monotonically decreases with increasing θ. However, we also observed that for certain values of θ there is a set of classes $\mathbb{I}$ for which classification accuracy improves with pruning (Section 8.4.2). To determine the conditions under which accuracy improves, we experimentally investigated the usage and contribution of individual filters for the classification of classes in $\mathbb{I}$ (Section 8.4.3). As a result, we extracted groups of the most active filters, specific for each class. A natural next step was to determine (a) the possible overlaps of used filters between classes in $\mathbb{I}$ (Section 8.4.4) and (b) the possible semantic relation between classes in $\mathbb{I}$ (Section 8.4.4). We observed (a) an existence of groups of classes $\mathbb{G}$ for which the classification accuracy improves by pruning a similar subset of filters (Section 8.4.5) and (b) that semantically related classes tend to prune similar subsets of filters (Section 8.4.5). Additionally, experiments in Section 8.4.5 showed that most improvements are observed within small groups, therefore, in the following experiment we studied the structure of $\mathbb{G}$ in more details. In particular, we looked at semantic relation with highly overlapping classes (Section 8.4.6) and how pruned filter similarity with these classes changed with increasing θ (Section 8.4.7) These experiments allowed determining that (a) classes, for which the classification accuracy is improved by pruning, have on average a higher number of semantically related neighbors, and (b) improved classes have on average a higher increase in correlation with semantically related classes. In addition, this experiment showed that there is an interference between filters learned for different classes, as classification accuracy improved by reducing filter overlap between the highly overlapping classes.

8.4.1 Experimental settings

For all experiments, we used AlexNet (Krizhevsky et al., 2012) trained on the ImageNet (Russakovsky et al., 2015) dataset.

ImageNet Dataset is an image classification dataset (Russakovsky et al., 2015) with 1.2 million training images, 50000 validation color images representing 1000 object classes. For evaluation, we used the ImageNet validation set. Following the convention, all images were resized to 256×256 resolution.

AlexNet consists of five convolutional and three fully connected layers. RBP was applied only to the convolutional layers, also referred to as the feature extractor. Filters of the first convolutional layer ($l = 1$) are referred to as early-layer filters. Filters of the second and third convolutional layers ($l = 2, 3$) are referred to as mid-layer filters. Finally, the filters of the fourth and fifth convolutional layers ($l = 4, 5$) are referred to as late-layer filters. Pruning ratio θ is set to 0 and increased by 0.05 until reaching $\theta = 0.5$ (representing 50% pruning of filters in the network). No retraining is performed after pruning.

8.4.2 Class-wise accuracy changes

We applied RBP to all classes $c \in \mathbb{C}$ in the ImageNet dataset and recorded their classification accuracies $\mathcal{A}_c^\theta$ for various $\theta \geq 0$.

As expected, the average accuracy monotonically decreases with increasing θ (see Fig. 8.2a). Fig. 8.2b shows the magnitude of change (increase or decrease) in accuracy for all classes at different pruning ratios (the x-axis is a pruning ratio θ, the y-axis represents class id, and color denotes the magnitude of change). A positive value (darker color) represents an increase, and a negative value (lighter color) represents a decrease in classification accuracy. As can be seen from Fig. 8.2b, despite the trend for average accuracy reduction, there are a significant number of classes $c \in \mathcal{C}$ in the network for which $\mathcal{A}_c^\theta - \mathcal{A}_c^{\theta=0} > 0$ (where $\mathcal{A}_c^{\theta=0}$ is the original accuracy for class c before pruning). For simplicity, $\mathcal{A}_c^{\theta=0}$ will be referred to as $\mathcal{A}_c^0$ in the follow-up sections.

Fig. 8.2c reflects the number of improved classes per pruning ratio θ and Fig. 8.2d shows average improvements in class-wise classification accuracy for each pruning ratio θ. One can observe from Fig. 8.2c that the highest number of classes with improved classification accuracy is observed at smaller $\theta \in \{0.05, 0.1\}$, 272 and 208, respectively, while the highest average improvement (Fig. 8.2d) in accuracy 5% is observed at large $\theta = 0.45$. The possible reason for this phenomenon is that classes which got improved at higher values of θ had strong interference from filters which were pruned only at later

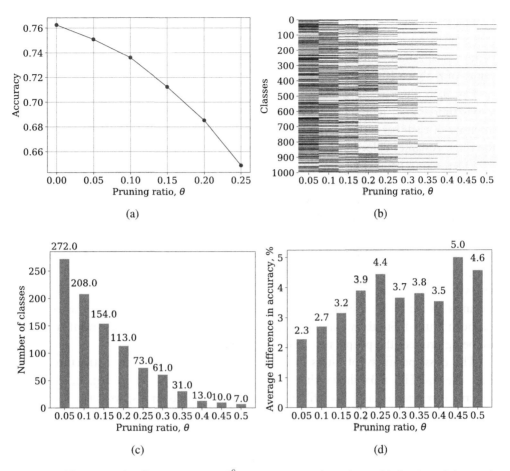

Figure 8.2 (a) Average classification accuracy $\mathcal{A}^\theta$ vs pruning ratio dependency, (b) direction of changes in accuracy for each class for different pruning ratios (dark spots represent increase in accuracy), (c) number of improved classes per pruning ratio (relative to the original accuracy), and (d) average class-wise accuracy improvements per pruning ratio (counted only over classes with improved classification accuracy).

pruning ratios, and hence got larger accuracy improvements. To investigate this phenomenon in more details, we need to study the contribution of each individual filter to class recognition, and what filters are getting removed by pruning.

8.4.3 Filters' contribution for each class recognition

The next step was to investigate the accumulated response value of each filter toward recognition of each class, and identify what groups of filters strongly contributed (had the highest values of accumulated responses) to each class recognition.

Fig. 8.3a shows accumulated response r_i^c of each filter $\mathbf{F}_i$ for each class c, the x-axis (horizontal) represents $\mathbf{F}_i$, while the y-axis (vertical axis) represent classes $c \in \mathbb{C}$. For better visualization, values of r_i^c below -10 were set to -10; however, there were no values of r_i^c above 10.6.

Fig. 8.3b illustrates how many classes pruned a particular filter at threshold θ, the x-axis (horizontal) represents $\mathbf{F}_i$ and the y-axis (vertical) is the pruning ratio θ. The intensity of each bar in the graph is proportional to the number of classes that pruned the filter. A darker color indicates a higher number of classes.

On the one hand, one can observe from Fig. 8.3a that the early-layer filters (the red rectangle in Fig. 8.3a) contributed almost equally to the recognition of all classes and were mostly not pruned at any thresholds (the red rectangle in Fig. 8.3b has mainly zeros). On the other hand, mid-layer (the green rectangle in Fig. 8.3a) and late-layer (the purple rectangle in Fig. 8.3a) filters are expected to be more class specific. As a result, we expect that mostly filters from later layers will be pruned. This expectation can be observed in Fig. 8.3a that shows pruning at smaller θ from 0.05 to 0.15: only filters from mid-layers are pruned. The pruned filters can be observed in the green rectangle in Fig. 8.3b: the intensity of each bar indicates for how many classes a filter has been pruned. Similarly, when pruning using higher $\theta \geq 0.15$, filters from late-layers are being pruned (the purple rectangle in Fig. 8.3b).

The class specificity of filters in mid- and late layers results in a structured class-wise overlap. Fig. 8.3a shows that classes 0–400 (rectangle A in Fig. 8.3a) have a structured overlap in mid-layer filters. This overlap results in a sparse class specificity: constant-colored rows show many filters' specific response. A similar type of overlap (to rectangle A) is also observed for classes 414–966 (rectangle B in Fig. 8.3a). Note that rectangles A and B show strong contrast of filter-accumulated responses to more homogeneous regions of late (purple square) filters and early (red square) filters. Additionally, rectangle A in Fig. 8.3a shows that filters in the range between 200 and 600 have specific accumulated responses for classes 0–400, while at the same time rectangle B shows that the same filters have an even smaller accumulated responses for classes 400–900. The observations in Fig. 8.3a suggest that there are groups of classes $\mathbb{G}$ which use and prune similar subsets of filters. It can be explained by the fact that class labels in ImageNet are organized according to the WordNet semantic hierarchy. Based on the observations from Figs. 8.3a and 8.3b, we hypothesize that classes using and pruning similar filters are located closely in the WordNet semantic hierarchy.

The next set of experiments will therefore provide a more precise quantitative evaluation of groups formed and intra-group pruned filter similarity ($\mathcal{P}$).

8.4.4 Class-wise pruned filter similarity and semantic similarity

Previous experiments showed that there are groups of classes $\mathbb{G}$ which share and prune similar subsets of filters. The next set of experiments was conducted to identify a more

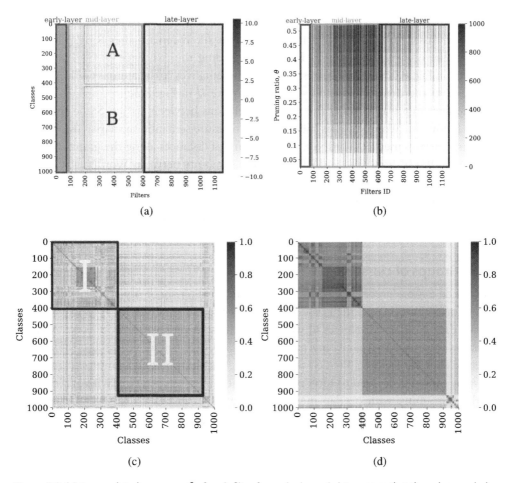

Figure 8.3 (a) Accumulated response r_i^c of each filter for each class c (white means that the value was below -10), (b) number of classes that pruned each filter $\mathbf{F}_i$ at different θ, (c) pruned filter similarity $\mathcal{P}$ for $\theta = 0.05$; the intensity of a pixel is proportional to the number of filters that overlap for the corresponding classes, and (d) semantic similarity $\mathcal{S}$.

precise quantitative evaluation of groups formed and their properties. In particular, we focused on investigating the dependencies between a class–wise pruned filter similarity $\mathcal{P}$ and a semantic similarity $\mathcal{S}$.

Fig. 8.3c shows results of pruned filter similarity $\mathcal{P}$ between all classes in $\mathbb{C}$ for $\theta = 0.05$. Initially we pruned each class independently for $\theta = 0.05$ to get $\bar{\mathbb{F}}_c$ for all $c \in \mathbb{C}$. Then, to generate Fig. 8.3c, we computed pruned filter similarity $\mathcal{P}$ between all $\bar{\mathbb{F}}_c$ of all $c \in \mathbb{C}$. Both axes in Fig. 8.3c represent the classes, and the intensity of each pixel is proportional to the pruned filter similarity for the classes corresponding to the row and column (the darker the color at the intersection, the higher is the pruned filter similarity between two classes). Fig. 8.3c shows that indeed there are easily identifiable groups of classes for which a large number of same filters remain after RBP. This result supports the observation made in Fig. 8.3a regarding the existence of $\mathbb{G}$. The groups observed in Fig. 8.3c roughly correspond to representatives of the animal world (square I in Fig. 8.3c) and items produced by humans (square II in Fig. 8.3c).

The next step was to study the semantic relations between classes. Since ImageNet classes follow the WordNet class hierarchy, we measure semantic similarity using corresponding metrics used in WordNet, e.g., in terms of distances along the graph structure. We use the Wu–Palmer (Wu and Palmer, 1994) similarity between WordNet nodes corresponding to the ImageNet class names. Fig. 8.3d shows the magnitude of Wu–Palmer semantic similarity between all classes in $\mathbb{C}$. The high similarity in Figs. 8.3d and 8.3c hypothesizes that semantically similar classes use similar filters, and hence prune similar filters as well.

8.4.5 Groups of classes $\mathbb{G}$

To provide a more precise quantitative evaluation of filter similarity and class grouping, we perform clustering on the classes based on pruned filter similarity $\mathcal{P}$ (Table 8.1).

For each considered value of θ, we calculate how many HOC groups exist. A group of classes is formed by calculating pairwise $\mathcal{P}(c_1, c_2)$ between all classes and then group together classes for which $\mathcal{P}(c_1, c_2) > 0.5$. As one class can belong to multiple groups at the same time, we decided to look at two separate cases, by grouping with and without overlap. Grouping with overlap means that one class can belong to several classes. To form groups without overlap, for classes which belonged to multiple groups, we assigned the group label based on most recent group (latest in the order of processing).

8.4.5.1 Nonoverlapping groups of classes

The column entitled "Average $\mathcal{P}$," shows the minimal, maximal, median, and average (mean) intra-group pruned filter similarity $\mathcal{P}$. As can be seen from Table 8.1, the number of groups of classes sharing similar pruned filters is decreasing with increasing θ: the more pruning is done, the more classes are encoded by the similar groups of filters. The pruning ratio $\theta = 0.4$ resulted in a single group of classes: all learned classes were pruning similar filters and therefore the experiment stopped.

The column named "Average $\mathcal{S}$" in Table 8.1 shows the results of computing semantic similarity $\mathcal{S}$ of groups of classes $\mathbb{G}$. The semantic similarity $\mathcal{S}$ is decreasing linearly with increasing θ. This observation confirms that larger groups are formed as a result of pruning: large groups of classes increasingly include classes that are less and less semantically related. Observe that on average the pruned filter similarity is growing inversely to the semantic similarity. This means that initially the average pruned filter similarity is divided among larger number of groups of classes while later larger groups have in general lower semantic similarity between classes within each group.

Table 8.1 Grouping based on $\mathcal{P} \geq 0.5$, * represents that groups which had only a single class as a member were removed from the statistics

θ	Number of $\mathbb{G}^*$	Average $\mathcal{P}$				Average $\mathcal{S}$			
		(min)	(max)	(median)	(mean)	(min)	(max)	(median)	(mean)
0.05	70	0.468	0.750	0.552	0.559	0.325	0.933	0.586	0.592
0.10	21	0.485	0.694	0.565	0.591	0.346	0.765	0.552	0.539
0.15	11	0.553	0.705	0.648	0.642	0.400	0.668	0.541	0.531
0.20	8	0.639	0.711	0.681	0.675	0.454	0.648	0.534	0.548
0.35	2	0.692	0.729	0.711	0.711	0.472	0.497	0.484	0.484
0.40	1	0.710	0.710	0.710	0.710	0.445	0.445	0.445	0.445

An even more detailed study of each group of classes $\mathbb{G}$ is shown in Table 8.2. In particular, Table 8.2 shows the number improved classes for each pruning ratio θ.

For every pruning ratio θ (rows two to five), we split the obtained groups of classes into four evenly size intervals (columns four to seven). Each row shows, for one θ and for each interval, the number of classes with improved classification accuracy (NIC), plus the range of values for the groups' sizes ($|\mathbb{G}|$) and the number of groups of classes $\mathbb{G}$ with the particular size. Note that because for each θ the largest and smallest group sizes are different, the intervals are different for each θ.

As can be seen from Table 8.2, for small $\theta = 0.05$, most of the classes with improved classification accuracy are in smaller groups (containing from 1 to 19 classes per group), see row 2, column 4. The total number of groups (N) at $\theta = 0.05$ and $\theta = 0.1$ in Tables 8.1 and 8.2 differs by 26 and 2, respectively, because Table 8.1 excludes groups which have only a single class inside (singleton-groups). Singleton groups were removed from Table 8.1 to provide a better trend statistics. Despite the fact that, according to Table 8.2, most of the improvements occur for small group size, only 6 classes improved with pruning from singleton-groups. This observation can be interpreted by saying that smaller groups offer more inter-group space that can be used for class movement during the pruning process.

8.4.5.2 Overlapping groups of classes

During the formation of groups in the previous section, we used nonoverlapping group assignment, in other words, each sample belonged to a single group only. For the next set of experiments, we decided to study similarity $\mathcal{G}$ between groups of classes when we assign the same class to multiple groups based on pruned filter similarity $\mathcal{P}$. To illustrate the concept, let us look at Fig. 8.4a. Allocating classes to all groups which satisfied the condition $\mathcal{P}(c_i, c_j) > \sigma$, we formed $\mathbb{G}_1$, $\mathbb{G}_2$, $\mathbb{G}_3$, and $\mathbb{G}_4$. As can be seen from Fig. 8.4a, $\mathbb{G}_4$ has one and three classes shared with $\mathbb{G}_1$ and $\mathbb{G}_2$, respectively. In order to quantify such overlaps between groups of classes and compute $\mathcal{G}$, we used intersection over union

Table 8.2 Number of improved classes (NIC) per interval. The size of group $\mathbb{G}$ is denoted as $|\mathbb{G}|$ and the total number of groups is denoted as N.

θ	N	Measure	Number of improved classes (NIC) per interval			
0.05	96	NIC	127.0	71.0	44.0	30.0
		$|\mathbb{G}|$	[1.0, 18.5)	[18.5, 36.0)	[36.0, 53.5)	[53.5, 71.0)
		N	80	9	5	2
0.1	23	NIC	103.0	54.0	0.0	51.0
		$|\mathbb{G}|$	[1.0, 90.5)	[90.5, 180.0)	[180.0, 269.5)	[269.5, 359.0)
		N	20	2	0	1
0.15	11	NIC	86.0	0.0	0.0	68.0
		$|\mathbb{G}|$	[6.0, 120.8)	[120.8, 235.5)	[235.5, 350.2)	[350.2, 465.0)
		N	10	0	0	1
0.2	8	NIC	0.0	53.0	19.0	41.0
		$|\mathbb{G}|$	[7.0, 81.2)	[81.2, 155.5)	[155.5, 229.8)	[229.8, 304.0)
		N	2	4	1	1

metrics using

$$\mathcal{G}(\mathbb{G}_1, \mathbb{G}_2) = \frac{|\mathbb{G}_1 \cap \mathbb{G}_2|}{|\mathbb{G}_1 \cup \mathbb{G}_2|}, \tag{8.6}$$

where $|\cdot|$ is the cardinality of a set.

To accurately estimate the neighborhood of each individual class c, we created a group $\mathbb{G}_c$ for each class $c \in \mathbb{C}$ by allocating all classes with $\mathcal{P}(c, c_i) > \sigma$. Next, for all $\mathbb{G}_c$, we computed group-wise similarity between all formed groups and only the maximum similarity with another group was recorded, $\mathcal{G}_c^{max} = \max_i(\mathcal{G}(\mathbb{G}_c, \mathbb{G}_{c_i}))$.

The main reason for keeping only the maximum similarity between two groups was to identify the existence of isolated groups which did not have overlap with other groups of classes. However, only a few groups satisfied this condition. Therefore we asked the question if a clear distinction between groups' overlap formed for improved and reduced classes can be found. To provide separate statistics on improved/reduced classes, we selected a subset of improved/reduced classes and computed average similarity $\bar{\mathcal{G}}^{max}$ over $\mathcal{G}_c^{max}$ for $c \in \mathbb{C}$. For simplicity, for the rest of the chapter $\bar{\mathcal{G}}^{max}$ will be referred to as $\bar{\mathcal{G}}$, which was computed for multiple similarity threshold values $\sigma \in \{0.4, 0.5, 0.6\}$, and resultant values are given in Fig. 8.4b. One can observe from Fig. 8.4b that, for all σ, the average similarity between groups for improved classes (blue, green, purple) is lower than for reduced accuracy classes (orange, red, brown). In addition, one can observe that, for higher σ, the gap between the average similarity of improving and reducing groups of classes is increasing. This observation implies that for groups formed at higher similarity σ, classes that improved after pruning were in a sparser space. Thus, the classes that stay in a sparse space as a result of pruning have a higher chance of a class-wise accuracy improvement: the movement of classes' samples within a sparser

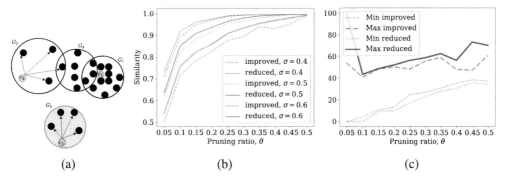

Figure 8.4 (a) Schematic representation of groups of classes and their intersection, (b) average similarity ($\bar{\mathcal{G}}$) between groups of classes for $\sigma = 0.4, 0.5, 0.6$; $\bar{\mathcal{G}}$ was computed separately for classes that increased/reduced classification accuracy after pruning, and (c) min/max average distance $\bar{\mathcal{F}}$ for improved/reduced classes.

feature space has a smaller chance to get closer to samples from a different class and therefore has a larger chance to increase the classification accuracy rather than to reduce it. Classes that have their classification accuracy reduced by pruning are thus in a denser space, increasing the possibility of classification mismatch.

Mapping to lower-dimensional space

In all the previous experiments, we considered only the presence and absence of filters and their overlap for different classes. For the next set of experiments, we take into account the values of the responses (accumulated response r^c). We construct a feature space from the accumulated responses $r^c = \{r_1^c, \ldots, r_f^c\}$ for all filters in AlexNet and map them to 2D space through t-SNE (van der Maaten and Hinton, 2008). We measured the average distances $\bar{\mathcal{F}}$ between a pruned class c and all neighbors in the group of classes $\mathbb{G}$. For example, let us look at Fig. 8.4a and on the group $\mathbb{G}_2$, which was formed from classes with $\mathcal{P}(c_2, c_i) > \sigma$ to c_2. As a result, class c_2 got 4 neighbors. Hence, average distances $\bar{\mathcal{F}}_{c_2}$ is computed as

$$\bar{\mathcal{F}}_{c_2} = \frac{1}{4} \sum_{i=1}^{4} \mathcal{F}(c_2, c_i).$$

Once $\bar{\mathcal{F}}$ for all $c \in \mathbb{C}$ was computed, similarly to the previous section experiments, we split $\mathbb{C}$ into two subsets of classes: improved (I) and reduced (R) accuracy classes. Next, for each subset of classes, we computed the minimum and maximum values of $\bar{\mathcal{F}}$. Fig. 8.4c shows the resultant values. One can observe that the minimum $\bar{\mathcal{F}}$ for improved classes (blue dashed line) is higher than the minimum feature distance $\bar{\mathcal{F}}$ for reduced classes (green line). This implies that classes, that have neighbors relatively close, have a smaller chance of getting improved by pruning. On the other hand, the maximum $\bar{\mathcal{F}}$ for reduced classes (red line) is always higher than $\bar{\mathcal{F}}$ for improved classes (yellow dashed line) for all θ. This implies that classes which were located far away from their neighbors have small confusion with other classes; however, during pruning they moved closer to other classes, thus increasing confusion with other classes.

8.4.6 Pruned filter similarity and semantic similarity between k-closest neighbors

Previous experiments showed that there are groups of classes $\mathbb{G}$ which share and prune similar subsets of filters. The next set of experiments was conducted to identify a more precise quantitative evaluation of groups formed and their properties. In particular, we focused on investigating the dependencies between a class-wise pruned filter similarity $\mathcal{P}$ and a semantic similarity $\mathcal{S}$.

To quantify the pruned filter similarity and semantic similarity between classes within each group $\mathbb{G}$, for each class $c \in \mathbb{G}$, we took $k = 5$ classes with the highest pruned filter similarity $\mathcal{P}$ (k-closest neighbors). We then calculated how many out of $k = 5$ neighboring classes were semantically related to c. We also looked at how the number of semantically related classes changed for different pruning ratios θ.

Let $\mathbb{K} = \{c_1, \ldots, c_k\}$ be a set containing k classes with the highest pruned filter similarity $\mathcal{P}$ to a class c. Then, let $\mathbf{s}^c = \{\mathcal{S}_1, \ldots, \mathcal{S}_k\}$ be a vector containing the semantic similarity between a class c with all classes in $\mathbb{K}$, where $\mathcal{S}_j = \mathcal{S}(c, c_j)$ and $k = 5$.

We counted how many classes in $\mathbb{K}$ are Semantically Related Neighbors (SRN, i.e., $\mathcal{S}(c, c_j) > \sigma$) and Semantically Unrelated Neighbors (SUN) to class c. We selected a similarity threshold $\sigma = 0.5$ for identifying SRN and SUN.

Column AV in Table 8.3 shows how many neighbors are SRN (Eq. (8.7)) on average over the whole set of classes $\mathbb{C}$ (including improved, reduced, and classes that did not change classification accuracy). The average number of SUN is complementary to the average number of SRN in the sense that $AV(SUN) = k - AV(SRN)$, where k is a number of classes in $\mathbb{K}$, and $k = 5$ in our experiments. Equations (8.7) and (8.8) provide equation for computing $AV(SRN)$ and $AV(SUN)$, respectively:

$$AV(SRN) = \frac{1}{m} \sum_{i=1}^{m} \sum_{j=1}^{k} g(\mathcal{S}(c_i, c_j)), \quad \text{where } g(x) := \begin{cases} 0, & \text{if } x \leq \sigma, \\ 1, & \text{if } x > \sigma, \end{cases} \tag{8.7}$$

$$AV(SUN) = \frac{1}{m} \sum_{i=1}^{m} \sum_{j=1}^{k} h(\mathcal{S}(c_i, c_j)), \quad \text{where } h(x) := \begin{cases} 1, & \text{if } x \leq \sigma, \\ 0, & \text{if } x > \sigma, \end{cases} \tag{8.8}$$

where m is a total number of classes in $\mathbb{C}$ and k is a number of classes in $\mathbb{K}$ for each class c_i.

Column I in Table 8.3 shows how many SRN classes are on average among the five closest neighbors for classes that improve classification accuracy after pruning at θ ($\mathcal{A}_c^\theta - \mathcal{A}_c^0 > 0$). The column entitled R shows the average number of SRN for classes

Table 8.3 An average number of Semantically Related (SRN) and Unrelated (SUN) Neighbors. Columns I and R represent average numbers for improved and reduced accuracy classes; AV is the average number of SRN and SUN for all classes.

Pruning ratio	AV		I		R	
	(SRN)	(SUN)	(SRN)	(SUN)	(SRN)	(SUN)
$\theta = 0.05$	3.932	1.068	4.033	0.967	3.935	1.065
$\theta = 0.10$	4.030	0.970	4.192	0.808	3.994	1.006
$\theta = 0.15$	4.051	0.949	3.922	1.078	4.077	0.923
$\theta = 0.20$	4.079	0.921	3.991	1.009	4.115	0.885
$\theta = 0.25$	4.110	0.890	3.973	1.027	4.124	0.876
$\theta = 0.30$	4.125	0.875	3.918	1.082	4.137	0.863

for which the classification accuracy is reduced after pruning at θ ($\mathcal{A}_c^\theta - \mathcal{A}_c^0 < 0$). As the number of classes that did not change classification accuracy by pruning was too small, we did not study them in more details. The number of semantically unrelated neighbors (SUN) is complementary to SRN for each case in Table 8.3.

Previous experiments (Figs. 8.3c and 8.3d) showed that semantically similar classes tend to prune similar filters. Hence, one can expect that the number of SRN in $\mathbb{K}$ will be approaching k. This hypothesis is supported by the results in Table 8.3, where values for SRN are much higher than for SUN. One can observe from Table 8.3 that for the first two pruning ratios $\theta = 0.05$ and $\theta = 0.10$, the highest values for SRN (4.033 and 4.192, respectively) are observed for classes for which the classification accuracy increased after pruning (Column I). However, once the pruning ratio gets above $\theta \geq 0.1$, the highest values of SRN (4.077, 4.115, 4124, and 4.137, respectively) are observed for classes with the reduced accuracy (Table 8.3, Column R). This observation can be explained as follows. At a small θ, pruning removes interfering filters that were introducing distortion into the target class classification. Therefore, for a small θ, pruning moves SRNs closer together. However, once we start to prune a more significant portion of the filters ($\theta \geq 0.1$), pruning starts to remove filters that allowed the discrimination between similar/semantically related classes. Now, the network tends to confuse more classes belonging to SRN and, hence, reduces the classification accuracy.

One of the possible conclusions from Table 8.3 is that, for small θ (with the highest number of classes with improved accuracy according to Fig. 8.2b) and for classes for which the classification accuracy $\mathcal{A}_c^\theta$ improves, the pruning tends to group SRN together. Hence, the next set of experiments aims to investigate how pruned filter similarity is changing by pruning.

8.4.7 Changes in pruned filter similarity with k-closest neighbors with pruning

We have seen that there are identifiable groups of classes $\mathbb{G}$ with a high pruned filter similarity. We also have observed that a high pruned filter similarity between classes also implies a high semantic similarity. Besides, it turns out that classes for which the classification accuracy had improved at smaller pruning ratios ($\theta \in \{0.05, 0.1\}$) also had a higher number of semantically related neighbors (SRN) than classes for which the classification accuracy was not improved by pruning. Based on this observation, we hypothesize that for a small θ (i.e., $\theta \in \{0.05, 0.1\}$), classes for which pruning increases the number of closest SRN have a higher chance to increase the classification accuracy. In addition, classes with increased accuracy by pruning have less SUN than classes for which the classification accuracy is reduced by pruning at lower θ. To verify this hypothesis, in this section, we experimentally determine how the pruned filter similarity between the semantic neighbors of improved and unimproved classes changes with an increase in θ.

Let $\mathbf{p}_c^\theta$ be a vector containing the pruned filter similarity between a class c and its k-closest neighbors $\mathbb{K}$ at θ ($k = 5$). For the simplicity of visualization, $\mathbf{p}_c^\theta$ will be denoted as $\mathbf{p}^\theta$ in the rest of the chapter. To determine the change in the pruned filter similarity, we calculate the element-wise difference (Δ) between $\mathbf{p}^{\theta_t}$ and $\mathbf{p}^{\theta_{t-1}}$ for class $c_i \in \mathbb{C}$ using Eqs. (8.9) and (8.10), where θ_t and θ_{t-1} stand for the current and previous pruning ratios, respectively. We separate $\mathbb{K}$ into Semantically Related neighbors (SRN) and Semantically Unrelated neighbors (SUN). Then we compute the Gradient of Pruned Filter Similarity separately for SRN (Δ_{SRN}) and SUN (Δ_{SUN}) as

$$\Delta_{SRN}(\mathbf{p}^{\theta_t}, \mathbf{p}^{\theta_{t-1}}) = \frac{1}{k'} \sum_{j=1}^{k} g(\mathcal{S}(c_i, c_j)) f(p_j^{\theta_t} - p_j^{\theta_{t-1}}), \quad \text{where } f(x) := \begin{cases} 0, & \text{if } x \le 0, \\ 1, & \text{if } x > 0, \end{cases} \quad (8.9)$$

where k is a total number of classes in $\mathbb{K}$, k' is a number of SRN in $\mathbb{K}$, $g(\cdot)$ is the same function as defined in Eq. (8.7), $\mathcal{S}$ is the semantic similarity between two classes, and $p_j^{\theta_t} = \mathcal{P}(c_i, c_j)$. Similarly,

$$\Delta_{SUN}(\mathbf{p}^{\theta_t}, \mathbf{p}^{\theta_{t-1}}) = \frac{1}{k''} \sum_{j=1}^{k} h(\mathcal{S}(c_i, c_j)) * f(p_j^{\theta_t} - p_j^{\theta_{t-1}}), \quad \text{where } f(x) := \begin{cases} 0, & \text{if } x \le 0, \\ 1, & \text{if } x > 0, \end{cases}$$
$$(8.10)$$

where k is a total number of classes in $\mathbb{K}$, k'' is a number of SUN in $\mathbb{K}$, $h(\cdot)$ is the same function as defined in Eq. (8.8), $\mathcal{S}$ is the semantic similarity between two classes, and $p_j^{\theta_t} = \mathcal{P}(c_i, c_j)$.

Table 8.4 shows the results of calculating the Gradient of Pruned Filter Similarity for Δ_{SRN} and Δ_{SUN} in pruned filter similarity over all classes $c_i \in \mathbb{C}$ and their corresponding k-closest neighbors for $\theta_t = 0.1, 0.15, 0.2, 0.25, 0.3$.

Table 8.4 Gradient of Pruned Filter Similarity for semantically related (Δ_{SRN}) and unrelated (Δ_{SUN}) neighbors. The higher the value in the table, the higher the number of neighboring classes with which the pruned filter similarity increases. Columns I and R represent the average change in pruned filter similarity for improved and reduced classes.

Pruning ratio	AV		I		R	
	(SRN)	(SUN)	(SRN)	(SUN)	(SRN)	(SUN)
$\theta_{t-1} = 0.05, \theta_t = 0.10$	0.948	0.918	0.969	0.905	0.943	0.918
$\theta_{t-1} = 0.10, \theta_t = 0.15$	0.647	0.672	0.688	0.659	0.637	0.667
$\theta_{t-1} = 0.15, \theta_t = 0.20$	0.572	0.590	0.654	0.642	0.560	0.581
$\theta_{t-1} = 0.20, \theta_t = 0.25$	0.710	0.738	0.732	0.790	0.708	0.731
$\theta_{t-1} = 0.25, \theta_t = 0.30$	0.697	0.696	0.699	0.638	0.695	0.700

The values of Gradient of Pruned Filter Similarity in Table 8.4 can be interpreted as follows. For example, let $\mathbb{K} = \{c_1, c_2, c_3, c_4, c_5\}$ be the 5 closest neighbors of the class c at θ_{t-1}. Let classes c_1, c_2, c_3 be SRN to c ($k' = 3$) and classes c_4, c_5 be SUN ($k'' = 2$). Then, for both θ_{t-1} and θ_t, we measure the pruned filter similarity $\mathcal{P}$ between the class c and its SRN classes ($\mathcal{P}(c, c_1)$, $\mathcal{P}(c, c_2)$, $\mathcal{P}(c, c_3)$). If the magnitude of $\mathcal{P}$ increased when moving from θ_{t-1} to θ_t for all SRN classes then Δ_{SRN} will be equal to 1. Otherwise, we take a ratio between the number of SRN classes for which the pruned filter similarity increased vs the total number of SRN (k'). For instance, assume that the value of $\mathcal{P}$ increased only for c_1 and c_2 then $\Delta_{SRN} = \frac{2}{3} = 0.67$. The value of Δ_{SUN} can be interpreted in a similar manner.

Table 8.4 shows the values of Δ_{SRN} and Δ_{SUN} averaged over all classes $c \in \mathbb{C}$ (column AV), all improved classes $c \in \mathbb{I}$ (column I), and all reduced classes $c \in \mathbb{R}$ (column R).

The most notable observation in Table 8.4 is that for the majority of θ_t, the values in Column I (Δ_{SRN}) values are higher than those in Column I (Δ_{SUN}). At the same time, the majority of the values in Column R (Δ_{SRN}) are lower than those in Column R (Δ_{SUN}). In addition, all values in Column I (Δ_{SRN}) are always higher than those in Column R (Δ_{SRN}). This observation suggests that the classes for which Δ_{SRN} is higher than Δ_{SUN} have a higher chance of classification accuracy to be improved by pruning.

Once the pruning is performed, we are left with a smaller number of features to discriminate classes. We hypothesize that with fewer filters, it is easier to encode semantically similar classes rather than classes from completely different groups. This hypothesis is supported by the results observed in Table 8.4. On the one hand, for classes where pruning increases the pruned filter similarity with SUN, the classification accuracy decreases. The possible explanation for such a behavior is that it is harder to capture the diversity of unrelated classes with a smaller number of filters. On the other hand, for classes where pruning increases the pruned filter similarity with SRN, we observed an increase in the classification accuracy. This observation supported the original hypothesis that semantically similar classes are easier to encode with a smaller set of filters. However, once we prune too many filters, it is becoming much harder to discriminate between similar classes as well.

Experiments conducted in this section showed a correlation between changes in pruned filter similarity $\mathcal{P}$ and improvement in accuracy for low values of θ. In particular, improved classes have higher increase in $\mathcal{P}$ with semantically related neighbors, while reduced accuracy classes have higher increase in $\mathcal{P}$ with semantically unrelated classes. The fact that we have an increase in both pruned filter similarity and accuracy indicates that the discriminative power of unpruned filters improved as a result of removing similar filters between neighboring classes. This implies that the closest neighbors are increasing their mutual filter similarity up to such θ so they can be distinguished by the filter response. It also can imply that by increasing $\mathcal{P}$ with SRN, classes are removing inferring filters, which is leading to accuracy improvements.

8.5. Model selection

Previous sections provided an experimental study of the effects of pruning on class-specific classification accuracy. As an extension to this study, we design a pruned model selection approach for improving a specific groups of classes. The principle behind the selection is the maximization of the number of classes that a pruned model is improving. At the same time, the selection attempts to minimize the intersection between classes that are improved by different selected models.

During the model selection process, the following conditions should be satisfied: the candidate model should improve the highest number of classes and those classes should have similarity above threshold σ. In this section we compared two similarity measures:
1. Pruned Filter Similarity, $\mathcal{P}(c_i, c_j) \geq \sigma$;
2. Semantic Similarity, $\mathcal{S}(c_i, c_j) \geq \sigma$.

The methodology for model selection proceeds as follows. Let $\mathbb{M}$ be the set of all pruned models available, $\mathbb{C}$ be the set of all classes in the dataset, and $\mathbb{C}^M \subset \mathbb{C}$ be the set of classes that model $M \in \mathbb{M}$ improves. The process of model selection is illustrated in Algorithm 8.1.

Line 1 in Algorithm 8.1 returns the set of all pruned models $\mathbb{M}$ in descending order, sorted based on the number of classes $c \in \mathbb{C}$ each pruned model $M \in \mathbb{M}$ improves. Line 2 initializes the target set of selected models $\mathbb{M}^{selected} \subset \mathbb{M}$. Line 3 returns the model M which improves the highest number of classes in $\mathbb{C}$. Then the set of classes $\mathbb{C}^M$ improved by model M is returned (line 4 of Algorithm 8.1). The selection of the models will continue until the selected model M improves at least ten classes (line 5). Lines 6 to 7 add the current selected model M to the set of selected models and remove the classes model M is improving from the set of all classes $\mathbb{C}$. The remaining pruned models in $\mathbb{M}$ are again sorted in descending order based on the number of classes the models improve (line 8). Once the sorting is done, we again remove the model with the highest number

---

Algorithm 8.1 Model Selection Algorithm.

1: $\mathbb{M}_{\prec} \leftarrow orderDescending(\mathbb{M}, \mathbb{C})$
2: $\mathbb{M}^{selected} \leftarrow \{\}$
3: $M \leftarrow pop(\mathbb{M}_{\prec})$
4: $\mathbb{C}^M \leftarrow classPerModel(M, \mathbb{C})$
5: **while** $|\mathbb{C}^M| > 10$ **do**
6:     $\mathbb{M}^{selected} \leftarrow \mathbb{M}^{selected} \cup M$
7:     $\mathbb{C} \leftarrow \mathbb{C} \setminus \mathbb{C}^M$
8:     $\mathbb{M}_{\prec} \leftarrow orderDescending(\mathbb{M}, \mathbb{C})$
9:     $M \leftarrow pop(\mathbb{M}_{\prec})$
10:     $\mathbb{C}^M \leftarrow classPerModel(M, \mathbb{C})$
11: **end while**

---

of improved classes (among remaining in $\mathbb{C}$) from the list of all remaining in $\mathbb{M}$ models (line 9) and repeat steps 6–7 for the new selected model, unless termination criteria are met.

For the rest of the chapter, the model accuracy will be referred to as the classification accuracy over the classes $\mathbb{C}^M$ for which the model M was selected. Therefore, the accuracy reported in this section might be different from the accuracy reported in other sections of this chapter. In addition, note that the order in which the model was selected may affect its classification accuracy, as the same model can be picked for a different subset of classes $\mathbb{C}^M$.

The experimental results of the model selection using Algorithm 8.1 are summarized in Figs. 8.5–8.8. All figures show different measures for several similarity thresholds σ used during the creation of the groups. In particular, for each $\sigma \in [0.25, 0.65]$ (with increment of 0.1) a plot is provided. The upper similarity threshold of 0.65 was determined experimentally so that both semantic similarity and pruned filter similarity could be compared for the sufficient number of models (more than two). The x-axis represents the ID of the models in descending order based on the number of improved classes. This is the same order by which Algorithm 8.1 selected the models.

Fig. 8.5 shows the number of classes improved by each model. The y-axis shows the number of classes and the x-axis shows the model ID. As can be seen from Fig. 8.5, the main difference between the model selection using pruned filter similarity (Fig. 8.5(a)) versus semantic similarity (Fig. 8.5(b)) is that for pruned filter similarity the number of classes across similarity thresholds has a higher variation. For instance, for the model selection using pruned filter similarity, the model improving the largest number of classes (model with ID 1 and $\sigma = 0.25$) contains more than 250 classes while the model (ID 1, $\sigma = 0.65$) improves less than 50 classes. The difference between these values is ≈ 200. At the same time, the largest and smallest numbers of classes improved by models selected

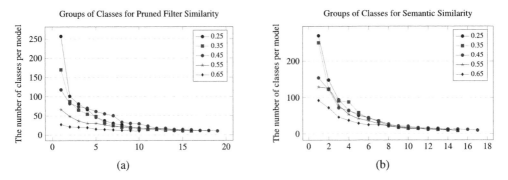

Figure 8.5 Number of classes per model used in the target set of selected models using (a) pruned filter similarity and (b) semantic similarity.

using semantic similarity (ID 1, $\sigma = 0.25$ and ID 1, $\sigma = 0.65$) are ≈ 270 and ≈ 100, respectively. This results in a difference of ≈ 170 (Fig. 8.5(b)).

Fig. 8.6 shows the average classification accuracy of each model on the classes $\mathbb{C}^M$ for original unpruned model (Figs. 8.6(a) and 8.6(b)), and for the selected pruned model (Figs. 8.6(c) and 8.6(d)). The y-axis shows the accuracy in percents, and the x-axis shows the model ID.

The first observation from Fig. 8.6 is that the average improvement of classification accuracy for the selected pruned models (Fig. 8.6(a) vs Fig. 8.6(c) and Fig. 8.6(b) vs Fig. 8.6(d)) is as expected higher than the accuracy of the original unpruned models. The second observation is that models selected using pruned filters similarity have higher variations in average accuracy for different similarity thresholds. For instance, the difference in classification accuracy between models with highest number of improving classes (Fig. 8.6(c)–(d), model ID 1) for $\sigma = 0.25$ and $\sigma = 0.65$ is around 20 while the accuracy difference between models selected using semantic similarity is ≈ 5.

Fig. 8.7 shows the improvement of average accuracy between the accuracy of the unpruned model and the accuracy of the selected pruned model evaluated on the subset of classes $\mathbb{C}^M$. The y-axis shows the difference in accuracy (ΔAcc) in percents, and the x-axis shows the model ID.

The most noticeable observation from Fig. 8.7 is that the models selected using semantic similarity (see Fig. 8.7(b)) have smaller variations in ΔAcc across similarity threshold σ.

In addition, the difference of classification accuracy improvement in Fig. 8.7(b) is approximately linearly decreasing with any additional models after the first one. This can be observed in Fig. 8.8(b). Fig. 8.8 shows the averaged measures for a number of classes, accuracy, and accuracy improvements across all similarity thresholds. Note that Fig. 8.8 has two y-axes. The right y-axis shows the difference in accuracy (ΔAcc) and

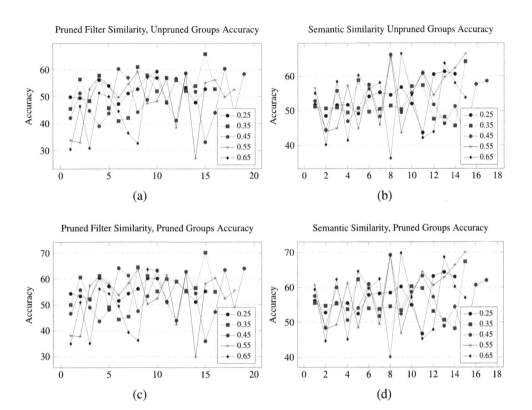

Figure 8.6 Accuracy of each model evaluated on the $\mathbb{C}^M$ classes before and after pruning. Note that before pruning only one model is evaluated on different $\mathcal{C}^M$.

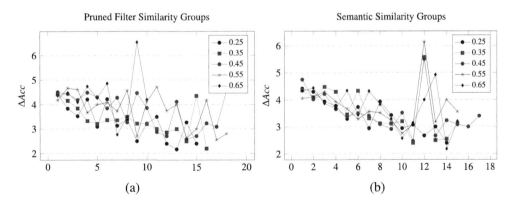

Figure 8.7 Differences in accuracy (ΔAcc) between unpruned and pruned models for the groups of classes at different similarity thresholds σ using (a) pruned filter similarity and (b) semantic similarity.

the left y-axis represents the accuracy in percents and average $|\mathbb{C}^M|$ (Count). The x-axis shows the model ID.

The fact that classification accuracy improvements are linearly decreasing is quite interesting because the models are ordered in the descending order by the number of improved classes. Therefore, one could expect that models improving less classes would have a higher average improvement in classification accuracy. However, the ranking of the models is done after previously improved classes are removed (line 7 in Algorithm 8.1) and each model is ranked using only the model-unique improved classes. The reduction of average improvement ΔAcc (observed in Fig. 8.7(b)) suggests that on average models' relative improvements rate (ΔAcc) correlates with the number of classes the model improves.

Another observation is that the semantic similarity seems to provide more stable model selection. This can be deduced from the fact that according to Fig. 8.5, using semantic similarity results in smaller variations in $|\mathbb{C}^M|$ across similarity thresholds σ. This observation would imply that the groups formed by using semantic similarity are more stable: groups unite classes that have higher semantic and higher pruned filter similarity. On the other hand, when using the pruned filter similarity selection criteria, the $\mathbb{C}^M$ groups contain also semantically unrelated classes: groups $\mathbb{C}^M$ contain classes that are close in pruned filter similarity but are semantically unrelated. As a result, grouping classes by pruned filter similarity would tend to have more variation in improvement across the similarity threshold.

In our previous experiments (Section 8.4.7) we determined that classes that had more semantic neighbors (in the pruned filter space) had higher probability to get improved after pruning. Hence, using pruned filter similarity for grouping together semantically related and unrelated classes can cause more unpredictable improvements behavior. This is also supported by the observations from Fig. 8.8, where it can be seen that the average improvement in classification accuracy for semantic similarity selection based approach is slightly higher and is decreasing in a more monotone manner.

8.6. Discussion and conclusions

The results presented in this work show several properties of pruning and classification. First, as shown in Section 8.4.5, the improvement in the accuracy of a set of classes due to RBP is directly related to the initial distance among the classes. Second, classes whose closest neighbors are semantically related have a higher probability of being improved by RBP (Section 8.4.6). Third, as a result of RBP, in Section 8.4.7 classes whose accuracy improved had a larger increase in pruned filter similarity with semantically related neighbors than with semantically unrelated. These observations imply that if a class is surrounded by mostly semantically related neighbors, then, if the neighbors are not too close, the pruning can be beneficial to the classification accuracy. This is because the

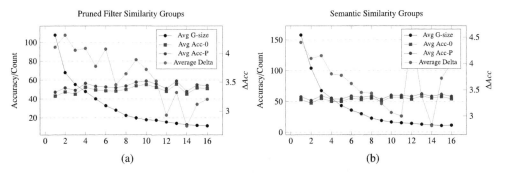

Figure 8.8 Averaged number of classes per group, initial unpruned accuracy, pruned accuracy, and the improvement across all evaluated similarity thresholds for (a) pruned filter and (b) for semantic similarity based group creation approach.

compression resulting from the pruning brings all classes closer, but also brings data samples closer together. If there is enough space between classes, the samples will be compressed enough for higher accuracy before classes will interfere with each other. Finally, in Section 8.5 we showed that a class-targeted model pruning can indeed improve classes and can be used to build ensemble models. For this to work, models must be selected in an efficient approach using a semantic similarity.

Our results could be used to design filter selection masks to increase the classification accuracy of a group of classes. Such masked networks then could be combined into ensembles for decision making. Based on our experiments, we can conclude that whether the classification accuracy for a given set of classes can be potentially improved by pruning can be determined by checking if the classes are located sparsely, a large fraction of neighbors is semantically related, and there is an initial increase in pruned filter similarity with semantically related neighbors.

Glossary

CNN Convolutional Neural Network

Acknowledgments

This work was funded by the FCDRGP research grant from Nazarbayev University with reference number 240919FD3936. Narendra Ahuja was supported by Office of Naval Research under grant N00014-20-1-2444.

References

Anwar, Sajid, Hwang, Kyuyeon, Sung, Wonyong, 2015. Structured pruning of deep convolutional neural networks. CoRR. arXiv:1512.08571 [abs].

Carter, Shan, Armstrong, Zan, Schubert, Ludwig, Johnson, Ian, Olah, Chris, 2019. Activation atlas. Distill.

Girshick, Ross, Donahue, Jeff, Darrell, Trevor, Malik, Jitendra, 2014. Rich feature hierarchies for accurate object detection and semantic segmentation. In: Proceedings of the IEEE CVPR, pp. 580–587.

Hu, Jie, Shen, Li, Sun, Gang, 2019. Squeeze-and-excitation networks. arXiv:1709.01507v4.

Husain, Farzad, Dellen, Babette, Torras, Carme, 2017. Chapter 20 – Scene understanding using deep learning. In: Samui, Pijush, Sekhar, Sanjiban, Balas, Valentina E. (Eds.), Handbook of Neural Computation. Academic Press, pp. 373–382.

Iandola, Forrest N., Han, Song, Moskewicz, Matthew W., Ashraf, Khalid, Dally, William J., Keutzer, Kurt, 2016. SqueezeNet: AlexNet-level accuracy with 50× fewer parameters and < 0.5 MB model size. arXiv:1602.07360.

Kindermans, Pieter-Jan, Schütt, Kristof T., Alber, Maximilian, Müller, Klaus-Robert, Erhan, Dumitru, Kim, Been, Dähne, Sven, 2017. Learning how to explain neural networks. arXiv:1705.05598.

Krizhevsky, A., Sutskever, I., Hinton, G.E., 2012. ImageNet classification with deep convolutional neural networks. In: NIPS.

Li, Hao, Kadav, Asim, Durdanovic, Igor, Samet, Hanan, Graf, Hans Peter, 2016. Pruning filters for efficient ConvNets. CoRR. arXiv:1608.08710 [abs].

Lin, Tsung Yi, Goyal, Priya, Girshick, Ross, He, Kaiming, Dollar, Piotr, 2017. Focal loss for dense object detection. In: ICCV, 2017, pp. 2999–3007.

Luo, Jian-Hao, Wu, Jianxin, Lin, Weiyao, 2017. ThiNet: A filter level pruning method for deep neural network compression. In: ICCV, pp. 5058–5066.

Ma, Xiaolong, Yuan, Geng, Lin, Sheng, Li, Zhengang, Sun, Hao, Wang, Yanzhi, 2019. ResNet Can Be Pruned 60×: Introducing Network Purification and Unused Path Removal (P-RM) after Weight Pruning.

Molchanov, Pavlo, Tyree, Stephen, Karras, Tero, Aila, Timo, Kautz, Jan, 2017. Pruning convolutional neural networks for resource efficient transfer learning. arXiv:1611.06440v2.

Morcos, Ari S., Barrett, David G.T., Rabinowitz, Neil C., Botvinick, Matthew, 2018. On the importance of single directions for generalization. arXiv:1803.06959.

Najafabadi, Maryam M., Villanustre, Flavio, Khoshgoftaar, Taghi M., Seliya, Naeem, Wald, Randall, Muharemagic, Edin, 2015. Deep learning applications and challenges in big data analytics. Journal of Big Data 2 (1), 1.

Olah, Chris, Satyanarayan, Arvind, Johnson, Ian, Carter, Shan, Schubert, Ludwig, Ye, Katherine, Mordvintsev, Alexander, 2018. The building blocks of interpretability. Distill.

Ouyang, Wanli, Wang, Xiaogang, Zeng, Xingyu, Qiu, Shi, Luo, Ping, Tian, Yonglong, Li, Hongsheng, Yang, Shuo, Wang, Zhe, Loy, Chen-Change, Tang, Xiaoou, 2015. DeepID-Net: Deformable deep convolutional neural networks for object detection. In: Computer Vision and Pattern Recognition (CVPR), 2015 IEEE Conference on, pp. 2403–2412.

Raghu, M., Gilmer, J., Yosinski, J., Sohl-Dickstein, J., 2017. SVCCA: singular vector canonical correlation analysis for deep learning dynamics and interpretability. arXiv:1706.05806.

Ren, Haoyu, Li, Ze-Nian, 2015. Object detection using generalization and efficiency balanced co-occurrence features. In: 2015 IEEE International Conference on Computer Vision (ICCV), pp. 46–54.

Russakovsky, Olga, Deng, Jia, Su, Hao, Krause, Jonathan, Satheesh, Sanjeev, Ma, Sean, Huang, Zhiheng, Karpathy, Andrej, Khosla, Aditya, Bernstein, Michael, Berg, Alexander C., Fei-Fei, Li, 2015. ImageNet large scale visual recognition challenge. International Journal of Computer Vision 115 (3), 211–252.

Suzuki, Taiji, Abe, Hiroshi, Murata, Tomoya, Horiuchi, Shingo, Ito, Kotaro, Wachi, Tokuma, Hirai, So, Yukishima, Masatoshi, Nishimura, Tomoaki, 2020. Spectral-pruning: Compressing deep neural network via spectral analysis. arXiv:1808.08558v2.

van der Maaten, Laurens, Hinton, Geoffrey, 2008. Visualizing data using t-SNE. Journal of Machine Learning Research 9, 2579–2605.

van den Oord, Aäron, Dieleman, Sander, Zen, Heiga, Simonyan, Karen, Vinyals, Oriol, Graves, Alexander, Kalchbrenner, Nal, Senior, Andrew, Kavukcuoglu, Koray, 2016. WaveNet: A generative model for raw audio. arXiv:1609.03499.

Wang, Ziyu, Schaul, Tom, Hessel, Matteo, van Hasselt, Hado, Lanctot, Marc, de Freitas, Nando, 2016. Dueling network architectures for deep reinforcement learning. In: Proceedings of the 33rd International Conference on Machine Learning. New York, NY, USA. In: JMLR: W&CP, vol. 48.

Wu, Zhibiao, Palmer, Martha, 1994. Verbs semantics and lexical selection. In: ACL'94: Proceedings of the 32nd Annual Meeting on Association for Computational Linguistics, pp. 133–138.

Yosinski, Jason, Clune, Jeff, Nguyen, Anh Mai, Fuchs, Thomas J., Lipson, Hod, 2015. Understanding neural networks through deep visualization. arXiv:1506.06579.

Zhou, Bolei, Bau, David, Oliva, Aude, Torralba, Antonio, 2019. Interpreting deep visual representations via network dissection. IEEE Transactions on Pattern Analysis and Machine Intelligence 41 (9), 2131–2145.

Zhou, Bolei, Lapedriza, Agata, Xiao, Jianxiong, Torralba, Antonio, Oliva, Aude, 2014. Learning deep features for scene recognition using places database. In: Proceedings of the 27th International Conference on Neural Information Processing Systems – Volume 1, NIPS'14. MIT Press, Cambridge, MA, USA, pp. 487–495.

Zhu, Michael, Gupta, Suyog, 2017. To prune, or not to prune: exploring the efficacy of pruning for model compression. arXiv:1710.01878.

CHAPTER 9

Explaining CNN classifier using association rule mining methods on time-series

Manjunatha Veerappa[a]**, Mathias Anneken**[a]**, Nadia Burkart**[a]**, and Marco F. Huber**[b,c]

[a]Fraunhofer Institute of Optronics, System Technologies and Image Exploitation, Interactive Analysis and Diagnosis, Karlsruhe, Germany
[b]Institute of Industrial Manufacturing and Management IFF, University of Stuttgart, Stuttgart, Germany
[c]Center for Cyber Cognitive Intelligence (CCI), Fraunhofer IPA, Stuttgart, Germany

9.1. Introduction

In order to support the understanding of today's surveillance systems, a large number of heterogeneous sensors are used in a system network. However, due to the large number of sensors, the volume of data to be processed is also growing rapidly. Therefore, automatic systems for supporting decision making are increasingly used.

An AI application of interest to us is maritime surveillance. About 80% of the global trade in 2019 was handled by the shipping industry (UNCTAD, 2019). Reliable vessel identification is thus necessary in order to combat illegal activities such as unregulated fishing and smuggling operations. Here, a *convolutional neural network* (CNN) is used as a classifier for the identification or classification of vessel types: by analyzing the movement patterns of vessels, the trained model is able to distinguish common vessel types. This can be seen as a building block for more advanced decision support systems. However, one major drawback for the acceptance of such systems is the unexplainable nature of black-box models.

The black-box models are the models whose internal workings are more difficult to understand. In particular, the deep neural networks, which have become increasingly successful in recent years, are often considered as black-box models (Russell and Norvig, 2010; Buhrmester et al., 2019; Sheu, 2020). Although they deliver highly accurate results, they fail to provide an estimate of the importance of each feature for the model predictions. This means that the results generated by black-box models such as state-of-the-art deep learning based classifiers raise questions regarding their explainability. In order to ensure the trust of operators in these systems, an explanation of the reasons behind the predictions is crucial. Hence, to make the results of such models more interpretable, different rule mining methods are evaluated in this work.

Explainable Deep Learning AI
https://doi.org/10.1016/B978-0-32-396098-4.00015-6
173

The structure of this chapter is as follows: A brief state-of-the-art regarding explainable artificial intelligence (XAI) methods is presented in Section 9.2. Section 9.3 describes the foundation towards classification, data preprocessing along with the AIS dataset, and association rule mining (ARM). The three evaluated rule mining approaches are discussed in Section 9.4. Section 9.5 contains a list of quality measures that are used for comparison of the implemented methods. Afterwards, in Section 9.6 the results of the experiments are illustrated. The chapter finishes in Section 9.7 with a conclusion and a short outlook for future work.

9.2. Related work

The research field of XAI deals with the generation of comprehensible explanations and justifications for results from complex dynamic and nonlinearly programmed systems. Model explainability allows one to better understand the function of a model by making its working mechanism transparent. This increases the confidence in such models and thus the acceptance of their introduction into real systems. For this purpose, a few model-agnostic methods such as Local Interpretable Model-Agnostic Explanation (LIME), Shapley Additive Explanations (SHAP), etc., have been introduced.

LIME technique (Ribeiro et al., 2016) was proposed by Ribeiro et al., which provides insights into the prediction of a single instance and is therefore suitable for a local explanation. This method tests what happens to the prediction by varying the data around the instance and trains a local interpretable model on this varied dataset. This allows us to create a picture that the model focuses on and uses to make its predictions. On the other hand, SHAP (Lundberg and Lee, 2017) explains the output of any machine learning model and is suitable for local explanation as well as global explanation. It is based on concepts borrowed from cooperative game theory.

The above mentioned XAI methods are typically highly focused on image, text, and tabular data. Unfortunately, the consideration of time-series is only limited for these methods. In comparison, an XAI method evaluated on time-series is presented in Schlegel et al. (2019). This method produces explanations in the form of heatmaps. The authors state that this reliance on visual saliency masks can be quite challenging for the users to interpret.

Another work on time-series is Hsu et al. (2019), where the attention mechanism concept is used to propose a deep-learning framework for interpretability. It identifies critical segments that are necessary for the classification performance. In other words, it highlights the important areas of the original data accountable for its corresponding prediction.

In healthcare, a prototype based time-series classification is proposed for interpretability (Gee et al., 2019), where prototypes are learned during the training of the classification model. These prototypes are then used to explain which features in the training data are responsible for the time-series classification.

In maritime domain application, Veerappa et al. (2021) evaluated three interpretable rule mining methods on time series datasets. Each one was a surrogate model which mimics the behavior of the MLP classifier. It was found that two out of the three rule mining methods performed quite well on every dataset, making a model less complex to interpret.

9.3. Background

In this section, the necessary background required for classification and rule mining is described. Firstly, the classification model, in particular the convolutional neural network, is introduced. This is followed by information on data acquisitions along with required preprocessing. Lastly, a brief description of association rule mining is stated.

9.3.1 Classification

Classification is a type of supervised learning in which the targets are also provided with the input data. It categorizes the output based on the input data, where categories are often referred to as targets, labels, or classes. Basically, the classifier learns from the training data to understand how the input data is related to the output. It can either be a binary classification or a multiclass classification problem. In this study, we are addressing a multiclass classification of maritime vessel types, i.e., to classify a vessel/ship-type based on its trajectories over time.

Given $\mathcal{X}$ as all possible inputs and $\mathcal{Y}$ as all possible outputs, multiclass classification can be defined as the mapping C_{multi} of an input $x \in \mathcal{X}$ to a single class $\hat{y} \in \mathcal{Y}$ and is given by

$$C_{\text{multi}} : x \mapsto \hat{y}. \tag{9.1}$$

9.3.1.1 Convolutional Neural Network — CNN

A convolutional neural network (CNN) is a deep learning algorithm that works with multidimensional data. This means that, although it was initially developed for two-dimensional image data, it can be used for one- and three-dimensional data. These networks are most often used in image related tasks, since they are able to successfully capture the spatial and temporal dependencies in the data. However, these networks can also be used for capturing the patterns on time-series data using the application of relevant filters.

Generally, CNNs consist of different layers that are stacked on top of one another. The most common layers used are the following:

- **Convolutional Layer.** As the name itself suggests, the convolutional layer performs convolution over the input. A single convolutional kernel (also called a filter) acts as a feature detector and its parameters are learned during the training phase of the neural network.

The kernel is basically a matrix of weights, which moves over the input data with a stride of 1 (default). Stride is a distance that the kernel moves over the input. For every move, a single output is produced, which is a scalar value. This process is repeated until the kernel moves over the entire input, resulting in a creation of a feature map. Once a feature map is created, which is a reduced version of the input, it is sent as input to the next layer.

- **Pooling Layer.** Similar to the convolutional layer, a pooling layer reduces the number of parameters in the input. By doing so, it serves two purposes: dimensionality reduction and introduction of invariance to small displacements. The dimensionality reduction is achieved by computing aggregation functions such as maximum, minimum, or average, over a moving portion of the input. If the filter computes the maximum value from the portion of the data covered by it, then it is referred to as max pooling, while the filter computing an average over the portion of the data referred to as average pooling. Although the pooling layer loses a lot of information, it reduces the computational power required to process the data and also avoid overfitting.

  On the other hand, it also introduces invariance to small position differences. This means that, when the pooling layer computes, e.g., a maximum value, it does not matter where exactly in the portion the feature is, but at least the feature is present.

- **Activation Layer.** Another important layer of CNNs is an activation layer. The main objective of this layer is to add nonlinearity. Typically, the activation layer is directly linked to the convolutional layer, ensuring that each convolutional layer is followed by an activation layer. The commonly used activation functions in CNNs are ReLU or variants of ReLU.

9.3.2 Data preprocessing

The dataset used in this work was Automatic Identification System (AIS). AIS is an automated tracking system equipped with transponders that can transmit and receive navigational information. Vessels equipped with onboard transceivers will continuously broadcast information about the vessel, together with identifiers such as the Maritime Mobile Service Identity (MMSI). This allows the movement of vehicles to be monitored and recorded (Raymond, 2019).

Three kinds of AIS information are transmitted by a vessel: static, dynamic, and voyage information. Dynamic information consists of position, speed over ground, course over ground, heading, etc., which is sent at intervals of two to ten seconds while underway and three minutes otherwise, whereas static and voyage information such as ship type, vessel dimensions, draught, as well as destination and ETA, is sent every six minutes (Raymond, 2019).

The vessels are divided into a set of ship types. Since most of them are relatively rare, for the evaluation only the most frequent ones (with cargo and tanker due to their similar moving patterns being fused to a single type) are used: *Cargo–Tanker, Fishing, Passenger, Pleasure-Craft,* and *Tug.*

Before the data is usable for training the classifier, preprocessing is necessary. This includes the same steps as described in Anneken et al. (2020) and Burkart et al. (2021), namely segmentation, filtering, transformation, and normalization.

Segmentation

The raw data extracted from the database consists of all received GNSS position, along with other information. Since most of the vessels are stationary, the data will have gaps because either AIS equipment is turned off or less data is transmitted often. The raw data for every vessel is segmented using

1. Temporal Gap. If the timestamp difference between successive samples in every vessel is greater than 2 hours, the data is split at every gap into separate sequences.
2. Spatial Gap. As compared to the temporal gap, the difference in position is used with a threshold of 10^{-4}. For this purpose, squared Euclidean distance is used (Dokmanic et al., 2015).
3. Sequence Length. As the above two segmentation criteria generate a wide range of different sequence lengths, the sequences are cut and padded to get the desired length with conditions as follows: If a sequence is longer than the desired sequence length, it is sliced into as many smaller sequences as necessary. After that, if a sequence is shorter than 80% of the sequence length, it is discarded, otherwise it is padded with zeros.

For each MMSI, a segmentation step is performed, which will result in trajectories. In this work, a trajectory T is defined as a sequence of n tuples, each containing the position P_i of an object at time t_i,

$$T = \{(t_1, P_1), (t_2, P_2), \ldots, (t_n, P_n)\}, \tag{9.2}$$

where the points $P_1, P_2, \ldots, P_n$ are the real positions on the surface of the earth as provided by the AIS.

Filtering

Large numbers of sequences are not relevant after segmentation, i.e., since this study classifies ship types via GNSS trajectories, the stationary vessels and the vessels traveling on rivers are filtered out.

Transformation

"Relative-to-first" transformation is used to add the invariance to the dataset. It maps the trajectory relative to the initial starting point. More detailed information can be found in Anneken et al. (2020).

Normalization

To speed up the training process of neural networks, the input features are normalized to the [0, 1] interval. This is achieved using

$$X' = \frac{X - X_{\min}}{X_{\max} - X_{\min}}. \tag{9.3}$$

After the data has gone through the preprocessing steps, nine features are extracted for each sample: Firstly, the speed over ground, the course over ground, the position in longitude and latitude (in a global and local manner), as well as the time difference between two samples, can directly be used. Based on the positional feature, additional features are derived, namely the distance to the coastline and the distance to the closest harbor. The global position is a position normalization over the whole dataset, while the local position is a normalization over the trajectory itself.

9.3.3 Association Rule Mining — ARM

ARM is one of the six tasks in data mining (Fayyad et al., 1996), which uncovers interesting relations between variables from a large dataset. A rule is basically an if–then condition/statement which has 2 items, an antecedent p and a consequent q, and takes the form $p \rightarrow q$. It can be seen as a tuple $(A, \hat{y})$, where A is a list of k predicates, the antecedents of the rule, and a prediction $\hat{y}$ as its consequent. Typically, the rules can be expressed in the form of

$$\begin{aligned} &\textbf{IF } \text{feature}_n = \alpha \textbf{ AND } \text{feature}_m < \beta \textbf{ AND } \dots \\ &\textbf{THEN } \text{class } \hat{y}. \end{aligned} \tag{9.4}$$

These rules are generated by looking for frequent patterns in data. Well-known measures that are used to generate each rule are support and confidence. In general, the aim is to create association rules for which the support and confidence is greater than the user-defined thresholds.

The association rules are derived from itemsets, which consist of two or more items. Let $I = \{i_1, i_2, \dots, i_m\}$ be a set of all items and $T = \{t_1, t_2, \dots, t_n\}$ be a set of all transactions. The *support* S can be defined as an indication of how frequently the itemset appears in all the transactions. It is the ratio of the number of transactions that contain p and q to the total number of transactions:

$$S(p \rightarrow q) = \frac{\text{Transactions containing both } p \text{ and } q}{\text{Total number of transactions}} = \frac{frq(p, q)}{|T|}. \tag{9.5}$$

The *confidence* C is defined as an indication of how often the generated association rule has been found to be true. It is defined as the ratio of the number of transactions that contain p and q to the number of transactions that contain p:

$$C(p \rightarrow q) = \frac{S(p \rightarrow q)}{S(p)} = \frac{frq(p, q)}{frq(p)}. \qquad (9.6)$$

Association rules are generated by using these two criteria. As for large datasets, the mining of all datasets is not necessarily feasible. Therefore, frequent pattern mining algorithms (Aggarwal et al., 2014) are introduced to speed up the computation.

A pattern is said to be frequent if feature values are cooccurring in many transactions. A pattern can be a single feature or a combination of features. In the dataset, the frequency of a pattern is determined by its support (Burkart et al., 2020),

$$S(\mathcal{P}) = \{(x, \cdot) \in \mathcal{D} \mid \forall p \in \mathcal{P} : p(x) = \text{True}\}, \qquad (9.7)$$

where $\mathcal{P}$ is a set of antecedents p. Algorithms for determining these patterns are called *Frequent Pattern Mining* (Letham et al., 2015). In this study, the *Equivalence Class Transformation (ECLAT)* algorithm (Zaki, 2000) is used to find frequent itemsets.

9.4. Methods

In this section, for each of the three evaluated ARM methods, a brief description is given. For the purpose of clarity, the notation found in Burkart et al. (2019) is adopted for all three methods.

9.4.1 Scalable Bayesian Rule Lists — SBRL

The first method is known as the *Scalable Bayesian Rule Lists (SBRL)*, which explains a model's prediction using a decision list generated by the Bayesian rule lists algorithm (Yang et al., 2017). A decision list is a set of rules with simple if–then statements consisting of an antecedent and a consequent. Here, the antecedents are conditions on the input features and the consequent is the predicted outcome of interest.

The scheme of this method is as shown in Fig. 9.1a. The typical objective of a model is to find a function $f : \mathcal{X} \rightarrow \mathcal{Y}$, given $\mathcal{X}$ as the space of all possible inputs and $\mathcal{Y}$ as the set of all possible outputs. The dataset $\mathcal{D}$ of size N, described by

$$\mathcal{D} = \left\{(x_i, y_i) \mid x_i \in \mathcal{X}, \ y_i \in \mathcal{Y}\right\}_{i=1}^{N}, \qquad (9.8)$$

consisting of the feature vectors $x_i \in X$ and the target classes $y_i \in Y$, is passed onto the data preprocessing section before training a model. The preprocessing steps include transformation, segmentation, filtering, and normalization as described in Section 9.3.2. The output of the preprocessing step is continuous numeric data which is then used to train the main model. Here, the main model is a *Neural Network (NN)*, denoted by

M_θ, given by its parameters $\theta \in \Theta$. The aim of the main model is to minimize the loss function $L(\theta, \mathcal{D})$, which optimizes the algorithm by estimating the classification performance,

$$\theta^* = \arg\min_{\theta \in \Theta} L(\theta, \mathcal{D}) . \tag{9.9}$$

Since the surrogate model in our case is an *SBRL* algorithm, which expects categorical features as input, the output of the preprocessing data (numeric) must be converted to categorical data. To achieve this, numerical features are binned, i.e., the range of numerical values is divided into discrete intervals. For the experiment, the number of bins is varied between 5 and 30 bins. Now, each categorical feature shows which interval contains the original numeric value. So we obtain a new dataset $\mathcal{D}'$ of size N,

$$\mathcal{D}' = \left\{ (x_i', M_\theta(x_i)) \mid x_i' \in X' \right\}_{i=1}^N . \tag{9.10}$$

The preprocessed input data x_i' along with $M_\theta(x_i)$ is then fed to the surrogate model, denoted by N_ρ, ρ being the surrogate rule list containing rules in the form of $(A, \hat{y})$. The surrogate model first mines the rules by extracting frequently occurring feature values/patterns from the dataset $\mathcal{D}'$ by using the *ECLAT* algorithm (Zaki, 2000). Next, the surrogate model learns a decision list from the premined rules and generates high confidence rules from each frequent itemset by ensuring high posterior probability. In general, we could say that the surrogate model aims to optimize the posterior probability

$$P(d \mid x, y, \mathcal{A}, \alpha, \lambda, \eta) \propto \underbrace{P(y \mid x, d, \alpha)}_{\text{likelihood}} \underbrace{P(d \mid \mathcal{A}, \lambda, \eta)}_{\text{prior}} \tag{9.11}$$

to obtain the best rule lists, where d denotes the rules in the list, λ is the desired size of the rule list, $\mathcal{A}$ is the set of premined rules, η is the desired number of terms in each rule and the preference over labels α, usually set to 1 to avoid preference over target labels. Finally, with the help of a decision list, the surrogate model N_ρ that mimics the output of the main model M_θ, will be able to explain a model's prediction.

9.4.2 Rule-based regularization method

Unlike the first method, which is an unregularized method, *Rule-based Regularization (RuleReg)* (Burkart et al., 2019) is a technique where a metric for complexity that acts as a degree of explainability is obtained from the surrogate model and fed back to the training of the main model as a regularization term. This method, similar to the *SBRL*, explains a model's prediction using a decision list consisting of a set of antecedents and consequent.

The scheme of the *RuleReg* technique is shown in Fig. 9.1b. In contrast to the *SBRL* method, both the main and surrogate models are trained simultaneously. Thus, the

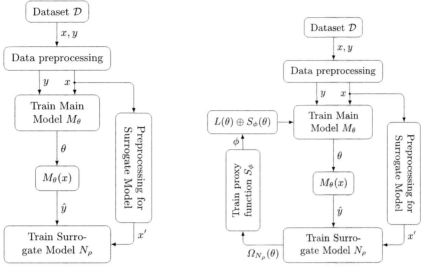

(a) The scheme of the *SBRL* method.   (b) The scheme of the *Rule Regularization* method (Burkart et al., 2019).

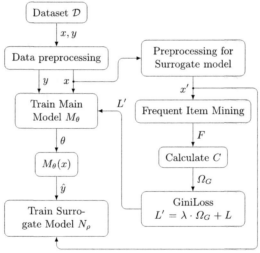

(c) The scheme of the *Gini Regularization* method.

Figure 9.1 The schemes of all three rule mining methods.

dataset $\mathcal{D} = \{(x_i, y_i)\}_{i=1}^{N}$ is passed through the preprocessing steps to the main model M_θ. As usual, the main model aims at optimizing the objective function such as the loss function L. Since it is a regularization technique, the regularization term Ω is added to the actual loss L, resulting in the new loss function

$$L'(\theta, \mathcal{D}) = \lambda \cdot \Omega(\theta) + L(\theta, \mathcal{D}), \tag{9.12}$$

where λ is the regularization strength. Please note that the term Ω is derived from the surrogate model to add a penalty to the cost function.

During the training of the main model, *RuleReg* often builds a new surrogate model for every training batch, and the metric Ω_{N_ρ} is calculated using the function

$$\Omega_{N_\rho}(\theta) = 1 + \sum_{(A,\hat{y}) \in \rho} |A|, \tag{9.13}$$

which sums up the number of antecedents for all rule lists. And this metric cannot be used directly in Eq. (9.12) as it is not differentiable. In order to overcome the problem of the regularization term not being differentiable, a proxy function is used to approximate Ω. Now, the actual loss function is

$$L''(\theta, \mathcal{D}) = \lambda \cdot S_\phi(\theta) + L(\theta, \mathcal{D}). \tag{9.14}$$

The inputs to fit the proxy function are the vectors of the main model parameters collected during the training of the main model and its corresponding complexity obtained from the surrogate model N_ρ.

And certainly, the surrogate model is fitted with the dataset $\mathcal{D}'$ of size N, namely $\{(x_i', M_\theta(x_i))\}_{i=1}^N$, where the numerical features are converted to categorical because of the requirement of the rule-mining algorithm such as *SBRL*. Once both the main and surrogate models have been trained successfully, a surrogate rule list is generated by the surrogate model which is human-simulatable. This is then used to explain a model's prediction.

9.4.3 Gini regularization method

Similar to the *RuleReg* method, *Gini Regularization* (Burkart et al., 2020) is a regularization technique which fits a global surrogate model to a deep NN for interpretability. But instead of repeatedly building a new surrogate model for every training batch as in *RuleReg*, this method focuses on training only one surrogate model. In addition, a differentiable regularization term Ω allowing gradient-based optimization is used to penalize the inhomogeneous predictions.

The scheme of this method is as shown in Fig. 9.1c. The dataset $\mathcal{D} = \{(x_i, y_i)\}_{i=1}^N$, with N being the size, is fed into the preprocessing section and then to train the main model (NN), denoted by M_θ. Before training a main model, frequent item mining is performed on an input data x' (categorical data) to obtain a set of frequent items F. For this purpose, the *ECLAT* algorithm (Zaki, 2000) is used. Once the frequent itemsets are mined, a binary matrix called *Caught-Matrix* C is calculated using

$$C_{i,j} = \begin{cases} 1, & x_i \in F_j, \\ 0, & \text{otherwise,} \end{cases} \tag{9.15}$$

indicating whether a datapoint is a member of the set F, i.e., if a datapoint x_i is in frequent itemset F_j, then the *Caught-Matrix* C at position (i, j) is 1, and 0 otherwise. Now, a differentiable loss function L' is constructed using *Caught-Matrix* and a classification loss function,

$$L'(\theta, D) = \lambda \cdot \Omega(\theta) + L(\theta, D),\qquad(9.16)$$

where Ω is the regularization term obtained despite constructing a rule–based model and λ is the regularization strength.

The main model is then trained on a dataset $\mathcal{D}$ with regard to L'. To mimic the output of the main model, the surrogate model N_ρ is trained on a dataset $\mathcal{D}' = \{(x_i', M_\theta(x_i))\}_{i=1}^{N}$ where $x' \in X'$ is the preprocessed input data. This means the numerical features are binned in order to convert them into a categorical data. To put in short, the surrogate model such as the SBRL algorithm then mines the rules and generates a decision list containing set of rules, which is used to explain a model's prediction.

9.5. Evaluation metrics

Evaluating any machine learning or deep learning algorithms is an essential part of the task. In this section, the list of quality measures that are used to compare the performance of the three methods are listed.

F_1–score of the main model ($F_{1,main}$)   is the harmonic mean between precision and recall of the main model M_θ, which seeks a balance between precision and recall. It is defined as

$$F_1 = 2 \cdot \frac{precision \cdot recall}{precision + recall}.\qquad(9.17)$$

Typically, the F_1-*score* is more useful than accuracy, particularly if the class distribution is uneven. Here, the prediction function is a CNN algorithm.

F_1–score of the surrogate model ($F_{1,surr}$)   is the harmonic mean between precision and recall of the surrogate model N_ρ and defined as shown in equation (9.17). Here, the prediction function is an SBRL algorithm, which is used to mimic the behavior of the main model M_θ.

Fidelity   is an accuracy score which measures the predictions of the surrogate model to the predictions of the main model. This means that it computes the subset accuracy: The set of labels predicted for a sample by the surrogate model must exactly match with the corresponding labels predicted by the main model. This metric matters the most, as the surrogate model tries to mimic the behavior of the main model.

Average Number of Rules (ANR)   is the number of rules which a decision list uses to classify a single sample. It should be noted that the notion of Average Path Length (APL) is not explicitly transferable to rule lists, but for comparison purposes APL has been replaced with ANR.

9.6. Experimental results

The derived datasets and experimental setup employed to train both the main model and the surrogate model for all three techniques are described in this section. In addition, all three methods are evaluated. Each method is evaluated on every dataset. Finally, the results are examined and compared to other methods.

9.6.1 Datasets

The data used in this study were based on the AIS. The experiments are conducted on four datasets. As described in Section 9.3.2, each dataset was extracted from the raw AIS data. The spatial and temporal thresholds are the same in all datasets. The only difference between the datasets is the sample count per sequence. The chosen lengths are 15, 30, 45, and 60, which correspond to 15, 30, 45, and 60 min of data, respectively, with a sampling time of 1 min. In general, each dataset has 10000 sequences with the sequence length varying depending on the chosen timespan, and each sample in turn has nine features as specified in Section 9.3.2. The target is to classify a vessel/ship-type: *Cargo–Tanker, Fishing, Passenger, Pleasure-Craft*, and *Tug*.

9.6.2 Experimental setup

The main model in all of our experiments was a simple CNN because the focus of this study was to generate a surrogate model that can imitate the behavior of the CNN classifier rather than to build a best performing main model (CNN). The network consists of layers such as input, convolution, MaxPooling, activation, and Dense. The input to the network depends on the number of samples present in a dataset, which results in a shape of "(number of samples, number of features)." A filter or kernel value of 3 is chosen to perform the multiplication between an array of input data and an array of weights. A *sparse categorical cross-entropy* is used as a classification loss function, *ReLU* as an activation function in all hidden layers, and *softmax* for the output. The main model uses the Adam optimization algorithm with a learning-rate of 0.001. In order to make *GiniReg* and *RuleReg* methods suitable for CNN models, the same architecture mentioned above, along with the same specifications, has been employed. Numerical features were binned in order to train the surrogate model. The surrogate model is trained with default hyperparameters of *SBRL* (as pysbrl on pip), except for a *support* parameter which is varied and evaluated the models performance. The *max_rule_len* parameter is chosen as 2, keeping in mind the processor and the RAM available to carry out our experiments, as well as the complexity of the local explanation. The experiments were executed on the following system:

- CPU: AMD Ryzen Threadripper 1920X 12–Core Processor
- RAM: 64 GB

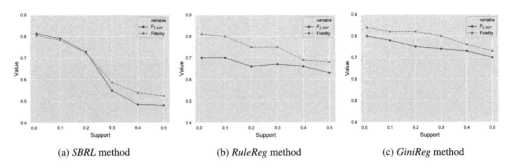

(a) *SBRL* method   (b) *RuleReg* method   (c) *GiniReg* method

Figure 9.2 The performance of the surrogate model (F_1, Fidelity) against different *support* parameter values on 30 min AIS dataset.

9.6.3 Results

The focus of this study was, on the one hand, to adapt the three ARM methods, which were proposed on MLP classifier, for a CNN-based classifier and, on the other hand, to evaluate the results of each method that are accurate and interpretable. For the adaptation, the architecture of CNN mentioned in Section 9.6.2 was used throughout our experiments. And for the evaluation, each method was implemented on every dataset. Before continuing with the evaluation, there were two parameters that had to be chosen in order to train the surrogate model, namely the *support* parameter and the number of bins considered for data preprocessing of the surrogate model. Firstly, since the *support* parameter plays a significant role while training the surrogate model, we trained all the three methods with several variations as shown in Fig. 9.2. We can observe that the performance of the surrogate model ($F_{1,surr}$) decreases with increase in the *support* value. Hence, all the models were further trained with a value of 0.01. Secondly, numerical features must be binned (number of discrete intervals) before training a surrogate model. Therefore, we trained the models with different bins as shown in Fig. 9.3. It can be observed that the performance of all three models increases to some extent and starts decreasing gradually with an increase in the number of bins. This means that the models are able to learn better if the features are categorized into more discrete intervals. But it should be noted that large discrete intervals make the model fail in learning the patterns in the trajectories of the ships.

Based on the evaluation results shown in Table 9.1, *SBRL* outperforms the other two methods in terms of metrics such as $F_{1,main}$, $F_{1,surr}$. However, due to the higher length (number of rules) of the surrogate list, it makes a model relatively more complex to interpret. Also, the fidelity between the main and surrogate models is not relatively high. *GiniReg*, on the other hand, though the F_1-score of both the main and surrogate models is a bit less compared to *SBRL*, relatively higher fidelity is achieved and the length of the resulting surrogate list is reduced, making the behavior of the model less complex to interpret. One such example of a surrogate model on 15 min dataset is shown in

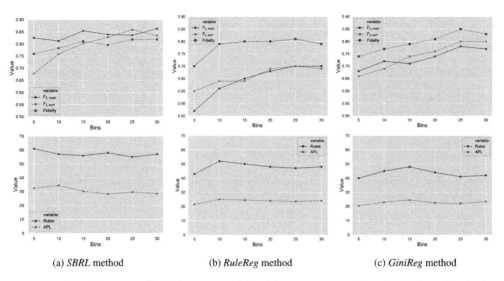

(a) *SBRL* method   (b) *RuleReg* method   (c) *GiniReg* method

Figure 9.3 The performance of both the main model and the surrogate model against different bins in the preprocessing for surrogate model on 15 min AIS dataset.

Fig. 9.4. This is the rule list that would be used in order to provide the reason for the classifier prediction. Currently, this study did not focus on the representation of the rules in a more intuitive way to the user, but it will be considered for the future work. The performance of the *RuleReg* is the worst out of all the three methods maybe because it trains multiple surrogate models during training of the main model as compared to the other two methods which train only one surrogate model. In case of *RuleReg*, choosing the correct batch size while training plays a major role. This is because training the models with smaller batch size decreases the performance of the surrogate model and with larger batch size decreases the performance of the main model.

In addition, we examined the execution time of all three methods on each dataset. The execution time is the duration of the time the method takes to train both the main model and surrogate models. For our experiments, we used a computing system as mentioned in Section 9.6.2. It can be seen in Table 9.2 that *SBRL* is faster in all circumstances, while *RuleReg* is slower. *RuleReg* generates several surrogate models while training in comparison to the other two approaches, making it rather slow.

Furthermore, the preceding experiment was carried out with the *max_rule_len* parameter set to 2 as specified in Section 9.6.2. The significance of this parameter is that at most 2 rules can be utilized in order to explain the prediction of a single instance (local explanation). That is, the shorter the rules, the longer the surrogate rule list. Similarly, the surrogate rule list gets shorter as this parameter is increased. Although a higher value of this parameter results in a shorter surrogate rule list, the increased number of rules may make the local explanation more difficult to understand for the user. As a result, this

Table 9.1 Performance of all three methods.

Method	Duration	Model	$F_{1,main}$	$F_{1,surr}$	Fidelity	No. of rules	APL/ANR	λ
SBRL			**0.84**	**0.86**	0.81	55	29.60	0.0
RuleReg	15 min	CNN	0.70	0.70	0.81	47	23.11	1
GiniReg			0.78	0.80	**0.85**	**41**	**22.11**	0.01
SBRL			**0.86**	**0.82**	0.81	54	23.50	0.0
RuleReg	30 min	CNN	0.70	0.70	0.81	47	22.52	1
GiniReg			0.82	0.80	**0.86**	**41**	**21.90**	0.1
SBRL			**0.86**	**0.84**	0.82	56	28.75	0.0
RuleReg	45 min	CNN	0.71	0.72	0.82	45	23.71	10
GiniReg			0.84	0.82	**0.85**	**42**	**22.63**	0.01
SBRL			**0.87**	**0.85**	0.82	59	30.50	0.0
RuleReg	60 min	CNN	0.70	0.72	0.80	47	23.70	1
GiniReg			0.85	0.84	**0.86**	**43**	**22.20**	0.1

linecolor@default@ @middlelinecolor@default

IF DisToCoast_14 in (0.866, 1.031] **AND** Course_17 in (1.401, 2.338]
   THEN Shiptype = Cargo-Tanker (0.94)[†]
ELSE IF (DisToCoast_23 in (0.0254, 0.194]) **AND** (DisToHarbor_24 in (-1.316, -1.182])
   THEN Shiptype = Tug (0.92)[†]
ELSE IF (Time_Diff_58 in (-0.884, -0.0441]) **AND** (DisToHarbor_6 in (-1.047, -0.913])
   THEN Shiptype = Cargo-Tanker (0.96)[†]
ELSE IF (DisToHarbor_78 in (1.498, 1.632])
   THEN Shiptype = Passenger (0.77)[†]
ELSE IF (Course_35 in (2.548, 3.552]) **AND** (Time_Diff_76 in (-0.752, 0.937])
   THEN Shiptype = Pleasure-Craft (0.95)[†]
ELSE IF (DisToCoast_41 in (-1.141, -0.974]) **AND** (DisToHarbor_60 in ((1.77, 1.904])
   THEN Shiptype = Fishing (0.98)[†]
ELSE IF (Speed_16 in (1.269, 1.396]) **AND** (DisToharbor_51 in (0.564, 0.699])
   THEN Shiptype = Passenger (0.94)[†]
ELSE IF (Course_17 in (-0.498, 0.463]) **AND** (Global_X_81 in (0.0113, 0.519])
   THEN Shiptype = Cargo-Tanker (0.47)[†]
   ⋮

ELSE Shiptype = Cargo-Tanker (0.73)[†]

―――――――――――――――――――――――――――――――
[†] predicted class with prediction probability in brackets

Figure 9.4 Example Surrogate Model for 15 min AIS dataset.

parameter must be chosen while taking into account the complexity of the explanation as well as the computing power available.

9.7. Conclusion and future work

In this study, three ARM methods have been adapted and implemented to imitate the behavior of the CNN classifier on time-series data. The results show that the methods

Table 9.2 Execution time of all the methods.

Method	Dataset	Execution time in *s*
SBRL		225
RuleReg	15 min	2221
GiniReg		316
SBRL		495
RuleReg	30 min	5010
GiniReg		1053
SBRL		914
RuleReg	45 min	12061
GiniReg		1995
SBRL		2760
RuleReg	60 min	25570
GiniReg		3769

which were initially proposed for MLP classifiers, also work well for CNN classifiers. In terms of classification, *SBRL* performs the best on almost all datasets, however, with more rules in the surrogate list, making a model more complex to interpret. In terms of explanation, *GiniReg* works the best on every dataset having high fidelity to the main model and a lower number of rules, making a model less complex to interpret. *RuleReg*, on the other hand, achieves higher fidelity but with low performance of the main and surrogate models. In comparison to the previous study, where MLP was the main model, the GiniReg method is again found to be the most effective with CNN as the main model in creating surrogate models that can mimic the predictive model's behavior. Besides, this chapter also illustrates the impact of *support* and *bins* parameters on the performance of the model. Furthermore, the execution time of all the methods was examined, where *SBRL* was faster and *RuleReg* was a lot slower.

Thus far, ARM methods were able to create a surrogate model for an MLP and a simple CNN classifier. Therefore, it would be interesting to see how these methods perform on complex CNNs such as deep CNN, recurrent neural network, residual neural network, etc., which would eventually yield new insights and should be considered. In addition, work on the representation of rules to make them more intuitive to the user is necessary.

References

Aggarwal, Charu C., Bhuiyan, Mansurul A., Hasan, Mohammad Al, 2014. Frequent pattern mining algorithms: A survey. In: Frequent Pattern Mining. Springer, pp. 19–64.

Anneken, Mathias, Strenger, Moritz, Robert, Sebastian, Beyerer, Jürgen, 2020. Classification of maritime vessels using convolutional neural networks. In: Christ, Andreas, Quint, Franz (Eds.), Artificial Intelligence: Research Impact on Key Industries; the Upper-Rhine Artificial Intelligence Symposium (UR-AI 2020). ISBN 978-3-943301-28-1, pp. 103–114. arXiv:2010.16241.

Buhrmester, Vanessa, Münch, David, Arens, Michael, 2019. Analysis of explainers of black box deep neural networks for computer vision: A survey. CoRR. arXiv:1911.12116 [abs].

Burkart, N., Faller, P.M., Peinsipp, E., Huber, M.F., 2020. Batch-wise regularization of deep neural networks for interpretability. In: 2020 IEEE International Conference on Multisensor Fusion and Integration for Intelligent Systems (MFI), pp. 216–222. https://doi.org/10.1109/MFI49285.2020.9235209.

Burkart, Nadia, Huber, Marco F., Anneken, Mathias, 2021. Supported decision-making by explainable predictions of ship trajectories. In: 15th International Conference on Soft Computing Models in Industrial and Environmental Applications (SOCO 2020). Springer International Publishing, Cham, pp. 44–54.

Burkart, N., Huber, M., Faller, P., 2019. Forcing interpretability for deep neural networks through rule-based regularization. In: 2019 18th IEEE International Conference on Machine Learning and Applications (ICMLA), pp. 700–705.

Dokmanic, Ivan, Parhizkar, Reza, Ranieri, Juri, Vetterli, Martin, 2015. Euclidean distance matrices: Essential theory, algorithms, and applications. IEEE Signal Processing Magazine 32 (6), 12–30.

Fayyad, Usama, Piatetsky-Shapiro, Gregory, Smyth, Padhraic, 1996. From data mining to knowledge discovery in databases. AI Magazine 17 (3), 37–54.

Gee, Alan, Garcia-Olano, Diego, Ghosh, Joydeep, Paydarfar, David, 2019. Explaining deep classification of time-series data with learned prototypes. arXiv:1904.08935.

Hsu, En-Yu, Liu, Chien-Liang, Tseng, Vincent, 2019. Multivariate time series early classification with interpretability using deep learning and attention mechanism. In: Pacific-Asia Conference on Knowledge Discovery and Data Mining, pp. 541–553.

Letham, Benjamin, Rudin, Cynthia, McCormick, Tyler H., Madigan, David, 2015. Interpretable classifiers using rules and Bayesian analysis: Building a better stroke prediction model. Annals of Applied Statistics 9 (3), 1350–1371.

Lundberg, Scott M., Lee, Su-In, 2017. A unified approach to interpreting model predictions. In: Proceedings of the 31st International Conference on Neural Information Processing Systems. Curran Associates Inc., Red Hook, NY, USA. ISBN 9781510860964, pp. 4768–4777. https://doi.org/10.48550/ARXIV.1705.07874.

Raymond, Eric S., 2019 AIVDM/AIVDO protocol decoding. (Accessed 28 September 2020).

Ribeiro, Marco Tulio, Singh, Sameer, Guestrin, Carlos, 2016. "Why should I trust you?": Explaining the predictions of any classifier. In: Proceedings of the 22nd ACM SIGKDD International Conference on Knowledge Discovery and Data Mining. Association for Computing Machinery, New York, NY, USA. ISBN 9781450342322, pp. 1135–1144. https://doi.org/10.18653/v1/n16-3020.

Russell, Stuart J., Norvig, Peter, 2010. Artificial Intelligence: A Modern Approach, 3rd ed. Prentice-Hall Series in Artificial Intelligence. Pearson, Boston.

Schlegel, Udo, Arnout, Hiba, El-Assady, Mennatallah, Oelke, Daniela, Keim, Daniel, 2019. Towards a rigorous evaluation of XAI methods on time series. In: 2019 IEEE/CVF International Conference on Computer Vision Workshop (ICCVW).

Sheu, Yi-han, 2020. Illuminating the black box: Interpreting deep neural network models for psychiatric research. Frontiers in Psychiatry 11, 1091.

UNCTAD: United Nations Conference on Trade and Development, 2019. UNCTAD Review of Maritime Transport. https://unctad.org/system/files/official-document/rmt2019_en.pdf.

Veerappa, Manjunatha, Anneken, Mathias, Burkart, Nadia, 2021. Evaluation of interpretable association rule mining methods on time-series in the maritime domain. In: Pattern Recognition. ICPR International Workshops and Challenges, pp. 204–218. https://doi.org/10.1007/978-3-030-68796-0_15.

Yang, Hongyu, Rudin, Cynthia, Seltzer, Margo, 2017. Scalable Bayesian rule lists. In: International Conference on Machine Learning. PMLR, pp. 3921–3930.

Zaki, Mohammed Javeed, 2000. Scalable algorithms for association mining. IEEE Transactions on Knowledge and Data Engineering 12 (3), 372–390.

CHAPTER 10

A methodology to compare XAI explanations on natural language processing

Gaëlle Jouis[a,b], **Harold Mouchère**[a], **Fabien Picarougne**[a], **and Alexandre Hardouin**[b]

[a]Nantes Université, École Centrale Nantes, CNRS, LS2N, UMR 6004, Nantes, France
[b]Pôle emploi, Information Technology Department, Nantes, France

Chapter points

- Introduction to various explanation principles
- A process to evaluate explanations without domain expert users
- A process to evaluate explanations with domain expert users
- An application of both processes
- An example of leads to adjust quantitative metric for a specific use case

10.1. Introduction

Artificial intelligence, and specifically machine learning, has been thriving for the past few years. Deep learning has proven its ability to perform in many tasks, such as image processing, object recognition, and natural language processing (Zou et al., 2019). Unlike other approaches such as linear models, deep learning models are considered as *black boxes* because their processing is quite opaque. Hence, explaining the result of a deep learning algorithm is a difficult task.

This chapter presents two context-dependent experiments to evaluate explanation methods. The first experiment is designed to provide a first evaluation when there are no end-users available. It can be conducted early and needs a few prerequisites. The second experiment provides an evaluation based on end-user preferences. It is more costly as the collection of data from users might take time.

This chapter is illustrated with a real-life use case of text classification for a French Institution, *Pôle emploi*. The classification consists in the detection of uncompliant job offers with the use of machine learning, and will later be called "LEGO" ("Légalité des Offres" in French). As an example, the sentence "We seek to hire a woman to take care of our children" is illegal, as there is discrimination over the candidate's gender. The label would be: "illegal: discriminative over gender". The institution has a legal duty of transparency about its algorithms and seeks to provide explanations alongside the tool's results. In our previous example, an explanation could be the presence of the word "woman". The "Why" and the "How" of eXplainable Artificial Intelligence (XAI) are now being tackled by the scientific community. To the best of our knowledge, proposed solutions are not systematically evaluated. Thus, choosing which method would best suit a particular AI project is not straightforward.

After presenting related works in Section 10.2, this contribution compares different explanation methods in the two different experiments. Methods are the anchors (Ribeiro et al., 2018), a method suitable for black-box models, and an attention-based white-box method, both being classic and based on distinct mechanisms. In Section 10.3 we provide our implementation of such methods. The two experiments are then detailed and applied as an illustration. The first experiment with no end user is defined in Section 10.4. The second experiment with domain expert users is detailed in Section 10.5.

The LEGO use case and Yelp (a rating app for local shops) dataset are used to generate explanations, as shown in Section 10.3. In Section 10.4 we ensure with Yelp that the process can be generalized to multiple use cases. The full evaluation process is tested on the LEGO use case with users involved in Section 10.4, suggesting best practices for XAI method comparison. Results of the process are analyzed and lead to an improvement of a quantitative metric, which is pointed out as an illustration.

10.1.1 Mathematical notations

Let us define a model $f : X \rightarrow \hat{Y}$. Let $x \in X$ be the input set of the model, and $y \in Y$ the desired output, also called ground truth. These X and Y are required in the train, validation, and test set. When the model is used for inferences, $\hat{y} \in \hat{Y}$ is the set of its outputs. Our model is the best function (linear or not) that answers for each instance $x \in X, f(x) = \hat{y} \approx y$. An explanation as a local or feature explanation is a subpart of the input x. It can be expressed as a set $Explanation = \{$"word1", "word2"$\}$ as in Ribeiro et al. (2018).

10.2. Related works

Local explanations, as named in Arrieta et al. (2020), are amongst the most used. They are mostly based on post-hoc methods, gradient analysis, and attention weights (see Section 10.2.1). They consist in highlighting parts of the input, such as variables for tabular data, n–grams for texts, and areas of pixels for images. One of the first popular local explanation is LIME (Local Interpretable Model-agnostic Explanations) (Ribeiro et al., 2016). Counterfactual explanations are also a simple way of generating explanations. Those explanations are often input samples extracted from the train dataset, sometimes generated via GANs (Charachon et al., 2020). Their main advantage is their clarity for the user. Counterfactuals can be given under the form "If only... the result will be different" (Miller, 2019). Based on the same idea, semifactual explanations are instances with the same output as the studied instance, but at the decision boundary, in other words, "right before the output changes" (Kenny and Keane, 2020).

In the rest of this section, we will present various types of methods. Then we will focus on the approaches used in our experiments, before tackling the evaluation of explanations.

10.2.1 Types of approaches

One can group the numerous existing XAI approaches according to the taxonomy found in Gilpin et al. (2018) and Guidotti et al. (2018). Hence three categories are defined:

1. Explain a *black-box* model based on its inputs and outputs.
2. Observe internal mechanisms of a system (*gray box*) after it was trained.
3. Design a transparent solution (*white box*) explaining itself.

Explaining black-box models induces the use of a proxy model. One well-known method is LIME (Ribeiro et al., 2016) and its improvement called anchors (Ribeiro et al., 2018). *LIME* is an approximation of a black-box model with a linear regression. The regression weighs the inputs by importance. Similarly, the anchors method explains a result with a rule. The rule presents a set of words leading to the decision of the model. These methods are designed to explain one instance at a time and are only accurate for close examples. Further details will be given later in Section 10.2.2.

Convolutional Neural Networks' (CNNs) internal processing has been analyzed and visualized (Zeiler and Fergus, 2014). The authors used a neural network they named *De-convolutional Network* to visualize patterns that activate neurons layer-wise. Also based on weight computation and gradient analysis, the authors of *Grad-CAM++* (Chattopadhay et al., 2018) detected regions and patterns of an image helping in class detection. Similar work has been done on semantic analysis with LSTM (Long Short-Term Memory) networks (Karpathy et al., 2015).

On the other hand, transparent solutions are inherent to the developed model. In Lin et al. (2017), the authors create an attention-based word embedding called *Structured self-attentive embedding*. Words associated with high attention weights are used by the model to classify text. Another attention-based visualization is shown in Olah and Carter (2016). Compared to black-box strategies, which are approximating the trained model, attention is a core component of this model. After training, there is no need for more computing as inference will generate attention weights used for meaningful visualizations.

In this chapter we will consider two classical methods with more details: a black-box explainer, the anchors method, and an attention-based model inspired by the work of Lin et al. (2017).

10.2.2 Local explanation with LIME and anchors

As LIME and anchors are proposals from the same authors, we will first introduce LIME to give a better understanding for the reader. As we introduce the main idea for each method, we encourage the reading of the two papers as they are strong references for the XAI field.

LIME is a linear approximation of any complex model, in the proximity of one data point $x \in X$. The model is considered the best function (linear or not) that answers $f(x) = \hat{y} \approx y$.

Let x be an instance to explain. We will select useful input variables (in our use case, words) with the following steps. First we generate, for x, the local perturbed samples, D, based on masks for each instance; D corresponds to the set Z in the original LIME paper (Ribeiro et al., 2016). A concrete example for a mask in text analysis is a sentence with a subset of words replaced by the word "OOV" which stands for "Out Of Vocabulary." The original model f is applied to this subset of data. Then we compute an estimator g, which is a linear function of an input vector x that best fits the behavior of f locally. This matches the gray dotted line of Fig. 10.1. In the end, explanations are the linear function's weights. Each weight is a variable's estimated importance. By selecting variables with a threshold weight, we obtain most important variables explaining the result $f(x)$ for our specific instance x.

Now that we know how LIME works, we can extend this to anchors. As in LIME, an anchor A is a set of words explaining an instance x. To some extent, anchors help users to understand the behavior of the model on similar texts. We will define a distribution D of similar texts, close in our vector space. It is the same idea as the set Z from LIME, but we keep the paper's notation. Hence the reader willing to check the original paper will not be lost. As in LIME, we will apply the model f to this subset of data. We get $\hat{Y}$ answers from the model. Then, we seek a set of variables shared by instances with the same label $\hat{y} \in \hat{Y}$. We try to maximize two properties: the precision, showing that most sentences with the set of variables from the anchor will have the same label as our instance, and the coverage, telling if the anchor applies to a lot of sentences.

If we rephrase this in mathematical terms, an anchor A is a rule such that, if x follows it, there is a huge probability that $f(x) = \hat{y}$. However, it might be possible that $f(x) \neq \hat{y}$, and we seek to minimize it. Let $D(\cdot|A)$ be the set of $x \in X$ following the rule A. We seek an anchor A that maximizes $D(\cdot|A)$ compared to X.

To give a concrete example, let us study a toy model that would classify sentences with "positive" and "negative" sentiments. Fig. 10.1 illustrates the concepts of LIME and anchors, it is only a drawing for comprehension purpose of this toy example. The figure was made following the codes of the original papers for LIME and anchors (Ribeiro et al., 2018, 2016). The behavior of our model is illustrated by the background colors. Blue stands for the "positive" label, and red for the "negative" label. If there were

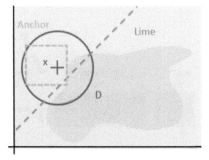

Figure 10.1 A toy example with the model's result as the background, LIME and anchors explanations are in dotted lines, for an instance *x* being the blue cross. The circle is the set *D* of variations of *x*. Illustration inspired from Ribeiro et al. (2018, 2016).

three or more labels, we would have one label versus the rest. The explained instance *x* is the blue cross in Fig. 10.1.

Let us take the sentence "This movie is not bad," which is labeled "positive" from the anchors' paper (Ribeiro et al., 2018). Hence our sentence *x* is the blue cross in Fig. 10.1. All sentences that would be in the blue parts of our vector space are classified as "positive" by our model. As LIME and anchors are local approximations, considered close sentences are in the blue circle, corresponding to the set of sentences *D*. The LIME explanation is the gray dotted line, dividing the circle to separate as well as possible the blue and red backgrounds. The anchor *A* is the rule $A = \{not, bad\} \rightarrow Positive$, and all sentences in the yellow rectangle comply to this rule. This subset is written $D(\cdot|A)$. In our example, this would refer to similar sentences containing the words "not" and "bad."

10.2.3 Attention mechanism

The attention mechanism is a useful layer in neural networks, aiming to focus on specific parts of the input to get the result (Bahdanau et al., 2015). If it has been widely used for performances gain, its inherent link with explainability has proven useful. Hence, there are many implementations of the attention mechanism for explainability purposes (Abnar and Zuidema, 2020; Yang et al., 2018; Bao et al., 2018).

There are two known attention mechanisms, namely General Attention and Self- (or Intra-)Attention. General Attention helps getting the link between two neuron layers. In Natural Language Processing (NLP) it can help associating an item of an output sequence to items in the input sequence. This is helpful in the case of translation as shown in Bahdanau et al. (2015). It is used in Transformers models to connect encoders and decoders (Vaswani et al., 2017). Self-Attention applies within the input of attention mechanism only.

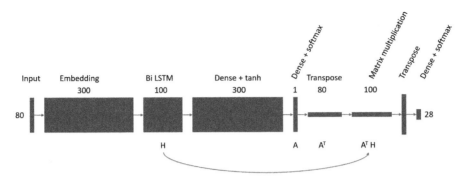

Figure 10.2 Architecture of the attention model used in this work. The output of attention layer *A* is multiplied to the output of the Bi-LSTM to compute the final decision.

Attention is made of learned weights such that every input variable gets an importance weight. This allows the next layers of the model to focus on specific parts of the input. Some implementations are designed to focus on word embeddings globally (Lin et al., 2017). This result in a network with a readable architecture. Self-Attention can be as simple as a dot product of two vectors with an activation such as a softmax activation function.

Others are designed to capture more details. These works aim to capture higher level concepts, despite adding the necessity of more complex models. In Wang et al. (2016), for instance, this means adding aspect-level attention as an input of the model.

In this work we will focus on Self-Attention, and will simply refer to it as attention. Fig. 10.2 details our reference layout (Lin et al., 2017). The attention matrix *A* is computed based on hidden states *H* of a Bi-LSTM layer. When applying a threshold on the highest attention weights, one can create explanations as the most considered inputs of the model. This allows one to highlight "most used" words by the model to compute its output.

Attention has been decried as multiple attention masks can lead to the very same result for a model input (Jain and Wallace, 2019). Hence, it is important to keep in mind that the attention mechanism is internal to the model. It might not provide the perfect desired explanation, compared to what a human could express. It will give users an insight of what triggers the most their model to explain a result (Wiegreffe and Pinter, 2019).

10.2.4 Evaluate explanations

Evaluating explanations can be done with two main approaches: (1) criteria and metrics, as well as (2) user evaluation.

Criteria and metrics

Explanations or models generating them are often evaluated with criteria and metrics in the literature. To evaluate proxy models, one most often used criterion is fidelity to the black-box model, measured by accuracy, or F1-score (Guidotti et al., 2018; Ribeiro et al., 2018). Interpretability is also measured, often as a size of the proxy model, such as the number of weights (Guidotti et al., 2018). The coverage can be measured as the number of instances that are in agreement with an explanation (Ribeiro et al., 2018). Metrics can also evaluate the explanation itself. In the case of natural language explanations, it is possible to use readability score such as the *Flesch-Reading-Ease* score, used in Costa et al. (2018). When required explanations are available, expected and obtained explanations can be compared as sets of features. Computing the Intersection Over Union (IOU) gives a score from 0 to 1. An IOU of 1 means explanations are identical. This metric is used in Bau et al. (2017) to evaluate interpretability in image-based problems. If only a few explanations are possible, the case can be considered as a classification problem, and usual accuracy metrics can be used (Codella et al., 2019).

Evaluation based on metrics allows working on huge test datasets. Without the need of finding users, it is also faster and cheaper to develop quantitative evaluations on any XAI method. However, explanations are designed to be an interface between algorithms and humans, hence they need to be evaluated by or with humans.

User evaluation

When conducting a user study on model explanations, evaluation can be objective or subjective. Subjective evaluation can be retrieved with a poll asking users if they are satisfied with a given explanation, or which explanation they prefer among a couple of them (Ribeiro et al., 2018). They might also be asked to choose between two classifiers, one being significantly better than the other, given only their explanations (Ribeiro et al., 2016). These evaluations are appropriate when the purpose is improving acceptance of a model. On the other hand, objective metrics can be extracted from user studies. In Iyer et al. (2018), users are given an explanation and must predict the next output of the system. Considering user's answers as results of binary classifiers, the authors compute an ROC curve and its area under curve to measure the success of their explanations. When the user must predict the output of the model, the response time of the user can be used as a measure of the user's confidence (Ribeiro et al., 2018).

The two proposed evaluation processes in this chapter are based on these two approaches. The first process is relying on metrics, and the second is based on users' preferences.

10.3. Generating explanations

In order to illustrate this chapter with an application of our evaluation processes, we generate various explanations to evaluate. We want here to compare two explanation methods: generation of anchors from Ribeiro et al. (2018) upon any model, and the use of attention within a transparent model from Lin et al. (2017). For each use case that follows, a transparent attention-based model will be trained, and anchors will be generated on the predictions of this same model. Quoting Ribeiro et al. (2018) again for the example, let us take the sentence "This movie is not bad," which is classified as "positive" by an attention-based model. As mentioned in Section 10.3, the anchors explanation would be $A = \{not, bad\} \rightarrow Positive$. Every word in the sentence would have an attention weight, and "not" and "bad" would have the highest weights.

The generation of anchors is made with the Python library developed by the authors of Ribeiro et al. (2018). Following the research of Lin et al. (2017), a neural network with a Bi-LSTM and the same attention mechanism was trained. The architecture was detailed in Fig. 10.2. The attention mechanism results in an attention matrix A, linking words to attention weights. Words of interest are filtered using a threshold t on attention values. In this section, attention models of each use case will be described, then the generation of ground truth will be discussed.

10.3.1 Yelp use case

The Yelp dataset contains user reviews about restaurants, associated with 1- to 5-star ratings. The training set contains 453 600 reviews. For this version of attention network, the embedding is a 100-dimensional English–based word2vec.[1] The optimizer is Adam with a learning rate of 0.0005. This network achieves an accuracy of 74.63% on its test set. In comparison, the authors of Lin et al. (2017) present in their paper an accuracy of 64.21% on their own test set.

Two explanations are extracted from this model: anchors' explanations and attention explanations with a threshold of $t = 0.15$. Table 10.1 illustrates these explanations over one rating from the Yelp dataset. A user study is not achieved for this use case, hence there is only one threshold of attention generated. As anchors explainer on large texts often leads to memory issues, anchors have been applied to a subset of 1060 shortest reviews over the 2653 reviews of the full test set.

10.3.2 LEGO use case

Pôle Emploi is the French national job center. One of its tools aims to automatically reject uncompliant job offers. Indeed, *Pôle Emploi* is legally bound to reject offers not complying with the Labor Code or being discriminative. The training dataset contains

---

[1] https://wikipedia2vec.github.io/wikipedia2vec/pretrained/.

Table 10.1 Yelp use case: Two reviews with ratings and explanations for anchors and attention methods. See text for other information.

Rating as stars	Anchors Expl.	Attention Expl. 0.15
"Wow! Superb maids did an amazing job cleaning my house. They stayed as long as it took to make sure everything was immaculate. I will be using them on a regular basis."		
5	[]	['superb', 'amazing', 'everything']
"For the record, this place is not gay friendly. Very homophobic and sad for 2019. Avoid at all costs."		
1	['not']	['record', 'not', 'homophobic', 'sad', 'avoid']

480000 sentences extracted from real offers. Retrieving the reason for rejection is a multiclass classification task, with 28 topics being targeted in this study. Offers used for the training of the classifier are already labeled in *Pôle Emploi*'s database, with labels predicted by the existing rule-based system.

The classifier for this use case is similar to that for the Yelp dataset. The embedding matrix used is a 300-dimensional GloVe embedding.[2] The optimizer is Adam with a learning rate of 0.0005. This network achieves an accuracy of 83.67% on its test set.

The old rule-based system, on which the Neural Network is trained, is prone to some errors. Thus, to accurately analyze explanations, a corrected test set was necessary. As the correction of labels is time-consuming, a test set of 208 sentences has been manually labeled and attributed the desired explanation. This explanation consists of highlighting keywords that led to rejection. As explanations are meaningful for uncompliant offers only, explanations for compliant offers are considered to be empty. The real world's class distribution has not been respected, and compliant explanations are underrepresented in this test set. Hence, the model's accuracy for this test set is lower and irrelevant (70.67%).

Later in this chapter, two subsamples of this test set of 208 sentences will be used. The test set of Good Predictions (GP), used in Section 10.4, is made of 147 sentences from the test set, correctly predicted. This dataset allows measuring explanations' performance when the model makes no error, preventing the measure to be affected in case of a poorly performing model. The test set of sentences with Different Explanations (DE), used in Section 10.5, is made of 106 sentences from the test set, with nonidentical explanations. This dataset focuses on the task for users to compare explanations, and avoid the situation where users have to choose between only identical explanations.

Three explanations are extracted from this model as shown in Table 10.2. Anchors' explanations are using the model as a black-box method, and two explanations rely on the attention mechanism, with threshold values of $t = 0.15$ and $t = 0.5$. The second explanation with a different threshold is used in the psychometric user study. As only

---

[2] https://dl.fbaipublicfiles.com/fasttext/vectors-crawl/cc.fr.300.vec.gz.

Table 10.2 LEGO use case: Sentences with their different explanations. See text for other information. Sentences are respectively numbered 0 and 73 from the LEGO - DE dataset.

Reject	Ground Truth	Anchors Expl.	Attention Expl. 0.15	Attention Expl. 0.5
"[...] Notre agence de Saint-Medard-en-Jalles recherche une Assistante Administrative pour completer son equipe."				
Genre[a]	['assistante administrative']	['recherche', 'Assistante', 'Jalles']	['assistante', 'administrative']	['assistante']
"Poste en CDD renouvelable en cdi."				
CDD possibilité CDI[b]	['CDD renouvelable en cdi']	['CDD renouvelable', 'cdi']	['cdi']	['cdi']

[a] Gender
[b] Fixed-term contract leading to permanent contract

the threshold is different, explanations with *attention* 0.5 are a subset of explanations with *attention* 0.15. When the model predicts no rejection, generated explanations are forced to be empty.

10.3.3 Generating human attention ground truth

To generate ground truth, some works are based on human attention (Mohseni et al., 2021). Hence there is a need for domain experts, or, if missing, strong reference documentation. A document containing law extracts and labeling guidelines was used to create the test LEGO dataset. For instance, gender discrimination is usually detected with the job title, hence it should be labeled as the explanation. We aim to compare explanations generated with a tool to an "ideal explanation." For a particular instance, we can separate "ideal explanation" (we will latter call it "ground truth") and "expected explanation." The difference between "ideal" and "expected explanation" is defined in the following two paragraphs.

Let us stay in the context of supervised learning. A ground-truth explanation consists of an input/output pair plus an "ideal explanation." It is ideal because it applies when everything runs smoothly. This explanation is based on domain expertise, which is why we call it "ground truth." If we wanted to train a model to give back those explanations, we would provide those as a training dataset. They are identical no matter which classifier one may use. In Mohseni et al. (2021), the authors refer to human attention, but explanations are based on a target label. Plus, no error is mentioned, hence we can deduce that only explanations on correct predictions were evaluated. This is an example of ground-truth explanations. In this chapter, ground-truth explanations are also being used as the reference in experiments achieved in Sections 10.4 and 10.5.

When a classifier gives the desired output, its explanation matches this ground truth. A model can also give an output that differs from expected label. In this very case, "ideal explanation" as previously defined does not reflect the model's behavior. It might be wished to get an explanation that answers the question "What was used by the model to give its answer?" To obtain this "expected explanation," one might ask users (domain experts, model experts). One could also ask domain experts to verify models' results and see where their attention is focused (oculometry, unbluring parts of an image...) (Das et al., 2017).

10.4. Evaluation without end users

Now that explanations have been generated, let us tackle the first experiment. In this section we will compare explanation methods with no end users, thanks to metrics. We will compare our two methods, anchors and attention. A threshold t is used in order to filter attention explanations, we only consider explanations with $t = 0.15$ in this section. This experiment seeks to provide a first evaluation, when there is no domain expert user available. We seek to know which explanation method best suits our use case in its given context. To do so, we divide our problem in two questions.

The first question is: "Is this explanation close to an ideal explanation?" A simple metric has been set, IOU, and used amongst other known metrics (accuracy, F1-score, etc.). These metrics compare the ground truth (see Section 10.3.3) to generated explanations for the LEGO dataset. As there was no domain expert's documentation for the Yelp use case, there was no ground truth for its dataset. Therefore, answering this question was not possible for this use case.

The second question is: "When there is no ground truth, how to assess explanation methods?" A qualitative human eye comes quickly with an answer, but it can be a very long (hence costly) task. In order to achieve it efficiently, IOU between anchors and attention explanations has been used to detect sentences of interest. In a context of an experiment without domain experts, this allows a data expert (e.g., a data scientist working on the use case) to proceed to a first evaluation of various explanation methods.

10.4.1 Quantitative analysis

As used in Bau et al. (2017), IOU will allow comparing ground truth to generated explanations. This means that ground truth serves as a reference and is, by design, considered as the best result. Accuracy and F1-score are also compared, plus recall and precision used in the F1-score. Recall is an interesting metric as it is not impacted by true negatives.

In the context of the LEGO dataset, to get fair measures, stop words are not taken into account. As the evaluation of the model is not the point in this experiment, the test set is a subset of 147 sentences out of 208 that have been correctly predicted.

Table 10.3 Comparison of anchors and attention explanations with ground truth, LEGO GP dataset. Best results are in bold. Attention gets slightly better results.

Measure	Anchors Expl.	Attention Expl. 0.15
IOU	0.938	**0.957**
Acc	0.980	0.987
Recall	0.970	0.964
Precision	0.961	**0.993**
F1	0.954	**0.969**

Results for all metrics for the LEGO use case are displayed in Table 10.3. Overall, when comparing to ground truth, attention explanations are slightly better than anchors, cf. Table 10.3. Scores are high, partially due to the number of sentences not rejected in the GP dataset, namely 131. These instances have no explanation, hence their metrics are equal to 1. Anchors and attention are also compared to one another. With no ground truth, metrics such as accuracy and F1-score are irrelevant. High IOU indicates that explanations are similar with both methods. The IOU between anchors and attention explanation is 0.947, which indicates that they give similar results. For the LEGO use case, anchors and attention explanations are both similar and close to the ideal explanation. Attention explanations seem to perform slightly better. Table 10.2 illustrates such slight variations in explanations.

For the Yelp use case, there is no ground truth. Hence, comparison is only possible between anchors and attention explanations. IOU indicates whether the given explanations are similar. Average IOU on the successful test set is 0.229, which shows strong differences between the two explanation methods. This can be explained by long texts and vast expected vocabulary in explanations. Hence, to assess explanation methods in Yelp use case, qualitative analysis is needed.

10.4.2 Qualitative analysis

As high IOU shows similarity between the two explanations, qualitative analysis can be more efficient with filtering texts with low IOU in the test set. Doing so will point out if one explanation method is more accurate when being different. Hence this filtering will be used in the following qualitative analysis for both use cases.

For the LEGO use case, anchors explanations are in average shorter than attention-based explanations. Average lengths are respectively 0.15 and 0.33 words in the test set. The mean value is low due to empty explanations. Table 10.2 gives examples where IOU is less than 0.5. This qualitative analysis is in agreement with the quantitative analysis, and points to attention weights as a better explanation method for this use case.

Table 10.4 Influence of rating shown by explanation in the Yelp use case.

Description	Rating	Predicted rating	Anchors Expl.	Attention Expl. 0.15
"[...] And this is the reason I gave them a mere 2 stars[...]"	3	2	['2', 'stars']	['2']

On the Yelp dataset, there is no possibility to compare explanations with any expected one. Still, it is interesting to have a look at explanations for extreme reviews (1 and 5 stars, well recognized) when IOU is 0, meaning explanations are very different.

For the Yelp use case, average explanation lengths are similar, 2.34 and 2.13 words for anchors and attention, respectively. Table 10.1 illustrates examples of Yelp ratings and associated explanations for extreme reviews (5 and 1 stars). It indicates a lack of meaningful words in anchors. For these sentences, attention-based explanations are performing better than anchors' explanations. The last line of Table 10.1 shows explanations based on different, but meaningful words. As average lengths are similar and attention seems more accurate when explanations are very different, this qualitative analysis indicates that attention-based explanations are a safer choice in this particular use case.

One interesting point for the Yelp use case is that both explanations are pointing to the same parts when reviewers mention their own rating. This even leads to a wrong prediction shown in Table 10.4. As the text mentions 2 stars, predicted rating is 2 stars. The real rating was 3 stars, but explanations both point out the "2" from the text.

The answer to our second question is the same for both use cases. Without using ground truth, IOU allows selecting interesting sentences to analyze. For both use cases, it pointed to attention explanations as a winning method. This first experiment has been designed to give a first evaluation of multiple explanation methods when domain experts and end users are out of reach. The following section presents a bigger experiment, with users involved.

10.5. Psychometric user study

The aim of this second study is to evaluate explanation methods when end users and/or domain experts are available. This user study is based on the LEGO use case. Yelp will no longer be treated as we do not have its corresponding end users. This experiment answers two questions: "Which explanation is preferred by domain expert?" and "How to make the quantitative metric match users' preference?"

As the goal is to work with preferences, the test dataset is different from that in Section 10.4. The DE dataset of 106 sentences will be used. This filter prevents users to be left with identical explanations to compare, which is meaningless.

To answer both questions, first of all, the experimental protocol is detailed. Then, results are presented and analyzed.

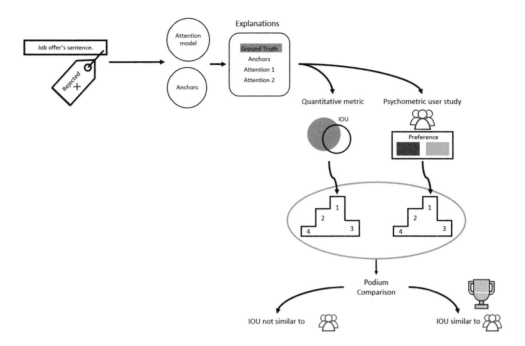

Figure 10.3 Global process of the experiment, with psychometric user study and quantitative analysis.

10.5.1 Experimental protocol

This section presents the global workflow for this second experiment. In a context where end users are available, this process allows for an evaluation of explanation methods that takes users' preferences into account. There are two goals: first, to collect users preferences for explanation methods, and second, to refine a quantitative metric to estimate users' preference. As in the previous experiment, the quantitative metric is IOU. Using Fig. 10.3 for support, the full process is now described following the arrows in the diagram.

First, labeled data are given to the model and explanation methods that we seek to evaluate. As peer-to-peer comparison is achieved later, we strongly recommend considering only a few evaluated explanation methods at a time.

To get the quantitative metric, explanations generated are compared with ground truth, in orange in Fig. 10.3. The first version is a simple metric, here IOU as seen in Section 10.4.1. Again, ground truth is considered the best option by design and gets the maximum score of 1. Other explanations get IOU scores between 0 and 1, with 1 being the best. Ordering explanation methods by their average IOU gives the quantitative ranking.

In parallel, a psychometric user study is achieved, as fully described in Section 10.5.2. As a quick brief, a peer-to-peer comparison is given to users, resulting in a preference matrix. The (i, j) element of the matrix indicates the number of times i has been preferred to j. In order to get a ranking from this matrix, the Bradley–Terry–Luce (BTL) algorithm was used. It gives a psychometric scale to rank the four explanations methods, namely ground truth and the generated ones.

Once rankings are defined, we can compare them in a podium comparison. If quantitative metric's ranking is similar to users' preferences, we can safely estimate that our metric reflects users' preference. The metric can be kept and reused with other explanation methods if needed.

If quantitative metric's ranking is not similar to users' preferences, then our quantitative metric needs to be improved. An analysis of this experiment's data will give leads on what to improve.

This illustration has been made on the LEGO use case for the sake of clarity, but can be generalized to other use cases, with a different set of data, other explanation methods, and a quantitative metric other than IOU. Data consists here of job offers' sentences as textual inputs with their associated labels: reason for rejection. Explanations are generated as described earlier in Section 10.3. As anchors need to be generated with a model, the attention model is used to generate the label. This ensures that model differences will not impact the experiment. In this work, we compare anchors and two attention explanations with thresholds values of $t = 0.15$ and $t = 0.5$. For each sentence, ground truth is also established, full details are given in Section 10.3.3. One input generates four elements to be compared.

Now that the overall experiment has been presented, the protocol for collecting users' preferences is detailed.

10.5.2 Collecting users' preferences

To collect their preferences, users are presented twice the same text, with the model's label and any needed material. For each extract, some of the words are highlighted. This constitutes an explanation. These elements can be seen in Fig. 10.4 in the two areas with white background color, for the LEGO use case. In this case, extra material is a rule for a quick reminder of the legal reason of rejection.

Users are asked to choose the explanation answering the question "Which explanation is the most useful in order to understand the alert?", the "alert" being the AI tool's answered reason of rejection. As shown in Fig. 10.4, the question is displayed on the top of screen during the entire experiment. The answer might be a mistake from the AI model. In this case, ground–truth explanations might seem off-topic to users, as discussed in Section 10.3.3.

The explanation can be "empty," meaning that there is no highlighted word. If users have no preference between the two explanations, they are asked to pick one according to their subjective feelings. As multiple users rate the same sentences, such cases will appear in data as difficult choices, where no explanation stands out.

Figure 10.4 The user interface for the experiment. Users are asked to choose between the two shown explanations and pick their preferred one. Above the explanations, the reason for rejection and associated rule are displayed. Explanations consist of highlighted words.

To reduce the risk of bias linked to users, the following precautions are recommended: first, to take into account users' focus, as the task is repetitive and can mix clear and nuanced preferences; second, to avoid any bias caused by tiredness or loss of attention, dividing the collection in smaller sessions. In users studies, another bias that can be encountered is the learning process of a given task. One strategy consists in asking expert users. Training users by having a set of learning instances that are not used in the analysis is another strategy. Finally, any accommodation for users in the design of the experiment must be made to ensure consistency of the results.

Applied to our end users of the LEGO use case, multiple actions have been taken. To avoid attention loss, they have been given small sessions of experimentation, namely 30 minutes per session. In the experiment, they have been given 9 sessions to do. They were also asked to switch off notification sources such as cellphones or company's communication software (emails and instant chat tools). Finally, each user saw pairs in a different order.

To tackle the learning bias, 14 users have been recruited through *Pôle Emploi*'s internal network. They were employees specializing in supporting recruiters, hence own domain experts. They were especially used to write and edit job offers and had been working with a rule-based (regex) old version of our AI solution that raises legal alerts for many years. Hence, users of this experiment were already aware of possible cases leading to false positives and negatives for an automatic reject of job offers. For sure, these experts were not prone to errors due to the discovery of the use case.

Users are experts and their schedule does not allow booking 4.5 hours of experiments in a row. The experiment has been designed to be carried out autonomously by users. First, the experiment has been divided in sessions of 30 minutes. The task was straightforward as they were given a single page with very few elements, as shown in Fig. 10.4. The experiment required no specific condition such as light level or screen colorimetry. Finally, at any time users were able to ask questions via a phone call or their usual tool for instant messaging.

The full procedure for this experiment has been detailed, now let us compute podiums from quantitative metric and users' preference.

Table 10.5 Objective comparison of anchors and attention explanations. Explanations are compared to ground truth with the IOU quantitative metric, on the LEGO DE dataset.

Explanation	Anchors Expl.	Attention Expl. 0.15	Attention Expl. 0.5
All (106)	0.269	0.230	0.231
Empty (53)	0.019	0.132	0.207
Simple (12)	0.534	0.583	0.458
Complex (41)	0.514	0.254	0.195

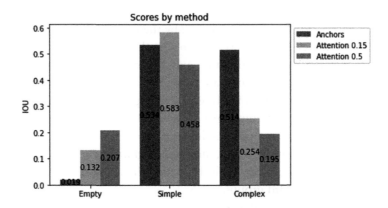

Figure 10.5 Scores obtained with IOU for each explanation method, on the LEGO DE dataset.

10.5.3 Computing IOU

As mentioned at the beginning of this section, this experiment is based on the DE dataset. This specific subdataset has no compliant sentences. Comparing quantitative metric with users' preference implies recomputing IOU in this dataset in order to define the podium for quantitative metric. Because of this variation on the design of the dataset, a consequent drop of IOU was expected, compared to IOU computed on the LEGO GP dataset in Section 10.4.

IOU was computed with the same protocol, with the stop words being ignored. As shown in Table 10.5, scores are dropping significantly, which was expected. Further analysis shows that, in our case, this decrease is due to working only with noncompliant sentences.

Results in Table 10.5 show a small difference between methods. Further analysis in this use case suggests differentiating sentences by their expected explanation, ground truth. Compliant sentences have no ground truth as discussed earlier. Those sentences will constitute the *empty* explanation category. Some sentences have *simple* expected explanations, made of one or two words. Finally, we will regroup expected explanations of three or more words in the *complex* category. This clustering gives us IOU scores for Fig. 10.5.

Table 10.6 Podium based on IOU, on the LEGO DE dataset, by category of explanation. Ground truth is the reference to compute, hence is not appearing in this table.

	First	Second	Third
Empty	Attention 0.5	Attention 0.15	Anchor
Simple	Attention 0.15	Anchor	Attention 0.5
Complex	Anchor	Attention 0.15	Attention 0.5

The first group of Fig. 10.5 shows that all three other methods have poor IOU, especially the anchors method. This is explained by the fact that IOU with empty ground truth can only be 0 or 1. An IOU of 0 is when a method gives any words as an explanation, hence intersection of this explanation and no explanation is of length 0. When a method gives no explanation, we compare two empty sets. As they are equal, IOU is 1. As anchors and attention methods rarely give nothing as an explanation, their IOU is very low when compared to an empty ground truth. The second group highlights good performance for anchor and attention method with $t = 0.15$ to imitate the given ground truth. The last group, for complex cases, indicates a significant divergence of both attention methods compared to ground truth. However, the anchors method keeps a stable IOU between the 2nd and 3rd groups.

For sure, IOU scores can be translated in the podium in Table 10.6. As a reminder, here the ground truth is our reference for IOU, hence it is considered as the best explanation for each case. Hence we have a ranking with ground truth as the reference, and the three other methods in an order as shown in Table 10.6. These podiums can now be compared to the users' preferences podiums. These users' preferences are discussed in the next section.

10.5.4 Users' preference

In this section we measure domain expert preferences by collecting peer-to-peer preferences, in the experiment detailed in Section 10.5.2.

Then we get preferences from the psychometric user experiment and obtain a preference matrix. Here $A = (a_{ij})_{m \times m}$ is the preference matrix, where each coefficient a_{ij} is the number of times the stimulus S_i has been preferred to the stimulus S_j. The matrix's diagonal is null. The number of comparisons is $n_{ij} = a_{ij} + a_{ji}$ and the probability that S_i is preferred over S_j is $P_{ij} = a_{ij}/n_{ij}$.

We will get a credit score from the preference matrix thanks to the Bradley–Terry–Luce (BTL) model. In this experiment, the credit score v_i represents the probability that one user chooses a method over the others. This algorithm has already been used in the literature when comparing users' preferences (Ak et al., 2021). We then obtain a psychometric scale such as in Fig. 10.6. A higher score indicates users preference. As v_i score is computed relatively to other elements, it should not be compared to any other scale. As this scale is transformed into a podium, this is not an issue here.

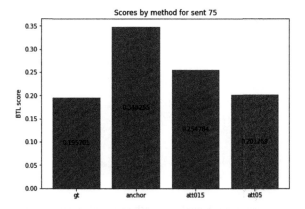

Figure 10.6 Example of scores obtained with the BTL model for each explanation method on one sentence. The value corresponds to the probability one user prefers one method over the others. Sentence extracted from the LEGO De dataset.

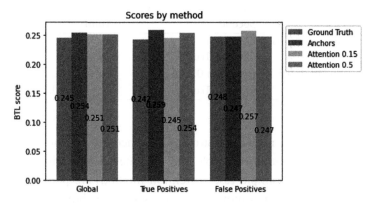

Figure 10.7 Scores obtained with the BTL model for each explanation method, on the LEGO DE dataset. True positives and false positives are shown. No strong difference appears between these two subsets.

The BTL scores can be evaluated sentence-wise. As shown in Fig. 10.6, for this specific sentence, the psychometric scale clearly points out attention with $t = 0.5$ as a preferred method, and anchors as least liked by users.

We then observe BTL scores on the entire LEGO DE dataset, and on two subsets, true positives and false positives, as we expect results to differ. The results are compared in Fig. 10.7. Unfortunately, this analysis shows no significant difference between the methods. Such a result points out that, globally, there is no method that wins it all.

Just like we did in Section 10.5.3, let us divide our dataset by sentences with *empty*, *simple* and *complex* ground-truth explanations. The BTL algorithm gives us the associated psychometric scale in Fig. 10.8.

Again, this psychometric scale can be turned into podiums, displayed in Table 10.7. Let us do a first analysis for all types of sentences. For sentences with empty ground-

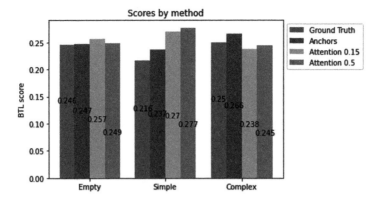

Figure 10.8 Scores obtained with the BTL model for each explanation method, on the LEGO DE dataset, by complexity. This clustering shows differences in users' preferences.

Table 10.7 Podium based on psychometric user study, on the LEGO DE dataset, by category of explanation.

	First	Second	Third	Fourth
Empty	Attention 0.15	(Attention 0.5, Anchor, Ground Truth)		
Simple	Attention 0.5	Attention 0.15	Anchor	Ground Truth
Complex	Anchor	Ground Truth	Attention 0.5	Attention 0.15

truth explanation, users do not have a strong preference for one method or another as shown in Fig. 10.8. The podium in Table 10.7 indicates that the slight preference goes to attention methods. For simple cases, attention methods are preferred, and ground truth is the least appreciated. For more complex cases, the anchors' explanation method has been preferred, and attention methods are struggling. In our use case, in other words, users do prefer attention methods in simple cases. When things are getting more complex, their preference goes to the anchors explanation method. This answers our first question regarding users' preference.

These podiums are compared to the qualitative metric podiums in the next section.

10.5.5 Analysis

We can now compare our results of quantitative analysis from Section 10.4.1 and user preference from Section 10.5.4. As we did before, let us stick to the analysis by complexity of ground-truth explanations. If we look at podiums from Tables 10.6 and 10.7, they do differ. One of the main reasons is the fact that the IOU metric is based on ground truth, which is not the method users prefer.

We can compare quantitative metric and users' podium regarding the category of explanation: empty, simple, and complex. The stacked barchart as shown in Fig. 10.9

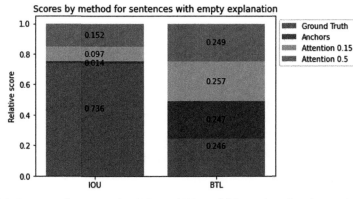

Figure 10.9 Relative scores from normalized IOU and BTL model for each explanation method, on the LEGO DE dataset, filtered on sentences with empty explanations. Normalization ensures that the sum of all scores is equal to one, helping to compare relative proportion between IOU and BTL.

allows comparing the relative proportion of methods in each case. IOU values are normalized for comparison, real values are presented in Table 10.5.

For sentences with empty ground-truth explanations, Fig. 10.9 shows that IOU and BTL reflect different explanations. As a reminder, the DE dataset is composed of sentences labeled as uncompliant by our model. Empty ground-truth explanations are associated with compliant sentences that have been wrongly predicted as uncompliant by the model. In this case, the ground truth might not be the right reference to compute IOU with. As explained in Section 10.3.3, we could prefer an expected explanation that should be defined for a specific model.

The case of sentences associated with simple ground-truth explanations is shown in Fig. 10.10. It highlights good quantitative results for *attention* 0.15 and anchors, *attention* 0.5 being the least matching method to ground truth. When it gets to users, they did not prefer ground truth over the other methods, and liked *attention* 0.5 more. Taking ground truth as a reference here does not make sense, and thus we can conclude that our IOU based on ground truth is not effective here either. However, users seem to like short explanations, as they preferred *attention* 0.5 over *attention* 0.15. For these simple cases, the length could help measure the relevance of any given explanation. Our quantitative metric should reflect this point, decreasing when the length of an explanation increases.

Podiums for sentences with more complex ground-truth explanations are compared in Fig. 10.11. IOU shows a good matching for anchors' explanations. This is reflected in the user study, as the preferred method is anchors, followed by ground truth. Considering IOU, *attention* 0.5 is less performing compared to *attention* 0.15. However, considering users, we see that their preference is actually the opposite. As *attention* 0.5 is a subset of *attention* 0.15, it indicates a preference for shorter explanations. Just like

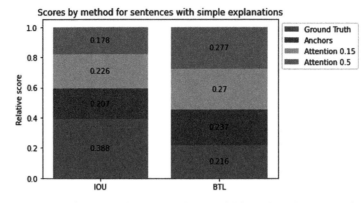

Figure 10.10 Relative scores from normalized IOU and BTL model for each explanation method, on the LEGO DE dataset, filtered on sentences with simple explanations. Normalization ensures that the sum of all scores is equal to one, helping to compare relative proportion between IOU and BTL.

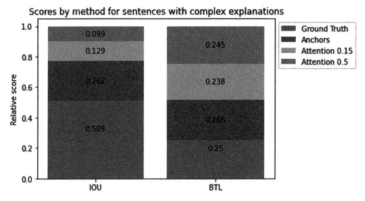

Figure 10.11 Relative scores from normalized IOU and BTL model for each explanation method, on the LEGO DE dataset, filtered on sentences with complex explanations. Normalization ensures that the sum of all scores is equal to one, helping to compare relative proportion between IOU and BTL.

for simple cases, our metric would better reflect users' preference if it took into account the explanations' length.

For all these categories, our podiums are different. According to our global experiment, we should then enhance our quantitative metric. To do so, the analysis gave us two leads. First, expected explanations, instead of ideal explanations (see the definition in Section 10.3.3), would be more efficient to serve as a reference. As they are more expensive, this could be done step by step. As we are aware, false positives are a source of great difference between expected and ideal explanations, they should be the first focus. The second lead is to take explanations' length into account in our experiment, as they seemed, for simple and complex cases, to be slightly preferred by users. These upgrades would lead to a change in our metric from

$$metric = \frac{e_{ideal} \cup e}{e_{ideal} \cup e} \tag{10.1}$$

to

$$metric = \frac{e_{expected} \cup e}{e_{expected} \cup e} \frac{\alpha}{len(e)}. \tag{10.2}$$

The formalization of this new equation for a quantitative metric is the answer to our second question of "How to make the quantitative metric match users' preference?". As we would need to recreate a new ground-truth dataset, the next step of this experiment is left off of this contribution. However, all the steps of this second experiment now have been illustrated.

10.6. Conclusion

The upcoming multiplicity of XAI methods leads to the necessity of choosing one method that suits each specific use case. Explanations can be counterfactual examples or input features that strongly impacted the models' result. In the case of natural language processing, explanations based on feature importance are sets of words. We presented comparisons of various XAI methods in two contexts, without and with end users at hand. Protocols have been designed to be generalized to any multiclass classification use case. Both methods can be applied on any explanation method, no matter if they are post-hoc or from self-explaining models. Two different use cases have been used, LEGO with French texts, and Yelp with English texts. This chapter helps fastening and reducing the cost of explanation analysis during system designing.

In the first experiment, we sought to know, with no end user available, which explanation method was best suiting a use case. On the LEGO use case, comparison with ground truth and qualitative analysis showed a slightly better performance for attention explanations. On the Yelp use case, qualitative analysis showed more interesting results for attention explanations, too. IOU can be used to focus on instances where compared explanations give different results, fastening explanation analysis.

In the second experiment, we compared explanation methods with users' preferences for the LEGO use case. Results' analysis showed that the preferred method depends on the complexity of the explanation. IOU is not representative of users' preference. Explanations' length seems to be an important criterion for users. They prefer, according to our analysis, shorter explanations. This analysis gives leads to improve our quantitative metric, the biggest change involving the need to refine the ground truth.

Ground truth as ideal explanation is meaningful, but it is not sufficient to be preferred by users. The main reasons for ground truth to differ from most preferred explanations are errors from the model and succinctness. The search for a ground truth that matches users' preference is crucial. Some work remains to be done to tackle the complexity of multilabel classification problems.

Glossary

Model In machine learning, a model is the result of training. It can be visualized as a virtual object taking inputs, and computing an output it has learned during the training phase.

Classifier A specific model designed to classify its inputs. Input data can be images, texts, sounds, etc.

Neural Network Specific model made of artificial neurons, organized in multiple interconnected layers. Neural Networks may have various architectures, defining the number and organization of its neurons.

Explanation In eXplainable Artificial Intelligence, a piece of information helping to understand how a model took a decision; often made from input variables or examples and counterfactuals.

Ideal explanation In this work, explanation associated with an input and its ground-truth label.

Expected explanation In this work, explanation associated with an input and a label given by a specific classification model. When a predicted label is the ground truth, expected explanation is equal to the ground-truth explanation.

IOU Short for Intersection Over Union, a metric measuring the similarity of two sets, $IOU = \frac{A \cup B}{A \cup B}$.

Accuracy A metric often used to measure a model's performance. It is the rate of correct predictions amongst all prediction, $Acc = \frac{TP+TN}{TP+TN+FP+FN}$.

Precision A metric often used to measure a model's performance. For a binary classifier, this it the rate of correct positive predictions amongst all positive predictions, $Prec = \frac{TP}{TP+FP}$.

Recall A metric often used to measure a model's performance. For a binary classifier, this is the rate of correct positive predictions amongst all positive elements, $Rec = \frac{TP}{TP+FN}$.

F1-score A metric often used to measure a model's performance; computed as the harmonic mean of precision and recall, $F1 = \begin{cases} \frac{2*(precision*recall)}{precision+recall} & \text{if } precision + recall > 0, \\ 0 & \text{if } precision + recall = 0. \end{cases}$

Stop words In Natural Language processing, common words in a language that are semantically meaningless, such as articles. A stop words' list is usually made for a use case, as some words might be considered as stop words in specific contexts.

References

Abnar, Samira, Zuidema, Willem, 2020. Quantifying attention flow in transformers. In: The 58th Annual Meeting of the Association for Computational Linguistics (ACL).

Ak, Ali, Abid, Mona, Da Silva, Matthieu Perreira, Le Callet, Patrick, 2021. On spammer detection in crowdsourcing pairwise comparison tasks: Case study on two multimedia QoE assessment scenarios. In: 2021 IEEE International Conference on Multimedia & Expo Workshops (ICMEW). IEEE, pp. 1–6.

Arrieta, Alejandro Barredo, Díaz-Rodríguez, Natalia, Del Ser, Javier, Bennetot, Adrien, Tabik, Siham, Barbado, Alberto, García, Salvador, Gil-López, Sergio, Molina, Daniel, Benjamins, Richard, et al., 2020. Explainable artificial intelligence (XAI): Concepts, taxonomies, opportunities and challenges toward responsible AI. Information Fusion 58, 82–115.

Bahdanau, Dzmitry, Cho, Kyunghyun, Bengio, Yoshua, 2015. Neural machine translation by jointly learning to align and translate. In: Bengio, Yoshua, LeCun, Yann (Eds.), 3rd International Conference on Learning Representations, ICLR 2015. May 7–9, 2015, San Diego, CA, USA. In: Conference Track Proceedings.

Bao, Yujia, Chang, Shiyu, Yu, Mo, Barzilay, Regina, 2018. Deriving machine attention from human rationales. arXiv:1808.09367.

Bau, David, Zhou, Bolei, Khosla, Aditya, Oliva, Aude, Torralba, Antonio, 2017. Network dissection: Quantifying interpretability of deep visual representations. In: Proc. of the IEEE Conf. on Computer Vision and Pattern Recognition, pp. 6541–6549.

Charachon, Martin, Hudelot, Céline, Cournède, Paul-Henry, Ruppli, Camille, Ardon, Roberto, 2020. Combining similarity and adversarial learning to generate visual explanation: Application to medical image classification. arXiv:2012.07332.

Chattopadhay, Aditya, Sarkar, Anirban, Howlader, Prantik, Balasubramanian, Vineeth N., 2018. Grad-CAM++: Generalized gradient-based visual explanations for deep convolutional networks. In: 2018 IEEE Winter Conference on Applications of Computer Vision (WACV). IEEE, pp. 839–847.

Codella, Noel C.F., Hind, Michael, Ramamurthy, Karthikeyan Natesan, Campbell, Murray, Dhurandhar, Amit, Varshney, Kush R., Wei, Dennis, Mojsilovic, Aleksandra, 2019. TED: Teaching AI to explain its decisions. In: Proceedings of the 2019 AAAI/ACM Conference on AI, Ethics, and Society.

Costa, Felipe, Ouyang, Sixun, Dolog, Peter, Lawlor, Aonghus, 2018. Automatic generation of natural language explanations. In: Proceedings of the 23rd International Conference on Intelligent User Interfaces Companion, pp. 1–2.

Das, Abhishek, Agrawal, Harsh, Zitnick, Larry, Parikh, Devi, Batra, Dhruv, 2017. Human attention in visual question answering: Do humans and deep networks look at the same regions? Computer Vision and Image Understanding 163, 90–100.

Gilpin, Leilani H., Bau, David, Yuan, Ben Z., Bajwa, Ayesha, Specter, Michael, Kagal, Lalana, 2018. Explaining explanations: An overview of interpretability of machine learning. In: 2018 IEEE 5th International Conference on Data Science and Advanced Analytics (DSAA), pp. 80–89.

Guidotti, Riccardo, Monreale, Anna, Ruggieri, Salvatore, Turini, Franco, Giannotti, Fosca, Pedreschi, Dino, 2018. A survey of methods for explaining black box models. ACM Computing Surveys (CSUR) 51 (5), 1–42.

Iyer, Rahul, Li, Yuezhang, Li, Huao, Lewis, Michael, Sundar, Ramitha, Sycara, Katia, 2018. Transparency and explanation in deep reinforcement learning neural networks. In: Proc. of the 2018 AAAI/ACM Conference on AI, Ethics, and Society.

Jain, Sarthak, Wallace, Byron C., 2019. Attention is not explanation. arXiv:1902.10186.

Karpathy, Andrej, Johnson, Justin, Li, Fei-Fei, 2015. Visualizing and understanding recurrent networks. CoRR. arXiv:1506.02078 [abs].

Kenny, Eoin M., Keane, Mark T., 2020. On generating plausible counterfactual and semi-factual explanations for deep learning. arXiv:2009.06399.

Lin, Zhouhan, Feng, Minwei, dos Santos, Cícero Nogueira, Yu, Mo, Xiang, Bing, Zhou, Bowen, Bengio, Yoshua, 2017. A structured self-attentive sentence embedding. In: 5th International Conference on Learning Representations, ICLR 2017. April 24–26, 2017, Toulon, France. In: Conference Track Proceedings.

Miller, Tim, 2019. Explanation in artificial intelligence: Insights from the social sciences. Artificial Intelligence 267, 1–38.

Mohseni, Sina, Block, Jeremy E., Ragan, Eric, 2021. Quantitative evaluation of machine learning explanations: A human-grounded benchmark. In: 26th International Conference on Intelligent User Interfaces, pp. 22–31.

Olah, Chris, Carter, Shan, 2016. Attention and augmented recurrent neural networks. Distill 1. https://doi.org/10.23915/distill.00001. http://distill.pub/2016/augmented-rnns.

Ribeiro, Marco Tulio, Singh, Sameer, Guestrin, Carlos, 2016. "Why should I trust you?": Explaining the predictions of any classifier. In: Proc. of the 22nd ACM Int. Conf. on Knowledge Discovery and Data Mining, pp. 1135–1144.

Ribeiro, Marco Tulio, Singh, Sameer, Guestrin, Carlos, 2018. Anchors: High-precision model-agnostic explanations. In: Proceedings of the Thirty-Second AAAI Conference on Artificial Intelligence, (AAAI-18), pp. 1527–1535.

Vaswani, Ashish, Shazeer, Noam, Parmar, Niki, Uszkoreit, Jakob, Jones, Llion, Gomez, Aidan N., Kaiser, Łukasz, Polosukhin, Illia, 2017. Attention is all you need. In: Advances in Neural Information Processing Systems, pp. 5998–6008.

Wang, Yequan, Huang, Minlie, Zhu, Xiaoyan, Zhao, Li, 2016. Attention-based LSTM for aspect-level sentiment classification. In: Proceedings of the 2016 Conference on Empirical Methods in Natural Language Processing, pp. 606–615.

Wiegreffe, Sarah, Pinter, Yuval, 2019. Attention is not not explanation. arXiv:1908.04626.

Yang, Zhengyuan, Li, Yuncheng, Yang, Jianchao, Luo, Jiebo, 2018. Action recognition with spatio-temporal visual attention on skeleton image sequences. IEEE Transactions on Circuits and Systems for Video Technology 29 (8), 2405–2415.

Zeiler, Matthew D., Fergus, Rob, 2014. Visualizing and understanding convolutional networks. In: European Conference on Computer Vision, pp. 818–833.

Zou, Zhengxia, Shi, Zhenwei, Guo, Yuhong, Ye, Jieping, 2019. Object detection in 20 years: A survey. arXiv:1905.05055.

CHAPTER 11

Improving malware detection with explainable machine learning

Michele Scalas[a], Konrad Rieck[b], and Giorgio Giacinto[a]

[a]University of Cagliari, Department of Electrical and Electronic Engineering, Piazza d'Armi, Cagliari, Italy
[b]Technische Universität Braunschweig, Institute of System Security, Braunschweig, Germany

Chapter points

- Explanations can be used to characterize malware
- The proposed approach enables the identification of the most influential features and the analysis of Android ransomware

11.1. Introduction

Malware detection is one of the areas where machine learning is successfully employed due to its high discriminating power and the capability of identifying novel malware variants. The typical problem formulation for malware detectors is strictly correlated to the use of a wide variety of features covering different characteristics of the entities to classify. This practice often provides considerable detection performance but hardly permits to gain insights into the knowledge extracted by the learning algorithm. Moreover, there is no guarantee that the detector modeled the malicious and legitimate classes correctly, paving the way to let an adversary craft malicious samples with the same representation as legitimate samples in the feature space, i.e., the so-called "adversarial examples." These samples are malicious applications that the learning model classifies as legitimate ones (Demetrio et al., 2019; Ilyas et al., 2019). In this sense, having the possibility to rely on explanations can improve the design process of such detectors, since they reveal characterizing patterns, thus guiding the human expert towards the understanding of the most relevant features.

While classic malware has focused on desktop systems and the Windows platform, recent attacks have started to target smartphones and mobile platforms, such as Android. In this chapter, we investigate a recent threat of this development, namely Android ransomware. The detection of such a threat represents a challenging, yet illustrative domain for assessing the impact of explainability. Ransomware acts by locking the compromised device or encrypting its data, then forcing the device owner to pay a ransom in order to restore the device functionality. Scalas et al. (2019) have shown that ransomware developers typically build such dangerous apps so that normally-legitimate components

Explainable Deep Learning AI
https://doi.org/10.1016/B978-0-32-396098-4.00017-X
217

and functionalities (e.g., encryption) perform malicious behavior; thus, making them harder to be distinguished from genuine applications. Given this context, and according to previous works (Maiorca et al., 2017; Scalas et al., 2019, 2021), we investigate if and to what extent state-of-the-art explainability techniques help to identify the features that characterize ransomware apps, i.e., the properties that are required to be present in order to combat ransomware offensives effectively. Our contribution is threefold:

1. Leveraging the approach of our previous work (Scalas et al., 2021), we propose practical strategies for identifying the features that characterize generic ransomware samples, specific families, and the evolution of such attacks over time;
2. We countercheck the effectiveness of our analysis by evaluating the prediction performance of classifiers trained with the discovered relevant features;
3. We discuss additional aspects to consider when selecting and tuning explanation methods, i.e., how they influence the questions to be answered.

We believe that our proposal can help cyber threat intelligence teams in the early detection of new ransomware families, and, above all, could be a starting point to help design other malware detection systems through the identification of their distinctive features. We first introduce background notions about Android, ransomware attacks, and their detection (Section 11.2), followed by a brief illustration of explanation methods (Section 11.3). Then, our approach is presented in Section 11.4. Since the explanation methods we consider have been originally designed to indicate the most influential features for a single prediction, we propose to evaluate the distribution of explanations rather than individual instances. This statistical view enables us to uncover characteristics of malware shared across variants of the same family. In our experimental analysis (Section 11.5), we analyze the output of explanation methods to extract information about the set of features that mostly characterize ransomware samples. Then, in Section 11.6 we present an analysis of additional aspects that might influence the questions that explanations are able to answer. We make conclusive remarks in Section 11.7.

11.2. Background

In this section, we introduce background notions about the domain under investigation in this chapter, namely Android ransomware. Starting from the essential elements that compose an Android app (Section 11.2.1), we describe the main traits of Android ransomware threats (Section 11.2.2), followed by the approach used in this work to detect such attacks (Section 11.2.3).

11.2.1 Android

Android applications are zipped archives inside the `apk` format, composed by the following elements: (*i*) the `AndroidManifest.xml` and other `xml` files that specify the application layout, (*ii*) one or more `classes.dex` files, and (*iii*) various resources, such as images, generic files (`assets`), and native libraries.

The elements we analyze in this work are the `AndroidManifest.xml` and the `classes.dex` files, since they provide relevant information for ransomware detection. The former lists the app's *components*, i.e., the elements that define its structure and functionalities. For example, the screens visualized by the user are built upon an `activity`, and background tasks are executed through `services`. One of the most important sections of the Manifest comes from the list of the *permissions* requested by the application (`uses-permission` tag). In fact, some functionalities require explicit consent by the user as they can affect her privacy. For example, they can be related either to the use of specific device modules (e.g., `ACCESS_NETWORK_STATE`) or sensitive functionalities (e.g., `SEND_SMS`). As regards the `classes.dex` file, it embeds the compiled source code of the applications, including all the user-implemented methods and classes.

11.2.2 Android ransomware

Mobile ransomware had a steep rise from 2015 to 2017, in terms of both the number of installation packages and the distribution share over all types of mobile threats. After that, a significant decrease in infections was observed. One of the reasons for this trend is the progress of security measures against such attacks. In this sense, Kaspersky (2020) highlights that most of the current spread families date back from 2017. This fact could indicate attacks target older versions of Android since − as of February 2022 − almost 20% of devices run Android Oreo 8.0 (API level 26, released in August 2017) or lower.[1]

Two common types of ransomware exist for the Android platform, namely locking ransomware and crypto ransomware, described in the following.

Locking ransomware

The goal is to *lock* the device screen. In this case, attackers typically take the following strategy: they create an `activity` upon which a nondismissable window is shown. This `activity` is forced to stay always in the foreground, and it can be restarted when killed or the device gets rebooted. Moreover, they disable the navigation buttons (e.g., the *back* functionality). Newer versions of Android, primarily since API level 28 (Android Pie), have implemented countermeasures in response to this strategy. For example, (*i*) the device can be booted in *Safe Mode*, where the system blocks third-party apps from running, (*ii*) when an activity is started from the background, a notification is always displayed, and (*iii*) the status bar takes priority and shows a specific notification that allows disabling overlay screens from the running app. However, as such recent Android versions do not reach the totality of the devices, locking behavior remains a relevant threat.

```
1
2    invoke-virtual {v9}, Landroid/app/admin/DevicePolicyManager;->lockNow()V
3    move-object v9, v0
```

---

[1] Data gathered from Android Studio's Android Platform Version Distribution.

```
4     move-object v10, v1
5
6     ...
7
8     move-result-object v9
9     move-object v10, v7
10    const/4 v11, 0x0
11    invoke-virtual {v9, v10, v11}, Landroid/app/admin/
12          DevicePolicyManager;->resetPassword(Ljava/
13          lang/String;I)Z
```

Listing 11.1: Part of the onPasswordChanged() method belonging to a locker–type ransomware sample.

As an example of its behavior, consider the dexcode snippet provided by Listing 11.1, belonging to *locker-type* ransomware.[2] In this example, it is possible to observe that the two function calls (expressed by invoke-virtual instructions) that are actually used to lock the screen (lockNow()) and reset the password (resetPassword()) are System API calls, belonging to the class DevicePolicyManager and to the package android.app.admin.

Crypto ransomware

Locking is generally preferred to the data encryption strategy because it does not require operating on high-privileged data. There are, however, *crypto*-ransomware apps that perform data encryption. Examples of crypto families are: Simplocker, Koler, Cokri, and Fobus. In this case, the attacker shows a window that could not necessarily be constantly displayed, because its main focus is to perform encryption of the user data (e.g., photos, videos, documents).

Listing 11.2 shows the encryption function employed by a *crypto-type* ransomware sample.[3] Again, the functions to manipulate the bytes to be encrypted belong to the System API (read() and close(), belonging to the FileInputStream class of the java.io package; flush() and close(), belonging to the CipherOutputStream class of the javax.crypto package).

```
1
2     Ljava/io/FileInputStream;->read([B)I
3     move-result v0
4     const/4 v5, -0x1
5     if-ne v0, v5, :cond_0
6     invoke-virtual {v1}, Ljavax/crypto/
7               CipherOutputStream;->flush()V
8     invoke-virtual {v1}, Ljavax/crypto/
9               CipherOutputStream;->close()V
10    invoke-virtual {v3}, Ljava/io/
11              FileInputStream;->close()V
```

Listing 11.2: Parts of the encrypt() method belonging to an encryption–type ransomware sample.

---

[2] MD5: 0cdb7171bcd94ab5ef8b4d461afc446c.
[3] MD5: 59909615d2977e0be29b3ab8707c903a.

In both ransomware types, the created window includes a threatening message that instructs the user to pay the ransom, which will theoretically permit to (*i*) suppress the permanent screen (locking case) or (*ii*) decipher the data (crypto case). As locking and encryption actions require the use of multiple functions that involve core functionalities of the system (e.g., managing entire arrays of bytes, displaying activities, manipulating buttons, and so on), *attackers tend to use functions that directly belong to the Android System API*. It would be extremely time-consuming and inefficient to build new APIs that perform the same actions as the original ones. This fact motivates the design choices we describe in the section that follows.

11.2.3 Ransomware detection

The method used for this work mostly follows the one proposed by Scalas et al. (2019), which relies on a small set of System API calls to discriminate Android ransomware samples. However, this work aims at understanding if the features identified both in such previous work and the literature turn out to be truly characteristic of the ransomware behavior, besides being effective for detection. Accordingly, we point this out through explainability techniques. Keeping a fully static analysis setting, we have chosen to start exploring our proposed approach making use of two types of features: (*i*) the occurrence of System API package calls and (*ii*) the request for permissions. This choice is motivated by the goal of understanding how two different kinds of features relate when inspected through explanation techniques. Moreover, with such an approach, the effectiveness of other types of features proposed in the literature – e.g., features extracted through dynamic analysis – could be evaluated so as to include them if they provide a positive contribution in the identification of ransomware actions. This work also differs from the one by Scalas et al. (2019) because here we consider a two-class problem, i.e., ransomware and legitimate classes, while the previous work included a third class related to generic malware.

Before illustrating how we employ explanations, we briefly recall the motivation for the usage of requested permissions as features: the Android operating system requires the app developer to request permission to use a particular functionality expressly. Permissions can be granted automatically or after explicit user consent, depending on the permission category. This distinction is also explicitly stated in the Android platform documentation as *protection level*; therefore, it is straightforward to consider permissions as useful features. For example, we can expect that common permissions (e.g., `INTERNET`, `ACCESS_NETWORK_STATE`) will be associated with trusted apps, while *dangerous* ones, such as `WRITE_EXTERNAL_STORAGE`, could be typical of ransomware samples.

11.3. Explanation methods

Several works in the literature proposed techniques to explain machine learning-based models, especially in the context of computer vision tasks. Besides the general aim of obtaining explanations from ML algorithms, this goal assumes peculiar traits depending on several factors, such as *why* the explanations are produced, *whom* they are addressed to, *what* they consist of. For example, we may produce explanations for knowledge extraction since we do not have a full understanding of the mechanisms of the problem under analysis. Other typical goals are (*i*) debugging a model when there is no certainty about the conditions under which the model could fail and (*ii*) satisfying legal or ethical requirements, e.g., ensuring no biases are present in the model. Also depending on the above goals, explanations can be addressed to different stakeholders (Preece et al., 2018), like (*i*) the designers of the ML models, e.g., to debug them, (*ii*) the theorists, e.g., to extract knowledge, (*iii*) the ethicists, e.g., to ensure models are fair, and (*iv*) the end-users, e.g., to gain trust about the decisions made by models. Lastly, explanations can be gathered from a model with external, specific techniques (*post-hoc* explanations) or inherently from the model, which is then considered as *transparent* by design. Since the models may be not fully accessible, some explainability techniques (called *black-box*) infer explanations only from models' outputs, as opposed to *white-box* techniques that can leverage the inner working of the algorithms. Moreover, explanations can be related to a single decision of the model (*local* explanations) or its whole logic (*global* explanations).

The typical output of a local explanation consists of a function $e : \mathbb{R}^n \times \Theta \to \mathbb{R}^n$, $e(\boldsymbol{x}, \theta) \mapsto a$ that takes a feature vector $\boldsymbol{x} = [x_1, x_2, \ldots, x_d]$ and a learning model θ and returns an attribution vector $\boldsymbol{a}$, where each component a_i is a real value − an *attribution*, or *relevance*, or *contribution* − associated with each of the d features. In the case of a two-class setting, the sign of the attribution indicates the class where the feature *moves to*. Another interesting venue is the generation of high-level *concepts* rather than feature attributions. In this sense, Kim et al. (2018) proposed a technique that introduces the notion of *Concept Activation Vectors* (CAVs), which evaluate the sensitivity of the models to user-defined examples defining particular concepts. Given this variety of possible methods, recent work such as the one by Warnecke et al. (2020) discussed general and security-specific criteria to evaluate explanation methods in different security domains. Moreover, the applicability of explainability techniques has been evaluated for explaining malware detectors through *gradient-based* techniques (Melis et al., 2018; Scalas et al., 2021). These are white-box, local, attribution methods. In this work, we consider three of them, as we describe in the section that follows.

11.3.1 Gradient-based explanation methods

One of the characteristics common to several explanation techniques is deriving them from the calculation of the gradient of the decision function with respect to the input.

In particular, the ones considered in this work – namely Gradient, Gradient⋆Input, and Integrated Gradients – are usually referred to as "gradient-based attribution methods." Before illustrating them, it is worth recalling that Sundararajan et al. (2017) have identified two axioms that attribution methods should satisfy, namely *implementation invariance* and *sensitivity*. These axioms, which are satisfied by Integrated Gradients, are convenient to introduce one important aspect for this work – the concept of *baseline*. This term refers to a reference vector that can model a neutral input (e.g., a black image) or other types of reference inputs. As we will discuss in detail in Section 11.6, depending on the chosen baseline, one can answer different questions when extracting explanations. Coming back to the first axiom by Sundararajan et al. (2017), the attributions should always be identical for two functionally-equivalent networks, e.g., they should be invariant to the differences in the training hyperparameters, which lead the network to learn the same function. The second axiom is satisfied if, for every input differing from the baseline even in one feature, the explanation has, for that feature, a nonzero attribution.

In the following, we briefly describe the three considered gradient-based techniques.

Gradient

The simplest method to obtain attributions is to compute the gradient of the classifier's discriminant function f with respect to the input sample $\boldsymbol{x}$. For image recognition models, it corresponds to the saliency map of the image (Baehrens et al., 2010). The attribution of the ith feature is computed as

$$\text{Gradient}_i(\boldsymbol{x}) := \frac{\partial f(\boldsymbol{x})}{\partial x_i}. \tag{11.1}$$

Gradient*Input

This technique has been proposed by Shrikumar et al. (2016) and is more suitable than the previously-proposed ones when the feature vectors are sparse. Given the input point $\boldsymbol{x}$, it projects the gradient $\nabla f(\boldsymbol{x})$ onto $\boldsymbol{x}$, to ensure that only the nonnull features are considered as relevant for the decision. More formally, the ith attribution is computed as

$$\text{Gradient}\star\text{Input}_i(\boldsymbol{x}) := \frac{\partial f(\boldsymbol{x})}{\partial x_i} \cdot x_i. \tag{11.2}$$

Integrated gradients

Sundararajan et al. (2017) have proposed a gradient-based explanation, called Integrated Gradients, that satisfies the axioms explained above. This method, firstly, considers the straight-line path from the baseline to the input sample and computes the gradients at all points along the path. Then, it obtains the attribution by accumulating those gradients. The attribution along the ith dimension for an input $\boldsymbol{x}$ and baseline $\boldsymbol{x}'$ is defined as

$$\text{IntegratedGrads}_i(\boldsymbol{x}) := (x_i - x_i') \cdot \int_{\alpha=0}^{1} \frac{\partial f\left(\boldsymbol{x}' + \alpha \cdot (\boldsymbol{x} - \boldsymbol{x}')\right)}{\partial x_i} d\alpha. \tag{11.3}$$

For linear classifiers, where $\partial f / \partial x_i = w_i$, this is equivalent to Gradient$\star$Input if $\boldsymbol{x}' = \boldsymbol{0}$ is used as the baseline. Therefore, in this particular case, also the Gradient$\star$Input method satisfies the above-mentioned axioms.

11.4. Explaining Android ransomware

In this section, we introduce our approach that proposes to leverage explanations in order to characterize Android ransomware and ultimately improve its detection. As stated in Section 11.1, machine learning systems are nowadays being extensively adopted in computer security applications, such as network intrusion and malware detection, as they have obtained remarkable performance even against the increasing complexity of modern attacks. More recently, learning-based techniques based on static analysis have proven to be especially effective at detecting Android malware, which constitutes one of the major threats in mobile security. In particular, these approaches have shown great accuracy even when traditional code concealing techniques (such as static obfuscation) are employed (Arp et al., 2014; Chen et al., 2016; Demontis et al., 2017; Scalas et al., 2019).

Despite the successful results reported by such approaches, the problem of designing effective malware detectors – or solving different cybersecurity tasks – through machine learning is still far from being solved. Moreover, several *pitfalls* may undermine the validity of such systems (Arp et al., 2022).

In the following, we illustrate our proposal on how to take advantage of gradient-based explanations, aiming to identify a unique, reliable, and coherent set of relevant features that is independent of the specific (*i*) model, (*ii*) explanation method, and (*iii*) dataset. Accordingly, we first describe the challenges that this goal raises (Section 11.4.1). Then, we illustrate our approach to addressing them (Section 11.4.2).

11.4.1 Challenges

Several challenges make the usage of explanations not straightforward. In the following, we list them starting from the ones that apply to all domains, which we tackle with specific tests. Then, we focus on the challenges that are specific to Android malware detection.

Domain-independent challenges

A first concern arises around the choice of the classifiers. Since several types of them can be used with success for this detection problem, *there could be as many different explanations as to the number of potential classifiers.* For this reason, it is necessary to verify if the specific learning algorithm affects the output of the attributions. Therefore, a reasonable check to perform is to compare the explanation vectors within a set of plausible classifiers, one explanation technique at a time.

Complementary to this aspect, it is of interest to get insights about which of the three explanation techniques is the most *accurate*, or to what extent they are equivalent. For example, if all the explanations are mostly similar, it is possible to consider only one of them. Therefore, for each model, we can compare its attributions across the different attribution techniques, similar to the procedure performed by Warnecke et al. (2020). It is worth noting that this approach gives rise to the following tricky issue: *How can we guarantee that similar attributions imply faithful explanations?* In this regard, in our setting, all the techniques are gradient-based, which are known to be reasonably effective; hence, we make the assumption that all of them are suitable despite their peculiarities.

The third concern comes from the influence of the data on the explanations; specifically, the possibility that *attributions could not be associated with the data labeling, and, consequently, to what the model learns.* For example, if the model is trained with a set of ransomware samples assigned to the trusted class on purpose and the attributions do not change, then the model would be bound by the samples themselves, rather than by what it learned through the training phase. This aspect can be of particular interest for Gradient★Input and Integrated Gradients, where the input is part of their computation. In this case, with a test following the method proposed by Adebayo et al. (2018), ordinary attributions of each classifier are compared to those of a correspondent classifier trained with randomized labels.

Malware-specific

Due to different factors, a new approach is necessary for investigating malware with explanation methods. First, gradient-based methods all operate on the level of instances. As a result, they only explain a single Android application. Android malware, however, is diverse and often *repackaged.* This term refers to the strategy by attackers of injecting malicious code into popular applications, so that the repackaged app appears legitimate. Because of such kinds of tactics, it is impossible to derive reasonable information from a single explanation.

Second, malware labels are noisy. It is hard to correctly attribute malware to given families. Consequently, samples might be mislabeled and explanations for these samples become misleading. Therefore, looking at individual explanations is not sufficient and a broader view to understand Android malware is needed.

Lastly, the typical features for Android malware detection, like those of our setting (API calls and permission requests) are examples of *sparse* features. More specifically, each application uses only a small amount of APIs and permissions; consequently, each sample exhibits a few nonzero (used) features. This fact makes a nonnegligible difference with respect to other domains, such as image recognition, where the features (typically raw pixels) are all always used. Therefore, when using explanations to characterize the Android ransomware samples under test, we expect the attributions to be sparse as well. Moreover, as investigated by Lage et al. (2019), sparsity is one of the factors that make explanations more *comprehensible* for the human expert. All other aspects being equal, explanation techniques that satisfy this requirement the most are preferable.

11.4.2 Approach

The above concerns and our proposed answers for them allow us to approach the problem with more awareness about the caveats that these explainability techniques pose. Once a single set of reliable attributions is established, we should find a strategy to analyze them and extract information. In particular, as the individual predictions' relevance values turned out to be misleading, we aim to catch the *average* role of the features onto the samples' characterization. Therefore, it is necessary to define the right concept of average in practice, i.e., the most suitable metric to express the central tendency of the distribution of the explanations.

Our approach starts by considering three typical synthetic measures of central tendency: mean, median, and variance. In particular, given an attribution vector $a = [a_1, a_2, \ldots, a_d]$, we consider the specific distribution value of each component over a certain set of N samples. Therefore, we obtain three potential vectors for the mean, median, and variance cases, respectively:

$$\gamma^1{}_i = \mathrm{mean}(a_i)_N, \tag{11.4}$$

$$\gamma^2{}_i = \mathrm{median}(a_i)_N, \tag{11.5}$$

$$\gamma^3{}_i = \mathrm{variance}(a_i)_N, \tag{11.6}$$

for $i = 1, 2, \ldots, d$, where d is the number of components (features).

Although using a unique, synthetic measure for describing the attributions could seem too limiting, we claim that useful information can actually be gathered by analyzing appropriate sets of samples, as we describe in Section 11.5.3. Starting from the above three metrics, we choose the one that best suits our specific problem (Section 11.5.2).

11.5. Experimental analysis

In this section, we leverage the attributions provided by the considered techniques to empirically find out the main characteristics of the ransomware samples. In particular, we seek to answer the following research questions:

- Is our approach helpful for understanding the discrimination of benign and malicious Android apps?
- Do the aggregated explanations provide information for analyzing malware families and their evaluation?
- Can the aggregated explanations serve as the basis for improving and reducing the number of features for malware detection?

To do so, after illustrating the experimental setting (Section 11.5.1), we analyze the generated explanations through different criteria (Section 11.5.3).

11.5.1 Setting

We operate in a two-class setting, where the learning algorithms are trained to classify the positive class of *ransomware* samples against the negative one of *trusted* samples. In the following, we briefly summarize the parameters and the implementation used for the experiments.

Dataset and features

We use the same dataset as Scalas et al. (2019, 2021), with 18396 trusted and 1945 ransomware samples, which span from 2011 to 2018 according to their dex last modification date. The feature vector consists of 731 features. Among them, 196 represent the occurrence of the API *package* calls. We cumulate all the Android platform APIs until level 26 (Android Oreo). Moreover, the set of APIs is strictly limited to the Android *platform* ones.[4] The remaining amount of features consists of checking the request of permissions extracted from the AndroidManifest.xml: when one permission is used, we assign to the correspondent feature a 1; 0 otherwise. In this case, we cumulate the list of permissions until level 29 (Android 10). Since each new API level typically adds new packages, the APIs introduced after 2018 cause the correspondent features to be not used. aapt[5] is employed to extract the permissions used by each APK. Permissions' names are indicated in capital letters.

Classifiers

Since we want our approach to be model-agnostic, for our preliminary evaluation (see Section 11.5.2) we initially consider three different classifiers, and we eventually se-

---

[4] https://developer.android.com/reference/packages.
[5] https://developer.android.com/studio/command-line/aapt2.

lect only a single representative one. The first two classifiers are a linear support-vector machine (SVM) and a support-vector machine with RBF kernel (SVM-RBF), both implemented with secml (Melis et al., 2019), a library for performing adversarial attacks and explaining machine learning models. The third classifier is a multilayer perceptron (MLP), implemented with Keras.[6] As illustrated at the end of Section 11.5.2, we eventually select and use the MLP only. Its performance is shown in the context of Section 11.5.3.4. Each classifier has been trained and optimized in its parameters with a repeated 5-fold cross-validation, using 50% of the dataset as the test set. Notably, these classifiers exhibit slightly lower performance with respect to a Random Forest classifier, which indeed had been used in Scalas et al. (2019). The reason for not using it is that this ensemble algorithm presents a nondifferentiable decision function; therefore, it is not possible to use gradient-based techniques on top of it.

Attribution computation

The attributions are calculated on the best classifier of the first iteration from the cross-validation. To produce the explanations for SVM and SVM-RBF we use secml; for MLP, we use DeepExplain.[7] We switch to iNNvestigate (Alber et al., 2019) for the computation of Gradient, since its implementation returns a signed attribution. We compute the attributions with respect to the ransomware class. Consequently, *a positive attribution value always identifies a feature that the classifier associates with ransomware.* As regards Integrated Gradients, since its computation includes an integral, this is approximated through a sum of n parts. We use $n = 130$, which is a manually-chosen value that ensures the approximation of the integral does not cause a high error. As a baseline, a zero-vector is used.

11.5.2 Explanation distribution

Starting from the three potential metrics described in Section 11.4.2, we choose the one that most suits our problem. Firstly, we excluded the variance metric (Eq. (11.6)) as it does not help in understanding the ranking of the most relevant attributions. Then, we manually observed the distribution of the attributions obtainable with our setting. Fig. 11.1 shows an example of it. In this figure, two features representing two permissions – we indicate permissions with capital letters – are shown; they are calculated with Integrated Gradients against ransomware samples for an MLP classifier.

The significant aspect to consider is that, in our setting, the distribution of relevance values is typically bimodal. The attribution values could be zero for some samples and be condensed around a certain value level for some others. In particular, they exhibit a positive value if the feature converges towards the ransomware class; negative otherwise.

---

[6] https://Keras.io/.
[7] https://github.com/marcoancona/DeepExplain.

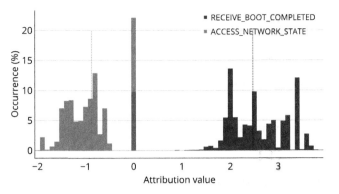

Figure 11.1 Attribution distribution of two features, calculated for a Multilayer Perceptron (MLP) classifier through Integrated Gradients. Positive values associate the feature to the ransomware class, negative values to the trusted one. The dotted lines represent the median value.

We observed that using the mean typically resulted in central tendency values too close to zero and did not highlight clearly the ranking of the different features. The synthetic metric that better expresses the central tendency of this kind of distribution is represented by the *median value*. Consequently, in our work, we consider the median value as defined in Eq. (11.5). In this way, we highlight a feature as relevant when, for most of the samples, it does not exhibit a zero value.

Preliminary evaluation

To overcome the challenges described in Section 11.4.1, we start our investigation through a set of tests where we compare and correlate median explanation vectors of the three classifiers according to different criteria, following the same procedure as described in Scalas et al. (2021). Overall, we came up with the conclusion that *the most suitable technique for our problem is Integrated Gradients, calculated on top of the MLP classifier.* Accordingly, all the following experiments and the related comments and discussion have been carried out using the MLP classifier and Integrated Gradients, the other two classifiers and explanation techniques resulting not being effective for extracting explanations related to ransomware detection.

11.5.3 Explanation analysis

In this section, we report the analysis of the explanations. After choosing a representative set of explanations, at this point we aim at understanding how – on average – the features can make a distinction between the trusted and the ransomware class. Moreover, we specifically characterize the behavior of the ransomware samples and their families by associating the most relevant features to the corresponding action in the app. Notably, we remark how features – especially in our case of system APIs and permissions – cannot

Table 11.1 Expected behavior associated with each feature depending on the sign of the attribution values and the samples used to calculate the explanations.

	Trusted sample	Ransomware sample
Positive attribution	Nontrusted	Ransomware
Negative attribution	Trusted	Nonransomware

be uniquely associated with ransomware since malicious behavior is a composition of essential actions that are not offensive by themselves.

In order to perform our analysis, we group the samples according to different criteria. The attributions are not normalized; consequently, there is no lower or upper bound to consider as a reference for the magnitude of each attribution. This choice also preserves the possibility to sort and compare them across the different features. If not stated differently, we consider the attributions calculated on all the dataset samples.

11.5.3.1 Evaluation by class

We consider the explanations' distribution separately for the trusted and ransomware class. In particular, we sort the attribution values of each group according to the median value of each feature, and we inspect the top features with positive values and the top ones with negative values. In this way, we can inspect how the features gravitate towards one of the two classes and reveal the kind of behavior they can be associated with. Table 11.1 exemplifies the interpretation of the four possible expected behaviors.

The top row of Fig. 11.2 shows the distribution of the attribution values for the top-8 positive and top-8 negative relevant features of the ransomware (Fig. 11.2a) and trusted (Fig. 11.2b) classes. As a first observation, we can notice that the highest median values are associated with the features that go into the direction of the ransomware class, while trusted samples' attributions exhibit lower sparsity and much higher variance. This fact suggests that trusted samples need a higher number of features to have them described, being the set of apps much broader and diversified. Going into more detail, let us consider Fig. 11.2a. The top-8 positive features can be reasonably associated with the behavior of generic malware. For example, `RECEIVE_BOOT_COMPLETED` enables an app to start after a device reboot, while `WAKE_LOCK` avoids it being killed by the operating system. Moreover, we can see the presence of a *ransomware-specific* feature — `SYSTEM_ALERT_WINDOW` — that is a permission allowing the attacker to display an overlay window (see Section 11.2.2), and that is often tied with `android.app.admin`. The top-8 negative features, such as `ACCESS_NETWORK_STATE`, should be interpreted as typical of *nonransomware* apps. Concerning the trusted samples, Fig. 11.2b shows as the most prominent feature `WRITE_EXTERNAL_STORAGE`, a permission that can be intuitively associated with crypto-ransomware apps. Nonetheless, it is worth noticing how its attributions also have zero or negative values. This fact indicates again how features considered alone do not often provide us with a full picture, but they become

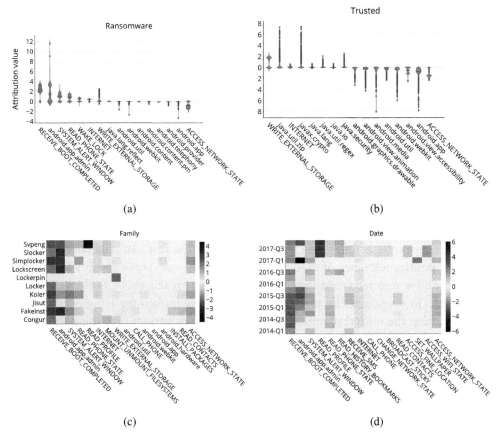

Figure 11.2 Top row: top-8 positive and top-8 negative feature attribution distribution for the ransomware (a) and trusted (b) samples of the dataset. Top-8 positive and top-8 negative attributions' median values for two grouping criteria: family (c) and date (d).

significant when tied with other ones in a specific attack pattern. Other positive values (*nontrusted* features) that emerge are `javax.crypto` and `java.security`, which are reasonably characteristic of crypto-ransomware apps as well. Among the *trusted-specific* features, an illustrative example comes from `android.app`, which provides a set of layout components that a developer of legitimate apps uses quite broadly.

11.5.3.2 Evaluation by ransomware family

Focusing on ransomware applications, we now inspect to what degree their different families exhibit shared and peculiar traits. AVClass[8] is used to extract the plausible fam-

---

[8] https://github.com/malicialab/avclass.

ilies from the VirusTotal reports of each sample. Moreover, the analysis is limited to the ransomware families with at least 30 samples, obtaining ten of them.

Fig. 11.2c shows the median values for the attributions of the main families. The list of the most relevant features is attained by considering the ransomware families together (same as Fig. 11.2a). This choice was made since the goal was to characterize common ransomware features: in principle, they might characterize new unseen families. Attributions for individual families have been computed as well, showing that each family exhibits a pattern of feature attributions similar to that of other ransomware families. As can be noticed by looking along the vertical axis of this plot, some features exhibit a stable relevance level across most of the families. In other words, features like SYS-TEM_ALERT_WINDOW can be considered to be a common characteristic of all ransomware apps. Other ones seem to be peculiar of specific families.

Looking at the properties of each family (rows of the plot), possible peculiarities can be noticed, such as for Svpeng and Lockerpin. In the first case, the family presents a strongly positive relevance of READ_PROFILE, while the Lockerpin family's attributions seem to exhibit zero relevance values instead, except for the WRITE_EXTERNAL_STORAGE permission. To investigate the reason for that, we have looked for representative samples by picking the ones that were closest to the median attributions, using the cosine similarity function. For the Svpeng family, we have obtained a locker ransomware sample[9] that, after hiding as a porn app, pretends to be the FBI enforcement and shows the victims messages that include the threat to send a supposed criminal record to their contacts, which are explicitly shown in the message. These contacts are gathered through the READ_PROFILE permission, which explains its relevance. In the second case[10] of Lockerpin, the anomalous explanation (we have checked the whole attribution vector) is due to the fact that the app contains, within its assets, another APK file that gets installed after the user opens the original app and grants the requested privileges. Therefore, the original app is merely a container.

11.5.3.3 Evaluation by ransomware date

The analysis of the evolution of malware is particularly relevant for machine learning-based detection systems. As a matter of fact, since they do not employ signatures to identify malicious behavior, they are often able to detect new variants of previously observed families. At the same time, they should be carefully evaluated over time to avoid experimental bias (Pendlebury et al., 2019). Therefore, it could be useful to understand what features do and do not possess a certain level of relevance, regardless of the ransomware evolution. To do so, we extract the last modification date from the dex file of each APK. We discard the samples with nonplausible dates (e.g., those with a *Unix*

---

[9] MD5: 8a7fea6a5279e8f64a56aa192d2e7cf0.
[10] MD5: 1fe4bc42222ec1119559f302ed8febfc.

epoch date), and we group the remaining ones in windows of three months. The result is shown in Fig. 11.2d. As can be noticed, some features maintain pretty much the same relevance values over time, which makes them *resilient* to new ransomware variants. In other words, some features describe essential components for ransomware samples. It should be noticed that also the types of features we employ – API calls and permission requests – change over time according to the Android development; therefore, both the attacker and the detector designer have to adapt to this progression. Fig. 11.2d also shows that the relevance of other features could depend on the spread of a particular family. For example, READ_PROFILE starts being relevant in 2017, when the previously-described Svpeng appeared.

11.5.3.4 Evaluation with a reduced feature set

We finally inspect if the explanations analyzed in the previous experiments, after helping with characterizing ransomware apps, can be used to change the group of features of the system under design. In other words, we aspire to build a feature set that, although it might cause accuracy loss, minimizes the learning of spurious patterns by the classifier. To do so, we construct a reduced feature set starting from the top-20 relevant attributions (10 positive and 10 negative) for both classes. Notably, we still use the attributions from Integrated Gradients for the MLP classifier, but we only consider training samples. We attain a set of 33 unique features, which means that 7 out of the initial 40 considered features are common to both ransomware and trusted apps. This result highlights again that features alone cannot necessarily be associated with malicious or legitimate behavior, but they become relevant in distinguishing the behavioral patterns when tied with other features.

Fig. 11.3 shows an ROC curve with a comparison between the original MLP classifier, trained with the full feature set, and the correspondent one trained with this reduced set of features. Despite the low number of features, the results at the threshold of FPR = 1% are quite close to those with the full feature set.

11.6. Discussion

In this section, we propose a discussion about additional criteria to consider when leveraging explanations. More specifically, we first illustrate three aspects that can *change the question explanations answer*. Then, we consider the impact relevant features might have in terms of robustness to *adversarial* attacks.

11.6.1 Explanation baseline

When thinking about explanations, we usually expect to understand what characteristics (features) *differ* from a reference – an event, a pixel, a software component. That is, we point out if and to what extent a feature indicates a certain element (e.g., event, pixel,

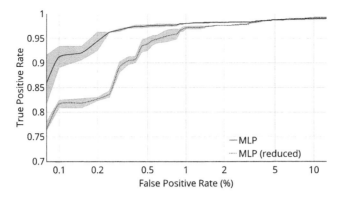

Figure 11.3 ROC curve comparison. The classifier with a solid line has been trained with the full feature set, the dotted one with a reduced feature set made of 33 features.

component) *instead of another one*. This idea is usually referred to as *foil*. As introduced in Section 11.3.1, explanation techniques such as Integrated Gradients embed a so-called *baseline* in order to explicitly set the foil to consider. In the experiments of Section 11.5, we employed a *neutral* input (corresponding to a zero-vector) as the baseline. This way, we extracted the characteristics of ransomware and trusted samples *per se*. However, using other baselines does change the meaning of the explanations, i.e., *answers different questions*, as in the examples that follow.

Fig. 11.4a shows the top absolute attributions calculated for *test ransomware* samples using as baseline the median feature vector of the *training trusted* samples. In this case, the resulting attributions answer the following question: *how ransomware is different from trusted samples?* Complementarily, Fig. 11.4b shows the top absolute attributions calculated for *test trusted* samples using as baseline the median feature vector of the *training ransomware* samples. In this case, the resulting attributions answer the following question: *How trusted apps are different from ransomware?*

Notably, other baselines could be defined, e.g., with a neutral (zero) value for certain features and median values for the other ones, in order to answer the following question: *How trusted (ransomware) samples are different from ransomware (trusted) for those specific features?*

11.6.2 Feature cardinality

Typical ML-based static analysis evaluates the presence or the usage frequency (as in this work) of software components. In the following, we evaluate a "binarized" version of the classifier, i.e., with features having the value of 1 or 0 whether the component (e.g., an API call) is present or not, respectively. By looking at the result in Figs. 11.4c and 11.4d, and comparing it with the original experiment in Figs. 11.2a and 11.2b, it is

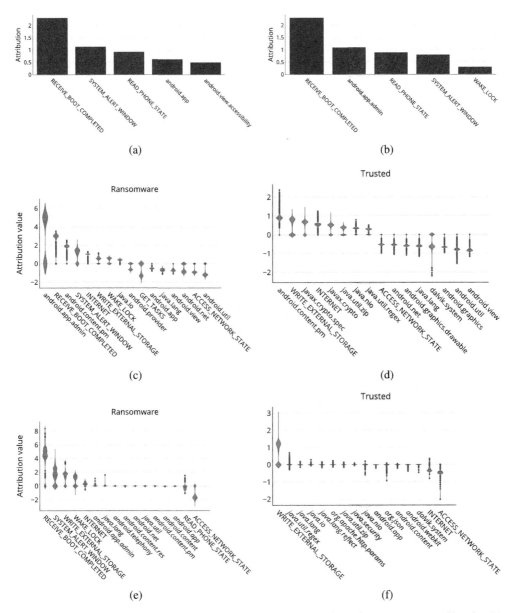

Figure 11.4 (Top row) Top-5 absolute attributions for ransomware samples with respect to a trusted baseline (a) and for trusted samples with respect to a ransomware baseline (b). (Middle row) Binarized feature vector. Top-8 positive and top-8 negative feature attribution distribution for the ransomware (c) and trusted (d) samples of the dataset. (Bottom row) Feature vector of API classes grouped by package. Grouped API class calls are indicated in italic font. Top-8 positive and top-8 negative feature attribution distribution for the ransomware (e) and trusted (f) samples of the dataset.

possible to see how – apparently – the classifier with binary features mostly considers as prominent the same features as the nonbinary one. However, the binary one does not highlight that trusted apps use layout components much more extensively than a ransomware sample. That is, binary features do not reveal that ransomware apps are usually composed of few screens.

11.6.3 Feature granularity

Using a different level of granularity for the features associated with API calls might imply different outcomes for classifiers in terms of detection performance, but also resilience to adversarial attacks or learned patterns (Scalas et al., 2019; Cara et al., 2020). Therefore, it is of interest to inspect how a variation in the feature vector influences explanations. In the following, we consider a classifier using calls to API *classes* instead of packages, resulting in 4676 features. Then, we group the attributions for each feature associated with an API class call into the correspondent API package, and we eventually calculate the mean attribution for that package. For example, calls to `android.app.admin.ConnectEvent` and `android.app.admin.SecurityLog` are both grouped into the `android.app.admin` package. The interesting, resulting point is that, by sorting the median explanations, the learned patterns shown in Figs. 11.4e and 11.4f are pretty much the same as those in Figs. 11.2a and 11.2b, respectively. This indicates that the conceptual idea behind the design and the associated structure (packages, classes, methods) of the Android APIs is correctly learned by the classifiers. Moreover, it also indicates how the difference between the possible three types of features is minor, as studied by Scalas et al. (2019).

11.6.4 Feature robustness

The experiment of Section 11.5.3.4 shows that detection performance with a reduced set of features – where the set is built on the basis of the most relevant ones – is only slightly lower than the case with the full feature set. This result might be interpreted in the light of *evasion* attacks, i.e., adversarial offensives that manipulate specific components of the Android apps in order to fool classifiers (Demontis et al., 2017; Cara et al., 2020; Melis et al., 2022). Relying only on a small set of features that have been recognized as characterizing ransomware behavior can be a defense mechanism against such attacks. Specifically, if attackers are obliged to alter the features corresponding to the components that perform the expected designed malicious actions, then the modification of the ransomware app might result in a nonworking application. Hence, attackers could only design theoretical evasion attacks in the so-called *feature space*, but they could not perform them concretely in the *problem space* (Cara et al., 2020; Pierazzi et al., 2020).

11.7. Conclusion

Through this work, we presented a method that helps designers in finding the features that have the highest importance in characterizing Android ransomware. By looking at the distribution of the importance of the features within domain-specific sets of samples, we showed (*i*) the Android ransomware's main traits that effectively distinguish malicious samples from legitimate ones, (*ii*) the different ransomware families and ransomware's evolution over time in terms of application components, and (*iii*) the effectiveness in terms of detection performance of a limited set of the most relevant features characterizing Android ransomware. Moreover, we suggested how other aspects, i.e., the explanation baseline, along with the cardinality and granularity of the features, can be considered in diverse ways in order to enhance and augment the capability of explanations in answering different questions for cyber threat intelligence teams, as well as to improve the robustness of detectors to adversarial attacks.

References

Adebayo, Julius, Gilmer, Justin, Muelly, Michael, Goodfellow, Ian, Hardt, Moritz, Kim, Been, 2018. Sanity checks for saliency maps. Advances in Neural Information Processing Systems 31, 9505–9515. Curran Associates, Inc..

Alber, Maximilian, Lapuschkin, Sebastian, Seegerer, Philipp, Hägele, Miriam, Schütt, Kristof T., Montavon, Grégoire, Samek, Wojciech, Müller, Klaus-Robert, Dähne, Sven, Kindermans, Pieter-Jan, 2019. iNNvestigate neural networks! Journal of Machine Learning Research 20 (93), 1–8.

Arp, Daniel, Quiring, Erwin, Pendlebury, Feargus, Warnecke, Alexander, Pierazzi, Fabio, Wressnegger, Christian, Cavallaro, Lorenzo, Rieck, Konrad, 2022. Dos and Don'ts of Machine Learning in Computer Security. In: 31st USENIX Security Symposium (USENIX Security 22). USENIX Association, Boston, MA. https://www.usenix.org/conference/usenixsecurity22/presentation/arp.

Arp, Daniel, Spreitzenbarth, Michael, Hübner, Malte, Gascon, Hugo, Rieck, Konrad, 2014. DREBIN: effective and explainable detection of Android malware in your pocket. In: Proceedings 2014 Network and Distributed System Security Symposium. Reston, VA. Internet Society, pp. 23–26.

Baehrens, David, Schroeter, Timon, Harmeling, Stefan, Kawanabe, Motoaki, Hansen, Katja, Müller, Klaus-Robert, 2010. How to explain individual classification decisions. Journal of Machine Learning Research 11, 1803–1831.

Cara, Fabrizio, Scalas, Michele, Giacinto, Giorgio, Maiorca, Davide, 2020. On the feasibility of adversarial sample creation using the Android system API. Information 11 (9), 433.

Chen, Sen, Xue, Minhui, Tang, Zhushou, Xu, Lihua, Zhu, Haojin, 2016. StormDroid. In: Proceedings of the 11th ACM on Asia Conference on Computer and Communications Security – ASIA CCS'16. New York, New York, USA. ACM Press, pp. 377–388.

Demetrio, Luca, Biggio, Battista, Lagorio, Giovanni, Roli, Fabio, Armando, Alessandro, 2019. Explaining vulnerabilities of deep learning to adversarial malware binaries. In: Proceedings of the Third Italian Conference on Cyber Security 2019. Pisa. CEUR-WS.org.

Demontis, Ambra, Melis, Marco, Biggio, Battista, Maiorca, Davide, Arp, Daniel, Rieck, Konrad, Corona, Igino, Giacinto, Giorgio, Roli, Fabio, 2017. Yes, machine learning can be more secure! A case study on Android malware detection. IEEE Transactions on Dependable and Secure Computing 16 (4), 711–724.

Ilyas, Andrew, Santurkar, Shibani, Tsipras, Dimitris, Engstrom, Logan, Tran, Brandon, Madry, Aleksander, 2019. Adversarial examples are not bugs, they are features. In: Advances in Neural Information Processing Systems 32 (NIPS 2019). Vancouver. Curran Associates, Inc., pp. 125–136.

Kaspersky, 2020. IT threat evolution Q2 2020. Mobile statistics. https://securelist.com/it-threat-evolution-q2-2020-mobile-statistics/98337/.

Kim, Been, Wattenberg, Martin, Gilmer, Justin, Cai, Carrie, Wexler, James, Viegas, Fernanda, Sayres, Rory, 2018. Interpretability beyond feature attribution: quantitative testing with concept activation vectors (TCAV). In: 35th International Conference on Machine Learning (ICML 2018), vol. 80. Stockholm, pp. 2668–2677.

Lage, Isaac, Chen, Emily, He, Jeffrey, Narayanan, Menaka, Kim, Been, Gershman, Samuel J., Doshi-Velez, Finale, 2019. An evaluation of the human-interpretability of explanation. In: Proceedings of the AAAI Conference on Human Computation and Crowdsourcing, vol. 7. Honolulu. AAAI Press, pp. 59–67.

Maiorca, Davide, Mercaldo, Francesco, Giacinto, Giorgio, Visaggio, Corrado Aaron, Martinelli, Fabio, 2017. R-PackDroid: API package-based characterization and detection of mobile ransomware. In: Proceedings of the Symposium on Applied Computing – SAC'17. New York, New York, USA. ACM Press, pp. 1718–1723.

Melis, Marco, Demontis, Ambra, Pintor, Maura, Sotgiu, Angelo, Biggio, Battista, 2019. secml: A Python library for secure and explainable machine learning. arXiv:1912.10013.

Melis, Marco, Maiorca, Davide, Biggio, Battista, Giacinto, Giorgio, Roli, Fabio, 2018. Explaining black-box Android malware detection. In: 2018 26th European Signal Processing Conference (EUSIPCO). IEEE, pp. 524–528.

Melis, Marco, Scalas, Michele, Demontis, Ambra, Maiorca, Davide, Biggio, Battista, Giacinto, Giorgio, Roli, Fabio, 2022. Do gradient-based explanations tell anything about adversarial robustness to Android malware? International Journal of Machine Learning and Cybernetics 13, 217–232. https://doi.org/10.1007/s13042-021-01393-7.

Pendlebury, Feargus, Pierazzi, Fabio, Jordaney, Roberto, Kinder, Johannes, Cavallaro, Lorenzo, 2019. TESSERACT: eliminating experimental bias in malware classification across space and time. In: 28th USENIX Security Symposium (USENIX Security 19). Santa Clara, CA, USA. USENIX Association, pp. 729–746.

Pierazzi, Fabio, Pendlebury, Feargus, Cortellazzi, Jacopo, Cavallaro, Lorenzo, 2020. Intriguing properties of adversarial ML attacks in the problem space. In: 2020 IEEE Symposium on Security and Privacy (SP). IEEE, pp. 1332–1349.

Preece, Alun, Harborne, Dan, Braines, Dave, Tomsett, Richard, Chakraborty, Supriyo, 2018. Stakeholders in explainable AI. In: AAAI Fall Symposium on Artificial Intelligence in Government and Public Sector. Arlington, Virginia, USA.

Scalas, Michele, Maiorca, Davide, Mercaldo, Francesco, Visaggio, Corrado Aaron, Martinelli, Fabio, Giacinto, Giorgio, 2019. On the effectiveness of system API-related information for Android ransomware detection. Computers & Security 86, 168–182.

Scalas, Michele, Rieck, Konrad, Giacinto, Giorgio, 2021. Explanation-driven characterization of Android ransomware. In: ICPR'2020 Workshop on Explainable Deep Learning – AI. Springer, Cham, pp. 228–242.

Shrikumar, Avanti, Greenside, Peyton, Shcherbina, Anna, Kundaje, Anshul, 2016. Not just a black box: learning important features through propagating activation differences. arXiv:1605.01713 [cs.LG].

Sundararajan, Mukund, Taly, Ankur, Yan, Qiqi, 2017. Axiomatic attribution for deep networks. In: Proceedings of the 34th International Conference on Machine Learning. Sidney. JMLR.org, pp. 3319–3328.

Warnecke, Alexander, Arp, Daniel, Wressnegger, Christian, Rieck, Konrad, 2020. Evaluating explanation methods for deep learning in security. In: 2020 IEEE European Symposium on Security and Privacy (EuroS&P). Genova. IEEE, pp. 158–174.

CHAPTER 12

Explainability in medical image captioning

Romaissa Beddiar[a] **and Mourad Oussalah**[a,b]

[a]University of Oulu, Faculty of ITEE, CMVS, Oulu, Finland
[b]University of Oulu, Faculty of Medicine, MIPT Unit, Oulu, Finland

Chapter points

- Attention-based encoder–decoder for medical image captioning is investigated.
- Self-attention is employed for word importance to highlight the most relevant semantic features viewed by the captioning model.
- Attention map visualization is employed for illustrating the most relevant regions of a medical image, corresponding to the essential visual features.

12.1. Introduction

Nowadays, with the advances in digital health technology and cloud infrastructure, hospitals and imaging centers produce an increasing number of medical images from different modalities. Being one of the best ways to investigate the inside of a human body without the need for surgery or other invasive procedures (Allaouzi et al., 2018), medical imaging provides important pathological information. Indeed, analyzing and exploiting this information could be useful to diagnose different diseases and therefore deliver appropriate treatment (Xiong et al., 2019). Medical imaging demonstrated its ability to identify and efficiently detect many diseases such as cancer, diabetic retinopathy diseases, and COVID-19, among others. However, manually analyzing and understanding the content of medical images can take a lot of time and may require extensive medical experience and expertise. This raises the crucial need to develop automatic tools to discover and extract the relevant information from images which will then be used to comprehend the content of these images and deliver accurate descriptions, which gave birth to (medical) *image captioning*. More specifically, image captioning is the task of extracting relevant information from an image and generating appropriate captions to describe the content of this image (Alsharid et al., 2019). In the health domain, this can help enrich the medical knowledge systems and facilitate the human–machine interactive diagnosis practice (Wang et al., 2019). From a multidisciplinary perspective, medical image captioning makes a bridge between computer vision and natural language processing (NLP) with an emphasis on medical image processing (Park et al., 2020; Oussalah, 2021). Besides, unlike natural image captioning, medical image captioning bears extra challenges in the sense that it generates, from the image, only captions that are relevant to clinically important observations instead of the whole description of image content as in standard image captioning systems. Boosted by several competitions organized by respected image processing, pattern recognition and medical artificial intelligence communities, several machine learning algorithms have been put forward in the literature with promising results in medical field. In overall, Allaouzi et al. (2018) categorized existing approaches for automatic image captioning proposed in the literature into four main classes: (i) template-based methods that rely on grammatical rules; (ii) retrieval-based models which rely on similarity among images to extrapolate captions from one image to another; (iii) generative models which use deep neural networks models to generate captions; and (iv) hybrid models which are based on a combination of generative models, retrieval systems, and template-based techniques to produce more relevant captions. Noticeably, deep learning models are those that achieved impressive results in most image captioning competitions, as well as related NLP and medical computer vision analysis tasks. However, one of the most annoying things about deep learning is its black-box nature, where explaining how the model arrived to this final decision is difficult. It is, for instance, unknown which features contributed the most to a model decision, which is crucial in many applications, especially in the medical field (Holzinger et al., 2019). This is because identifying responsibility is pivotal in the case of failure of medical system diagnosis. Indeed, these algorithms were implemented within the Computer Aided Diagnosis to help clinicians in their daily routine and diagnosis by highlighting critical findings and triggering alerts when a potentially dangerous disease is detected. Therefore, any technical interaction among clinicians would require highlighting arguments behind success or failure of the AI system. Besides, enforcing the adoption of a new AI technology by a health authority often requires a lengthy scrutinization and a full transparency of the functioning of the system. For example, promoting a new AI-based diagnosis system for cancer treatment requires some visible proofs and causal knowledge that explains why the system came up with such a diagnosis. Similarly, in precision-medicine, explanation is required to support system diagnosis outcome and clinical investigation. Strictly speaking, we shall also acknowledge other domains of AI where explainability (XAI) is not that crucial as in aircraft collision avoidance software, where algorithms have been operating for years without human interaction and the problem could be described and formulated mathematically precisely. In other words, explainability is often required when some aspects of the underlying system cannot be sufficiently encoded into the model (Doshi-Velez and Kim, 2017), or when there is a mismatch between the output of the model and the stackholders' expectations. Indeed, in general stakeholders are reluctant to adopt techniques that are not directly trustworthy, tractable, and interpretable (Grice, 1975), especially given the increasing scope of ethical AI (Conati et al., 2018). Besides, since the European Union's General Data Protection Regulation (GDPR) introduced the "right to explanation" which states that users can ask for an explanation of an algorithmic decision that was made about them (Goodman and Flaxman, 2017), a growing interest to XAI has been noticed from both academic and industry perspective. In an attempt to summarize the XAI needs, Samek et al. (2017) pointed out that the need of explainable systems is rooted in four distinct standpoints: (a) verification of the system, i.e., understanding the rules governing the decision process in order to detect possible biases; (b) improvement of the system, i.e., understanding the model and the dataset to compare different models and to avoid failures; (c) learning from the system, i.e., extracting the distilled knowledge from the AI system; (d) compliance with legislation (particularly with the "right to explanation" set by European Union), i.e., finding answers to legal questions and informing people affected by AI decisions. Since explainability is wise when critical decisions are to be made, understanding and interpreting a deep learning based captioning model, especially for medical images, is extremely desirable.

Efforts have been made recently to develop AI systems with an explainability module, aiming at providing a description and an interpretation to the implemented system. This motivated us to extend our proposed model for the ImageCLEFmedical 2021 (Beddiar et al., 2021) by adding an explainability module. The ImageCLEF medical (Pelka et al., 2021; Ionescu et al., 2021) task is organized each year as part of the CLEF initiative labs, aiming at developing machine learning methods for medical image understanding and description. It consists in generating coherent captions based on the visual content of the image and its related clinical concepts. We present therefore, in this chapter, an extension of our contribution of the ImageCLEF 2021 medical task with an explainability module. The caption generation model is based on an encoder–decoder network with an attention layer, where the encoder is based on a CNN feature extractor and the decoder is composed of an LSTM network with an attention mechanism. We employed a GRU based RNN with a self-attention mechanism to calculate semantic features from word embedding and generate attention vectors that helped us later in the explainability task. Furthermore, the attention mechanism of the encoder–decoder is also used to extract attention maps that exhibit the most relevant regions of the image considered by the model while generating new captions. To summarize, we use both attention mechanisms for our explainability module to visualize attention maps and word importance. The findings are reported in terms of qualitative and quantitative results after evaluating the ImageCLEF medical captioning dataset. Fig. 12.1 shows our proposed method with the explainability module.

After introducing the topic of medical image captioning, we briefly review some studies from the literature related to captioning of medical images in Section 12.2. Next, we detail our proposed methodology for predicting captions from medical images and their underlying concepts in Section 12.3. Furthermore, we provide a brief description of the ImageCLEF dataset used in this study, the evaluation metrics used to assess the performance of our methodology, the experimental setup, as well as the obtained results

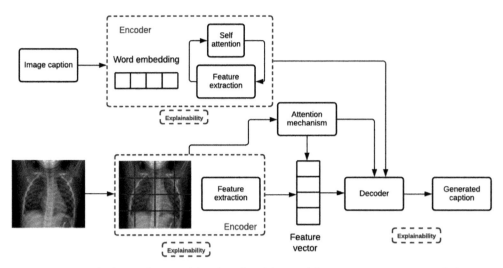

Figure 12.1 General scheme of our model with explainability module. Image captions are encoded using a self-attention GRU model and fitted to the decoder; visual features are encoded using a ResNet50 model and are then fitted to the decoder passing through an attention mechanism; captions are generated using both semantic and visual features. Explainability is introduced to explain visual features with convolutional layers' outputs, semantic features with word importance, and attention maps of generated words.

in Section 12.4. Finally, we finish with a conclusion where we highlight some key insights and future directions in Section 12.5.

12.2. Related work

Image captioning is the task of generating textual explanations to describe the image content (Alsharid et al., 2019). This is particularly of interest in applications such as semantic tagging, image retrieval, early childhood learning, human–like robot–robot interactions, and visual question answering tasks. On the other hand, AI explainability, or XAI, emerged as a set of tools and algorithms that help make deep learning models understandable. In this section, we first summarize some existing image captioning methods in the literature, focusing on their application in the medical field. Second, we enumerate and briefly outline some state–of–the–art explainable techniques.

12.2.1 Medical image captioning

In the medical domain, image captioning consists in generating medical reports to highlight the most important clinical findings observed in the image. As pointed out in the introduction section, four main classes of automatic medical image captioning can be distinguished (Allaouzi et al., 2018) where further exemplifications are provided:

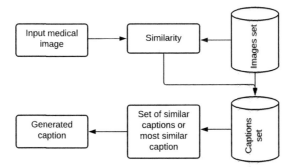

Figure 12.2 General architecture of retrieval-based captioning models. Similar images to the input image are selected and then their captions are either combined or the caption of the most similar image is used to generate a new caption.

1. **Template-based methods** rely on the use of templates caption that follow some grammar rules to generate captions for unseen image. They are in general simple, generate grammatically correct descriptions, but use hard-coded visual concepts, leading to low flexibility and less variety of the output (Ayesha et al., 2021). For instance, Harzig et al. (2019) proposed to use a deep CNN to detect diseases from gastrointestinal tract examinations by classifying images, identifying important regions using class activation maps, and generating descriptive reports from a template library.

2. **Retrieval-based models** use the similarity between images to extract a set of captions, speculating that similar images yield similar captions. Then, they either pick the most similar caption or combine many similar captions to generate a new one based on some rules (Ayesha et al., 2021) as illustrated by Fig. 12.2. For instance, Kisilev et al. (2015) proposed to generate breast radiology reports using lesion boundaries' detection and mapping of image measurements into semantic descriptors. The proposal is based on an SVM and a structured learning approach.

3. **Generative models** advocate deep learning networks that learn to generate captions from visual and semantic information of the image. They include encoder–decoder models as shown by Fig. 12.3, deep fully connected models, and merge models (Ayesha et al., 2021). In general, these techniques map features into captions or describe features with words and combine them at the end to generate captions using language models. For instance, merge models extract visual features using CNN models and learn the textual features using RNN models, and then both sets of features are merged to generate appropriate captions such as Rahman (2018). Moreover, encoder–decoder-based models extract features using a CNN network and feed them into an encoder to decode these features and generate a caption such as in Pelka and Friedrich (2017). To focus on particular areas of interest, researchers include attention mechanisms such as in Gajbhiye et al. (2020).

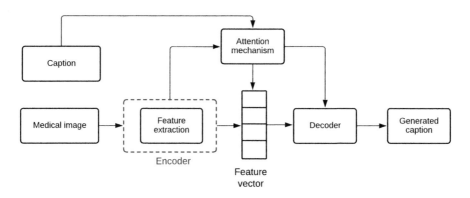

Figure 12.3 General architecture of encoder-decoder models with attention mechanism.

4. **Hybrid models** combine two or all of the above methods to produce more relevant and accurate captions. For instance, Xie et al. (2019) generate descriptions for abnormal observations by providing detailed visual evidence through a topic guided attention mechanism. Similarly, Li et al. (2018) proposed a novel Hybrid Retrieval-Generation Reinforced Agent (HRGR-Agent) guided by a retrieval policy to select whether to generate a new sentence or retrieve a template sentence. In the same spirit, Li et al. (2019) suggest to predict diseases using abnormality graph learning and then retrieve text templates using these abnormalities and natural language modeling.

The most common techniques proposed in the literature are the generative models. This is due to their effectiveness in many other NLP tasks and ability in generating new sentences for unseen images (Ayesha et al., 2021). However, the quality of the constructed captions is biased by the reliability of the model and the richness of the vocabulary used. In other words, if the vocabulary is not large enough, the generated captions are very limited in terms of word variety and the model will likely be unable to learn to construct grammatically correct sentences. Some researchers suggest to involve experts in the process of description generation by allowing them to correct and confirm the findings but this may slow down the diagnosis and the reporting processes leading to the loss of the most essential objective of these models, i.e., accelerating the automatic medical report generation (without human implication) (Yang et al., 2021).

12.2.2 AI explainability

A new trend in deep learning based AI suggests to explain the predictions made by the models to give more useful cues about why these results are obtained. Yoshua Bengio, a pioneer in the field of deep learning research, said that "As soon as you have a complicated enough machine, it becomes almost impossible to completely explain what it does" (Burkart and Huber, 2021). Similarly, Jason Yosinski from Uber (Voosen, 2017) declared: "We build amazing models. But we don't quite understand them." Motivated by this, much research has been conducted in this regard to deliver explainable deep learning based models for many computer vision and NLP tasks. Likewise, understanding why an automatic captioning system produced a specific description from a given image is very interesting, especially in the medical field. This augments the transparency and the credibility of the models, and provides clinicians with accurate reasoning on the medical findings. As of yet, there exists an active debate about usefulness of explainability in machine learning (Burkart and Huber, 2021), for which one side justifies the reliability of a system by its transparency and understandability. Opponents argue that sometimes human reasoning is not understandable, and therefore explainability is not required for every ML task, but limited to some specific purposes, while others view additional steps in ensuring system explainability as undermining the performance of the overall system due to increased computational cost and possible interaction modalities that may compromise security issues. Strictly speaking, the need for AI explainability was recognized much earlier, and was an inherent component of many of the first AI diagnostic systems where "IF–Then" rules and inference engine were widely employed to explain the actions of the underlined expert system, for instance. This was implemented in early MYCIN systems (Buchanan and Shortliffe, 1984) that formed the basis of many subsequent medical systems; although the exact scope and nature of these rules can be debatable. In the literature, the concept of explainability is related to transparency, interpretability, trust, fairness, and accountability, among others (Abdul et al., 2018).

Roughly speaking, many explanation methods have been proposed in the literature, such as gradient-based methods (Sundararajan et al., 2017; Selvaraju et al., 2017), decomposition-based methods (Murdoch et al., 2018; Lundberg and Lee, 2017), and sampling-based methods (Petsiuk et al., 2018; Luss et al., 2019), which could be adapted to explain captioning models. Only few works focused on interpreting captioning models so far. In general, attention heatmaps are considered as explanations for the attention-based captioning since they provide the locations of object words but cannot unravel the contributions of the image and the text (Sun et al., 2022). Moreover, gradient-based methods such as Grad-CAM have been exploited to explain predictions of image captioning models without attention module. For instance, Sun et al. (2022) use attention visualization to analyze the predictions of image captioning models by combining layer-wise relevance propagation (LRP) and gradient-based explanation methods. Likewise, the authors of Biswas et al. (2020) compute visual attention using high- and low-level features obtained from object specific salient regions of the input image. Then, they embed the content of bounding boxes from the pretrained Mask R-CNN model to provide explanatory features. Likewise, Han et al. (2020) presented an eXplainable AI (XAI) approach to image captioning, providing visual link between the region of image and the particular generated word. However, evaluating the provided explanation is still challenging since no standardized framework is put forward for implementing explainability, and no specific metrics are considered (Heuillet et al., 2021). Moreover, the explanation is planned exclusively for a specific audience who may have different levels of understanding and various interpretations leading to a subjective assessment of the explanation quality.

12.3. Methodology

We present in the current chapter an explainable approach to generate accurate captions for medical images. The model is based on an encoder–decoder architecture where visual and semantic features of the image are fused to efficiently describe the content of a given image with correct sentences. First, data is preprocessed to transform the text and the images into understandable units. Next, embeddings are calculated from image captions and images are augmented using some data augmentation techniques. In addition, visual features are extracted and used in accordance with semantic features to generate new captions by the decoder. The attention maps of the attention-based encoder–decoder model and the word importance are used to explain the captions generated in accordance with relevant image regions and highlighted words from original captions. The detail is provided in the next subsections.

12.3.1 Data preprocessing

Text preprocessing

We preprocess the captions using the NLTK package.[1] For that, each caption is first tokenized, while stop words and punctuation are removed using the NLTK's "English" stop-word list. Then, we lower case and retrieve the stem of each token using the NLTK's Snowball stemmer.[2] We add to each filtered sentence corresponding to a medical image, two tokens, namely '< start >' and '< end >' to help the RNN decoder identify the beginning and the end of each caption.

Image preprocessing

Before feature extraction, it is essential to perform some image preprocessing. For that, we create data generators that allow us to normalize, transform, and resize the images into adequate type and size to facilitate the features calculation and make them fit in the feature extractor size, which is $224 \times 224 \times 3$. Data augmentation is then applied by vertically and horizontally flipping and crop-centering with a fraction of 87.5%. Therefore, the training set and the validation set are then expanded without altering the visual content of the image.

---

[1] https://www.nltk.org/.
[2] https://www.nltk.org/api/nltk.stem.snowball.html.

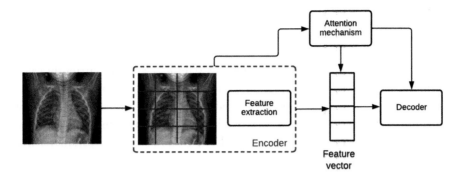

Figure 12.4 Scheme of visual features encoding with attention mechanism.

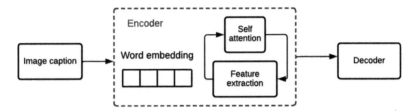

Figure 12.5 Scheme of self-attention GRU model used for text encoding.

12.3.2 Encoder–decoder with attention for caption prediction

We addressed the task of automatic captioning of medical images using an encoder–decoder architecture with an attention mechanism similar to Xu et al. (2015). Two encoders were used to encode the text and image inputs.

The first encoder is a pretrained ResNet50 model for which the last convolutional layer is removed and weights of ImageNet are frozen. It serves to extract visual features from raw medical images. In other words, for a given image I, the encoder produces m D-dimensional visual vectors V representing different parts of the image as $V = (v_1, \ldots, v_m)$, $v_i \in \mathbb{R}^D$, as shown in Fig. 12.4. Features are extracted from the convolutional layer instead of a flatten layer to help build the correspondence between image regions and extracted features. Therefore, the decoder will be able to generate a word for each region of the image by focusing on the most important parts.

The second GRU based RNN with self-attention acting as a multilabel classifier is used to extract semantic features from image captions. Self-attention is employed to highlight the most important words in the caption as shown in Fig. 12.5. GRU tracks the sequences' state without separate memory cells by dint of its gating mechanism that allows the system to control the added information to the state (Yang et al., 2016). A GRU employs two types of gates: the reset gate r_t which controls how much the past state contributes to the candidate state and the update gate z_t, and computes the new state at time t as

$$h_t = (1 - z_t) \odot h_{t-1} + z_t \odot \tilde{h}_t. \tag{12.1}$$

We demonstrate in (12.1) how the previous state h_{t-1} and the currently calculated state from the new sequence information $\tilde{h}_t$ are employed to compute the new state h_t. This linear interpolation is therefore controlled by the update gate z_t that decides which information is kept from the past or newly added; z_t is updated through (12.2), where x_t refers to the sequence vector at time t, and W, U, and b refer to parameter matrices and vector:

$$z_t = \sigma(W_z x_t + U_z h_{t-1} + b_z). \tag{12.2}$$

The candidate state $\tilde{h}_t$ is computed as

$$\tilde{h}_t = \tanh(W_h x_t + r_t \odot (U_h h_{t-1}) + b_h). \tag{12.3}$$

Similarly, the reset state r_t is computed as

$$r_t = \sigma(W_r x_t + U_r h_{t-1} + b_r). \tag{12.4}$$

Since it is difficult to fuse the semantic meaning of the image and the text in one vector using a single attention weight, we consider here two attention mechanisms. The first is related to the text, and the second is associated with the visual features while combining the encoders and decoder.

The self-attention mechanism related to text is used to extract words that are important to the meaning of the sentence. One-layer MLP is employed to compute the hidden representation u_{it} of the word embedding h_{it} as $u_{it} = \tanh(W_w h_{it} + b_w)$. Then, the similarity of u_{it} with a word level context vector u_w measures the importance of the word which is obtained through a softmax function as

$$\alpha_{it} = \frac{\exp(u_{it}^T u_w)}{\sum_t \exp(u_{it}^T u_w)}. \tag{12.5}$$

For the second attention mechanism, we use a multilayer perception MLP conditioned on the previous hidden state to focus on the most relevant parts of the image and generate weights accordingly. These weights serve to create the context vectors which are employed later by the decoder in addition to the previous hidden state and the previous word to generate a new word from the computed vocabulary at each time step. Therefore, visual features (represented by the context vector) and semantic features (represented by word embeddings) are employed by the LSTM based decoder to create new caption sequences word by word until the '$< end >$' token is met.

The context vector $\hat{z}_t$ represents each relevant part of the input image at time t. For each part of the image, a positive weight α_i is calculated to illustrate if this part is important for producing the next word. MLP is again used to compute the weights α associated with visual vectors V with the attention model f_{att} as follows:

$$e_{ti} = f_{att}(v_i, h_{t-1}), \tag{12.6}$$

$$\alpha_{ti} = \frac{\exp(e_{ti})}{\sum_{k=1}^{m} \exp(e_{tk})}. \tag{12.7}$$

Finally, the context vector $\hat{z}_t$ can be obtained as

$$\hat{z}_t = \phi(v_i, \alpha_i), \tag{12.8}$$

where ϕ is a function that selects a single vector given the set of visual vectors and their corresponding weights as demonstrated in Xu et al. (2015).

12.3.3 Caption generation explainability

First, we illustrate in Fig. 12.1 the context underpinning the introduction of explainability overall. Second, to explain the proposed medical image captioning model, we employ two main visualization schemes:

- First, we use the *word importance* to highlight the most important words in the caption. In other terms, we show which words were mainly considered by the GRU encoder while computing the word embeddings and fitting them to the decoder. For that, we used a self-attention mechanism as shown in the previous subsection. In fact, the contribution of single words in the construction of a given caption ranges from "most important" to "neglected" words. Attention weights can therefore be employed to reflect such importance. Weights or scores are generated for each word constituting the caption and then, based on the associated score value, we use color distribution to visualize words (the higher the score, the darker the color).
- Second, we use the attention maps to highlight the image regions for which words are generated as presented in the previous subsection. For that, we generate a weight matrix for input image regions and words of the original caption. Words are obtained from the decoder generation and image regions correspond to features extracted using the ResNet50 encoder from the convolutional layers which construct the correspondence between image regions and features extracted. The attention mechanism is a feed forward neural network which outputs a weight matrix. Each row of the matrix illustrates the relevance of the region and the word generated. This relevance is reflected through the context vectors $\hat{z}_t$ calculated above.

12.4. Experimental results

We describe in this section our experimental methodology, quantitative and qualitative results, which validate the effectiveness of our explainable medical image captioning model.

12.4.1 Dataset

For 2021 ImageCLEF edition (Pelka et al., 2021; Ionescu et al., 2021), data is shared between two ImageCLEF tasks: the ImageCLEFmed Caption and the ImageCLEF-VQAMed tasks. The dataset includes three sets: the training set composed of the VQA-Med 2020 training data with 2756 medical images, the validation set consisting of 500 radiology images, and the test set consisting of 444 radiology images. Two Excel files containing the medical image ID and the corresponding concepts CUIs (Concept Unique Identifiers) in the first file and the captions of each image in the second file are given to map each medical image onto its related concepts and caption. The first file is used for the concept detection task, whereas the second file is devoted to the caption prediction task. We present in Fig. 12.6 sample images with their underlying concepts and captions.

On further analysis of the dataset, we observed that the most frequent CUI is the "C0040398" corresponding to "Tomography, Emission-Computed" with 1159 images and that most of the medical images are attached to 2 to 3 concepts, whereas the maximum number of concept CUIs per image is 10. Moreover, we noticed that the

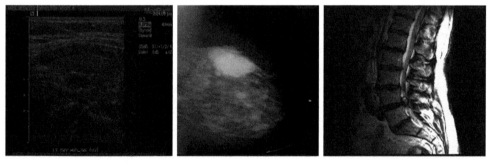

Medical concepts: Anatomical pole, structure of left lower lobe of lung, ultrasonography. **Caption:** Adjacent to the mid to lower pole of the left thyroid lobe posteriorly is a 1.5 x 0.5 x 0.8 cm ovoid homogeneous solid hypoechoic mass. It is well circumscribed.

Medical concepts: Mass of body structure, mammography. **Caption:** Left MLO view with mass seen in the upper quadrant.

Medical concepts: Mass of body structure, abnormal degeneration, disks, present, MRI. **Caption:** Sagittal T2W demonstrating a smoothly marginated extradural mass at the L4/5 level. Degenerative vertebral and disc changes are present at multiple levels.

Figure 12.6 Sample images from the ImageCLEF medical captioning dataset. For each image, some medical concepts are combined with the caption describing the semantic content of the image generated by professional annotators.

maximum number of sentences per image caption is 5 and the maximum length of any caption is 47 words before preprocessing, whereas it is 33 words after the preprocessing.

In addition, the dataset is very challenging. It includes data from different modalities (X-ray, ultrasound, CT scan, MRI, etc.), various body parts (brain, hand, knee, etc.), and acquisition conditions vary as well from one image to another (illumination, contrast, size, scale, etc.). This makes the visual features' extraction challenging, especially with few samples available for training.

12.4.2 Experimental setup

To validate the effectiveness of our captioning model, we present in the following qualitative and quantitative results. First, we compute the BLEU score over the validation set. More formally, for each image, we calculate the BLEU score between the original caption and the newly generated caption. Then, we average the score over the validation images to get the score for the proposed model. Next, we visualize some visual features extracted using the pretrained ResNet50 model from two images at different layers (layer 0, layer 20, and layer 40), as illustrated in Fig. 12.8. Then, we visualize some attention maps highlighting the most relevant regions of the image in addition to words generated by the captioning model. We compare the original caption to the generated caption by presenting the words existing in both captions in red color (mid gray in print version). Furthermore, we illustrate some examples where the model was not able to predict the caption and where only some or none of the words constituting the original caption are generated. Similarly, we show the attention maps for these wrong results as well to explain why the model failed to generate correct captions. We discuss the evaluation metrics used and report the results in the next subsections.

12.4.3 Evaluation metrics

To evaluate the performance of our model in generating accurate captions for medical images, we calculate the BLEU score by assuming that each caption is a single sentence even if it is actually composed of several sentences. For that, we use the default implementation of the Python NLTK based on Papineni et al. (2002):

$$BLEU = BP \cdot \exp\left(\sum_{n=1}^{N} W_n \cdot \log p_n\right), \tag{12.9}$$

where BP refers to the brevity penalty, N refers to the number of n_grams (uni-gram, bi-gram, 3-gram, and 4-gram), W_n refers to the weight of each modified precision, and P_n refers to the modified precision. By default, $N = 4$ and $W_n = 1/N = 1/4$.

Brevity Penalty (BP) allows us to pick the candidate caption which is most likely close in length, word choice, and word order to the reference caption. It is an exponential decay and is calculated as follows:

$$BP = \begin{cases} 1, & c > r, \\ \exp(1 - r/c), & c \leqslant r, \end{cases} \quad (12.10)$$

where r refers to the count of words in the reference caption and c refers to the count of words in the candidate caption.

Modified precision is computed for each n_gram as the sum of clipped n_gram counts of the candidate sentences in the corpus divided by the number of candidate n_grams as highlighted in (12.11) (Papineni et al., 2002). It allows us to compute the adequacy and the fluency of the candidate translation to the reference translation:

$$p_n = \frac{\displaystyle\sum_{C \in \{Candidates\}} \sum_{n\_gram \in C} Count_{clip}(n\_gram)}{\displaystyle\sum_{C' \in \{Candidates\}} \sum_{n\_gram' \in C'} Count(n\_gram')}. \quad (12.11)$$

12.4.4 Results

Quantitative results

We report in Table 12.1 the results of caption generation over the validation set in terms of BLEU score. The extended version achieved better results than our previous version (Beddiar et al., 2021). However, Tsuneda et al. (2021) obtained a better performance than ours even though our models are based on the "Show, Attend, and Tell" model. In addition, we present in Fig. 12.7 the evolution of the training and the validation losses over 50 epochs. We can see that the training loss is decreasing more rapidly than the validation loss.

Table 12.1 Comparison of our results to some state-of-the-art results.

Method	BLEU score
06 pattern 3 + Imaging Types_Anatomic Structure_Findings (Wang et al., 2021)	25.7
"Show, Attend, and Tell" with histogram normalization (Tsuneda et al., 2021)	43.7
Encoder–decoder with attention (Beddiar et al., 2021)	28.7
Our proposal	40.29

Qualitative results

We visualize the features extracted using the ResNet50 encoder at different convolutional layers. The used ResNet50 model contains 49 convolutional layers, whose outputs are exploited to obtain the visual features. Fig. 12.8 illustrates some features extracted at layer 0, layer 20, and layer 40. We choose to show these layers to illustrate the evolution

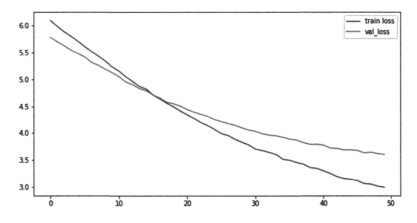

Figure 12.7 Training loss versus validation loss.

of the features over layers. Different general features such as contours, shape, contrast, etc., are computed, and, at each layer, more detailed features are obtained. If we compare features of different images at the same layer, we can see that features of different images are not similar and at least some visual features help to distinguish the body part of the study. Then, more detailed features can distinguish between various images of the same body part. Visualizing these features helps us to understand which features are extracted by the visual encoder and what is fed to the decoder.

Moreover, we visualize word importance of the image captions using the attention scores. The higher the score, the darker the color of the word, and the higher the degree of relevance of this word in the semantic features of the image, as illustrated by Fig. 12.9.

Furthermore, we visualize in Figs. 12.10 and 12.11 some attention maps for correctly generated captions. In Fig. 12.10, we can see from the original image and its original caption that the model was able to generate exactly the same caption by focusing on some parts of the image only. The yellow color (light gray in print version) of the attention maps illustrates the most relevant image region considered while generating the caption. For each important region, the model assigns a word from the vocabulary using the semantic features and the visual features learned from the image. Then the sequence of words is combined to create a coherent caption. The same finding is observed in Fig. 12.11, where the model generated word by word a correct caption for the image but missed the word "both." Similarly, the model focused on some parts is illustrated by the yellow color (light gray in print version) in the attention maps.

Finally, we visualize some wrong captions generated by the model in Fig. 12.12. The model failed to generate the correct captions partially or completely as illustrated by the three subfigures. In the first the model failed to generate C6-7 (place of the dislocation of the disc) maybe due to the preprocessing where characters are removed. In the second subfigure, the model encountered an unknown word that does not belong

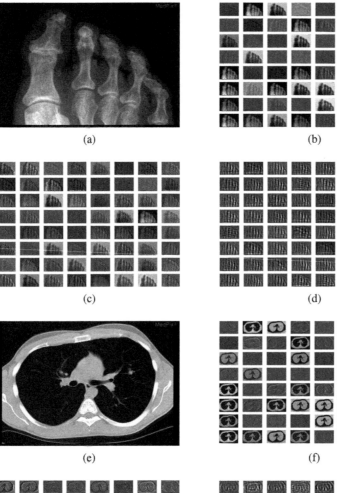

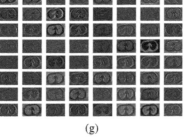

Figure 12.8 Visualization of features extracted from the ResNet encoder at different layers for one sample from the ImageCLEF medical captioning dataset: (a) original image, (b) visual features at layer 0, (c) visual features at layer 20, (d) visual features at layer 40 for the first sample, (e) original image, (f) visual features at layer 0, (g) visual features at layer 20, and (h) visual features at layer 40 for the second sample.

Word	Score
contrast	0.631746
enhanced	0.745938
axial	0.616506
CT	1.000000
images	0.762938
and	0.823625
oblique	0.934849
sagittal	0.470925
reconstructed	0.801451
images	0.800402
of	0.698901
the	0.632170
chest	0.624119
demonstrates	0.514835
a	0.851869
focal	0.750645
narrowing	0.553317
of	0.732408
the	0.690753
aorta	0.784924
just	0.514351
distal	0.689935
to	0.990118
the	0.829186
UNK	0.947459
of	0.842289
the	0.751287
left	0.777720
subclavian	0.733597
artery	0.657347
with	0.526815
post	0.244704
UNK	0.751891
dilation	0.949717
of	0.753076
the	0.558918
descending	0.505137
thoracic	0.504509
aorta	0.689161
PAD	0.683687

(a)

Word	Score
this	0.981197
is	0.904059
now	0.543213
a	0.894860
transverse	1.000000
_ UNK	0.775203
evaluation	0.861105
of	0.703457
the	0.603856
right	0.753450
kidney	0.469614
UNK	0.653602
superiorly	0.735162
and	0.630522
then	0.589518
UNK	0.714209
inferiorly	0.685258
this	0.727177
image	0.494226
is	0.729277
the	0.547256
initial	0.589878
image	0.450573
of	0.640012
right	0.736467
kidney	0.517799
transverse	0.820756
evaluation	0.728667
in	0.732342
the	0.436854
image	0.346563
the	0.473267
liver	0.597025
and	0.562813
kidney	0.450151
can	0.556699
be	0.438292
identified	0.670330
PAD	0.579648

(b)

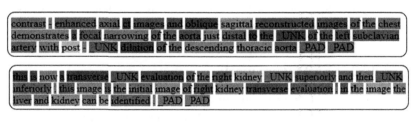

(c)

Figure 12.9 Word importance using images captions and self-attention scores.

to the vocabulary and was not able to construct a correct caption, but we see that the model recognized the breast even though the caption does not include the word "breast." In the third subfigure, the model failed completely to generate the caption and encountered many unknown words. By observing the attention maps, we see that the

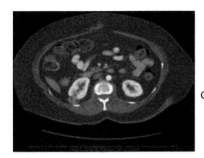

Original caption: Right renal complex cyst

Generated caption: right renal complex cyst

(a)

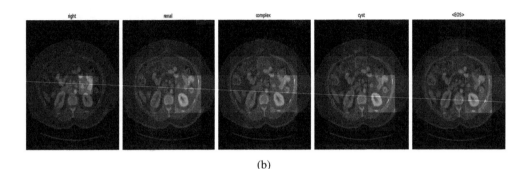

(b)

Figure 12.10 Visualization of attention maps of a correctly generated caption: (a) original image and (b) attention maps.

disc was recognized by focusing on it in the image and hence giving a partially correct caption. Similarly, for the second attention map, the model focused on different regions but could not generate a correct caption. However, for the last one, it focused on the same region and could not generate any correct word.

12.5. Conclusion and future work

We presented in this chapter an extension of our contribution to the ImageCLEF 2021 medical task. We proposed an attention-based encoder–decoder model for caption generation of medical images with an explainability module. We used a multilabel classifier with self-attention model for semantic features encoding and ResNet50 based model for visual features encoding. Attention mechanism is then employed to combine the encoders and the decoder. Some traditional data augmentation techniques are used to enrich the training set and preprocessing of both images and text is exploited. To explain the outputs of our model, we used the word importance derived from the scores of the self-attention classifier to visualize the most relevant words of the image captions. We visualized as well some visual features computed using by convolutional layers of

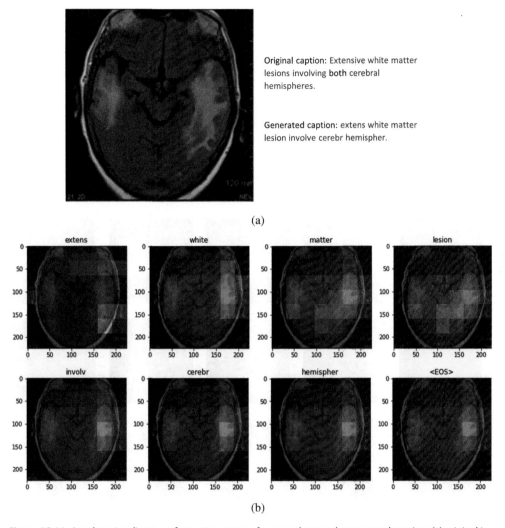

Figure 12.11 Another visualization of attention maps of a second correctly generated caption: (a) original image and (b) attention maps.

the visual encoder. In addition, we used the attention maps and their weights to visualize the most important regions of the images that were exploited by the model to generate accurate captions. Quantitative results are presented in terms of BLEU score, while qualitative results are shown by contrasting correctly generated and wrongly generated captions through our developed visualization module. Although, the developed approach yields satisfactory results that enable us to compete with top ImageCLEF participants, there is still room for further improvement and enhancement, especially whenever new large-scale and high quality dataset is released. Indeed, the used dataset

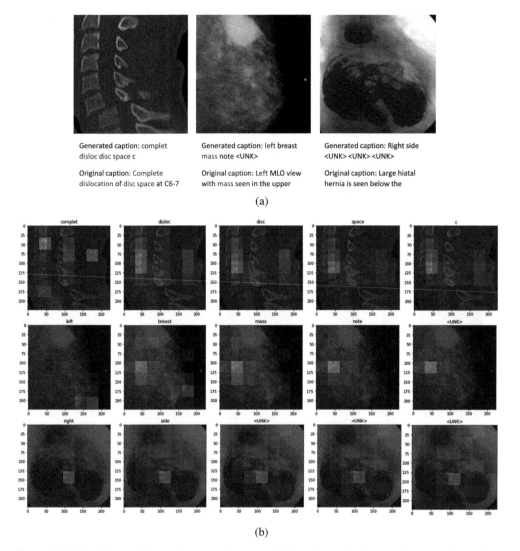

Figure 12.12 Visualization of attention maps of some partially and completely wrongly generated captions: (a) original images and (b) attention maps.

is very challenging, containing images of different modalities, different body parts and from various views and scales. This complexity can impact the quality of learning and generated model. It would be, for instance, interesting to investigate larger dataset of one modality only and see how to improve the parameters of the encoder and decoder to make the process of caption generation more efficient. In addition, specific embeddings, especially related to medical field, could be employed to help create more significant captions.

Acknowledgment

This work is supported by the Academy of Finland Profi5 DigiHealth project (#326291), which is gratefully acknowledged.

References

Abdul, A., Vermeulen, J., Wang, D., Lim, B.Y., Kankanhalli, M., 2018. Trends and trajectories for explainable, accountable and intelligible systems: An HCI research agenda. In: Proceedings of the 2018 CHI. Association for Computing Machinery.

Allaouzi, I., Ben Ahmed, M., Benamrou, B., Ouardouz, M., 2018. Automatic caption generation for medical images. In: Proceedings of the 3rd International Conference on Smart City Applications (SCA'18).

Alsharid, M., Sharma, H., Drukker, L., Chatelain, P., Papageorghiou, A.T., Noble, J.A., 2019. Captioning ultrasound images automatically. In: Medical Image Computing and Computer-Assisted Intervention: MICCAI, International Conference on Medical Image Computing and Computer-Assisted Intervention, p. 22.

Ayesha, H., Iqbal, S., Tariq, M., Abrar, M., Sanaullah, M., Abbas, I., Rehman, A., Niazi, M.F.K., Hussain, S., 2021. Automatic medical image interpretation: State of the art and future directions. Pattern Recognition 114, 107856.

Beddiar, D.R., Oussalah, M., Seppänen, T., 2021. Attention-based CNN-GRU model for automatic medical images captioning: ImageCLEF 2021. In: Working Notes of CLEF – Conference and Labs of the Evaluation Forum, CLEF-WN 2021. 21–24 September, Bucharest, Romania, pp. 1160–1173.

Biswas, R., Barz, M., Sonntag, D., 2020. Towards explanatory interactive image captioning using top-down and bottom-up features, beam search and re-ranking. KI-Künstliche Intelligenz 34 (4), 571–584.

Buchanan, B.G., Shortliffe, E.H., 1984. Rule Based Expert Systems: The MYCIN Experiment of the Stan-Ford Heuristic Programming Project. Addison-Wesley, Reading, MA.

Burkart, N., Huber, M.F., 2021. A survey on the explainability of supervised machine learning. Journal of Artificial Intelligence Research 70, 245–317.

Conati, C., Porayska-Pomsta, K., Mavrikis, M., 2018. AI in education needs interpretable machine learning: Lessons from open learner modelling. arXiv:1807.00154.

Doshi-Velez, F., Kim, B., 2017. Towards a rigorous science of interpretable machine learning. arXiv:1702.08608.

Gajbhiye, G.O., Nandedkar, A.V., Faye, I., 2020. Automatic report generation for chest X-ray images: A multilevel multi-attention approach. In: 4th International Conference on Computer Vision and Image Processing, CVIP 2019, vol. 1147, pp. 174–182.

Goodman, B., Flaxman, S., 2017. European Union regulations on algorithmic decision making and a "right to explanation". AI Magazine 38 (3).

Grice, H.P., 1975. Logic and conversation. In: Syntax and Semantics 3. Speech Arts, pp. 41–58.

Han, S.H., Kwon, M.S., Choi, H.J., 2020. Explainable AI (XAI) approach to image captioning. The Journal of Engineering 2020 (13), 589–594.

Harzig, P., Einfalt, M., Lienhart, R., 2019. Automatic disease detection and report generation for gastrointestinal tract examinations. In: 27th ACM International Conference on Multimedia, MM 2019, pp. 2573–2577.

Heuillet, A., Couthouis, F., Díaz-Rodríguez, N., 2021. Explainability in deep reinforcement learning. Knowledge-Based Systems 214, 106685.

Holzinger, A., Langs, G., Denk, H., Zatloukal, K., Müller, H., 2019. Causability and explainability of artificial intelligence in medicine. Wiley Interdisciplinary Reviews: Data Mining and Knowledge Discovery 9 (4), e1312.

Ionescu, B., Müller, H., Péteri, R., Ben-Abacha, A., Sarrouti, M., Demner-Fushman, D., Hasan, S.A., Kozlovski, S., Liauchuk, V., Dicente, Y., Kovalev, V., Pelka, O., Seco de Herrera, A.G., Jacutprakart, J., Friedrich, C.M., Berari, R., Tauteanu, A., Fichou, D., Brie, B., Dogariu, M., Ştefan, L.D., Constantin, M.G., Chamberlain, J., Campello, A., Clark, A., Oliver, T.A., Moustahfid, H., Popescu, A., Deshayes-Chossart, J., 2021. Overview of the ImageCLEF 2021: Multimedia retrieval in medical, nature, internet and social media applications. In: Experimental IR Meets Multilinguality, Multimodality, and Interaction, Proceedings of the 12th International Conference of the CLEF Association (CLEF 2021). Bucharest, Romania, September 21–24. In: LNCS Lecture Notes in Computer Science. Springer.

Kisilev, P., Walach, E., Barkan, E., Ophir, B., Alpert, S., Hashoul, S.Y., 2015. From medical image to automatic medical report generation. IBM Journal of Research and Development 59 (2).

Li, C.Y., Liang, X., Hu, Z., Xing, E.P., 2018. Hybrid retrieval-generation reinforced agent for medical image report generation. In: Advances in Neural Information Processing Systems 31 (NIPS 2018), p. 31.

Li, C.Y., Liang, X., Hu, Z., Xing, E.P., 2019. Knowledge-driven encode, retrieve, paraphrase for medical image report generation. In: Proceedings of the AAAI Conference on Artificial Intelligence, pp. 6666–6673.

Lundberg, S.M., Lee, S.I., 2017. A unified approach to interpreting model predictions. In: Proceedings of the 31st International Conference on Neural Information Processing Systems, pp. 4768–4777.

Luss, R., Chen, P.Y., Dhurandhar, A., Sattigeri, P., Zhang, Y., Shanmugam, K., Tu, C.C., 2019. Generating contrastive explanations with monotonic attribute functions. arXiv:1905.12698.

Murdoch, W.J., Liu, P.J., Yu, B., 2018. Beyond word importance: Contextual decomposition to extract interactions from LSTMs. arXiv:1801.05453.

Oussalah, M., 2021. AI explainability. A bridge between machine vision and natural language processing. In: Proceedings of the ICPR. Workshops and Challenges. Springer International Publishing, pp. 257–273.

Papineni, K., Roukos, S., Ward, T., Zhu, W.J., 2002. BLEU: a method for automatic evaluation of machine translation. In: Proceedings of the 40th Annual Meeting of the Association for Computational Linguistics, pp. 311–318.

Park, H., Kim, K., Yoon, J., Park, S., Choi, J., 2020. Feature difference makes sense: A medical image captioning model exploiting feature difference and tag information. In: Proceedings of the 58th Annual Meeting of the Association for Computational Linguistics: Student Research Workshop, pp. 95–102.

Pelka, O., Abacha, A.B., De Herrera, A.G.S., Jacutprakart, J., Friedrich, C.M., Müller, H., 2021. Overview of the ImageCLEFmed 2021 concept & caption prediction task. In: CLEF2021 Working Notes, CEUR Workshop Proceedings. Bucharest, Romania, September 21–24. CEUR-WS.org.

Pelka, O., Friedrich, C.M., 2017. Keyword generation for biomedical image retrieval with recurrent neural networks. In: 18th Working Notes of CLEF Conference and Labs of the Evaluation Forum, CLEF 2017, p. 1866.

Petsiuk, V., Das, A., Saenko, K., 2018. RISE: Randomized input sampling for explanation of black-box models. arXiv:1806.07421.

Rahman, M.M., 2018. A cross modal deep learning based approach for caption prediction and concept detection by CS Morgan state. In: 19th Working Notes of CLEF Conference and Labs of the Evaluation Forum, CLEF 2018, p. 2125.

Samek, W., Wiegand, T., Müller, K.R., 2017. Explainable artificial intelligence: Understanding, visualizing and interpreting deep learning models. ITU Journal: ICT Discoveries Special Issue, 39–48.

Selvaraju, R.R., Cogswell, M., Das, A., Vedantam, R., Parikh, D., Batra, D., 2017. Grad-CAM: Visual explanations from deep networks via gradient-based localization. In: Proceedings of the IEEE International Conference on Computer Vision, pp. 618–626.

Sun, J., Lapuschkin, S., Samek, W., Binder, A., 2022. Explain and improve: LRP-inference fine-tuning for image captioning models. Information Fusion 77, 233–246.

Sundararajan, M., Taly, A., Yan, Q., 2017. Axiomatic attribution for deep networks. In: International Conference on Machine Learning. PMLR, pp. 3319–3328.

Tsuneda, R., Asakawa, T., Aono, M., 2021. Kdelab at ImageCLEF2021: Medical caption prediction with effective data pre-processing and deep learning. In: CLEF2021 Working Notes, CEUR Workshop Proceedings. CEUR-WS.org, Bucharest, Romania.

Voosen, P., 2017. How AI detectives are cracking open the black box of deep learning. Science.

Wang, X., Guo, Z., Xu, C., Sun, L., Li, J., 2021. ImageSem group at ImageCLEFmed caption 2021 task: Exploring the clinical significance of the textual descriptions derived from medical images. In: CLEF2021 Working Notes, CEUR Workshop Proceedings. CEUR-WS.org, Bucharest, Romania.

Wang, X., Guo, Z., Zhang, Y., Li, J., 2019. Medical image labelling and semantic understanding for clinical applications. In: International Conference of the Cross-Language Evaluation Forum for European Languages. Springer, pp. 260–270.

Xie, X., Xiong, Y., Philip, S.Y., Li, K., Zhang, S., Zhu, Y., 2019. Attention-based abnormal-aware fusion network for radiology report generation. In: 24th International Conference on Database Systems for Advanced Applications, DASFAA 2019, vol. 11448, pp. 448–452.

Xiong, Y., Du, B., Yan, P., 2019. Reinforced transformer for medical image captioning. In: 10th International Workshop on Machine Learning in Medical Imaging, MLMI 2019 Held in Conjunction with the 22nd International Conference on Medical Image Computing and Computer-Assisted Intervention, MICCAI 2019, vol. 11861, pp. 673–680.

Xu, K., Ba, J., Kiros, R., Cho, K., Courville, A., Salakhudinov, R., Zemel, R., Bengio, Y., 2015. Show, attend and tell: Neural image caption generation with visual attention. In: International Conference on Machine Learning. PMLR, pp. 2048–2057.

Yang, S., Niu, J., Wu, J., Wang, Y., Liu, X., Li, Q., 2021. Automatic ultrasound image report generation with adaptive multimodal attention mechanism. Neurocomputing 427, 40–49.

Yang, Z., Yang, D., Dyer, C., He, X., Smola, A., Hovy, E., 2016. Hierarchical attention networks for document classification. In: Proceedings of the 2016 Conference of the North American Chapter of the Association for Computational Linguistics: Human Language Technologies, pp. 1480–1489.

CHAPTER 13

User tests & techniques for the post-hoc explanation of deep learning

Eoin Delaney[a,b], **Eoin M. Kenny**[a,b], **Derek Greene**[a,b], and **Mark T. Keane**[a,b]
[a]School of Computer Science, University College Dublin, Dublin, Ireland
[b]VistaMilk SFI Research Centre, Dublin, Dublin, Ireland

13.1. Introduction

In recent years, following the significant breakthroughs in Deep Learning, the Artificial Intelligence (AI) community has turned to the problem of eXplainable AI (XAI), mainly because of rising public concern about the use of these technologies in people's everyday lives, jobs, and leisure time (Ala-Pietilä and Smuha, 2021). Indeed, for the research community, there is very real worry that issues of interpretability, trust, and ethical usage will limit or block the deployment of these AI technologies. For these reasons, the DARPA XAI program has specifically targeted XAI research with a strong user testing emphasis to overcome such impasses (Gunning and Aha, 2019). At the same time, governments have also woken up to the need for regulation in this space; for example, the European Commission has established the High Level Expert Group on Artificial Intelligence to define guidelines for Trustworthy AI in the European Union, as a precursor to further legal steps (Ala-Pietilä and Smuha, 2021). Indeed, in the EU, GDPR places requirements on the need to explain automated decisions (Wachter et al., 2017). This wave of activity around the notion of explainability and XAI is also spawning new subareas of research; for example, XAI methods to support users in reversing algorithmic decisions – so-called *algorithmic recourse* – have emerged as a vibrant research topic (Karimi et al., 2020b). In this chapter, we present some recent solutions to the XAI problem using several variants of post-hoc explanations-by-example (Kenny et al., 2020; Keane et al., 2021). In the remainder of this introduction, we first consider the concept of "explanation" in XAI before outlining some of the different strategies explored in the literature. Then, in the remaining sections of the chapter we present new empirical evidence on how these different methods perform in dealing with image and time series datasets, along with reviewing what has been learned from user studies on their application.

13.1.1 What is an explanation? Pre-hoc versus post-hoc

One of the key problems facing XAI research is that the notion of "explanation" is not well defined and is still debated in Philosophy and Psychology (Sørmo et al., 2005).

Explainable Deep Learning AI
https://doi.org/10.1016/B978-0-32-396098-4.00019-3

One response to this issue in XAI has been to use terms other than "explanation", such as "interpretability," "transparency," and "simulatability"; but these renamings do not circumvent the fundamental problem that "explanation" is a slippery, hard-to-define concept. However, one broad distinction from philosophy that has gained general acceptance is the distinction between "explanation proper" and "explanation as justification." Sørmo et al. (2005) cast this philosophical distinction as the difference between explaining *how* the system reached some answer (what they call transparency) and explaining *why* the system produced a given answer (post-hoc justification). Lipton (2018) echoes these ideas with a similar distinction between transparency (i.e., "How does the model work?"; what we call pre-hoc explanation) and post-hoc explanation (i.e., "What else can the model tell me?").

Pre-hoc explanations promise to, in some sense, explain the Deep Learning model directly. So, the user can understand how the whole model works given some representation of it (Frosst and Hinton, 2017) via simplified model that "behaves similarly to the original model, but in a way that is easier to explain" (Lipton, 2018) (e.g., Frosst and Hinton (2017)). The claim here is that the model is inherently "transparent," "simulatable," or "interpretable" by virtue of how it runs. Rudin (2019) argues that this use of inherently transparent models is the only appropriate solution to XAI in sensitive, high-stakes domains; pointing to her own use of prototypes (Chen et al., 2018). However, the literature is not replete with many examples of this type of solution; indeed, the idea that one could "show" the inner workings of a Deep Learner to an "ordinary" end-user seems somewhat implausible as a proposition. Furthermore, many of the solutions which claim to be pre-hoc "transparent machine learning" are, actually, post-hoc solutions. For example, some model "simplifications" are really mappings of the Deep Learner into another modeling method (e.g., decision trees), what some call *proxy or surrogate models* (Gilpin et al., 2018), rather than direct renderings of the original neural network. As such, most of the XAI literature really concerns itself with post-hoc methods.

Post-hoc explanations provide after-the-fact justifications for what the Deep Learner has done. The key idea here is that one can explain/justify how a model reached some decision with reference to other information (e.g., "the model did this because it used such-and-such data"). This approach involves a broad spectrum of approaches involving many different techniques that try to provide evidential justifications for why a black-box model did what it did. Almost by definition, this means that these approaches are approximate; often, they do not directly show what was done to reach a prediction, but provide some basis for understanding why a prediction arose. There are probably four main approaches taken in the post-hoc explanation sphere: proxy-models, example-based explanations, natural language accounts and visualizations (see also Lipton (2018); Keane et al. (2021); Kenny et al. (2020)).

13.1.2 Post-hoc explanations: four approaches

The four main solutions to post-hoc explanation – proxy-models, example-based explanations, natural language accounts and visualizations – present quite different alternatives to the XAI problem. Here, we sketch each in turn, before going on to consider example-based explanations in some detail.

Proxy-model solutions provide some post-hoc mapping of some aspect of the Deep Learner into a "more transparent" modeling framework; for example, the Deep Learner is rerendered as a decision tree or a rule-based system that is said to explain its functioning. In general, these solutions assume that the proxy model is inherently transparent, as an article of faith without any substantiation for whether end-users actually find the proxy model comprehensible (Doshi-Velez and Kim, 2017). As Lipton (2018) points out "neither linear models, rule-based systems, nor decision trees are intrinsically interpretable... Sufficiently high-dimensional models, unwieldy rule lists, and deep decision trees could all be considered less transparent than comparatively compact neural networks." This means that to some degree, the jury is still out on the status and success of these proxy-model approaches. However, to be positive, there are now more user studies on people's understanding of rule-based explanations being carried out (Lage et al., 2019).

Example-based explanations arise out of long-standing case-based reasoning approaches to explanation (Sørmo et al., 2005; Nugent et al., 2009), where a case/precedent/example is used to provide a justification for a prediction (e.g., my house is valued at $400k because it is very similar to your house which sold for $400k). However, traditionally, example-based explanations were only used for k-NNs with only a handful of papers attempting to extend them to explaining multilayer perceptrons (Caruana et al., 1999; Shin and Park, 1999). More recent work has extended example-based explanation to Deep Learning models for classification, regression and natural language processing (Kenny and Keane, 2019, 2021a). The latter have been described as *twin-systems*, in which a black-box model is paired with a white-box model with the functionality of the former being mapped into the latter to find explanations (Kenny et al., 2021a; Kenny and Keane, 2021a). This twinning notion is very similar to the proxy-model idea, but subtly differs in that, typically, the white-box's function is purely explanatory; its sole role is to elucidate the predictions of the black box. In proxy-model approaches, the proxy often takes over the predictive role (as well as having an explanatory one), with evaluations being directed at establishing the fidelity of the proxy's predictions to those of the black box (see, e.g., White and d'Avila Garcez (2019); Guidotti et al. (2019)). A second major development in this example-based approach has been the proposal of different types of example-based explanations. Traditional case-based explanations use *factual examples*; they use instances from the dataset to directly explain a prediction (e.g., the house-price example). Recently, researchers have proposed counterfactual and semifactual example-based explanations, opening up whole new vistas for post-hoc explanations (see Section 13.1.3).

Natural language explanations are a third, post-hoc option reflecting a long history of attempts to turn AI model predictions or decision traces into natural language descriptions to be read by end-users (see, e.g., Camburu et al. (2020); Shortliffe et al. (1975); Nugent et al. (2009)). Traditionally, this approach tries to take some aspect of the model – such as its rules or outputs – and render it in a natural language description, on the assumption that users will then find the models workings more comprehensible. Obviously, this natural language processing step does not in itself guarantee that such an explanation will work, as it will also depend on what is being explained.

Visualizations are the final post-hoc XAI solution, one that has received significant attention in the literature. These methods attempt to surface significant aspects of a Deep Learner through visualizations using saliency maps, heat maps, and feature or class activation maps (Erhan et al., 2009; Simonyan et al., 2013; Zeiler and Fergus, 2014; Hohman et al., 2018; Zhou et al., 2016). As with the natural language solution, these methods to some extent depend on what is being highlighted for comprehension by end users.

13.1.3 Example-based explanations: factual, counterfactual, and semifactual

The present chapter focuses on recent advances in post-hoc example-based explanations and on the variety of solutions arising in this literature. Recently, the XAI literature has rapidly moved from traditional factual, example or case-based explanations to counterfactual (Byrne, 2019; Miller, 2019; Karimi et al., 2020a; Keane et al., 2021) and semifactual explanations (Kenny and Keane, 2021b). Here, we briefly sketch the ideas behind these explanation strategies, largely describing them using tabular-data content (see later sections for image and time series examples).

Factual Explanations. These explanations are the case-based examples discussed in hundreds, if not thousands of case-based reasoning (CBR) papers (Leake and McSherry, 2005; Sørmo et al., 2005); except that now the example-cases to explain Deep Learners are retrieved based on extracted feature-weighs from the Deep Learner (Kenny and Keane, 2019, 2021a). Imagine a SmartAg system, where a Deep Learning model for predicting crop growth tells a farmer that "in the next week, the grass yield on their farm will be 23 tons," and the farmer asks "Why?" (Kenny et al., 2021b). Using these techniques, a factual explanation could be found from historical instances in the dataset for this farm, to give the explanation "Well, next week is like week-12, two years ago, in terms of the weather and your use of fertilizer and that week yielded 22.5 tons of grass." This explanatory factual case comes from finding the nearest neighbor in the dataset (also known as the Deep Learner's training data) based on analyzing the feature weights contributing to the prediction made.

Counterfactual explanations. This explanation strategy is quite different to the factual option. It tells the end-user about how things would have to change for the model's predictions to change (hence, it can be used for algorithmic recourse; Karimi et al. (2020c)). Imagine the farmer thinks that the crop yield should be higher than 23 tons and asks, "Why not higher?"; now, the AI could provide advice for getting a better yield in the future, by explaining that "If you doubled your fertilizer use, then you could achieve a higher yield of 28 tons." So, unlike factual explanations which tend to merely justify the status quo, counterfactuals can provide a basis for actions that can change future outcomes (see, e.g., Byrne (2019); Miller (2019) on the psychology of counterfactual explanations for XAI).

Semifactual explanations. Finally, semifactual explanations also have the potential to guide future actions. Imagine again, the farmer thinks that the crop yield should be higher than 23 tons and asks, "Why not higher?"; now, the AI could provide a semi-factual "even-if" explanation that is also quite informative saying "Even if you doubled your fertilizer use, the yield would still be 23 tons." In this case, the farmer is potentially warned-off over-fertilizing and polluting the environment. Semifactuals have been examined occasionally in psychology (McCloy and Byrne, 2002), but hardly at all in AI (see discussion of a-fortiori reasoning for one notable exception in Nugent et al. (2009)).

13.1.4 Outline of chapter

In the remainder of this chapter, we focus on the different solutions we have found in the post-hoc example-based explanations across image and time series datasets. Most current research focuses on tabular datasets, but in this chapter we consider the, arguably more difficult, problem of XAI for image and time series datasets. This work introduces a suite of novel XAI methods for these domains, that have been supported by some user studies (though more are needed; see Keane et al. (2021)). The next three sections consider these different example-based solutions – factual, counterfactual, and semifactual – in which we describe the methods proposed, present some indicative results, and review the results from user testing. Section 13.2 considers factual example-based explanations for images and time series, before examining counterfactual and semifactual solutions for image data (Section 13.3) and for time series (Section 13.4). The latter two sections present novel extensions to our previous work. Finally, we conclude with a general discussion on the future directions for XAI and explainability in these domains.

13.2. Post-hoc explanations using factual examples

As we saw earlier, the use of factual explanations for neural networks emerged over 20 years ago in CBR, when the feature-weights of multilayered perceptrons (MLPs) were mapped into k-NN models to find nearest neighbors for a target query, to be used as example-based explanations (Caruana et al. (1999); Shin and Park (1999); see Keane and Kenny (2019) for a review). More recent work has extended this approach to convolutional neural networks (CNNs) exploring tabular, image, and time series datasets, though the specific solutions proposed are somewhat different. These techniques share the common idea that example-based explanations can be found using nearest neighbors to explain the predictions of a novel, unseen test instances.

13.2.1 Factual explanations of images

Kenny and Keane (2019, 2021a) extended factual explanations for tabular data involving MLPs to image datasets and generalized the approach – the *twin-systems* framework – to Deep Learners (mainly, CNNs). This approach relies on twinning the Neural Network model with a k-NN, where the feature-weights for a test-instance in the Neural Network are applied to a k-NN model, operating over the same dataset, to retrieve factual explanations (see Figs. 13.1, 13.2, and 13.3); notably, the feature-weights are based on feature contributions to the local prediction made.

The twin-systems framework proposes that an ANN may be abstracted in its entirety into a single proxy CBR system that mimics the ANN's predictive logic. Most methods for post-hoc explanation-by-example use feature activations to locate similar training examples to a test instance (also known as neuron activations in the ANN) (Papernot and McDaniel, 2018; Jeyakumar et al., 2020). In contrast, the twin-systems solution uses feature contributions, which weight these neuron activations by their connection weights to the predicted class (the so-called COLE Hadamard Product, C-HP, method). This approach has the effect of finding nearest neighbors that (i) are predicted to be in the same class as the test case, and (ii) have similarly-important features used in the prediction. This solution has a notable advantage over other explanation methods as CBR is nonlinear (e.g., as opposed to LIME (Ribeiro et al., 2016)) and can thus more accurately abstract the nonlinear ANN function using only a single proxy model.

Kenny and Keane (2019, 2021a) have shown that this contributions-based feature-weighting method provides the most accurate analysis of black-box ANNs, with a view to finding factual example-based explanations. This feature-weighting method – Contributions Oriented Local Explanations (COLE) – can be applied to both multilayered perceptrons (MLPs) and convolutional neural networks (CNNs) to find explanatory cases from the twinned k-NN/CBR model (i.e., a CNN-CBR twin) applied to the same dataset. Negative weights in the C-HP indicate that a certain feature map is not important for retrieving informative explanatory cases. COLE fits a k-NN model with feature contributions to abstract the ANN function, that are calculated by multiplying a data-instance by weights it used in the final prediction. To implement this in a CNN there are two possible options. Firstly, the CNN may have several fully connected layers post feature-extraction, in which case we have shown how saliency map techniques can be used to implement COLE (Kenny and Keane, 2019). Secondly, there may be a linear

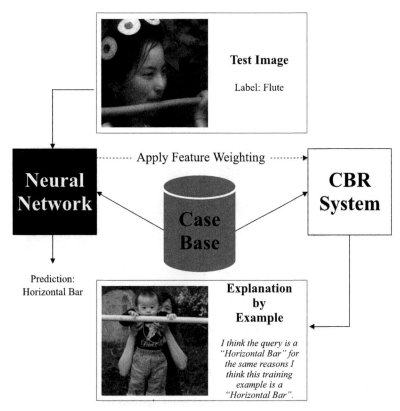

Figure 13.1 The Twin-Systems Explanation Framework: A deep learning model (Neural Network) produces a misclassification for an ImageNet test image, wrongly labeling a "Flute" as a "Horizontal Bar." This prediction is explained by analyzing the feature-weights of the network for that prediction and applying these to a twinned *k*-NN (Case Based Reasoner/CBR System) to retrieve a nearest neighbor to the test-image in the training set. This explanatory image shows that the model used an image of a "Horizontal Bar," where the bar looked very like the flute in the test image, to help make the classification. So, although the classification is wrong, it is somewhat understandable.

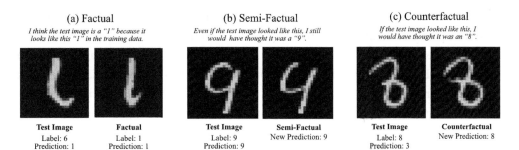

Figure 13.2 Factual, semifactual and counterfactual Explanations for a CNN's predictions applied on the MNIST dataset.

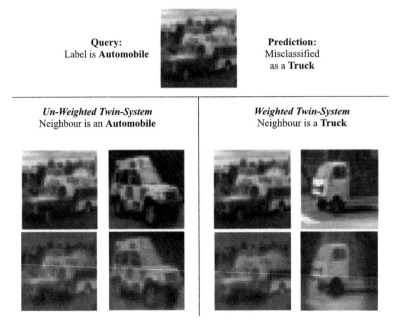

Figure 13.3 A CNN-CBR twin misclassifies an image of an automobile as a truck. Perhaps the main advantage of twin-systems is their ability to retrieve training examples predicted to be in the same class as the test instance. To illustrate this, in the unweighted twin-system, the explanation retrieved is an image of an automobile, which does not make sense since the test image was classified as a truck. To be explicit, this explanation is saying "I think the test image is a truck because it reminds me of this image I think is an automobile" (which makes no sense). In contrast, the weighted twin-system retrieves an image classified as a truck. This basic requirement of explanation-by-example (i.e., retrieving a training image predicted to be in the same class as the test image) is only guaranteed to be fulfilled if twin-systems (and their feature weighting) are used.

classifier post feature-extraction (e.g., the ResNet architectures), in which case contributions can be calculated by taking the Hadamard product of an instance's penultimate activations with the weight vector connected to its final classification (henceforth called C-HP). The saliency maps (i.e., FAMs here) are not used in the nearest neighbor search, they are a post-hoc addition after the neighbors are found (see Fig. 13.3).

C-HP has been extensively tested on 17 classification/regression datasets, which consistently showed C-HP to be the best for both MLPs and CNNs. Initially, twinning was demonstrated for classification (Kenny and Keane, 2019) but it has now been extended to regression problems and natural language domains (Kenny and Keane, 2021a). Kenny & Keane originally used feature-activation maps (FAMs) to show the important features in the explanatory images for the prediction (Kenny and Keane, 2019); however, FAMs can often produce unclear or unintuitive heat-maps for important features. So, KDK21-CCR has proposed a new method for finding *critical regions* in the explanatory image, to provide more information to users about the feature(s) that underlie the classifications.

Sample Factual Explanations for Images. Fig. 13.1 shows the general architecture for twinning between a Neural Network (CNN) and a k-NN (CBR) where the nearest neighboring image found hinges on finding critical regions in candidate images in the set of nearest neighbors; here, the original test image is misclassified but the explanation shows why the model failed because of the presence of a very similar image (with a Horizontal Bar instead of a Flute). Fig. 13.2(a) shows another factual explanation, again for a misclassification, but using the MNIST dataset. Here, a test image of a "1" is presented to a CNN and the model inaccurately labels it as a "6." When the feature-weights are abstracted from the CNN and mapped to the k-NN to retrieve nearest-neighbors of the test in the dataset, a similar instance is found showing a "1" that was annotated as a "1." Here, the example-based explanation shows the user why the model was in error; namely, that it has been presented with instances of ones that were very like badly-drawn sixes and, accordingly, misclassified the test instance. Fig. 13.3 shows a more complex case, using the CIFAR-10 dataset involving the misclassification of an automobile as a truck. This incorrect prediction is justified by the explanatory example from the weighted-twin, which essentially says to the user "I think this is a truck because it looks like the trucks I saw before." In addition, the FAMs highlight the most important (i.e., the most positively contributing) feature in the classification, which clearly focuses on the vehicle wheels in all images. Since these are a central aspect of both automobiles and trucks, it makes the misclassification more reasonable. In this case, the explanatory example found by the unweighted twin does not actually explain the misclassification, in a way that the weighed-twin does.

13.2.2 Factual explanations of time series

In the time series domain, factual explanations can be retrieved by identifying nearest neighbors to the to-be-explained test instance. Typically, either Euclidean distance or Dynamic Time Warping (if the instances are out of phase) is used in this nearest neighbor retrieval. However, it is generally agreed that comparing test instances with their nearest neighbors often yields little information about a classification decision (Ye and Keogh, 2011). Hence, factual explanations in this domain are often gained from retrieving class prototypes. *Class prototypes* are instances that are maximally representative of a class and have demonstrated promise in providing global explanations for time series classifiers in the healthcare domain (Gee et al., 2019). A simple method used to retrieve class prototypes is to extract medoids using the k-medoids clustering algorithm (Molnar, 2020).

However, one of the recognized problems with these techniques is that they typically fail to identify discriminative subsequences of the time series, that often contain semantically-meaningful information for both classification and explanation. In light of these issues, a variety of techniques such as Shapelet mining (Ye and Keogh, 2011; Grabocka et al., 2014) and Class Activation Mapping (Zhou et al., 2016; Wang et al., 2017) have been proposed to identify discriminative regions of the time series. These solutions can be cast as a type of explanation by visualization (Lipton, 2018), a very popular family of explanation methods in the time series domain. However, recent research has drawn attention to the unreliability of saliency-based approaches, especially for multivariate time series data in combination with deep learning classifiers, motivating a need for more robust forms of explanation (Adebayo et al., 2018; Ismail et al., 2020; Nguyen et al., 2020; Jeyakumar et al., 2020).

The twin-systems approach is still a relatively untapped, yet promising solution, to the development of factual explanations for time series classification. The closest works to this approach are those of Leonardi et al. (2020) and Sani et al. (2017) who suggested mapping features from a Deep Learner (typically a CNN) to a CBR system for interpretable time series classification. For global explanations, Gee et al. demonstrated the promise of leveraging an autoencoder to learn prototypes from the latent space. This design also enabled the extraction of real-world and semantically-meaningful global features (e.g., bradycardia in electrocardiogram waveforms), highlighting the advantages of combining Deep Learning and CBR for global factual explanations (Gee et al., 2019; Li et al., 2017). As we shall see in the later section on counterfactual explanations, the leveraging of discriminative features and instances from the training data also has a role to play in generating informative contrastive explanations.

13.2.3 User studies of post-hoc factual explanations

Even though factual example-based explanations are one of the oldest XAI solutions in the AI literature (in CBR see Sørmo et al. (2005); Leake and McSherry (2005), and in Recommender Systems, see Tintarev and Masthoff (2007); Nunes and Jannach (2017)), there are few well-designed user studies that test them. Keane and Kenny (2019), in a survey of the CBR literature, found < 1% of papers reported user studies (many of which were loose surveys of expert users). Furthermore, this literature also focuses more on tabular data (see, e.g., Nugent and Cunningham (2005); Cunningham et al. (2003); Dodge et al. (2019)) than on image or time series data (the latter receiving really no attention for the reasons outlined earlier).

The few papers on factual explanations for images focus on two questions: how do explanations (i) change people's subjective assessments of a model (e.g., in task performance, trust, and other judgments), and (ii) impact people's negative assessments of a model's errors (so-called *algorithmic aversion*, see Dietvorst et al. (2015)). On the question users' perceptions of the model, the few relevant studies show somewhat modest impacts for these explanations. Buçinca et al. (2020) reported two experiments examining how example-based explanations influenced people's use of an AI-model making predictions about fatty-ingredients from pictures of food-dishes; they used multiple examples (i.e., four photos of similar food dishes) or a single example with highlighted features (i.e., photo of one food-dish with identified ingredients). They found that providing explanations improved performance on the fat-estimating task and impacted trust measures in varied ways. However, these experiments have several design flaws that mean the results need to be considered with care (e.g., imperfectly matched materials, statistical comparisons between experiments as if they were conditions). Another study by Yang et al. (2020) tested users' ($N = 33$) trust in example-based explanations for a classifier's predictions for images of tree-leaves and found that specific visual representations improved "appropriate trust" in the system; their classifier had an accuracy of 71% but, notably, their participants were perhaps less expert (i.e., not botanists). Cai et al. (2019) used drawings of common objects as explanations for misclassifications by a classifier; their users ($N = 1150$) reported a better understanding of the model and viewed it as a more capable when given an explanation. Finally, there is a smattering of other studies, some using MNIST, that either have low N values (< 12) or are not reported in sufficient detail from which to draw conclusions (Bäuerle et al., 2018; Glickenhaus et al., 2019; Ross and Doshi-Velez, 2018). A notable and worrying finding from this work is the lack of evidence on people's performance on a target task. Many of them show that people's subjective assessments of the model change, but they do not show that explanations improve their performance on a task (which is generally assumed to be one of the goals of good explanation).

Finally, in a significant sequence of studies (involving several 100 participants), Kenny et al. (2021a) and Ford et al. (2020) showed that people's judgments of correctness of a CNN's errors on MNIST were subtly influenced by example-based explanations. Specifically, people (perhaps without them being aware of it) came to view the errors as "less incorrect" when given an explanation; ironically, it was also found that they came to blame the model more than the data (i.e., poorly written numbers) when explanations were provided. This work also systematically addressed the second question about the impact of errors on people's algorithmic aversion, by presenting different groups with different levels of errors (between 3% and 60%). In general, they found that people's trust in the model linearly decreased with increasing error-levels and explanations did not mitigate this decreasing trust. Indeed, beyond about 3–4% errors there is a steep shift in trust levels.

Taken together, all of these results suggest three significant conclusions. First, the provision of factual explanations is not a silver bullet for remedying algorithmic aversion. Second, explanations can subtly affect people's perceptions of a model (e.g., perceptions of correctness) in ways that could be unethically exploited. Third, the evidence for changes in people's performance on a task (e.g., debugging a CNN or learning about an unfamiliar domain), as a function of explanation, is, at best, weak. However, it should be said that these conclusions are made against a backdrop of a very poor programme of user testing.

13.3. Counterfactual & semifactual explanations: images

Although factual explanations have traditionally been the focus for example-based explanations, recently a huge research effort has focused on contrastive, example-based explanations (Kenny and Keane, 2021b; Miller, 2019; Byrne, 2019; Keane and Smyth, 2020). These developments have been partly motivated by the argument that contrastive explanations are much more causally-informative than factual ones, as well as being GDPR-compliant (Wachter et al., 2017). However, most current counterfactual methods only apply to tabular data (Wachter et al., 2017; Keane and Smyth, 2020), though recent work has begun to consider images (Goyal et al., 2019; Van Looveren and Klaise, 2019; Kenny and Keane, 2021b). Figs. 13.2(b) and 13.2(c) show some samples of explanations using contrastive, example-based explanations for a CNN's predictions on the MNIST dataset. In Fig. 13.2(c) the CNN misclassifies an image of an "8" as a "3" and the counterfactual explanation generated shows how the test instance would have to change to be correctly classified by the CNN as an "8". Fig. 13.2(b) shows the other type of contrastive explanation – a semifactual explanation – where a "9" is correctly classified by the CNN and the explanation shows a generated instance of a "9" essentially saying "even if the 9 changed to look like this, it would still be classified as a 9." One way to think about semifactuals is that they show users the "headroom" that exists just before the decision boundary is crossed, whereas the counterfactual shows users instances that occur after the decision boundary is crossed (see Fig. 13.4). In this section, we reprise our model of contrastive explanations – the PIECE model (Kenny and Keane, 2021b) – and propose some improvements to it, before testing it in a novel experiment.

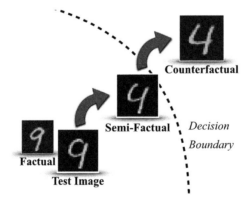

Figure 13.4 A test image from MNIST. A factual explanation could be presented (i.e., a nearest neighbor). Otherwise, a semifactual could be presented for an explanation which points towards the decision boundary (but does not cross it) to help convince the user the initial classification was correct. Lastly, a counterfactual could be presented for an explanation which explains how to modify the test image into a plausible example of the counterfactual class.

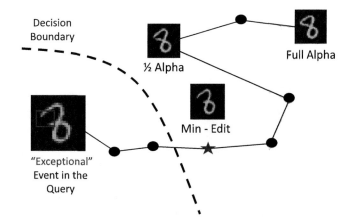

Figure 13.5 The PIECE counterfactual method. The alpha parameter controls the proportion of "exceptional" features that are modified to become "normal."

13.3.1 PIECE: generating contrastive explanations for images

Kenny and Keane (2021b) proposed the PlausIble Exceptionality-Based Contrastive Explanations (PIECE) method to generate counterfactuals for image datasets using a statistical technique combined with a generative model. PIECE generates counterfactual images by identifying "exceptional" features in the test image, and then perturbs these identified features in the test instance to be "normal." PIECE also generates semi-factuals, as a side effect of generating the counterfactual, as the latter is generated from perturbing exceptional features, just before crossing the decision boundary to generate the counterfactual.

PIECE works by identifying "exceptional features" in a test instance with reference to the training distribution; that is, features of a low probability in the counterfactual class are modified to be values that occur with a high probability in that class. For example, when a CNN has been trained on the MNIST dataset and a test image labeled as "8" is misclassified as "3," the exceptional features (i.e., low probability features in the counterfactual class 8) are identified in the extracted feature layer of the CNN via statistical modeling (i.e., a hurdle model to model ReLU activations) and modified to be their expected statistical values for the 8-counterfactual-class (see Fig. 13.5). PIECE has three main steps: (i) "exceptional" features are identified in the CNN for a test image from the perspective of the counterfactual class, (ii) these are then modified to be their expected values, and (iii) the resulting latent-feature representation of the explanatory counterfactual is visualized in the pixel-space with help from the GAN.

Fig. 13.5 illustrates how PIECE works in practice to generate a counterfactual image-explanation. Here, the counterfactuals to a test image I, in class c, with latent features x, are denoted as I', c' and x', respectively. Fig. 13.5 shows a test image labeled as class "8" (i.e., c) is misclassified as class "3" (i.e., c'). Exceptional features are identi-

(A) Semi-Factual Explanation   **(B) Counterfactual Explanation**

Test Image	**PIECE Semi-Factual**	**Test Image**	**PIECE Counterfactual**
Label: Smiling	New Prediction: Smiling	Label: Smiling	New Prediction: Smiling
Prediction: Smiling		Prediction: Not Smiling	

Figure 13.6 (A) A semifactual explanation justifying why the initial classification was definitely correct, in that, even if the image was smiling much less, it still would have classified it as "smiling." (B) A counterfactual explanation conveying to a user why the CNN made a mistake, and how the image would need to look for it to have classified it correctly (as computed by PIECE+ and Min-Edit).

fied using mathematical probability in the extracted feature layer X which have a low chance of occurrence in c'; these are then modified to be their expected feature values for class c' which modify the latent representation x to be x'. This new latent counterfactual representation x' is then visualized in the pixel space as the explanation I' using a GAN depending on the number of exceptional features changed, PIECE will produce a semifactual or counterfactual. To implement semifactual explanations for images, we used the PIECE algorithm, but stop the modification of exceptional features before the decision boundary is crossed. Figs. 13.6(A) and 13.6(B) illustrate other examples of semifactuals and counterfactuals for the CelebA dataset.

Reported experiments using PIECE have shown that it generates plausible counterfactuals and semifactuals, and is less likely than other models to generate out-of-distribution explanatory instances. It also may be unique in that it is (to our knowledge) the only method which produces counterfactuals for multiclass classification, without requiring human intervention to select the counterfactual class. However, as we shall see in the next subsection, PIECE is not as general as it could be and can be improved in several ways.

13.3.2 PIECE+: designing a better generative method

The generation of explanatory counterfactual images using deep learning hinges on finding key features in the image and then modifying these features in plausible, intuitive and informative ways. Several solutions to this problem have been proposed in the literature. He et al. (2019) proposed AttGAN, a method which produces very realistic-looking modifications to images. However, their method focuses only on a single dataset, and relies on class attribute labels, with no consideration given to counterfactual explanation or class modification. Liu et al. (2019) proposed that AttGAN could be used for counterfactual generation; however, their approach cannot be applied to a pretrained network, and again relies on attribute-labeling to work. Mertes et al. (2020) pursued a different approach based on modifying CycleGAN (Almahairi et al., 2018); this method produces quite realistic image modifications in radiology, but is limited to binary classification problems. In contrast to these methods, PIECE adopts another approach, utilizing statistical hurdle models alongside a GAN. However, PIECE is limited in its requirement for a well-trained GAN for the domain in question, alongside the ability to recover latent representations of test images in the GAN. This limits PIECE to relatively simple datasets such as MNIST, as locating a test image's latent representation in a GAN is far from a solved problem in AI currently (Zhu et al., 2020). The current improvement on PIECE – PIECE+ – builds upon AttGAN with three important modifications: (i) a pretrained CNN is incorporated into the PIECE framework, so that any CNN may be explained post-hoc, (ii) AttGAN is modified to handle multiclass classification, and (iii) the more flexible architecture allows handling of more complex datasets beyond MNIST (such as CelebA) by virtue of avoiding the need for latent recovery of test images in a GAN. In the next subsection, we describe PIECE+ in more detail, before reporting some preliminary observations.

13.3.2.1 PIECE+: the method

The PIECE+ method is trained over several steps using three distinct losses – the Reconstruction, Adversarial, and Classification Losses – combined using multiobjective optimization, which all start from the initial encoder/generator component (see Fig. 13.7). During training, the test image is encoded by E into a latent representation $z \in \mathbb{R}^{(4,4,k)}$, where k is the number of feature kernels. During training, the encoding z firstly has a label vector $C \in \mathbb{R}^{(1,1,n)}$ appended to it, to generate a reconstruction, and again a counterfactual label vector of the same shape (which is randomly chosen), to generate a counterfactual image (i.e., there are two separate forward passes). Either way, this additional vector is expanded into a matrix $C \in \mathbb{R}^{(4,4,n)}$, where n is the number of classes in the domain. Hence, the vector z has a $4 \times 4 \times 10$ matrix appended to it in MNIST here (since there are 10 digit classes), where one of these 4×4 "slices" is filled in with 1's (representing the class we are generating), and the rest 0's. This final representation is decoded through the generator G and (depending on what vector c was appended to it) generates either a target counterfactual image, or a reconstruction of the original image.

The *Reconstruction Loss* involves the reconstruction of the image compared to the original image, and the loss is taken to train the encoder/generator (L_1-loss is used here). Using *Adversarial Loss*, the generated counterfactual image is then input to the discriminator network (also known as a "critic" network), and an adversarial loss is taken by comparing it to the dataset of "real" images. WGAN-GP is used here (Gulrajani et al., 2017), and the typical hyperparameters associated with it (e.g., using an Adam

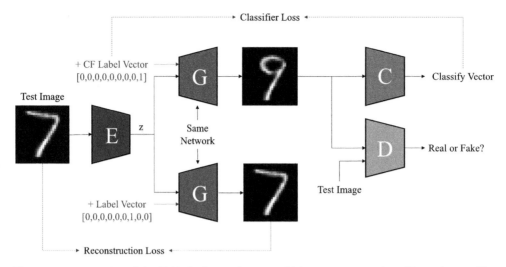

Figure 13.7 An overview of the CF Method: a combination of (1) a reconstruction loss, (2) an adversarial loss using the discriminator (D), and (3) a classifier (C) loss combine to train the encoder (E) and generator (G) architecture. Heavily adapted from He et al. (2019).

optimizer and training the generator every five steps). Then *Classification Loss* is used when the generated counterfactual image is passed into the CNN we are trying to explain, with the aim of classifying the image with a probability of 1.0 in the target counterfactual class, a cross-entropy loss is taken for multiclass classification as is typical. Following the typical WGAN–GP framework, we train the entire system as follows. The critic (also known as discriminator D) is trained for 4 iterations using the typical loss in addition to the gradient penalty, then on the 5th iteration the generator/encoder is trained using the Classification, Reconstruction, and Adversarial Losses (i.e., how good the generated images are measured by the critic). So, a combination of all these losses is backpropagated.

One limitation of this method is that the CNN is required to have been trained using the same activation functions/normalization as the critic network. Here we used leaky ReLU and instance normalization in both networks. However, there is some leeway to be found, in that the usage of leaky ReLU in the critic and ReLU in the CNN appears to produce almost optimal results, but we empirically found the best results to be using leaky ReLU and instance normalization in both networks. Future research would do well to investigate how to train this system without any limitations on the pretrained CNN architecture.

13.3.2.2 Results: PIECE+

Here the results of two brief evaluations are shown, the first of which is a demonstration of the method on MNIST, and the second a quantitative evaluation. Lastly, we conclude with a brief reflection on what improvements this new implementation of PIECE has brought, and what future challenges remain.

Sample explanations

In Fig. 13.8 we see an example of a straightforward transition from the digit 7 to the digit 9 in MNIST. Although the network is not trained to produce plausible images between the image reconstruction and the counterfactual image, it can nevertheless "fade" between both images by gradually adjusting the $C \in \mathbb{R}^{(4,4,n)}$ matrix accordingly, similar to the original AttGAN paper (He et al., 2019). During this transition, it is possible to generate either a semifactual image of a 7, or a counterfactual image of a 9; note, the red line (dark gray in print version) in Fig. 13.8 shows where the decision boundary falls, so semifactuals will occur before it and counterfactuals after it.

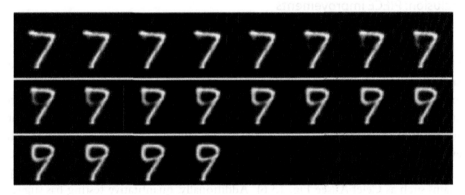

Figure 13.8 A test image of a 7 on MNIST is slowly transformed from a 7 to a 9. During the transition, it is possible to generate both a semifactual and a counterfactual. The red line (dark gray in print version) represents the model decision boundary.

Automatically selected counterfactuals

Perhaps the key novelty of PIECE is its ability to generate counterfactual images in multiclass classification problems, and being able to automatically select counterfactual classes in such an instance (most work in the area has focused on binary classification). Originally, PIECE did this by gradient ascent, were the full pipeline was able to automatically select the CF class (Kenny and Keane, 2021b), this was necessary as the GAN formed an integral part of the pipeline. Here however, that is not the case, and the CF class can be automatically selected simply by choosing the class of second highest probability in a classification. Hence, here we compare this against a baseline which randomly selects a CF class in 64 randomly selected test images. The main idea here is that the better the method, the closer the explanation should be in pixel-space. Hence, if allowing PIECE to automatically select the counterfactual is better, the generated explanations should be closer to the original test image.

For counterfactuals, the mean L_2 pixel-space distance between the original images and for PIECE selected CF classes was 14.65 ± 0.36, whilst it was 16.50 ± 0.51 for the randomly selected ones, showing a largely statistically significant difference with a two tailed, independent t-test ($p < 0.005$). For semifactuals, the mean L_2 pixel-space distance between the original images and for PIECE selected CF classes was 8.80 ± 0.23, whilst it was 17.44 ± 0.23 for the randomly selected ones, again showing a largely statistically significant difference with a two tailed, independent t-test ($p < 0.0001$). Overall, the results clearly show that PIECE's ability to automatically select the counterfactual class via simply choosing the class of second highest probability will result in better "closer" contrastive explanations than allowing users to manually select it, which should generally result in better explanations (Keane and Smyth, 2020).

Conclusion: PIECE improvements

The main problem with the original implementation of the PIECE framework by Kenny and Keane (2021b) is that it requires the recovery of a latent representation for a test image in a GAN. Whilst this works well on MNIST, it is still an open research area for more complex domains (Zhu et al., 2020). To solve these issues, PIECE+ has taken inspiration from AttGAN and designed a general framework for post-hoc contrastive explanations in image domains. Namely, to solve the issue of recovering a latent representation for a test image, PIECE+ has an encoder/decoder architecture which alleviates the issue completely by training the prior to encode these representations during training. This has the added benefit of allowing PIECE+ to work in more complex domains such as CelebA (see Fig. 13.6). Additionally, quantitative testing has suggested it is still beneficial in this new implementation of PIECE to allow automatic selection of the CF class, rather than trusting users to. Future work will examine the integration of modifying "exceptional features" within this new framework, which was shown to work well before (Kenny and Keane, 2021b). In the next section, we continue this examination of contrastive explanations by considering methods for time series data.

13.4. Contrastive explanations: time series

In the previous section, we reported on the explosion of research on counterfactual explanations and on how most of this research tends to focus on tabular rather than image datasets. Even less of this research has considered the time series domain. Interestingly, tabular methods for counterfactuals (Wachter et al., 2017; Keane and Smyth, 2020), quickly become intractable for time series data because of the massive number of possible feature dimensions and the utility of domain-specific distance measures (such as DTW) (Delaney et al., 2021). Indeed, much of the work reviewed here has only been published in the last two years (only the present work has even considered semifactuals). In this section, we reprise our model of contrastive explanations for time series – Native

Guide (Delaney et al., 2021) – and propose some improvements to it, before testing it in a novel experiment.

The current focus in XAI for time series mainly considers saliency-based approaches where important subsequences or features are highlighted (Wang et al., 2017; Fawaz et al., 2019b; Schlegel et al., 2019). However, it is quite unclear if these explanations are faithful to the underlying black-box model in providing informative explanations (Adebayo et al., 2018; Ismail et al., 2020; Nguyen et al., 2020)

Many have considered leveraging shapelets to generate contrastive explanations (Karlsson et al., 2018; Guidotti et al., 2020). However, issues have been raised about the interpretability of the shapelets produced by the frequently deployed shapelets learning algorithm (Grabocka et al., 2014), and many solutions are not model agnostic. By modifying the loss function proposed by Wachter et al. (2017) to generate counterfactuals, Ates et al. (2020) explored generating counterfactual explanations for multivariate time series classification problems. Labaien et al. (2020) have progressed contrastive explanations for the predictions of recurrent neural networks in time series prediction.

The Native Guide method (Delaney et al., 2020, 2021) adopts a different approach to these other methods and we demonstrate that it can work with any classifier (model-agnostic). In the next subsection, we sketch the essence of this method before proposing a novel extension to it using Gaussian noise.

13.4.1 Native guide: generating contrastive explanations for time series

Native Guide (Delaney et al., 2020, 2021) incorporates a strategy where the closest in-sample counterfactual instance to the test-instance is adapted to form a new counterfactual explanation (Keane and Smyth, 2020; Goyal et al., 2019). Here the "Native-Guide" is a counterfactual instance that already exists in the dataset (e.g., the nearest-neighbor time series to the test-instance that involves a class change; see Fig. 13.9). We can retrieve this in-sample counterfactual instance using a simple 1-NN search. Once this instance is found it is leveraged to guide the generation of the explanatory counterfactual T'. The generated counterfactual instance T' (the yellow square [light gray in print version] in Fig. 13.9), should offer better explanations than the original in-sample counterfactual as it is in closer to the test whilst still staying within the distribution of the data. As an aside, we note that Native Guide could also be used to compute plausible semifactual explanations by terminating the counterfactual generation process just before the explanatory instance enters the counterfactual class.

Native Guide generates counterfactual explanations for a to-be-explained query, T_q, by leveraging both (i) discriminative feature information and (ii) native counterfactual instances (e.g., the query's nearest unlike neighbor (T'_{NUN})). Blind perturbation techniques frequently fail to account for dependencies between features and leveraging information from native counterfactual instances in the training data can immensely aid the generation of meaningful explanations (Keane and Smyth, 2020; Delaney et al.,

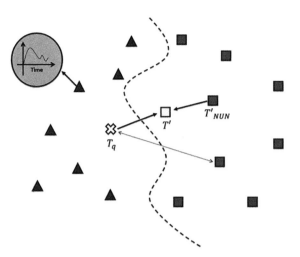

Figure 13.9 A query time series T_q (X with solid arrow) and a nearest-unlike neighbor T'_{NUN} (red square [dark gray in print version] with solid arrow) are used to guide the generation of counterfactual T' (see yellow square, light gray in print version) in a binary classification task. Another in-sample counterfactual (i.e., the *next* NUN; other red square [dark gray in print version] with dashed arrow) could also be used to generate another counterfactual for diverse explanations.

2021). However, gaining informative information from neighbors can be quite difficult when working with noisy time series data (Le Nguyen et al., 2019; Schäfer, 2016) and techniques such as dynamic time warping and weighted barycenter averaging (Petitjean et al., 2011; Forestier et al., 2017) are often required to generate meaningful explanations when instances are out of phase (Delaney et al., 2021). Moreover, access to neighbors from the training dataset may not always be available when generating explanations. So, a technique that purely utilizes discriminative feature information in generating counterfactual explanations bears practical utility. Hence, we considered an adjustment to Native Guide in a scenario where information from training instances is not readily available, greatly improving the flexibility of the technique.

13.4.2 Extending native guide: using Gaussian noise

Nguyen et al. (2020) analyzed the informativeness of different explanation techniques by adding Gaussian noise to discriminative subsequences and monitoring the degradation of classification performance. In this work, we demonstrate that Gaussian noise can be leveraged to generate counterfactual explanations without the need to access native counterfactual instances in the training data. In Native Guide, the counterfactual explanations are generated by modifying a contiguous subsequence of the to-be-explained test instance. As before, the most influential contiguous subsequence, T_{Sub}, according to a feature-weight vector, ω, is identified. This feature-weight vector can be retrieved from class activation maps (CAMs) when using convolutional architectures (Zhou et al.,

2016; Wang et al., 2017), or alternatively, from model agnostic techniques such as LIME (Ribeiro et al., 2016) or SHAP (Lundberg and Lee, 2017). However, instead of replacing the values of T_q with the corresponding region in T'_{Native}, Gaussian noise is added to the discriminative subsequence, $T_{Sub} + \mathcal{N}(\mu, \sigma^2)$, to generate a counterfactual, T'. This is an iterative process, initializing with a small subsequence and iteratively increasing the size of the perturbed subsequence and/or the magnitude of the Gaussian noise until a counterfactual is generated.

Experiment: extending native guide

In this experiment we demonstrate the model agnostic flexibility of Native Guide through implementing both Mr-SEQL (Le Nguyen et al., 2019) and a pretrained ResNet architecture (Fawaz et al., 2019b) as the base classifiers on two popular UCR datasets (Dau et al., 2019) (Coffee & Gunpoint). We compare the counterfactual generated across architectures when injecting Gaussian noise onto discriminative subsequences of the time series. We also compare the explanations to the counterfactuals generated by the original variant where access to instances from the training data are available. For the ResNet architecture, we use Class Activation Maps (CAMs) to extract the feature weight vector ω. MR–SEQL converts the time series to a symbolic representation and extracts discriminative feature information using a symbolic sequence learning algorithm. Following Keane and Smyth (2020); Delaney et al. (2021), we use a relative counterfactual distance measure to monitor the proximity and sparsity of the generated counterfactual with respect to existing in-sample counterfactual solutions.

Results and discussion

Native Guide consistently generates sparse counterfactuals that are closer to the to-be-explained query than in sample counterfactual instances when access to the training data available. Interestingly, when adding Gaussian noise into the input time series, the counterfactuals for the ResNet classifier typically required much fewer feature changes than the Mr-SEQL classifier. For example, in the coffee dataset the mean relative L_1 distance between the query and the counterfactual was 0.47 ± 0.08 for the ResNet architecture and significantly larger, 1.12 ± 0.12, for the MR–SEQL classifier (independent two tailed t–test $p < 0.01$). One possible explanation for this is that Deep learning architectures are very sensitive to slight perturbations on the input time series and prone to adversarial attack (Fawaz et al., 2019a). Access to neighbors in the training data guarantees the generation of plausible counterfactual instances (perfect coverage) (Delaney et al., 2021). Adding Gaussian noise to a discriminative subsequence sometimes failed to generate a counterfactual explanation for instances in the gunpoint dataset, especially for the more robust MR–SEQL classifier, indicating the importance of leveraging information from the training data in generating informative explanations. Different feature weight vectors often resulted in different counterfactual explanations (see Fig. 13.10).

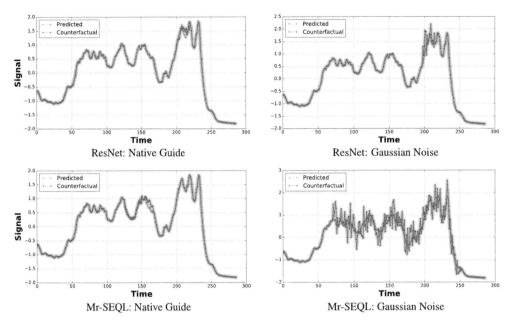

Figure 13.10 Counterfactual explanations for the predictions of both a ResNet architecture (Fawaz et al., 2019a) using Class Activation Mapping (Zhou et al., 2016; Wang et al., 2017), and Mr-SEQL (Le Nguyen et al., 2019) on an instance from the coffee dataset, where the task is to distinguish between Arabica and Robusta coffee beans from spectrographs. The ResNet architecture is more sensitive to slight perturbations on the input signal and the counterfactuals produced typically focus on a discriminative area of the time series that contains information about the caffeine content of the beans. Mr-SEQL is more robust to noise and the produced counterfactual explanations typically focus on an area containing information about the acid and lipid content of the coffee beans (Briandet et al., 1996).

For example on the coffee dataset, the counterfactuals generated from in symbolic sequence learning algorithm in Mr-SEQL typically focus on an area of the time series that contain information about the chlorogenic acid and lipid content of the coffee beans whist the class activation maps (CAMs) from the ResNet architecture often focused on a contiguous subsequence that contained discriminative information about the caffeine content of the beans (Briandet et al., 1996; Dau et al., 2019). As feature weighting techniques often highlight different regions in the input time series, the availability of ground truth domain knowledge expertise is crucial in assessing if the produced explanations are plausible as computational proxies are an imperfect proxy measure, further instilling the need for user studies with domain experts in the time series domain.

13.5. User studies on contrastive explanations

In the previous sections, we considered a variety of methods for computing contrastive explanations for images and time series datasets. For the most part, the focus of user studies in this area has been almost wholly on counterfactual explanations with most of these studies focusing on tabular data. Though semifactuals have been researched in psychology and philosophy (e.g., see McCloy and Byrne (2002)), they have yet to be explicitly tested in XAI (for a solitary exception see Doyle et al. (2004)). Indeed, arguably, even the user studies on counterfactuals seem to be behind the curve of computational advances in the area.

Keane et al. (2021) reviewed the user studies on counterfactual explanations based on a survey of > 100 distinct counterfactual methods in the recent literature. They found that only 31% of papers perform user studies (36 out of 117) and fewer (21%) directly test a specific method on users. This means that few of the features that are discussed in the AI literature have been explicitly tested with users. Furthermore, as was the case with tests of factual explanations, many of these studies are methodologically questionable (e.g., use low Ns, poor or inappropriate statistics, nonreproducible designs, inadequate materials).

The user-tests that have been done provide moderate support for the efficacy of counterfactual explanations under some conditions. Some studies show counterfactual explanations to be useful and preferred by end users (e.g., Lim et al. (2009); Dodge et al. (2019)). For instance, Lim et al. (2009) tested What-if, Why-not, How-to, and Why explanations, and found that they all improved performance relative to no-explanation controls. Dodge et al. (2019) assessed four different explanation strategies (e.g., case based, counterfactual, factual) on biased/unbiased classifiers and found counterfactual explanations to be the most impactful (though for a very limited set of problems). However, other studies show that counterfactual explanations often require greater cognitive effort and do not always outperform other methods (Lim et al., 2009; van der Waa et al., 2021; Lage et al., 2019; Dodge et al., 2019). Notably, however, few of these studies directly test specific facets of counterfactual algorithms (e.g., sparsity, plausibility, diversity) or compare competing methods (Goyal et al., 2019; Singla et al., 2019; Lucic et al., 2020; Akula et al., 2020; Förster et al., 2020a,b, 2021). This means that there is quite limited support for the specific properties of most counterfactual methods in the AI literature. Indeed, with respect to image and time series data, the literature is ever thinner and, as such, we await evidence to support the efficacy of these methods.

13.6. Conclusions

This chapter has considered state-of-the-art contributions to the rapidly evolving and increasingly important field of XAI; namely, the use of post-hoc explanations involving factual, counterfactual, and semifactual examples to elucidate a variety of Deep Learning models. There are many future directions in which this work can be taken. For instance, with respect to image data, we have begun to look at combining example-based explanations with visualizations of critical regions, reflecting important features impacting a Deep Learner's predictions. Parallel opportunities exist for similar developments in the time series domain. However, if we were pressed on what is the most important direction to pursue, it would have to be that of user testing. In many respects, XAI is starting to exhibit quite a dysfunctional research program, where 100s or 1000s of models are being developed without any consideration of their psychological validity. Recently, there has been a growing commentary on this deficit in XAI, on the failure to properly address user requirements (Anjomshoae et al., 2019; Hoffman and Zhao, 2020), on the "over-reliance on intuition-based approaches" (Leavitt and Morcos, 2020), and on the increasing disconnect between the features of models and actions in the real-world (Barocas et al., 2020; Keane et al., 2021). In short, it is our view that a significant program of carefully-controlled and properly-designed user studies needs to be carried out as a matter of urgency, if XAI is to avoid drowning in a sea of irrelevant models.

Acknowledgments

This chapter emanated from research funded by (i) Science Foundation Ireland (SFI) to the Insight Centre for Data Analytics (12/RC/2289-P2), (ii) SFI and DAFM on behalf of the Government of Ireland to the VistaMilk SFI Research Centre (16/RC/3835).

References

Adebayo, Julius, Gilmer, Justin, Muelly, Michael, Goodfellow, Ian, Hardt, Moritz, Kim, Been, 2018. Sanity checks for saliency maps. In: Advances in Neural Information Processing Systems, pp. 9505–9515.

Akula, Arjun, Wang, Shuai, Zhu, Song-Chun, 2020. CoCoX: Generating conceptual and counterfactual explanations via fault-lines. In: Proceedings of the AAAI Conference on Artificial Intelligence, vol. 34, pp. 2594–2601.

Ala-Pietilä, Pekka, Smuha, Nathalie A., 2021. A framework for global cooperation on artificial intelligence and its governance. In: Reflections on Artificial Intelligence for Humanity. Springer, pp. 237–265.

Almahairi, Amjad, Rajeshwar, Sai, Sordoni, Alessandro, Bachman, Philip, Courville, Aaron, 2018. Augmented CycleGAN: Learning many-to-many mappings from unpaired data. In: International Conference on Machine Learning. PMLR, pp. 195–204.

Anjomshoae, Sule, Najjar, Amro, Calvaresi, Davide, Främling, Kary, 2019. Explainable agents and robots: Results from a systematic literature review. In: 18th International Conference on Autonomous Agents and Multiagent Systems (AAMAS 2019). Montreal, Canada, May 13–17, 2019. International Foundation for Autonomous Agents and Multiagent Systems, pp. 1078–1088.

Ates, Emre, Aksar, Burak, Leung, Vitus J., Coskun, Ayse K., 2020. Counterfactual explanations for machine learning on multivariate time series data. arXiv:2008.10781.

Barocas, Solon, Selbst, Andrew D., Raghavan, Manish, 2020. The hidden assumptions behind counterfactual explanations and principal reasons. In: Proceedings of the 2020 Conference on Fairness, Accountability, and Transparency, pp. 80–89.

Bäuerle, Alex, Neumann, Heiko, Ropinski, Timo, 2018. Training de-confusion: An interactive, network-supported visual analysis system for resolving errors in image classification training data. arXiv:1808. 03114.

Briandet, Romain, Kemsley, E. Katherine, Wilson, Reginald H., 1996. Discrimination of Arabica and Robusta in instant coffee by Fourier transform infrared spectroscopy and chemometrics. Journal of Agricultural and Food Chemistry 44 (1), 170–174.

Buçinca, Zana, Lin, Phoebe, Gajos, Krzysztof Z., Glassman, Elena L., 2020. Proxy tasks and subjective measures can be misleading in evaluating explainable AI systems. In: Proceedings of the 25th International Conference on Intelligent User Interfaces, pp. 454–464.

Byrne, Ruth M.J., 2019. Counterfactuals in explainable artificial intelligence (XAI): Evidence from human reasoning. In: IJCAI-19, pp. 6276–6282.

Cai, Carrie J., Jongejan, Jonas, Holbrook, Jess, 2019. The effects of example-based explanations in a machine learning interface. In: Proceedings of the 24th International Conference on Intelligent User Interfaces, pp. 258–262.

Camburu, Oana-Maria, Shillingford, Brendan, Minervini, Pasquale, Lukasiewicz, Thomas, Blunsom, Phil, Xie, Linhai, Miao, Yishu, Wang, Sen, Blunsom, Phil, Wang, Zhihua, et al., 2020. Make up your mind! Adversarial generation of inconsistent natural language explanations. In: Proceedings of the 58th Annual Meeting of the Association for Computational Linguistics, ACL 2020. Seattle, Washington, USA, July 5–10, 2020. Association for Computational Linguistics, pp. 116–125.

Caruana, Rich, Kangarloo, Hooshang, Dionisio, J.D., Sinha, Usha, Johnson, David, 1999. Case-based explanation of non-case-based learning methods. In: Proceedings of the AMIA Symposium. American Medical Informatics Association, p. 212.

Chen, Chaofan, Li, Oscar, Barnett, Alina, Su, Jonathan, Rudin, Cynthia, 2018. This looks like that: Deep learning for interpretable image recognition. arXiv:1806.10574.

Cunningham, Pádraig, Doyle, Dónal, Loughrey, John, 2003. An evaluation of the usefulness of case-based explanation. In: International Conference on Case-Based Reasoning. Springer, pp. 122–130.

Dau, Hoang Anh, Bagnall, Anthony, Kamgar, Kaveh, Yeh, Chin-Chia Michael, Zhu, Yan, Gharghabi, Shaghayegh, Ratanamahatana, Chotirat Annh, Keogh, Eamonn, 2019. The UCR time series archive. IEEE/CAA Journal of Automatica Sinica 6 (6), 1293–1305.

Delaney, Eoin, Greene, Derek, Keane, Mark T., 2020. Instance-based counterfactual explanations for time series classification. arXiv:2009.13211.

Delaney, Eoin, Greene, Derek, Keane, Mark T., 2021. Instance-based counterfactual explanations for time series classification. In: International Conference on Case-Based Reasoning. Springer, pp. 32–47.

Dietvorst, Berkeley J., Simmons, Joseph P., Massey, Cade, 2015. Algorithm aversion: People erroneously avoid algorithms after seeing them err. Journal of Experimental Psychology: General 144 (1), 114.

Dodge, Jonathan, Liao, Q. Vera, Zhang, Yunfeng, Bellamy, Rachel K.E., Dugan, Casey, 2019. Explaining models: an empirical study of how explanations impact fairness judgment. In: Proceedings of the 24th International Conference on Intelligent User Interfaces, pp. 275–285.

Doshi-Velez, Finale, Kim, Been, 2017. Towards a rigorous science of interpretable machine learning. arXiv:1702.08608.

Doyle, Dónal, Cunningham, Pádraig, Bridge, Derek, Rahman, Yusof, 2004. Explanation oriented retrieval. In: European Conference on Case-Based Reasoning. Springer, pp. 157–168.

Erhan, Dumitru, Bengio, Yoshua, Courville, Aaron, Vincent, Pascal, 2009. Visualizing higher-layer features of a deep network. University of Montreal 1341 (3), 1.

Fawaz, Hassan Ismail, Forestier, Germain, Weber, Jonathan, Idoumghar, Lhassane, Muller, Pierre-Alain, 2019a. Adversarial attacks on deep neural networks for time series classification. In: 2019 International Joint Conference on Neural Networks (IJCNN). IEEE, pp. 1–8.

Fawaz, Hassan Ismail, Forestier, Germain, Weber, Jonathan, Idoumghar, Lhassane, Muller, Pierre-Alain, 2019b. Deep learning for time series classification: a review. Data Mining and Knowledge Discovery 33 (4), 917–963.

Ford, Courtney, Kenny, Eoin M., Keane, Mark T., 2020. Play MNIST for me! User studies on the effects of post-hoc, example-based explanations & error rates on debugging a deep learning, black-box classifier. arXiv:2009.06349.

Forestier, Germain, Petitjean, François, Dau, Hoang Anh, Webb, Geoffrey I., Keogh, Eamonn, 2017. Generating synthetic time series to augment sparse datasets. In: ICDM. IEEE, pp. 865–870.

Förster, Maximilian, Hühn, Philipp, Klier, Mathias, Kluge, Kilian, 2021. Capturing users' reality: A novel approach to generate coherent counterfactual explanations. In: Proceedings of the 54th Hawaii International Conference on System Sciences, p. 1274.

Förster, Maximilian, Klier, Mathias, Kluge, Kilian, Sigler, Irina, 2020a. Evaluating explainable artificial intelligence–what users really appreciate. In: Proceedings of the 28th European Conference on Information Systems.

Förster, Maximilian, Klier, Mathias, Kluge, Kilian, Sigler, Irina, 2020b. Fostering human agency: A process for the design of user-centric XAI systems. In: Proceedings ICIS.

Frosst, Nicholas, Hinton, Geoffrey, 2017. Distilling a neural network into a soft decision tree. arXiv:1711.09784.

Gee, Alan H., Garcia-Olano, Diego, Ghosh, Joydeep, Paydarfar, David, 2019. Explaining deep classification of time-series data with learned prototypes. CEUR Workshop Proceedings 2429, 15–22.

Gilpin, Leilani H., Bau, David, Yuan, Ben Z., Bajwa, Ayesha, Specter, Michael, Kagal, Lalana, 2018. Explaining explanations: An approach to evaluating interpretability of machine learning. arXiv:1806.00069.

Glickenhaus, B., Karneeb, J., Aha, D.W., 2019. DARPA XAI phase 1 evaluations report. In: DARPA XAI Program. Report.

Goyal, Yash, Wu, Ziyan, Ernst, Jan, Batra, Dhruv, Parikh, Devi, Lee, Stefan, 2019. Counterfactual visual explanations. arXiv:1904.07451.

Grabocka, Josif, Schilling, Nicolas, Wistuba, Martin, Schmidt-Thieme, Lars, 2014. Learning time-series shapelets. In: ACM SIGKDD, pp. 392–401.

Guidotti, Riccardo, Monreale, Anna, Giannotti, Fosca, Pedreschi, Dino, Ruggieri, Salvatore, Turini, Franco, 2019. Factual and counterfactual explanations for black box decision making. IEEE Intelligent Systems 34 (6), 14–23.

Guidotti, Riccardo, Monreale, Anna, Spinnato, Francesco, Pedreschi, Dino, Giannotti, Fosca, 2020. Explaining any time series classifier. In: IEEE Second International Conference on Cognitive Machine Intelligence (CogMI). IEEE, pp. 167–176.

Gulrajani, Ishaan, Ahmed, Faruk, 2017, Arjovsky, Martin, Dumoulin, Vincent, Courville, Aaron C. Improved training of wasserstein gans. In: Advances in Neural Information Processing Systems.

Gunning, David, Aha, David W., 2019. DARPA's explainable artificial intelligence program. AI Magazine 40 (2), 44–58.

He, Zhenliang, Zuo, Wangmeng, Kan, Meina, Shan, Shiguang, Chen, Xilin, 2019. AttGAN: Facial attribute editing by only changing what you want. IEEE Transactions on Image Processing 28 (11), 5464–5478.

Hoffman, Guy, Zhao, Xuan, 2020. A primer for conducting experiments in human–robot interaction. ACM Transactions on Human–Robot Interaction (THRI) 10 (1), 1–31.

Hohman, Fred, Kahng, Minsuk, Pienta, Robert, Chau, Duen Horng, 2018. Visual analytics in deep learning: An interrogative survey for the next frontiers. IEEE Transactions on Visualization and Computer Graphics 25 (8), 2674–2693.

Ismail, Aya Abdelsalam, Gunady, Mohamed, Bravo, Héctor Corrada, Feizi, Soheil, 2020. Benchmarking deep learning interpretability in time series predictions. arXiv:2010.13924.

Jeyakumar, Jeya Vikranth, Noor, Joseph, Cheng, Yu-Hsi, Garcia, Luis, Srivastava, Mani, 2020. How can I explain this to you? An empirical study of deep neural network explanation methods. Advances in Neural Information Processing Systems 33.

Karimi, Amir-Hossein, Barthe, Gilles, Balle, Borja, Valera, Isabel, 2020a. Model-agnostic counterfactual explanations for consequential decisions. In: International Conference on Artificial Intelligence and Statistics, pp. 895–905.

Karimi, Amir-Hossein, Schölkopf, Bernhard, Valera, Isabel, 2020b. Algorithmic recourse: from counterfactual explanations to interventions. arXiv:2002.06278.

Karimi, Amir-Hossein, von Kügelgen, Julius, Schölkopf, Bernhard, Valera, Isabel, 2020c. Algorithmic recourse under imperfect causal knowledge: a probabilistic approach. Advances in Neural Information Processing Systems 33.

Karlsson, Isak, Rebane, Jonathan, Papapetrou, Panagiotis, Gionis, Aristides, 2018. Explainable time series tweaking via irreversible and reversible temporal transformations. In: ICDM.

Keane, Mark T., Kenny, Eoin M., 2019. How case-based reasoning explains neural networks: A theoretical analysis of XAI using post-hoc explanation-by-example from a survey of ANN-CBR twin-systems. In: Proceedings of the 27th International Conference on Case-Based Reasoning (ICCBR-19). Springer, pp. 155–171.

Keane, Mark T., Kenny, Eoin M., Delaney, Eoin, Smyth, Barry, 2021. If only we had better counterfactual explanations: Five key deficits to rectify in the evaluation of counterfactual XAI techniques. In: Proceedings of the 30th International Joint Conference on Artificial Intelligence (IJCAI-21).

Keane, Mark T., Smyth, Barry, 2020. Good counterfactuals and where to find them: A case-based technique for generating counterfactuals for explainable AI (XAI). In: ICCBR. Springer, pp. 163–178.

Kenny, Eoin M., Delaney, Eoin D., Greene, Derek, Keane, Mark T., 2020. Post-hoc explanation options for XAI in deep learning: The insight centre for data analytics perspective. In: International Conference on Pattern Recognition. Springer.

Kenny, Eoin M., Ford, Courtney, Quinn, Molly, Keane, Mark T., 2021a. Explaining black-box classifiers using post-hoc explanations-by-example: The effect of explanations and error-rates in XAI user studies. Artificial Intelligence 294, 1–25.

Kenny, Eoin M., Keane, Mark T., 2019. Twin-systems to explain artificial neural networks using case-based reasoning: Comparative tests of feature-weighting methods in ANN-CBR twins for XAI. In: Proceedings of the 28th International Joint Conferences on Artificial Intelligence (IJCAI-19), pp. 2708–2715.

Kenny, Eoin M., Keane, Mark T., 2021a. Explaining deep learning using examples: Optimal feature weighting methods for twin systems using post-hoc, explanation-by-example in XAI. Knowledge-Based Systems 233, 107530.

Kenny, Eoin M., Keane, Mark T., 2021b. On generating plausible counterfactual and semi-factual explanations for deep learning. In: Proceedings of the 35th AAAI Conference on Artificial Intelligence (AAAI-21), pp. 11575–11585.

Kenny, Eoin M., Ruelle, Elodie, Geoghegan, Anne, Shalloo, Laurence, O'Leary, Micheál, O'Donovan, Michael, Temraz, Mohammed, Keane, Mark T., 2021b. Bayesian case-exclusion and personalized explanations for sustainable dairy farming. In: International Joint Conference on Artificial Intelligence.

Labaien, Jokin, Zugasti, Ekhi, De Carlos, Xabier, 2020. Contrastive explanations for a deep learning model on time-series data. In: International Conference on Big Data Analytics and Knowledge Discovery. Springer, pp. 235–244.

Lage, Isaac, Chen, Emily, He, Jeffrey, Narayanan, Menaka, Kim, Been, Gershman, Sam, Doshi-Velez, Finale, 2019. An evaluation of the human-interpretability of explanation. arXiv:1902.00006.

Le Nguyen, Thach, Gsponer, Severin, Ilie, Iulia, O'Reilly, Martin, Ifrim, Georgiana, 2019. Interpretable time series classification using linear models and multi-resolution multi-domain symbolic representations. Data Mining and Knowledge Discovery 33 (4), 1183–1222.

Leake, David, McSherry, David, 2005. Introduction to the special issue on explanation in case-based reasoning. Artificial Intelligence Review 24 (2), 103.

Leavitt, Matthew L., Morcos, Ari, 2020. Towards falsifiable interpretability research. arXiv:2010.12016.

Leonardi, Giorgio, Montani, Stefania, Striani, Manuel, 2020. Deep feature extraction for representing and classifying time series cases: Towards an interpretable approach in haemodialysis. In: Flairs-2020. AAAI Press.

Li, Oscar, Liu, Hao, Chen, Chaofan, Rudin, Cynthia, 2017. Deep learning for case-based reasoning through prototypes: A neural network that explains its predictions. arXiv:1710.04806.

Lim, Brian Y., Dey, Anind K., Avrahami, Daniel, 2009. Why and why not explanations improve the intelligibility of context-aware intelligent systems. In: Proceedings of the SIGCHI Conference on Human Factors in Computing Systems, pp. 2119–2128.

Lipton, Zach C., 2018. The mythos of model interpretability. Queue 16 (3), 30.

Liu, Shusen, Kailkhura, Bhavya, Loveland, Donald, Han, Yong, 2019. Generative counterfactual introspection for explainable deep learning. In: 2019 IEEE Global Conference on Signal and Information Processing (GlobalSIP). IEEE, pp. 1–5.

Lucic, Ana, Haned, Hinda, de Rijke, Maarten, 2020. Why does my model fail? Contrastive local explanations for retail forecasting. In: Proceedings of the 2020 Conference on Fairness, Accountability, and Transparency, pp. 90–98.

Lundberg, Scott M., Lee, Su-In, 2017. A unified approach to interpreting model predictions. In: Advances in Neural Information Processing Systems, pp. 4765–4774.

McCloy, Rachel, Byrne, Ruth M.J., 2002. Semifactual "even if" thinking. Thinking & Reasoning 8 (1), 41–67.

Mertes, Silvan, Huber, Tobias, Weitz, Katharina, Heimerl, Alexander, André, Elisabeth, 2020. This is not the texture you are looking for! Introducing novel counterfactual explanations for non-experts using generative adversarial learning. arXiv:2012.11905.

Miller, Tim, 2019. Explanation in artificial intelligence: Insights from the social sciences. Artificial Intelligence 267, 1–38.

Molnar, Christoph, 2020. Interpretable Machine Learning. Lulu.com.

Nguyen, Thu Trang, Le Nguyen, Thach, Ifrim, Georgiana, 2020. A model-agnostic approach to quantifying the informativeness of explanation methods for time series classification. In: Proceedings of the 5th Workshop on Advanced Analytics and Learning on Temporal Data at ECML 2020. Springer.

Nugent, Conor, Cunningham, Pádraig, 2005. A case-based explanation system for black-box systems. Artificial Intelligence Review 24 (2), 163–178.

Nugent, Conor, Doyle, Dónal, Cunningham, Pádraig, 2009. Gaining insight through case-based explanation. Journal of Intelligent Information Systems 32 (3), 267–295.

Nunes, Ingrid, Jannach, Dietmar, 2017. A systematic review and taxonomy of explanations in decision support and recommender systems. User Modeling and User-Adapted Interaction 27 (3–5), 393–444.

Papernot, Nicolas, McDaniel, Patrick, 2018. Deep k-nearest neighbors: Towards confident, interpretable and robust deep learning. arXiv:1803.04765.

Petitjean, François, Ketterlin, Alain, Gançarski, Pierre, 2011. A global averaging method for dynamic time warping, with applications to clustering. Pattern Recognition 44 (3), 678–693.

Ribeiro, Marco Tulio, Singh, Sameer, Guestrin, Carlos, 2016. "Why should I trust you?": Explaining the predictions of any classifier. In: Proceedings of the 22nd ACM SIGKDD International Conference on Knowledge Discovery and Data Mining. ACM, pp. 1135–1144.

Ross, Andrew Slavin, Doshi-Velez, Finale, 2018. Improving the adversarial robustness and interpretability of deep neural networks by regularizing their input gradients. In: Thirty-Second AAAI Conference on Artificial Intelligence.

Rudin, Cynthia, 2019. Stop explaining black box machine learning models for high stakes decisions and use interpretable models instead. Nature Machine Intelligence 1 (5), 206–215.

Sani, Sadiq, Wiratunga, Nirmalie, Massie, Stewart, 2017. Learning deep features for k-NN-based human activity recognition. In: Proceedings of the ICCBR-17 Workshop. ICCBR (Organisers).

Schäfer, Patrick, 2016. Scalable time series classification. Data Mining and Knowledge Discovery 30 (5), 1273–1298.

Schlegel, Udo, Arnout, Hiba, El-Assady, Mennatallah, Oelke, Daniela, Keim, Daniel A., 2019. Towards a rigorous evaluation of XAI methods on time series. arXiv:1909.07082.

Shin, Chung Kwan, Park, Sang Chan, 1999. Memory and neural network based expert system. Expert Systems with Applications 16 (2), 145–155.

Shortliffe, Edward H., Davis, Randall, Axline, Stanton G., Buchanan, Bruce G., Green, C. Cordell, Cohen, Stanley N., 1975. Computer-based consultations in clinical therapeutics: Explanation and rule acquisition capabilities of the MYCIN system. Computers and Biomedical Research 8 (4), 303–320.

Simonyan, Karen, Vedaldi, Andrea, Zisserman, Andrew, 2013. Deep inside convolutional networks: Visualising image classification models and saliency maps. arXiv:1312.6034.

Singla, Sumedha, Pollack, Brian, Chen, Junxiang, Batmanghelich, Kayhan, 2019. Explanation by progressive exaggeration. arXiv:1911.00483.

Sørmo, Frode, Cassens, Jörg, Aamodt, Agnar, 2005. Explanation in case-based reasoning–perspectives and goals. Artificial Intelligence Review 24 (2), 109–143.

Tintarev, Nava, Masthoff, Judith, 2007. A survey of explanations in recommender systems. In: 2007 IEEE 23rd International Conference on Data Engineering Workshop. IEEE, Istanbul, Turkey, pp. 801–810.

van der Waa, Jasper, Nieuwburg, Elisabeth, Cremers, Anita, Neerincx, Mark, 2021. Evaluating XAI: A comparison of rule-based and example-based explanations. Artificial Intelligence 291, 103404.

Van Looveren, Arnaud, Klaise, Janis, 2019. Interpretable counterfactual explanations guided by prototypes. arXiv:1907.02584.

Wachter, Sandra, Mittelstadt, Brent, Russell, Chris, 2017. Counterfactual explanations without opening the black box: automated decisions and the GDPR. Harvard Journal of Law & Technology 31, 841.

Wang, Zhiguang, Yan, Weizhong, Oates, Tim, 2017. Time series classification from scratch with deep neural networks: A strong baseline. In: IJCNN. IEEE, pp. 1578–1585.

White, Adam, d'Avila Garcez, Artur, 2019. Measurable counterfactual local explanations for any classifier. arXiv:1908.03020.

Yang, Linyi, Kenny, Eoin, Lok, Tin, Ng, James, Yang, Yi, Smyth, Barry, Dong, Ruihai, 2020. Generating plausible counterfactual explanations for deep transformers in financial text classification. In: Proceedings of the 28th International Conference on Computational Linguistics, pp. 6150–6160.

Ye, Lexiang, Keogh, Eamonn, 2011. Time series shapelets: A novel technique that allows accurate, interpretable and fast classification. Data Mining and Knowledge Discovery 22 (1–2), 149–182.

Zeiler, Matthew D., Fergus, Rob, 2014. Visualizing and understanding convolutional networks. In: European Conference on Computer Vision. Springer, pp. 818–833.

Zhou, Bolei, Khosla, Aditya, Lapedriza, Agata, Oliva, Aude, Torralba, Antonio, 2016. Learning deep features for discriminative localization. In: Proceedings of the IEEE Conference on Computer Vision and Pattern Recognition, pp. 2921–2929.

Zhu, Jiapeng, Shen, Yujun, Zhao, Deli, Zhou, Bolei, 2020. In-domain GAN inversion for real image editing. In: European Conference on Computer Vision. Springer, pp. 592–608.

CHAPTER 14

Theoretical analysis of LIME

Damien Garreau
Université Côte d'Azur, Inria, CNRS, LJAD, UMR 7351, Nice CEDEX 2, France

Chapter points

- Precise exposition of LIME's operating scheme in its public implementation for three datatypes: image, text, and tabular
- Behavior of the interpretable coefficients when the number of perturbed samples is large
- Role of the hyperparameters (bandwidth, number of bins, etc.)
- Specific points of caution raised by the analysis

14.1. Introduction

When trying to explain the prediction of a given model for a fixed example, it is very natural to try and perturb this example and see how the predictions of the model are changing in the process. Surely, if moving in a certain direction drastically changes the prediction, then this direction is important for the model's prediction. In a seminal paper from 2016, Ribeiro et al. (2016) proposed LIME (Locally Interpretable Model-agnostic Explanations), a method based upon this intuition. In a nutshell, LIME's procedure to explain the prediction of a model f, for example, ξ is the following:

1. Creating interpretable features;
2. Creating perturbed samples $x_1, \ldots, x_n$ by removing interpretable features at random, where n is a number of samples fixed in advance by the user;
3. Getting the model predictions at these perturbed samples, $y_i := f(x_i)$ for all $i \in [n]$;
4. Giving a weight to these predictions with respect to the distance between x_i and ξ;
5. Training a linear model on these (weighted) examples.

The end-user is generally presented with the top coefficients of this linear model, highlighting the importance of the most relevant interpretable features. For instance, in the image setting, LIME will highlight specific parts of the image that are deemed important for prediction (see Fig. 14.1).

Its ubiquity, understandable results, and speed quickly made of LIME one of the top contenders when it comes to explaining a black-box model. Before diving deeper into the implementation details, let us develop further these three points:

Explainable Deep Learning AI
https://doi.org/10.1016/B978-0-32-396098-4.00020-X

- *ubiquity* – LIME can be used on any model, taking as input nearly every datatype. One notable exception in the publicly released version[1] was time-series input, but some recent work filled this gap (see, e.g., Mishra et al. (2017); Guillemé et al. (2019); Neves et al. (2021)).
- *understandable results* – one of the key points of the method is to create *interpretable features*, therefore providing the user with a clear take-home message. For instance, in the case of images, some higher-level portions of the image are highlighted in opposition to pixelwise explanations given by saliency maps such as integrated gradient (Sundararajan et al., 2017).
- *speed* – the sampling is deterministic, and the main computational cost is Step 3, calling f on each perturbed sample, $n = 10^3$ times by default. Unless the model to explain is incredibly large, this cost is very reasonable. Moreover, this step is parallelizable in nature.

Together with SHAP (Lundberg and Lee, 2017), with which it shares a similar global structure, LIME is one of the "go to" interpretability method for black-box models. Besides its widespread use in practice, LIME also stemmed numerous extensions. One branch of research focuses on extending the framework to different data type. We already mentioned the case of time series, but LIME has also received attention in the world of survival analysis (Kovalev et al., 2020; Utkin et al., 2020). Another branch aims at improving the method itself. For instance, in the case of images, Agarwal and Nguyen (2020) proposes to use generative models in the sampling step. It is therefore doubly important to understand precisely how LIME operates: both from a practical standpoint (in order to use it properly), and from a theoretical standpoint (in order to see where the potential improvements lie).

This chapter is organized as follows: in Section 14.2, we present the detailed operation of LIME for images. Section 14.3 is dedicated to text data and Section 14.4 to tabular data. In each section, we present the precise operation of LIME in its public implementation, as well as some theoretical analysis in each case. We conclude in Section 14.5.

General setting

Before jumping to specific settings, we want to precise the framework of our exposition:
- *focus on a class* – the model to explain f does not take values in a vector space. To put it simply, when the model to explain makes predictions for several outputs (or several classes), we focus on a single one of them.
- *regression setting* – in the following, we are concerned with the explanation of an unknown model f taking values in a continuous set, not a discrete one. One way to think about it is to imagine the output of a model trained for regression. It is also

---

[1] https://github.com/marcotcr/lime.

possible to use LIME for classification, but in that event one should consider as f the likelihood function, not the predicted class. Using LIME with discrete outputs can lead to unwanted behaviors.

Notation

To conclude this introduction, let us fix some rudimentary notation. The model to explain is always denoted by f, and the example to explain by ξ. For any integer $k \in \mathbb{N}$, we denote by $[k]$ the finite set $\{1, 2, \ldots, k\}$. We index the features by j and the samples by i. We denote by $\| \cdot \|$ the Euclidean norm on $\mathbb{R}^d$.

14.2. LIME for images

In this section, we start looking at the specifics of LIME in the case of images. Namely, in the usual case of RGB images, our model f takes as input $x \in \mathbb{R}^{H \times W \times 3}$. It is perhaps in this setting that the experimental results are the most striking (an example is provided in Fig. 14.1). Indeed, the parts of the image highlighted by LIME often make sense: we can believe that they are important parts of the image for the classification In the same time, these explanations are simple enough that we can understand them easily. For instance, in Fig. 14.1, a gradient-based explanation method would give as explanation many pixels not necessarily grouped around the truck. We note that the visualization of the explanations is done here for the *positive* explanation (parts of the image contributing positively to the classification), but one can equally easily obtain the explanations for the negative prediction (parts of the image contributing negatively to the prediction).

Figure 14.1 For this image of the ILSVRC dataset (Russakovsky et al., 2015), InceptionV3 (Szegedy and Van-houcke, 2016) predicts the class `truck` with a confidence of 35%. In green (mid gray in print version), the explanation given by LIME for this prediction. We used 1000 perturbed samples and chose $\nu = 0.25$.

14.2.1 Overview of the method

Now as promised we look into more details into LIME operating procedure for image data. We first look into the creation of interpretable features.

Interpretable features

In the case of images, a natural idea is to consider groups of adjacent pixels as interpretable feature, what is often called a *superpixel*. Therefore, before generating the perturbed samples, LIME produces a superpixel decomposition of the image ξ. By default, the quickshift algorithm is used (Vedaldi and Soatto, 2008) (see Fig. 14.2 for an illustration), though any other superpixel algorithm can be used. For instance, Agarwal and Nguyen (2020) use SLIC (Achanta et al., 2012). We note that the superpixels are often connected components, but we do not use this in our analysis. Slightly more formally, we call J_j the jth superpixel associated to ξ and set d the number of superpixels associated to ξ. Then the J_js form a partition of the pixel set, that is, $J_1 \cup \cdots \cup J_d = [H] \times [W]$ and $J_k \cap J_\ell = \emptyset$ for all distinct k, ℓ.

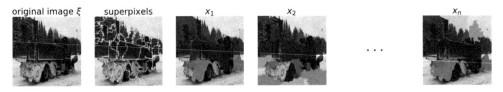

Figure 14.2 LIME default sampling process for images: from the original image, superpixels are generated. Here we used quickshift (Vedaldi and Soatto, 2008), obtaining $d = 56$ superpixels whose boundaries are marked in yellow (light gray in print version). Subsequently, n new images are created by replacing randomly selected superpixels by their mean RGB value.

Sampling

Using these superpixels, a very reasonable way to perturb ξ is to *erase randomly* a subset thereof. Here an interesting question arises: How does one erase a part of the image? The immediate answer, replacing the superpixel by a given color (say, black), is not always satisfying: this given color could be meaningful for our predictor. The choice that is made in the default implementation is to use the average RGB value on the superpixel as a replacement. Formally, for a given ξ to explain, the *replacement image* is defined as

$$\forall u \in J_k, \qquad \overline{\xi}_u := \frac{1}{|J_k|} \sum_{v \in J_k} \xi_v, \tag{14.1}$$

where $|\cdot|$ denotes the cardinality of a finite set. We can now be more precise regarding the sampling mechanism: for each new sample $i \in [n]$, LIME draws a vector $z_i \in \{0, 1\}^d$ with i.i.d. Bernoulli components with parameter $1/2$. Intuitively, $z_{i,j}$ is equal to 0 if superpixel j is replaced in sample i, and 1 otherwise (and therefore the vector $\mathbf{1}$ corresponds to ξ). In other words, the perturbed sample i has pixel values given by

$$\forall u \in J_k, \qquad x_{i,u} = z_{i,j}\xi_u + (1 - z_{i,j})\overline{\xi}_u, \tag{14.2}$$

where J_k is the superpixel containing u. The sampling process is illustrated in Fig. 14.2. It is interesting at this point to notice that when the superpixels boundaries are regular enough, it can happen that state-of-the-art image classifiers recognize most (if not all) perturbed samples as belonging to a specific class such as "puzzle" or "maze" (see Fig. 8 in Agarwal and Nguyen (2020)). A good practice is to check manually the predicted class for the perturbed samples in order to avoid this phenomenon.

Weighting the perturbed samples

As mentioned earlier, each perturbed sample receives a positive weight π_i. These weights are defined by

$$\forall i \in [n], \qquad \pi_i := \exp\left(\frac{-d_{\cos}(\mathbf{1}, z_i)}{2\nu^2}\right), \qquad (14.3)$$

where $d_{\cos}$ is the cosine distance and ν is a bandwidth parameter (which value is set to 0.25 by default). Let us recall that, for any two vectors $u, v \in \mathbb{R}^d$, the cosine distance is defined by

$$d_{\cos}(u, v) := 1 - \frac{u^\top v}{\|u\| \cdot \|v\|}. \qquad (14.4)$$

Whenever $u = \mathbf{1}$ and v is 0–1-valued, Eq. (14.4) simplifies greatly. Indeed, denoting by s the number of 0s in z_i, one can show that $d_{\cos}(\mathbf{1}, z_i) = 1 - \sqrt{1 - s/d}$. It is important to notice that, since the cosine distance depends only on the size of the intersection between activated and inactivated superpixels, that is also the case for the weights π_i. In particular, they *do not depend on the shape of the superpixels*. The weights can only diminish the importance of perturbed samples that are far away from the original image in terms of sheer number of replaced superpixels. If only one superpixel is replaced, the distance to ξ will be the same, be that superpixel half the image or a very small fraction thereof. See Fig. 14.3 for an illustration.

Figure 14.3 From the original image (left), LIME sampling produces perturbed samples by replacing random superpixels by their mean RGB value. In x_1, 10 superpixels were replaced, 43 in x_2. As a result, x_2 is further away from ξ than x_1, and LIME gives a smaller weight to x_2 then to x_1.

Building the surrogate model

The final step of LIME is to create a locally interpretable model, often called the *surrogate model*, fitting the responses $y_i = f(x_i)$ to the interpretable features z_i for $i \in [n]$. By default, weighted ridge regression (Hoerl and Kennard, 1970) is used. Namely, LIME outputs

$$\hat{\beta}^{(n)} \in \underset{\beta \in \mathbb{R}^{d+1}}{\arg\min} \left\{ \sum_{i=1}^{n} \pi_i (y_i - \beta^{\top} \tilde{z}_i)^2 + \lambda \| \beta \|^2 \right\}, \tag{14.5}$$

where $\tilde{z}_i = [1, z_i^{\top}]$ and $\lambda > 0$ is a regularization parameter (equal to 1 by default). Note that the extra component corresponding to the bias is given index 0. We emphasize the dependency on the number of perturbed samples by the superscript n in $\hat{\beta}^{(n)}$, dropping this superscript when n is clear from context.

It is important to understand that the interpretable coefficients, in this setting, are each associated to a superpixel. To summarize, the interpretable features are the absence or presence of a given superpixel, and *the associated interpretable coefficient corresponds to the amount by which the prediction decreases when removing the superpixel from the image.* In the previous sentence, removing should of course be understood as replacing by $\bar{\xi}$ as defined in Eq. (14.1) (or a user-defined constant).

14.2.2 Theoretical analysis

As we have seen in the previous section, creating the explanations is a complex process. Therefore, a question arises: Can we be sure that the proposed explanations are, indeed, explanations, and not an artifact of the method? To be more precise, let us say that LIME highlights superpixel J_1 as an important part of the image for the prediction. Can we be sure that J_1 is highlighted because it is important to predict $f(\xi)$? This question seems quite challenging to address in the general case, that is, for an arbitrary f. In what follows, we give minimalist answers to this question by making a key simplification that we describe in the next paragraph.

No regularization and consequences

In general, the number of superpixels is quite low with respect to the number of perturbed samples. Since the sum of errors in Eq. (14.5) scales as n whereas the $\| \beta \|^2$ scales as d, the effect of regularization for small λ is, in practice, negligible. Therefore *we assume that $\lambda = 0$* in Eq. (14.5). With this in mind, the $\hat{\beta}^{(n)}$ coefficients are solution of a weighted least-squares problem, which is found in closed-form. Namely, let $Z \in \{0, 1\}^{n \times (d+1)}$ be the matrix such that $Z_{i,.} = \tilde{z}_i^{\top}$, $W \in \mathbb{R}^{n \times n}$ the diagonal matrix such that $W_{i,i} = \pi_i$, and $y \in \mathbb{R}^n$ the vector such that $y_i = f(x_i)$. Then

$$\hat{\beta}^{(n)} = (Z^{\top} W Z)^{-1} Z^{\top} W y.$$

We will now look at the previous display when the sample size is large, that is, when $n \to +\infty$. In that event, the finite-sample explanations $(\hat{\beta}^{(n)})$ stabilize around a limit value, which we call β, and which *can be written explicitly in function of the hyperparameters of the problem*. This is the content of proposition below, whose main consequence is that one can focus on the limit explanations in order to understand LIME for images: up to noise coming from the sampling, LIME empirical explanations $\hat{\beta}^{(n)}$ are close to the limit explanations given by β.

Proposition 14.1 (Limit explanations, images (Proposition 2 in Garreau and Mardaoui (2021))). *Assume that $|f|$ is bounded and that $\lambda = 0$ in Eq. (14.5). Then, for any given ξ, when $n \to +\infty$, $\hat{\beta}^{(n)}$ converges in probability towards $\beta \in \mathbb{R}^{d+1}$, with*

$$\forall j \in [d], \quad \beta_j = c_d^{-1} \left\{ \sigma_1 \mathbb{E}\left[\pi f(x)\right] + \sigma_2 \mathbb{E}\left[\pi z_j f(x)\right] + \sigma_3 \sum_{\substack{k=1 \\ k \neq j}}^{d} \mathbb{E}\left[\pi z_k f(x)\right] \right\}, \quad (14.6)$$

where $c_d, \sigma_1, \sigma_2, \sigma_3$ are quantities depending explicitly on d and ν.

An expression for the intercept of the surrogate model (β_0) is also readily available, we refer to Garreau and Mardaoui (2021) for this expression as well as for a rigorous proof of Proposition 14.1. We note that, in this last display, the expectations are taken with respect to $z \in \mathbb{R}^d$, the random draw of Bernoulli random variables corresponding to the activation / inactivation of superpixels. All other quantities inside the expectation depend explicitly on z by means of Eqs. (14.2) and (14.3).

Linearity of the explanations

Now, Eq. (14.6) can be a bit intimidating. However, it has one striking feature: it is linear in the model to explain f. To put it plainly, let us write f as the sum of two models $f_1 + f_2$, and let us emphasize the dependency of β to any given model f by writing $\beta = \beta(f)$. Then, the corresponding limit interpretable coefficients at a given ξ satisfy

$$\forall j \in [d], \qquad \beta_j(f) = \beta_j(f_1) + \beta_j(f_2). \quad (14.7)$$

Since the empirical interpretable coefficients are close to the limit interpretable coefficients when the number of perturbed samples is large, Eq. (14.7) remains true for the empirical interpretable coefficients, up to noise coming from the sampling. This is an interesting feature, though we want to point out that it is true only in the limit $\lambda \to 0$. For larger values of λ or other penalization choices, Eq. (14.7) has no reason to be true.

Dependency on the bandwidth

Another avenue of investigation opened by Proposition 14.1 is the influence of the bandwidth parameter on the interpretable coefficients. We first note that, when $\nu \to 0$, all weights are 0. Therefore, the limit interpretable coefficients are all equal to zero, and the same holds for the empirical interpretable coefficients. We can then try and take $\nu \to +\infty$. In that event, it is clear from their expression (Eq. (14.3)) that the weights π_i tend to 1 for all $i \in [n]$. As a consequence, the expression of β simplifies greatly. Namely, up to a numerical constant,

$$\forall j \in [d], \qquad \beta_j \xrightarrow[\nu \to +\infty]{} \beta_j^\infty \propto \mathbb{E}\left[f(x)\big|z_j = 1\right] - \mathbb{E}\left[f(x)\right], \qquad (14.8)$$

where $\mathbb{E}\left[f(x)\big|z_j = 1\right]$ is the expected value of $f(x)$ *conditionally to superpixel J_j being present in the image*. In other words, the LIME coefficient associated to superpixel j is high if the average prediction around ξ is typically higher when superpixel J_j is present in the image.

Specializing Proposition 14.1

Another way to better comprehend Eq. (14.6) is to specialize it for an explicit model f. Perhaps the simplest way to do so is to consider a *linear model*. Let $x \in \mathbb{R}^{H \times W \times 3}$ be any given array. For each pixel position $u \in [H] \times [W]$, we denote by x_u the vector $(x_{u,1}, x_{u,2}, x_{u,3})^\top \in \mathbb{R}^3$. With this convention in mind, any linear model can be written

$$\forall x \in \mathbb{R}^{H \times W \times 3}, \qquad f(x) = \sum_{u \in [H] \times [W]} \lambda_u^\top x_u,$$

where $\lambda \in \mathbb{R}^{H \times W \times 3}$ are fixed, arbitrary coefficients. In that event, it is possible to show that Eq. (14.6) simplifies greatly to the following:

$$\forall j \in [d], \qquad \beta_j = \sum_{u \in J_j} \lambda_u^\top (\xi_i - \overline{\xi}_u). \qquad (14.9)$$

In other words, the limit interpretable coefficient associated to superpixel j is the sum over J_j of the linear coefficients multiplied by the difference between pixel values of the image to explain and pixel values of the replacement image. This is a satisfying property: indeed, this expression is reminiscent of "gradient times input" explanations (Shrikumar et al., 2017), which is also a widespread, simple method to get explanations for images when a gradient of the model is easily obtainable. To be more precise, here the gradient of the model is simply λ anywhere, and thus multiplying by the input ξ pixelwise, we find $\lambda \odot \xi$. Considering instead the normalized input $\xi - \overline{\xi}$, and summing over each superpixel, we recover Eq. (14.9). We demonstrate the accuracy of the predictions of Eq. (14.9) in Fig. 14.4. We conclude this paragraph by noting that, at least

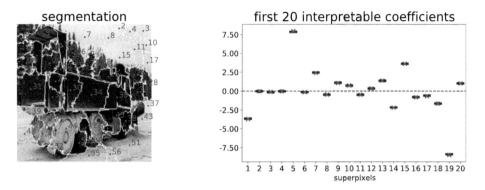

Figure 14.4 In this figure, we display LIME empirical explanations for a linear model. The coefficients of the linear model were chosen at random according to a Gaussian i.i.d. sampling. The left panel shows the image to explain and its superpixels, whereas the right panel displays LIME interpretable coefficients values (in blue [mid gray in print version], 10 repetitions) and the theoretical values given by Eq. (14.6) (red crosses, light gray in print version). With $n = 10^3$ perturbed samples, there is near perfect agreement.

in the simple case of a linear model, the question raised at the beginning of this section receives a positive answer: LIME explanations do make sense. It is also possible to look at other models such as simple shape detectors, for which the answer is also positive (see Section 4.1 in Garreau and Mardaoui (2021)).

Looking closer to the replacement image

An interesting consequence of Eq. (14.9) is that, for a linear model, LIME explanations are close to zero for superpixels such that the replacement image is close to the original image. This can happen, for instance, in the background of the image, when all pixels in a superpixel have a similar color, be it the sky or a far away landscape (see Eq. (14.1)). On these superpixels, one has $\xi_u \approx \overline{\xi}_u$ for all $u \in J_j$, and $\beta_j \approx 0$ whatever the values of λ_u may be. This effect is visible in Fig. 14.4. Looking for instance at superpixels 2 to 4, located in the upper right corner of the image, the white background will be replaced by white and we can see that the corresponding coefficients are at zero.

The phenomenon described in the previous paragraph is in fact a more general phenomenon, not limited to linear models: informally speaking, if $\overline{\xi}$ is locally very similar to ξ, then replacing ξ by $\overline{\xi}$ has little to no effect on the model prediction. Therefore, LIME will most certainly give a small coefficient for this superpixel in the proposed explanation. This can be a desirable property: background is often unimportant for the classification task that we are trying to explain, which is generally focused on objects, animals, or persons, that are usually located in the foreground of the image. Thus there is a natural bias in LIME to give small weights to the background superpixels. On the other side, it can sometimes be devastating if the relevant part of the image for the classifier has a plain color. There is some ongoing effort to improve LIME sampling in the case of images, the most notable being the generative approach proposed by Agarwal and Nguyen (2020), which proposes to use an in-painting algorithm (Yu et al., 2018) to replace the missing superpixels.

Back to the bandwidth

It is important to notice that whereas Eq. (14.9) does not depend on the bandwidth parameter ν, the general expression given in Proposition 14.1 does. And the dependency of a given β_j in ν, in the general case, is not trivial. It is neither monotonic, nor sign-constant: increasing ν can increase or decrease the value of β_j, and sometimes even make it change of sign. The only known and stable behavior are when $\nu \approx 0$ (where β_j approaches 0 for all $j \in [d]$ since the weights are negligible in that case), and at $\nu \to +\infty$ as discussed previously. We demonstrate this effect in Fig. 14.5. A very interesting avenue for research is to propose a founded way to choose ν, a parameter of the method which is often overlooked by the practitioner.

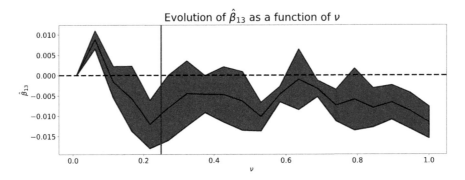

Figure 14.5 Evolution of $\hat{\beta}_{13}$, the interpretable coefficient associated to superpixel 13 of the segmentation displayed in the left panel of Fig. 14.4, as a function of the bandwidth parameter ν. For different values of ν, we report the average value of $\hat{\beta}_{13}$ over 5 runs of LIME. The shaded part corresponds to the standard deviation over these repetitions. The model explained in that case is the InceptionV3 network. In red (mid gray in print version), we report the default value of $\nu = 0.25$. As we can see, the magnitude and the sign of the explanation can change drastically when changing the bandwidth parameter.

Limits of the analysis

Since we take them as a given, the analysis is robust to a change of superpixel algorithm. Another definition of the sampling and / or the weights would lead to different computations but also seems manageable. Extending the analysis to more complicated models seems quite challenging. Another idea is to consider that any smooth model can be locally approximated by a linear model. This link is explored further in Garreau and Mardaoui (2021), where it is shown that LIME explanations are empirically close to the sum of integrated gradient times input on each superpixel. Of course, this link is tenuous for highly nonlinear models such as deep convolutional networks.

14.3. LIME for text data

We now move to the text version of LIME: the example to explain is now a document, that is, an ordered sequence of words. The global operation of the method is the same as announced in Section 14.1, with two key differences: what is now considered as interpretable features and the sampling scheme. We describe these differences in Section 14.3.1, before showing how the theoretical insights transform in Section 14.3.2.

14.3.1 Overview of the method

In this section, we briefly summarize LIME's operating procedure on text data.

Interpretable features

The first step of the method, as we have seen in Section 14.1, is the creation of interpretable features. Documents come with a very natural notion of interpretable features: the (unique) words composing the document. This is the notion of interpretable feature chosen by LIME in this setting: *the absence or presence of a given word in the document*. Let us formalize this: first, we define $\mathcal{D}$ to be the global dictionary containing all individual words used in our dataset and D its cardinality (the total number of words in the English language, for instance). Here we note that generally a preprocessing step is taken to remove all noninformative words and token. We do not consider this step here to avoid unnecessary complications. In any case, for a given document ξ to explain, only a certain number $d \ll D$ of words from our dictionary $\mathcal{D}$ are used. We collect these d words in a local dictionary, which we call $\mathcal{D}_\xi$. Without loss of generality, we can write $\mathcal{D}_\xi = \{w_1, \ldots, w_d\}$, so that the document to explain is written as an ordained sequence of w_js (with possible repetitions). The interpretable features in the case of text data for a document x are the $z_i \in \{0, 1\}^d$, where $z_{i,j} = 1$ if and only if $w_j \in x$.

Sampling mechanism

It is, of course, not possible to use the sampling scheme described in Section 14.2.1 for documents, but it is straightforward to adapt it by *removing words at random in the document*. There are different ways for this process to happen, and we now dive deeper into the details of this removal. For each $i \in [n]$, the default sampling process is to select a certain number of words to be removed s, uniformly at random in $[d]$. Then, a subset $S \subseteq [d]$ with cardinality s is chosen uniformly at random among all subsets of size s, and all words with indices belonging to S are removed from ξ. This process is repeated independently n times, to generate perturbed samples $x_1, \ldots, x_n$. We illustrate this process in Table 14.1.

Table 14.1 Sampling scheme for text data on an example from the Yelp reviews dataset (Zhang et al., 2015). In this example, the local dictionary has size $d = 11$ whereas the global dictionary has size 10,450.

ξ	"Can't say enough good things about Sens. Excellent food and excellent service."	$s = 0$
x_1	"Can't say enough food service"	$s = 6$
x_2	"Can't say enough good things about Sens excellent food excellent service"	$s = 1$
$\vdots$		$\vdots$
x_n	"Say enough good things Sens food service"	$s = 4$

A major problem with this sampling technique, as becomes apparent going through Table 14.1, is that the perturbed samples are generally not meaningful documents anymore. Removing words at random destroys the semantic structure of most sentences, and one can wonder if providing these inputs to the model to explain makes sense. A slightly more evolved possibility is to use a placeholder instead of total removing. For instance, one can opt for UNKWORDZ in the public implementation, with the right option choice. Further down this line of reasoning, one can imagine using a generative model to propose for each missing word a list of candidates keeping the sentence together. This is for instance a possibility when using Anchors (Ribeiro et al., 2018) where DistilBERT, a lighter version of BERT (Devlin et al., 2019), can be used instead of a token replacement. We do not consider these possibilities here and focus on straight removal of words.

Weights and surrogate model

The next step is to assign positive weights to each perturbed sample. Denoting by $z_i \in \mathbb{R}^d$, again, the associated 0–1-valued vector corresponding to the absence or presence of a word in the perturbed sample, the positive weights are given by Eq. (14.3). As in the image setting, the same remarks are true: these weights depend only on the number of deletions. In particular, they do not depend on the number of repetitions of the deleted words. For instance, if $s = 1$, the weight given to the sample is the same if the removed word is present one time or 100 in the original document. Finally, the output of LIME for text data is given by the linear model trained as in Eq. (14.5).

14.3.2 Theoretical analysis

We now show how to transpose the theoretical analysis presented in Section 14.2.2 to text data. In what follows, we address this complicated task by doing one main assumption on the model to explain: f takes as input *vector features*. More precisely, before going through f, the data first goes through a *vectorizer*, which we denote by ϕ. Namely, instead of looking at explanations for $f(x)$, we consider explanations for $f(\phi(x))$, where f is still considered as black-box but ϕ is known. More precisely, we assume this vectorizer to be the *TF-IDF transform*, which is the case in the publicly released version of the code.

TF-IDF

The term "frequency-inverse document frequency" is a frequently-used statistic, giving a measure of importance to each word of a document. It is defined as the product of two terms: the term frequency (TF), measuring how frequent a word is in the document (Luhn, 1957), and the inverse document frequency (IDF), measuring how unfrequent it is in our corpus (Spärck Jones, 1972). The obtained vector (one component for each word of the global dictionary $\mathcal{D}$) is usually normalized, by default by its Euclidean norm. More formally, let $\mathcal{C}$ be our corpus of documents and set $N = |\mathcal{C}|$. Then the (normalized) TF–IDF of document x is defined as

$$\forall j \in [D], \qquad \phi(x)_j := \frac{m_j v_j}{\sqrt{\sum_{k=1}^{D} m_k^2 v_k^2}}, \tag{14.10}$$

where m_j is the *multiplicity* of word j in x, and $v_j := \log \frac{N+1}{N_j+1} + 1$, where N_j is the number of documents in $\mathcal{C}$ containing w_j. Intuitively, individual components of $\phi(x)$ take high values for words that are frequent in x but not in the global corpus. In the opposite direction, $\phi(x)_j = 0$ for all w_js not contained in x.

Limit explanations

With these notations in hand, we can prove a convergence result for the LIME empirical explanations for text data, reasoning exactly as we did in Section 14.2.2.

Proposition 14.2 (Limit explanations, text data (Proposition 2 in Mardaoui and Garreau (2021))). *Assume that $|f|$ is bounded and that $\lambda = 0$ in Eq. (14.5). Assume further that the data goes through the TF-IDF vectorizer ϕ defined by Eq. (14.10) before being passed to the model to explain. Then, for any given document ξ, when $n \to +\infty$, $\hat{\beta}^{(n)}$ converges in probability towards $\beta \in \mathbb{R}^{d+1}$, with*

$$\forall j \in [d], \quad \beta_j = c_d^{-1} \left\{ \sigma_1 \mathbb{E}\left[\pi f(\phi(x))\right] + \sigma_2 \mathbb{E}\left[\pi z_j f(\phi(x))\right] + \sigma_3 \sum_{\substack{k=1 \\ k \neq j}}^{d} \mathbb{E}\left[\pi z_k f(\phi(x))\right] \right\},$$
$$\tag{14.11}$$

where $c_d, \sigma_1, \sigma_2, \sigma_3$ are quantities depending explicitly on d and v.

As in the image case, an expression for the intercept of the surrogate model (β_0) is available, we refer to Mardaoui and Garreau (2021) for this expression and a complete proof of Proposition 14.2. The expression given in Proposition 14.2 is very similar to the one given by Proposition 14.1. The key differences are (i) the exact expression of the σ coefficients and the normalization constant c, which is of little importance here, and (ii) the presence of the vectorizer ϕ, as per our assumptions. This last point, as we will see, brings additional complexity in the analysis when specializing Proposition 14.2 to simple models.

Dependency on the bandwidth

As in the image setting, the dependency of the interpretable coefficients in the bandwidth is complicated. In fact, one can obtain plots similar to Fig. 14.5 in the text setting (see Fig. 4 in Mardaoui and Garreau (2021) for instance). However, we can get more precise insights for specific values of ν. For instance, it is possible to take $\nu \to +\infty$ in Proposition 14.2 and by doing so get rid of the dependency on π. Up to numerical constants, we obtain a very similar expression to Eq. (14.8), namely

$$\forall j \in [d], \qquad \beta_j \xrightarrow[\nu \to +\infty]{} \beta_j^\infty \propto \mathbb{E}\left[f(\phi(x))\big|w_j \in x\right] - \mathbb{E}\left[f(\phi(x))\right], \qquad (14.12)$$

where $\mathbb{E}\left[f(\phi(x))\big|w_j \in x\right]$ denotes the conditional expectation of $f(\phi(x))$ conditionally to the word w_j being present in x. Again, Eq. (14.12) makes great sense: in the large sample / large bandwidth limit, LIME gives a high, positive coefficient to word j if the model takes higher values than average when the word is present.

Specializing Proposition 14.2

To make the most from Proposition 14.2, one is tempted to specialize it, again, to simple models such as the linear model. Here, a few technical difficulties arise, and we choose to avoid the most minor by sticking to the infinite bandwidth behavior. In other terms, we will now specialize Eq. (14.12) to the linear model, and not Eq. (14.11). Let us recall that, by linear model, we mean that for any document x,

$$f(\phi(x)) = \sum_{j=1}^{d} \lambda_j \phi(x)_j \,.$$

In view of the previous display and Eq. (14.12), by linearity, it is sufficient to investigate the computation of $\mathbb{E}\left[\phi(x)_j\big|w_k \in x\right]$, with $j, k \in [d]$. In other terms, we need to obtain *the average value of the TF-IDF transform of a document obtained by removing words at random in ξ*. Let us consider the case $j = k$, the other cases being somewhat similar. Let us remind ourselves the definition of the TF-IDF transform (Eq. (14.10)): it is equal to the product of the term frequency and the inverse document frequency. Since this last term does not change when words are removed at random (the inverse frequencies are calibrated on the corpus beforehand), we can focus on the term frequency. Conditionally to $w_j \in x$, the term frequency of w_j in the perturbed document x does not change: only the normalization does. More precisely, recall that we set S the (random) set of words to be removed. Then, conditionally to $w_j \in x$,

$$\phi(x)_j = \frac{m_j v_j}{\sqrt{\sum_{k \notin S} m_k^2 v_k^2}} = \phi(\xi)_j \cdot \frac{1}{\sqrt{1 - H_S}} \,, \qquad (14.13)$$

where we set $H_S := \sum_{j \in S} \omega_j$, with $\omega_j := m_j^2 v_j^2 / \sum_{k=1}^d m_k^2 v_k^2$. Again by linearity, it remains to evaluate $\mathbb{E}\left[(1 - H_S)^{-1/2} | S \not\ni j\right]$. When ω_j is not too large, it is shown in Mardaoui and Garreau (2021) that this last expression can be well approximated by $\sqrt{6}/2$ (and $2\sqrt{3}/3$ in the $j \neq k$ case). Therefore, in the infinite bandwidth regime, we have the following approximate expression for the limit interpretable coefficients of a linear model:

$$\forall j \in [d], \qquad \beta_j^\infty \approx 1.36 \cdot \lambda_j \phi(x)_j. \tag{14.14}$$

In other terms, the limit explanations for any given word are close to *the product of the TF-IDF of that word multiplied by the coefficient appearing in the linear model*. We illustrate Eq. (14.14) on an example in Fig. 14.6. It is interesting to note that, even though we made computations in the infinite bandwidth regime, the approximate values hold pretty well for much smaller values of v, and in particular for the default value $v = 0.25$. We notice that, once more, Eq. (14.14) is reminiscent of a "gradient times input" interpretation. It seems intuitively satisfying: features corresponding to large variations of the function are given large weights, if their TF–IDF transform is not too small.

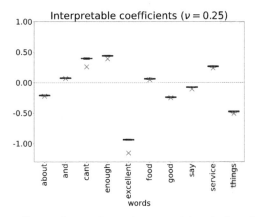

Figure 14.6 Interpretable coefficients for an arbitrary linear model applied on the same example as in Table 14.1. In blue (dark gray in print version), the empirical values given by LIME ($n = 5000$, 10 repetitions). In red (light gray in print version), the values given by Eq. (14.14). We see that the approximate values are quite close to the empirical values, even though the bandwidth in this experiment is 0.25 (which is the default value).

Limits of the analysis

Some minor changes in the pipeline are amenable to the analysis. For instance, while L_2 normalization is most widespread when using TF-IDF, one can also use L_1 normalization. Then the discussion of the previous paragraph is modified in the following way: one must now look at $\mathbb{E}\left[(1 - H_S)^{-1} | S \not\ni j\right]$. The same arguments apply readily, and it is also possible to provide numerical approximate values in that case. Using other vectorizers, such as Word2Vec (Mikolov et al., 2013) seems quite challenging since the link between individual words and their vector representation is not explicitly known. Finally, looking at more complicated models promises to be challenging, as already looking at the random perturbations of the TF-IDF under LIME sampling is demanding.

14.4. LIME for tabular data

We now turn to tabular data, that is, unstructured input data which can be seen as living in $\mathbb{R}^d$. For simplicity's sake, we will focus on the case where each input feature is *continuous* (we discuss briefly the case of categorical data at the end of this section). Therefore, for any given example to explain ξ, we assume that all features are real-valued.

14.4.1 Overview of the method

As in the case of images and text data, the first step is to create interpretable features. The default way this is done is (i) to discretize the input space, and (ii) to encode the presence of a feature by *falling into the same box as the example to explain*. Let us detail both these steps, starting with the discretization step, before turning to the sampling mechanism.

Interpretable features

LIME for tabular data creates, on each input feature, a partition of the space in p consecutive bins, with $p = 5$ by default. More precisely, given some train data $\mathcal{X}$, the quantiles of order $1/p$ of the projection of $\mathcal{X}$ on each dimension are computed. Therefore, for each $j \in [d]$, we have boundaries $q_{j,0} < q_{j,1} < \cdots < q_{j,p}$ such that a proportion $1/p$ of the train data falls into each $[q_{j,b-1}, q_{j,b}]$ for all $b \in [p]$. By convention, we set $q_{j,0} = -\infty$ and $q_{j,p} = +\infty$. We note that it is also possible to directly provide to LIME the boundaries of these d-dimensional bins, although this can be problematic later on in the sampling step if the provided bins are not adapted to the distribution of the data. We refer to Fig. 14.7 for an illustration of the discretization step. The interpretable features are then defined as follows: $z_{i,j} = 1$ if x_i falls into the same bin as ξ on direction j, and 0 otherwise. Formally, let us denote by $b_j^\star$ the bin index of ξ_j in each dimension j. Then $z_{i,j} = \mathbf{1}_{x_{i,j} \in [q_{j,b_j^\star}, q_{j,b_j^\star+1})}$.

Sampling

From the d-dimensional bins described in the previous paragraph, we can now detail the sampling mechanism of LIME for tabular data. The overall idea is to mimic the distribution of $\mathcal{X}$. For each perturbed sample x_i, a random bin is chosen independently at random in each direction, with probability $1/p$. On this bin, LIME then proceeds to sample a *truncated normal distribution* with parameters given by the mean and standard

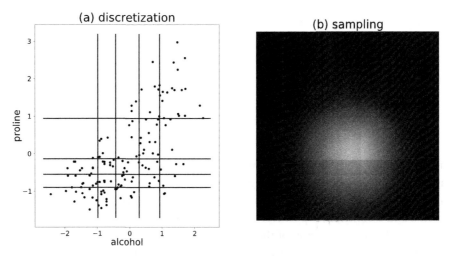

Figure 14.7 (*Left*) Tabular LIME discretization step visualized on the `wine` dataset (Cortez et al., 1998). In black, a 2-dimensional slice of the dataset. In blue (dark gray in print version), the lines corresponding to the quantiles of the training data on each input feature. Here we took $p = 5$, hence 20% of the train data falls into each bin when projected on the axis. (*Right*) Density used for the sampling step, pointwise product of truncated Gaussian with boundaries given by the d-dimensional bins and position and scale parameters given by the mean and standard deviation on the bins.

deviation of $\mathcal{X}$ in this bin. That is, a normal distribution with prescribed mean and standard deviation conditioned to take values in the bin. We illustrate the density of the sampling distribution in Fig. 14.7.

It is important to realize that this sampling has several important caveats. First, the sampling is done independently on each direction, therefore ignoring any dependency that could occur in the training data. Second, the data marginal distribution may not be Gaussian at all inside any given bin. For instance, when projected on the axis, the marginal data could be bimodal. Finally, each d-dimensional box receives (roughly) a proportion $1/p^2$ of the perturbed sample data. This can be a problem if there is no training data in this box: LIME will query the model in a corner of the input space which is out of distribution. We can witness this phenomenon in Fig. 14.7: the upper left corner contains no train data, but will nonetheless contain a nonzero proportion of the x_is.

While we do not consider this case here, let us note that the sampling mechanism is quite straightforward when dealing with categorical data. In that event, LIME simply evaluates the frequency of occurrence of each alternative on $\mathcal{X}$, and subsequently samples according to this probability. For instance, if feature j has two possible outcomes A and B, each occurring in $\mathcal{X}$ with frequency 0.3 and 0.7, then LIME sampling will be A with probability 0.3 and B with probability 0.7, independently of all other features.

Weights and surrogate model

As in the image and text data setting, each perturbed sample x_i receives a positive weight π_i for all $i \in [n]$. These weights also stem from the Gaussian kernel, but with a slightly different expression:

$$\forall i \in [n], \qquad \pi_i := \exp\left(\frac{-\|\mathbf{1} - z_i\|^2}{2v^2}\right), \tag{14.15}$$

where v is a bandwidth parameter, equal to $\sqrt{0.75 \cdot d}$ by default. The surrogate model is built in similar fashion than for images and text data. Given the nature of the interpretable features, a positive weight for feature j will be interpreted as "feature j being between a and b contributes positively to the prediction."

To conclude this description of the default implementation of LIME for tabular data, let us note that the original description of the method in Ribeiro et al. (2016) allows for great flexibility in the choice of the interpretable features, the weights, and the regularization. For instance, one popular choice is to take $p = 1$, that is, *no discretization* of the input space. In that event, the perturbed samples are simply a Gaussian perturbation ξ. The analysis simplifies greatly, and some links with gradient-based explanations were noted by Agarwal et al. (2021). We do not consider this case here, and assume that $p > 1$ from now on. Another popular choice is to use L_1 penalization instead of L_2 in Eq. (14.5) (that is, weighted LASSO (Tibshirani, 1996)), in order to limit the number of interpretable features in the surrogate model. This is a very sensible choice, since the number of interpretable features should be low in order for the end-user to understand the explanation well. The analysis in that case is much more challenging, in the same way the analysis from LASSO differs from that of least squares (Bühlmann and Van De Geer, 2011).

14.4.2 Theoretical analysis

As in the image (Section 14.2) and text (Section 14.3) settings, we can give the closed-formula expressions of the interpretable coefficients when the sample size goes to infinity. This is the content of the next result:

Proposition 14.3 (Limit explanations, tabular data (adapted from Theorem 1 in Garreau and von Luxburg (2020))). *Suppose that $|f|$ is bounded and that $\lambda = 0$ in Eq. (14.5). Then, for any given ξ, when $n \to +\infty$, $\hat{\beta}^{(n)}$ converges in probability towards $\beta \in \mathbb{R}^{d+1}$, with*

$$\forall j \in [d], \qquad \beta_j = c_d^{-1}\left\{\sigma_1 \mathbb{E}\left[\pi f(x)\right] + \sigma_2 \mathbb{E}[\pi z_j f(x)]\right\}, \tag{14.16}$$

where c_d, σ_1, σ_2 are quantities depending explicitly on d, p, and v.

We refer to Garreau and von Luxburg (2020) for a proof of Proposition 14.3, as well as an expression for the intercept. Similarly to the image and text settings, we notice immediately the linearity of Eq. (14.16) in the model. We now list a few less obvious consequences of Proposition 14.3, some of them quite different from the image and text settings.

Locality of the observations

A first observation that can be made is the locality of Eq. (14.16): all quantities depend on ξ only through the boundaries of the d-dimensional bin immediately surrounding ξ. More precisely, let us call B this d-dimensional bin, and consider ξ_1 and ξ_2 two points belonging to B. Then the weights of the perturbed samples with respect to ξ_1 and ξ_2 are the same, since they only depend on the projections onto the axes and their relative positions with respect to the box boundaries. As a consequence, *the limit explanations are the same for all examples lying in B*. This can be a problem since B can be quite large (one can think, for instance, to the case where B contains half-axes in some directions), and one can imagine that examples far from each other are classified for very different reasons. Tabular LIME will ignore these differences if the distribution of the input data is flat in this region.

Dependency on the bandwidth

Unlike the image and text settings, the expressions of σ_1, σ_2, and c are not overly complicated here, thus we can provide them in order to understand better how the interpretable coefficients depend on the bandwidth. Namely, $c_d = c^d$, $\sigma_1 = -pc/(pc - 1)$, and $\sigma_2 = p^2c^2/(pc - 1)$ with

$$c := \frac{1}{p} + \left(1 - \frac{1}{p}\right) e^{\frac{-1}{2\nu^2}} .$$

We see that even in this simple case (in comparison to image and text data) the dependency in ν is nonlinear, and *a priori* nonmonotonous. In fact, one can obtain graphs similar to Fig. 14.5 for tabular data as well (see Fig. 7 in Garreau and von Luxburg (2020), for instance).

It is, however, possible to be more precise for the two extremes: $\nu = 0$ and $\nu \to +\infty$. As before, when $\nu = 0$ all interpretable coefficients are 0. On the other hand, when $\nu \to +\infty$, $c \to 1$, and the weights converge to 1 almost surely as well. Coming back to Eq. (14.11), we see that $\sigma_1 \to -p/(p - 1)$ and $\sigma_2 \to p^2/(p - 1)$. Since $\mathbb{E}\left[z_j f(x)\right] = \frac{1}{p}\mathbb{E}\left[f(x)\middle| b_j = b_j^\star\right]$, the expectation of the model conditionally to x falling into the same bin as ξ on axis j, we have obtained the expression of the limit interpretable coefficients as $\nu \to_\infty$:

$$\forall j \in [d], \qquad \beta_j \xrightarrow[\nu \to +\infty]{} \frac{p}{p - 1}\left(\mathbb{E}\left[f(x)\middle| b_j = b_j^\star\right] - \mathbb{E}\left[f(x)\right]\right) .$$

Here the conclusion is the same, namely, the interpretable coefficients take large values if the model takes significantly higher values when the data has values similar to ξ on axis j.

Ignoring unused coordinates

Another consequence of the expression of the limit interpretable coefficients in the tabular case (Eq. (14.16)) is the following corollary:

Corollary 14.1 (adapted from Proposition 9 in Garreau and von Luxburg (2020)). *Assume that f is bounded and only depends on a subset $S \subseteq [d]$ of the features. Then, for any $j \in \overline{S}$, $\beta_j = 0$.*

In other words, *if the model does not depend on a subset of features, the limit interpretable coefficients associated to those features are put to zero* by tabular LIME. This is an attractive feature of tabular LIME, since it is very intuitive that coordinates unused by the model should not appear important in the explanation. Interestingly, this result was only proven for the tabular version and does not seem to hold in the text and image settings. We illustrate this phenomenon in Fig. 14.8.

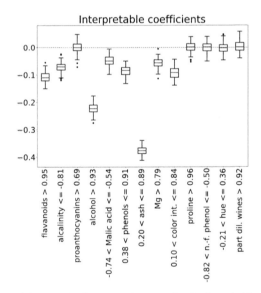

Figure 14.8 Ignoring unused features. In this example, we trained a kernel ridge regressor g on the Wine dataset, which has 13 features. We then consider the model f, equal to the restriction of g to a subset of 9 features (therefore, 4 features are unused by f to make predictions). We computed LIME's explanation for f at a given example 10 times. As predicted by Corollary 14.1, the explanations given by tabular LIME are zero for the four unused features, up to noise coming from the sampling.

Specializing Proposition 14.3

Since the expression of the limit interpretable coefficients is simpler, it is easier to specialize Proposition 14.3 to explicit models. Here, we will only consider the case of a linear model, given by

$$\forall x \in \mathbb{R}^d, \qquad f(x) = \sum_{i=1}^{d} \lambda_j x_j \,,$$

where $\lambda \in \mathbb{R}^d$ is a fixed vector of coefficients. In that case, it is possible to show (Corollary 4 in Garreau and von Luxburg (2020)) that

$$\forall j \in [d], \qquad \beta_j = \left(\tilde{\mu}_{j,b_j^\star} - \frac{1}{p-1} \sum_{\substack{b=1 \\ b \neq b_j^\star}}^{p} \tilde{\mu}_{j,b} \right) \cdot \lambda_j \,, \tag{14.17}$$

where $\tilde{\mu}_{j,b}$ denotes the mean of the truncated Gaussian used for the sampling on dimension j in bin b. To put it simply, the limit interpretable coefficients in that case are *proportional to the coefficients of the linear model.* Moreover, on a given axis, the proportionality coefficient is equal to the difference between the mean of the truncated Gaussian used for the sampling on the bin containing ξ and the average of the means on the other bins. An interesting consequence of Eq. (14.17) is that the limit interpretable coefficient can be zero whereas λ_j is not. This can be a problem, since this effect comes solely from the data distribution, not from the example of the model: tabular LIME would put weight zero on a potentially important feature only because p is chosen in such a manner that the means "compensate." We refer to Garreau and von Luxburg (2020) (more specifically Section 1.1.1) for more details.

Limits of the analysis

We conclude this section by noticing that the analysis is quite robust to other choices of weights and distances between the z_is as in the image and text setting. In fact, we note that the original analysis (Garreau and Luxburg, 2020) was about a modified version of tabular LIME (notably the distance in Eq. (14.15) is the Euclidean distance between ξ and x_i). It is therefore possible to try different design choices and look at their repercussions onto the limit interpretable coefficients. With respect to more complicated models, the analysis can be extended to quite a large class of additive and multiplicative models, including in particular CART trees, see Garreau and von Luxburg (2020).

14.5. Conclusion

As deep learning architectures come and go, we believe that there will always be a privileged place for *post hoc* interpretability in the future. Among them, LIME stands out as a seminal work, and we believe that it is important to have a solid understanding of this method. We note that the complexity arising from considering the exact implementation details is often overlooked. The interplay between the construction of interpretable features, the sampling mechanism, the definition of the weights, the distance between perturbed samples and the example to explain, and the choice of hyperparameters is often ignored by the end-user. In this chapter, we demonstrated that looking closely at all these elements is essential since some default choices seem to lead to unwanted behavior even for simple models.

As future work, we see several interesting directions to pursue. To mention only one of them, a problem often occurring when using LIME or other perturbation-based methods is the robustness (or rather lack thereof) of the provided explanations. In a nutshell, running LIME twice on the same model—example pair will not necessarily yield the same explanations. A simple way to visualize this phenomenon is to look at the size of the boxplots in Fig. 14.8, for instance. While some approaches have been proposed to alleviate this effect (Visani et al., 2020), we believe that this variability is intrinsic to the method. We offer a new perspective on this problem: by taking a large enough sample size, since the empirical explanations converge to a given limit, the variability problem disappears. Of course, the main challenge is to define what "large" means in the previous sentence in a quantitative way. Bettering the rates of convergence in Propositions 14.1, 14.2, and 14.3 would yield a first answer.

Acknowledgments

The author thanks Ulrike von Luxburg and Dina Mardaoui: without them none of this work would have been completed. We acknowledge the funding of ANR (project NIM-ML).

References

Achanta, Radhakrishna, Shaji, Appu, Smith, Kevin, Lucchi, Aurelien, Fua, Pascal, Süsstrunk, Sabine, 2012. SLIC superpixels compared to state-of-the-art superpixel methods. IEEE Transactions on Pattern Analysis and Machine Intelligence 34 (11), 2274–2282.

Agarwal, Sushant, Jabbari, Shahin, Agarwal, Chirag, Upadhyay, Sohini, Wu, Steven, Lakkaraju, Himabindu, 2021. Towards the unification and robustness of perturbation and gradient based explanations. In: Meila, Marina, Zhang, Tong (Eds.), Proceedings of the 38th International Conference on Machine Learning. 18–24 Jul 2021. In: Proceedings of Machine Learning Research, vol. 139. PMLR, pp. 110–119.

Agarwal, Chirag, Nguyen, Anh, 2020. Explaining image classifiers by removing input features using generative models. In: Proceedings of the Asian Conference on Computer Vision.

Bühlmann, Peter, Van De Geer, Sara, 2011. Statistics for High-Dimensional Data: Methods, Theory and Applications. Springer Science & Business Media.

Cortez, P., Cerdeira, A., Almeida, F., Matos, T., Reis, J., 1998. Modeling wine preferences by data mining from physicochemical properties. Decision Support Systems 47 (4), 547–553.

Devlin, Jacob, Chang, Ming-Wei, Lee, Kenton, Toutanova, Kristina, 2019. BERT: pre-training of deep bidirectional transformers for language understanding. In: Proceedings of the 2019 Conference of the North American Chapter of the Association for Computational Linguistics: Human Language Technologies, Volume 1 (Long and Short Papers). Association for Computational Linguistics, Stroudsburg, PA, USA, pp. 4171–4186.

Garreau, Damien, Luxburg, Ulrike, 2020. Explaining the explainer: A first theoretical analysis of LIME. In: International Conference on Artificial Intelligence and Statistics. PMLR, pp. 1287–1296.

Garreau, Damien, Mardaoui, Dina, 2021. What does LIME really see in images? In: Meila, Marina, Zhang, Tong (Eds.), Proceedings of the 38th International Conference on Machine Learning. 18–24 Jul 2021. In: Proceedings of Machine Learning Research, vol. 139. PMLR, pp. 3620–3629.

Garreau, Damien, von Luxburg, Ulrike, 2020. Looking deeper into tabular LIME. Preprint, available at https://arxiv.org/abs/2008.11092v2.

Guillemé, Maël, Masson, Véronique, Rozé, Laurence, Termier, Alexandre, 2019. Agnostic local explanation for time series classification. In: 2019 IEEE 31st International Conference on Tools with Artificial Intelligence (ICTAI). IEEE, pp. 432–439.

Hoerl, Arthur E., Kennard, Robert W., 1970. Ridge regression: Biased estimation for nonorthogonal problems. Technometrics 12 (1), 55–67.

Kovalev, Maxim S., Utkin, Lev V., Kasimov, Ernest M., 2020. SurvLIME: A method for explaining machine learning survival models. Knowledge-Based Systems 203, 106164.

Luhn, Hans Peter, 1957. A statistical approach to mechanized encoding and searching of literary information. IBM Journal of Research and Development 1 (4), 309–317.

Lundberg, Scott M., Lee, Su-In, 2017. A unified approach to interpreting model predictions. In: Advances in Neural Information Processing Systems, pp. 4765–4774.

Mardaoui, Dina, Garreau, Damien, 2021. An analysis of LIME for text data. In: Banerjee, Arindam, Fukumizu, Kenji (Eds.), Proceedings of the 24th International Conference on Artificial Intelligence and Statistics. 13–15 Apr 2021. In: Proceedings of Machine Learning Research, vol. 130. PMLR, pp. 3493–3501.

Mikolov, Tomas, Sutskever, Ilya, Chen, Kai, Corrado, Greg S., Dean, Jeff, 2013. Distributed representations of words and phrases and their compositionality. In: Advances in Neural Information Processing Systems, pp. 3111–3119.

Mishra, Saumitra, Sturm, Bob L., Dixon, Simon, 2017. Local interpretable model-agnostic explanations for music content analysis. In: ISMIR, pp. 537–543.

Neves, Inês, Folgado, Duarte, Santos, Sara, Barandas, Marília, Campagner, Andrea, Ronzio, Luca, Cabitza, Federico, Gamboa, Hugo, 2021. Interpretable heartbeat classification using local model-agnostic explanations on ECGs. Computers in Biology and Medicine 133, 104393.

Ribeiro, Marco Tulio, Singh, Sameer, Guestrin, Carlos, 2016. "Why should I trust you?": Explaining the predictions of any classifier. In: Proceedings of the 22nd ACM SIGKDD International Conference on Knowledge Discovery and Data Mining. ACM, pp. 1135–1144.

Ribeiro, Marco Tulio, Singh, Sameer, Guestrin, Carlos, 2018. Anchors: High-precision model-agnostic explanations. In: Proceedings of the AAAI Conference on Artificial Intelligence, vol. 32.

Russakovsky, Olga, Deng, Jia, Su, Hao, Krause, Jonathan, Satheesh, Sanjeev, Ma, Sean, Huang, Zhiheng, Karpathy, Andrej, Khosla, Aditya, Bernstein, Michael, Berg, Alexander C., Fei-Fei, Li, 2015. ImageNet large scale visual recognition challenge. International Journal of Computer Vision (IJCV) 115 (3), 211–252.

Shrikumar, Avanti, Greenside, Peyton, Kundaje, Anshul, 2017. Learning important features through propagating activation differences. In: International Conference on Machine Learning. PMLR, pp. 3145–3153.

Spärck Jones, Karen, 1972. A statistical interpretation of term specificity and its application in retrieval. Journal of Documentation 28 (1), 11–21.

Sundararajan, Mukund, Taly, Ankur, Yan, Qiqi, 2017. Axiomatic attribution for deep networks. In: Proceedings of the 34th International Conference on Machine Learning (ICML).

Szegedy, Christian, Vanhoucke, Vincent, Ioffe, Sergey, Shlens, Jon, Wojna, Zbigniew, 2016. Rethinking the inception architecture for computer vision. In: Proceedings of the IEEE Conference on Computer Vision and Pattern Recognition, pp. 2818–2826.

Tibshirani, Robert, 1996. Regression shrinkage and selection via the lasso. Journal of the Royal Statistical Society: Series B (Methodological) 58 (1), 267–288.

Utkin, Lev V., Kovalev, Maxim S., Kasimov, Ernest M., 2020. SurvLIME-Inf: A simplified modification of SurvLIME for explanation of machine learning survival models. Preprint, available at https://arxiv.org/abs/2005.02387v1.

Vedaldi, Andrea, Soatto, Stefano, 2008. Quick shift and kernel methods for mode seeking. In: European Conference on Computer Vision, pp. 705–718.

Visani, Giorgio, Bagli, Enrico, Chesani, Federico, Poluzzi, Alessandro, Capuzzo, Davide, 2020. Statistical stability indices for LIME: Obtaining reliable explanations for machine learning models. Journal of the Operational Research Society, 1–11.

Yu, Jiahui, Lin, Zhe, Yang, Jimei, Shen, Xiaohui, Lu, Xin, Huang, Thomas S., 2018. Generative image inpainting with contextual attention. In: Proceedings of the IEEE Conference on Computer Vision and Pattern Recognition, pp. 5505–5514.

Zhang, Xiang, Zhao, Junbo, LeCun, Yann, 2015. Character-level convolutional networks for text classification. Advances in Neural Information Processing Systems 28, 649–657.

CHAPTER 15

Conclusion

Romain Bourqui[a] and Georges Quénot[b]

[a]Univ. Bordeaux, CNRS, Bordeaux INP, LaBRI, UMR 5800, Talence, France
[b]Univ. Grenoble Alpes, CNRS, Grenoble INP, LIG, Grenoble, France

Chapter points

- Sums up of the previous chapters
- Opens challenges and directions for future work

As Deep Learning models have been widely adopted in many application domains, explanations of these models are becoming of utmost importance in order to foster trust and to favor their adoptions by end-users. In this book, we have presented the main concepts behind eXplainable AI and made a particular focus on Deep Learning models.

The various aspects of XAI are reflected by the large variety of methods proposed by the community. This book covers many methods that try to capture one or several of these aspects. For instance, model- and sample-based methods have different objectives. While model-based methods seem rather to be a means for AI expert users to identify (un)expected behaviors, they do not seem appropriate for decision-makers or for a general audience. On the other hand, sample-based methods can help the general audience to understand a particular prediction for a particular data sample. To illustrate how these methods can be implemented in practice, the book also presents their applications to various application domains, e.g. language processing, medical image processing, malware detection, scene recognition, etc. It shows that, whatever the considered application domains are, expert knowledge is mandatory to implement but also and most importantly to interpret the provided explanation. The XAI domain is in full effervescence and is constantly evolving, introducing new methods at high frequency. This raises questions that should be addressed in the next few years. One of the key questions relates to the evaluation of the explanations for assessing their effectiveness but also for enabling the comparison of XAI methods. That question is not purely technical or theoretical, it also relates to the visualization and to the perception of an explanation, which have to be considered within various contexts. Indeed, the form used to present the explanation to the user has a strong impact on her understanding and trust in the proposed explanation.

The other key question relates to the semantics associated to an explanation. While many research works focus on identifying the features that drive a prediction of a model, these features often do not bring any semantics. AI experts might be able to infer the semantics behind such an explanation thanks to their prior knowledge in the domain, combined with an expertise in their model. However, the general audience and the stakeholders cannot infer in the general case the semantics of the provided explanation. It is therefore necessary for the XAI community to design new techniques that produce semantically enriched explanations.

Hence concluding this book, we state that this research direction XAI (explainable AI), despite a very intensive research presented in its chapters, has large perspectives. We see today the paths to follow and we are just at the beginning of them.

Index

A

Absolute coloring, 40, 42
Accumulated responses, 149, 153, 154, 159
Accuracy
  classes, 159
  classification, 46, 104, 133, 136, 138, 147, 151, 152, 157, 159–166, 168
  explanations, 126
  improvements, 153, 164, 166
  metrics, 197
  models, 45, 148
  network, 42, 49, 136
  prediction, 28
  score, 105, 183
Activations, 39, 40, 79, 80, 84, 148
  layer, 49, 176
  neurons, 41, 101
  ReLU, 275
  visualization, 148
Adam optimizer, 108, 135, 136, 278
Aggregated
  attribution evidences, 59
  explanations, 227
Anchors, 20, 192, 194, 195, 198, 201, 202, 205, 208, 304
  explainer, 198
  explanation, 198, 202, 210
  method, 193, 208
Android ransomware, 5, 217–219, 224, 237
  explaining, 224
  samples, 221, 226
  threats, 218
Aquatic semantic classes, 67, 69
Architecture
  model, 44, 48, 127
  modification, 48
  network, 40, 44, 48, 52, 79, 89
Artificial intelligence (AI), 7, 125, 263
  explainability, 2, 242, 244, 245
  explainable, 2, 7, 8, 79, 104, 245, 263, 317, 318
  systems, 1, 2, 126, 241
  systems explainability, 2
Artificial neural network (ANN), 125

Association rule mining (ARM), 174, 178, 179, 185
Attention explanations, 201
Attribution
  evidences, 59, 67
  maps, 3, 9–11, 14, 26, 56, 57, 75, 104
  methods, 9, 16, 56, 57, 59, 66, 222, 223
  processes, 59
  regions, 57, 65
  results, 59, 64, 67
  scheme, 3
  scores, 57, 63
  statistics, 69, 72
  study, 57
  techniques, 225
  values, 228, 230
  vector, 222, 226, 232
Automatic Identification System (AIS), 176, 177, 184
  dataset, 174
  equipment, 177
  information, 176
Average Number of Rules (ANR), 183
Average Path Length (APL), 183

B

Background superpixels, 301
Backpropagation (BP), 3, 4, 80, 98, 100, 102, 118, 127
  algorithm, 100
  gradient, 80–82
  guided, 4, 98, 102
  map, 101
Base classifiers, 283
Benchmarking metrics, 87
Binary
  classification, 13, 175, 279
  classification datasets, 135
  classification problems, 150, 277
  classifier, 197
  classifier explanation maps, 91
  classifier networks, 91
  feature, 236
  feature map, 86